The State of the Nations 2003

The State of the Nations 2003

The Third Year of Devolution in the United Kingdom

Edited by Robert Hazell

SCHOOL *of* PUBLIC POLICY

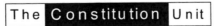

IMPRINT ACADEMIC

Published in the UK by Imprint Academic
PO Box 200, Exeter EX5 5YX, UK

Published in the USA by Imprint Academic
Philosophy Documentation Center
PO Box 7147, Charlottesville, VA 22906-7147, USA

ISBN 0 907845 49 5

British Library Cataloguing in Publication Data
A catalogue record for this book is available from the
British Library and the US Library of Congress

Front cover: architectural visuals and work in progress for
the new Scottish Parliament building, Holyrood
© Parliamentary copyright.
Scottish Parliamentary Corporate Body, 2002

Contents

PART II: THE STATE

6   Intergovernmental Relations
    Officialdom Still in Control? 143
    Alan Trench

7   Evolution from Devolution
    The Experience at Westminster. 169
    Oonagh Gay

PART III: PUBLIC POLICY DIVERGENCE

List of Contributors

John Curtice is Professor of Politics and Director of the Social Statistics Laboratory at Strathclyde University and Deputy Director of the Centre for Research into Elections and Social Trends. He has written widely on public attitudes and voting behaviour in the wake of devolution and is co-editor of *New Scotland, New Society?* (Polygon, 2002).

Oonagh Gay is currently on secondment to the Constitution Unit from the House of Commons Library, where she is a specialist in constitutional affairs. She is responsible for the Unit's project on Devolution at Westminster, funded by Leverhulme.

Scott Greer is Research Fellow at the Constitution Unit, UCL, and lead researcher on the Devolution and Health project. A political scientist who has researched territorial politics and health in Spain, the United States, France and the UK, he looks at the four health systems of the UK to see what devolution has done to politics, and what the conduct of health policy tells us about them.

Robert Hazell is the Director of the Constitution Unit and Professor of Government and the Constitution in the School of Public Policy, University College London. Originally a barrister, he spent most of his working life at the Home Office. He left Whitehall to become director of the Nuffield Foundation and founded the Constitution Unit in 1995. He is the director of a five year research programme into the Dynamics of Devolution, funded by the Leverhulme Trust.

Peter Hetherington is *The Guardian*'s Regional Affairs Editor and chairs the Commission on Local Governance, which recently suggested a raft of measures to revive local democracy and put town and county halls on a sounder constitutional footing. He helps produce the quarterly ESRC-funded 'Monitoring the English Regions' reports for the Constitution Unit.

Dan Hough is a Lecturer in Politics at the University of Nottingham. His recent publications include *The Fall and Rise of the PDS in Eastern Germany, 1989–2000* (Birmingham: Birmingham University Press, 2002) and "The Electoral Cycle and Multi-Level Voting in Germany" (with Charlie Jeffery), in Stephen Padgett und Thomas Poguntke (Hrsg.): *Continuity and Change in German Politics: Beyond the Politics of Centrality* (London: Frank Cass, 2001), pp. 73–98.

Charlie Jeffery is Director of the ESRC's Devolution and Constitutional Change Programme and Deputy Director of the Institute for German Studies at the University of Birmingham. His most recent publications include *Germany's European Diplomacy: Shaping the Regional Milieu* (Manchester: Manchester University Press, 2000, with Simon Bulmer and William E. Paterson), "Regionalwahlen in Mehr-Ebenen-Systemen" (with Dan Hough), in Thomas Conzelmann und Michele Knodt (Hrsg.): *Regionales Europa, europäisierte Regionen: Mannheimer Jahrbuch für Europäische Sozialforschung* (Frankfurt am Main: Campus Verlag, Band 6, 2002), pp.213–237 and 'Party Politics and Territorial Representation in the Federal Republic of Germany', in *West European Politics*, 22, 1999, pp. 130–166.

James Mitchell is Professor of Politics at Strathclyde University and heads the Scottish Monitoring team. He is the author of numerous book and articles on Scottish and UK politics and devolution.

John Osmond is Director of the Institute of Welsh Affairs, a policy think tank based in Cardiff. He is a former political journalist and television producer and has written widely on Welsh politics and devolution. His most recent books are *Welsh Europeans* (Seren, 1997); *The National Assembly Agenda* (Editor, 1998); and *Building a Civic Culture: Institutional Change, Policy Development, and Political Dynamics in the National Assembly for Wales* (co-editor with J. Barry Jones, 2001) both published by the Institute.

Rachel Simeon is a Senior Policy Analyst with the government of Ontario, Canada, specialising in intergovernmental social policy. She recently completed a master's degree in public policy at University College London.

John Tomaney works in the Centre for Urban and Regional Development Studies at Newcastle University. His research interests include the political economy of regional development and the politics of devolution in England. Among his recent publications is *England: The State of the Regions*, edited with John Mawson (Bristol: Policy Press, 2002).

Alan Trench is a Senior Research Fellow at the Constitution Unit, working on issues of devolution and intergovernmental relations in the United Kingdom. A solicitor by profession, he has been specialist adviser to the House of Lords Select Committee on the Constitution for their inquiry into *Devolution: Inter-Institutional Relations in the United Kingdom*.

Rick Wilford is a Professor of Politics at Queen's University Belfast. He has written extensively on both devolution and politics in Northern Ireland. His most recent works include articles on public opinion and devolution in *Government and Opposition* and *Regional and Federal Studies* and he was contributing editor of *Aspects of the Belfast Agreement* (OUP: 2001). He is currently researching the operation of the Northern Ireland Assembly between 1998 and 2002.

Robin Wilson is director of the Belfast-based think tank Democratic Dialogue, co-leader with Professor Rick Wilford of the Northern Ireland devolution monitoring project team and an honorary senior research fellow of the Constitution Unit. He is a member of the board of the Institute of Governance, Public Policy and Social Research at Queen's University Belfast, of the advisory council of the Dublin-based think tank TASC, and of the Northern Ireland Community Relations Council.

List of Figures

THIRD YEAR: THIRD FIRST MINISTER

INTERGOVERNMENTAL RELATIONS
OFFICIALDOM STILL IN CONTROL?

EVOLUTION FROM DEVOLUTION —
THE EXPERIENCE AT WESTMINSTER

FREE PERSONAL CARE
POLICY DIVERGENCE AND SOCIAL CITIZENSHIP

ELECTIONS IN MULTI-TIER SYSTEMS
LESSONS FOR THE UK FROM ABROAD

DEVOLUTION MEETS THE VOTERS: THE PROSPECTS FOR 2003

CONCLUSION: THE DEVOLUTION SCORECARD AS THE DEVOLVED ASSEMBLIES HEAD TO THE POLLS

Abbreviations

AM	Assembly Member
AMS	Additional Member Electoral System
BIC	British-Irish Council
BMA	British Medical Association
CBI	Confederation of British Industry
CCEA	Council on the Curriculum, Examinations and Assessments
CFER	Campaign for English Regions
CFP	Common Fisheries Program
DCMS	Department for Culture, Media and Sport
DEFRA	Department for Environment, Food and Rural Affairs
DEL	Departmental Expenditure Limit
DPM	Deputy Prime Minister
DTI	Department of Trade and Industry
DTLR	Department for Transport, Local Government and the Regions
DUP	Democratic Unionist Party
DWP	Department of Work and Pensions
EC	Executive Committee
ELWa	Education and Learning Wales
EP	European Parliament
ESRC	Economic and Social Research Council
EU	European Union
FBI	Federal Bureau of Investigation
FF	Fianna Fáil
FM	First Minister
FOI	Freedom of Information
GLA	Greater London Authority
IDB	Industrial Development Board
IGR	Intergovernmental Relations
ILP	Independent Labour Party
INI	Invest Northern Ireland
IRA	Irish Republican Army
JMC	Joint Ministerial Committee
LGA	Local Government Association
LEA	Local Education Authority
LHB	Local Health Board
MLA	Member of the Legislative Assembly
MPA	Ministerial Parliamentary Aide

MSP	Member of the Scottish Parliament
NHS	National Health Service
NICS	Northern Ireland Civil Service
NILTS	Northern Ireland Life and Times Survey
NIO	Northern Ireland Office
NSMC	North/South Ministerial Council
ODPM	Office of the Deputy Prime Minister
OFMDFM	Office of the First Minister and Deputy First Minister
PDS	Party of Democratic Socialism
PC	Plaid Cymru
PCT	Primary Care Trusts
PFI	Private Finance Initiative
PPP	Public-Private Partnership
PQ	Parliamentary Questions
PR	Proportional Representation
PSA	Public Service Agreements
PSNI	Police Service Northern Ireland
RDA	Regional Development Agency
RRI	Reinvestment and Reform Initiative
RUC	Royal Ulster Constabulary
SDLP	Social Democratic and Labour Party
SDS	Sustainable Development Strategy
SF	Sinn Féin
SNP	Scottish National Party
SRB	Single Regeneration Budget
SSP	Scottish Socialist Party
STV	Single Transferable Vote
SWRDA	South West Regional Development Agency
TD	Member of the House (Republic of Ireland Parliamentarian)
UDA	Ulster Defence Association
UUP	Ulster Unionist Party
WC	Women's Coalition
WGLA	Welsh Local Government Association

Foreword

This is the third in our series of annual reviews recording the progress of devolution in the UK, and bringing together the fruits of a major five-year research programme into devolution funded by the Leverhulme Trust. The book records the main developments in the third year of devolution, and looks ahead to the devolved assembly elections in May 2003. To bring publication closer to the elections we are bringing this year's review out in January 2003. This is why we have called the book The State of the Nations 2003; but the year on which it reports is 2002 (to be precise, the political year from October 2001 to October 2002).

The first two parts of the book are the same as in previous years, in providing an up to date and comprehensive record of the latest developments. Part 1, The Nations, contains four chapters which are a distillation of our quarterly monitoring reports on the progress of devolution in Scotland, Wales, Northern Ireland and the English regions. Those who want to keep bang up to date can view the more detailed quarterly monitoring reports on the Constitution Unit's website (http://www.ucl.ac.uk/constitution-unit) on the Nations and Regions pages. They can also be received every quarter by email: if you want to go on the list of email recipients, please drop us a line at constitution@ucl.ac.uk.

The monitoring reports are written by teams of experts in Scotland, Wales, Northern Ireland and the English regions (the latter with funding from the ESRC). The leaders of those teams are the authors of the first part of the book. The four chapters on the nations are written by James Mitchell in Scotland, John Osmond in Wales, Robin Wilson and Rick Wilford in Northern Ireland, and John Tomaney and Peter Hetherington covering the regions of England. Their chapters are a pleasure to read, offering real insights alongside the hard facts we ask for to make this a volume of record. And as partners they continue to be a pleasure to work with, delivering their chapters to very tight deadlines, and producing monitoring reports of consistently high quality.

Part 2 of the book covers the impact of devolution on the centre (on which we also produce quarterly reports, published on our website address above). From the start we have maintained a strong interest in the centre, and in how devolution reshapes the British state. This year we have detailed chapters by Alan Trench, on Intergovernmental Relations and the changes it has brought in Whitehall; and by Oonagh Gay on the changes at Westminster.

Parts 3 and 4 of the book constitute a new departure. We have tried each year to record the main differences in public policy which result from devolution, and this year we have included a separate Part, Part 3, with two chapters which analyse the reasons for policy divergence. Scott Greer looks at divergence in the health service, and Rachel Simeon takes as a case study the decision in Scotland to introduce free long term care for the elderly.

Finally Part 4 looks ahead to the Assembly elections in May 2003. Charlie Jeffery and Dan Hough explain why Labour is likely to perform badly, and the nationalist parties better, by comparison with the general election in 2001. John Curtice reads the opinion polls to explain the underlying trends in voting behaviour. And the final chapter looks ahead beyond the Assembly elections to the issues which will face the devolved governments in their second term.

As with previous volumes, the book has been written and published in record time. For that we owe special thanks to all the contributors and to Keith Sutherland and Sandra Good at Imprint Academic, who turned everything round with their usual speed and efficiency. And in the Constitution Unit special thanks go to Catherine Flew, who bravely took on the role of editing the book in her very first month with the Unit. To her and to all our partners and contributors, many thanks.

Robert Hazell   School of Public Policy
October 2002   University College London

1

Introduction: The Dynamism of Devolution in its Third Year

Robert Hazell

Devolution is never dull. The third year of devolution saw significant developments in all parts of the UK as devolution continued to unfold, and the dynamic forces released by devolution continued to work their way through the system. Scotland saw another change of First Minister; the Welsh First Minister established an independent commission to review the devolution settlement in Wales; in Northern Ireland the roller coaster came off the rails once more, when the British government suspended the devolved institutions for the fourth time in three years. Meanwhile in England the campaign for regional government continued, and the government responded by publishing its plans for directly elected regional assemblies in the long awaited regional government White Paper.

Devolution has certainly not reached a steady state, and the dynamic continues to unfold. In some places this is clearly visible, as in the developments highlighted above from England, Wales and Northern Ireland; in others the currents are deeper, working below the surface, and their effect is harder to discern. This opening chapter will briefly describe the dynamics which are at work, and set the scene for the subsequent chapters which explain the developments in detail.

THE STRUCTURE OF THIS BOOK

The book is organised into four parts. Part 1, the Nations, tells the story of the third year of devolution in the four countries of the UK. There have been dramatic developments in each, so each country is given extended treatment in separate chapters on Scotland, Wales, Northern Ireland and the English regions. Part 2 brings the reader back to the centre, with chapters describing the main developments in intergovernmental relations and Whitehall, and the impact of devolution on Westminster. Here the story is more one of very gradual evolution, with the institutions of central government making the minimal changes necessary to adjust to the realities of devolution.

In the second half of the book the focus shifts from telling the story of the third year to more analytical chapters set in a longer time frame. Part 3 takes a step back, to analyse how devolution has caused divergence in two key areas of public policy. Chapter 8 analyses the reasons for divergence in health policy during the first four years of devolution. Chapter 9 is a detailed case study of the biggest policy divergence which occurred in that period: the decision by the Scottish Executive to introduce free long term care for the elderly.

Finally Part 4 looks ahead to the devolved assembly elections which will take place in May 2003. Chapter 10 analyses to what extent the devolved elections in the UK are 'second order' elections with different voting behaviour from general elections, based on comparisons with the different voting behaviour in state elections in Germany, provincial elections in Canada and the regional elections in Spain. Chapter 11 explains how we should evaluate the election results, based upon the first devolved assembly elections and more recent opinion polls. The final chapter, chapter 12, sums up the achievements of the devolved administrations in their first term, and sets out some of the challenges they will face in the second.

The remainder of this opening chapter contains an introduction to the four main parts of the book. Before that, the key developments of the third year of devolution are set out in Figure 1.1.

Figure 1.1: Key events in the third year of devolution 2001–02

2001	
18 September	Seamus Mallon (SDLP) announces he will not seek re-election as Deputy First Minister in Northern Ireland.
30 October	Plenary meeting of Joint Ministerial Committee in Cardiff. Tony Blair gives speech in National Assembly for Wales.
6 November	David Trimble (UUP) and Mark Durkan (SDLP) elected as First and Deputy First Minister in Northern Ireland, after Alliance Party re-designates 3 of its 5 MLAs as 'Unionists' to secure cross-community consent.
8 November	Resignation of Henry McLeish MSP as Scottish First Minister.
22 November	Jack McConnell MSP elected as Scottish First Minister.
27 November	Rhodri Morgan announces Welsh Executive will be known as the 'Welsh Assembly Government'.
2002	
14 February	Final report of Welsh Assembly Review of Procedure, set up in December 2000 and chaired by Lord Elis-Thomas.
27 February	House of Lords Select Committee on the Constitution start inquiry into Devolution: Inter-institutional Relations in the UK.

18 April	Labour Peer Lord Richard appointed to chair independent Commission into Powers of National Assembly for Wales.
2 May	Tony Blair and Gordon Brown visit Belfast to announce Reinvestment and Reform initiative, conferring borrowing powers on Northern Ireland government.
2 May	First elections for directly elected Mayors in 7 local authorities in England.
9 May	Publication of English regions White Paper, *Your Region, Your Choice*.
17 May	In Irish general election Sinn Féin increases representation in the Dail from one to five TDs.
29 May	DTLR broken up into Office of Deputy Prime Minister, headed by John Prescott and responsible for local and regional government in England; and Department of Transport headed by Alistair Darling.
17 June	Mike German AM cleared of criminal charges, returns to Welsh Cabinet as Deputy First Minister and Minister for Rural Development and Wales Abroad.
3 July	Sunderland Commission reports recommending introduction of STV for local government elections in Wales.
15 July	Treasury Spending Review announces New Public Spending Plans 2003–2006.
31 July	Members announced of Richard Commission into Powers of Welsh Assembly.
14 October	Suspension of devolution to Northern Ireland. Two extra Ministers appointed to complement three-strong NIO team.
22 October	Plenary meeting of Joint Ministerial Committee in London.
28 October	Paul Murphy replaces John Reid as Secretary of State for Northern Ireland. Peter Hain appointed to replace Paul Murphy as Secretary of State for Wales.

THE NATIONS: WALES

The main developments in 2001–02 were in the two nations bringing up the rear of the devolution stakes: Wales and England. In Wales the trajectory continued in the direction described by John Osmond in previous years. Some steps are small, some large, but every step increases the separation of powers in Wales and takes the Assembly in a parliamentary direction. The changes in designation say it all. The 'Assembly Secretaries' of the Government of Wales Act now call themselves Ministers, and the Executive

Committee has become the Cabinet. The Executive as a whole is now known as the 'Welsh Assembly Government', and the Management Board of senior civil servants has become the Executive Board. Within the peculiar body corporate structure prescribed by the Government of Wales Act the elastic has been stretched as far as it possibly can to create a more conventional division of functions between executive and legislature.

The two reviews announced by Rhodri Morgan as part of the Partnership Agreement with the Liberal Democrats will continue this process. The first was an internal review chaired by the Presiding Officer, Lord Elis-Thomas, which looked at how to strengthen the way the Assembly works without any changes to the statutory framework. Its report, the product of a year's work, was presented to the Assembly in February 2002 and adopted unanimously. The main issues it addressed included the relationship between the Assembly's executive, legislative and deliberative functions, the role of its various committees, and the making of new Westminster legislation affecting Assembly functions. The key institutional change it called for was to sharpen and clarify the split between the Assembly's executive and the legislative/ scrutiny side. It was as a consequence that the Welsh Assembly Government came formally into being in March 2002, with some 3,800 civil servants working for it. The remaining 200 are assigned to the renamed Presiding Office, which is responsible for providing support to Assembly Members in plenary and in their committee work, and for running the Assembly's debating, scrutinising and law-making functions.

The second review is an independent Commission, chaired by Lord Richard, which is expressly charged with reviewing the limitations imposed by the Government of Wales Act, and in particular the central limitation that the National Assembly has no primary legislative powers. It was established in the third year of devolution, in July 2002, but invited to report back 18 months later, by the end of 2003. In terms of the Assembly's long march towards becoming a parliament, the Richard Commission represents the biggest single step. Previous steps have taken the Assembly as far as it can go within the existing statutory framework. If the Richard Commission recommends that the Assembly should have primary legislative powers, they would in effect be recommending that the Assembly become a parliament, with powers much closer to those of the Scottish Parliament and Northern Ireland Assembly.

They would also be recommending a further evolution which appears to accord to the wishes of the people of Wales. Chapter 2 reports on major surveys done by the Institute of Welsh Politics at Aberystwyth which show support for a parliament (with law making and tax raising powers) going up in leaps and bounds, from 20 per cent at the time of the referendum in 1997, to 30 per cent at the time of the first Assembly elections in 1999, and almost

40 per cent in summer 2001 (overtaking those supporting an Assembly with its current limited powers, who in 2001 fell to 25 per cent: see Figure 2.9).

THE NATIONS: ENGLAND

In England the long march to regional government has a long way to go yet, but 2002 heralded a major development with the government's July White Paper *Your Region, Your Choice*, which charted a way forward for those regions that want to proceed to directly elected regional assemblies. But campaigners could raise only two cheers, because the assemblies proposed would have strategic powers only and limited budgets, and the way forward was potentially blocked by a major obstacle, in the form of local government reorganisation. But another obstacle, or rather diversion, of an alternative model of city regions based on major provincial cities run by mayors, was effectively removed when no big cities in the 28 mayoral referendums held in 2001-02 opted to have a directly elected mayor.

As in Wales, the direction of devolutionary travel continues to be one way, towards stronger regional government for England; but the destination is much less certain. Even though city regions may now be out of the running, there are other alternative models for strengthening the regional tier of government without going as far as directly elected regional assemblies. The White Paper set out these alternatives in chapter 2. The Government Offices for the Regions could be further strengthened. Regional Development Agencies could be given bigger budgets and a wider range of functions. The existing voluntary Regional Chambers could be constituted on a statutory basis, and given formal powers over the RDAs. All these existing regional bodies have been growing fast in terms of budgets and functions, albeit from a low base, and all have something to lose if some of their powers and functions were transferred to elected regional assemblies.

Within the government John Prescott continues to be the sole champion of regional assemblies for England. Tony Blair is lukewarm at best, as are most of his Cabinet colleagues. None was prepared to offer up significant powers or budgets for transfer to regional assemblies, which is why the model on offer in the White Paper is so slimline and strategic. The potentially fatal blow dealt by the Cabinet was to insist on unitary local government as a precondition for regional government, so that regional government could not be vulnerable to attack as an 'additional tier'. Privately many ministers are in favour of unitary local government (as is John Prescott himself). But it did not need to be so tightly linked to regional government, or made a formal precondition. Local government restructuring risks requiring a major diversion of energy and resources, and could tip the balance in any referendum against the introduction of regional government.

THE NATIONS: NORTHERN IRELAND

Northern Ireland has a dynamic of a different kind. As chapter 4 relates, it is the ups and downs of the peace process which have derailed devolution, rather than withdrawal of confidence in devolution itself. On the unionist side the Belfast Agreement was meant to lead to decommissioning of weapons as well as to devolution, and it was the continuing failure of the IRA to engage in the decommissioning process which led unionists to lose confidence in the institutions of the Belfast Agreement, and in particular power sharing with Sinn Féin, the political wing of the IRA.

Ironically the third year of devolution, from November 2001 to October 2002, saw the longest phase of concerted implementation of the Belfast Agreement. It was the first time that the Assembly operated for a full year, and with a reformed legislative process its legislative output increased significantly, the committees got down to work and began to scrutinise the executive and the public finances. But it was not to last. Rising loyalist paramilitary violence and, in Belfast, naked intercommunal hostility, further undermined the confidence of both communities. A crisis was already looming when it was discovered that Sinn Féin sympathisers had apparently been carrying out espionage against ministers in the Northern Ireland Office. That was enough to bring about a complete collapse of confidence, and rather than have David Trimble walk out of government, the UK government suspended the institutions. The suspension, which began in October 2002, looked likely to last a long time, with no certainty that the next Assembly elections will be held in May 2003.

THE NATIONS: SCOTLAND

Scotland is presented last in this year's tour of the nations, because it is where the least happened. But here too there was some turbulence, indicated in the title of chapter 5: 'Third Year, Third First Minister'. The third year of devolution opened with the downfall of Henry McLeish, who was replaced in November 2001 as First Minister by Jack McConnell, who had been Dewar's Finance Minister, and then served as Education Minister. McConnell had almost a clean sweep of the Cabinet, so that its longest serving members are the two Liberal Democrat Ministers, Jim Wallace and Ross Finnie. They have provided continuity and stability to the coalition government while their Labour colleagues have changed around them.

Stability has been the watchword under McConnell, with the only further turbulence during his first year being the departure in May 2002 of Wendy Alexander, his main rival and Minister for Enterprise. With her departure the Cabinet lost its most 'business friendly' minister, and one of its rising stars.

As Scotland heads for the polls in May 2003, one of the questions which may be asked of the McConnell administration is what it stands for. McConnell is a Labour party machine politician (and former General Secretary of the party), with no strong policy views. If he forms another coalition with the Liberal Democrats, it may turn out, as with the first Labour/Liberal Democrat partnership, that the policy drive comes disproportionately from the junior partner. In Labour's first term the two biggest policy changes, on student tuition fees and free long term care for the elderly, both came from the Liberal Democrats.

THE CENTRE

Back in Westminster and Whitehall it was business as usual in the third year of devolution. The sustained period of apparent calm in Northern Ireland meant that all strands of the Belfast Agreement were in operation, including north-south (the North South Ministerial Council) and east-west (the British-Irish Council). Intergovernmental relations between the UK and the devolved administrations continued relatively smoothly, with just two plenary meetings of the Joint Ministerial Committee (the annual meetings in October 2001 and October 2002); although the JMC (Europe) met five times, and the JMC (Poverty) was revived in September 2002. The UK government remains clearly the dominant partner: intergovernmental meetings are convened to suit its agenda (eg the JMC (Poverty) was revived by Gordon Brown to pursue his social policies); and UK dominance is reinforced through London's complete control of finance.

At Westminster the new Parliament elected in June 2001 has strongly reforming Leaders in both Houses, in Robin Cook and Lord Williams of Mostyn, but neither includes adjustments in response to devolution as part of their modernising agenda. In the Commons the full panoply of pre-devolution territorial committees continues, with separate Select Committees for Scottish, Welsh and Northern Ireland Affairs, and the continuation of three Grand Committees for Scotland, Wales and Northern Ireland. The most significant development took place in the Lords, with the new Constitution Committee's inquiry into *Devolution: Inter-institutional Relations in the United Kingdom*. Because the Lords committee structure is not so fragmented, they can take a view of devolution in the round which is denied to the Commons; their report will be the most important parliamentary report on the subject since devolution began.

DIVERGING PUBLIC POLICIES

The Lords report will focus on institutions. More important for the public is the impact the new institutions have on their daily lives. What are the

differences in public policy as a result of devolution, and are there any limits
to how far public policy might diverge? Chapters 8 and 9 focus on policy
divergence in health and social rights, an area where the devolved countries
have some of their greatest room to make their mark and where the political,
economic, and social stakes are very high.

Chapter 8 looks at three high-profile areas of health policy, namely organisation, public health, and the public-private relationship. It finds remarkable
divergence for such a short period of time (even if health policy takes years to
affect people's lives) and suggests that it is because each of the four systems
has a different balance of policy advocates who can work with their differing
party systems to change policy. Chapter 9 is a case study of the most visible,
important, and expensive policy change made by a devolved government:
Scotland's decision to fund long-term personal care for the elderly. It shows
the combination of institutional constraint and political forces that led the
Scottish government to dramatically break with Westminster. It also highlights a surprising aspect of the unique UK structure of devolution: the relative absence of constraints on the policies of substate governments. There is
always tension in any system between unity and diversity: between the
opposing values of devolution/divergence on the one hand, and unifor-
mity/equity on the other. What is surprising in a system thought to place a
high value on equity is that both chapters suggest that the UK may have a bias
towards divergence. Between the diverging political systems and the weak
constraints on policy change and divergence, the United Kingdom might,
compared to its peers internationally, prove to be a particularly propitious
environment for policy divergence within one country.

THE DEVOLVED ASSEMBLY ELECTIONS IN 2003

Devolution has introduced a new electoral dynamic to British politics. At
Westminster the electoral battle is between Labour and the Conservatives,
and Labour achieved landslide victories over the Conservatives in the last
two general elections (1997 and 2001), with the third party, the Liberal
Democrats, also doing well. This pattern is not reproduced in Scotland and
Wales, which are four-party systems. The Conservatives are not nearly so
strong, and the main opposition to Labour comes from the nationalist parties,
the Scottish National Party in Scotland, and Plaid Cymru in Wales.

Chapter 10 shows how the devolved assembly elections may develop their
own regional dynamic, separate from the elections to Westminster. In the
first devolved elections in Scotland and Wales in 1999 Labour did very badly
by comparison with its general election performance two years before, with
its share of the vote down 19 percentage points in Wales, and 12 per cent in
Scotland. By contrast the nationalist parties did very well, with Plaid

Cymru's vote share going up by 20 percentage points, and the SNP by a more modest 7 per cent compared with the general election. The issue to watch in the 2003 elections is whether this pattern repeats itself, suggesting that the devolved elections are uncoupled from the national electoral process, but follow a specific regional dynamic of their own. It will also be interesting to see whether the media begin to grasp this, and report the election from a base-line of the last devolved elections in 1999; or whether they take as their base-line the most recent general election results in 2001, and continue to view devolution through a Westminster lens.

The other thing to watch in the 2003 elections is turnout. Chapter 11 expects turnout to be lower than in 1999, for three reasons: because West-minster is now more clearly seen as the more important institution; because of devolution's failure to meet the high expectations of 1999; and because of decline in the perceived importance of the election outcome. (This last is not a problem unique to the devolved assemblies, but applies also to Westmin-ster.) If turnout does fall significantly, then parties stand to gain if they can get more of their supporters out. But even if the nationalists do better than Labour in this respect, they are unlikely to form an administration in Scot-land or Wales. The electoral system is not fully proportional, but is biased to Labour in both countries. Chapter 11 shows how if the nationalist parties won an equal share of the vote with Labour, they would be left with six fewer seats than Labour in Scotland and four fewer in Wales: leaving Labour free to form a government with the Liberal Democrats, but denying the national-ists the same opportunity. So the probability is that we shall see Labour-led administrations re-elected in both countries in 2003.

ISSUES IN THE SECOND TERM

How will the dynamics of devolution play out in the devolved assemblies' second term? At the constitutional level, the big issues will be how to handle the demand from Wales for primary legislative powers, and the next steps towards regional government in England. Welsh devolution had few strong supporters in Blair's first Cabinet, and it will be interesting to see how the second Blair government handles demands from Wales for more. Some will be anxious that the devolution bandwagon is running away with them, and may also get nervous about regional government in England, as the first Blair government did back in 1997. It will also be interesting to see the reaction of the other devolved administrations. Will the Scots (and Northern Ireland, if devolution is restored) support a demand from Wales for greater powers, which would take the National Assembly closer to the model of the Scottish Parliament, and the Northern Ireland Assembly? Or will they sit on their hands and let the Welsh fight their case on their own?

The pattern so far has been for the devolved governments to pursue things bilaterally with the British government. The asymmetry in the devolution settlement has reinforced this tendency, and has helped to reinforce the dominance of the UK government in intergovernmental relations. But the devolved governments have more in common than perhaps they realise, especially over issues like finance. So far they have not come together, and they have not even held a separate meeting just of the devolved governments: which is in marked contrast to the regular gatherings of state premiers in federal systems like Australia, Canada or Germany. In the second term there may develop a greater solidarity amongst the devolved administrations, and a greater consciousness of the issues on which they should develop a common cause against the British government.

The third issue to watch in the second term is further divergence in public policies. The main items are those where a different path was marked out in the first term: free long term care for the elderly, students' tuition fees, and in health the growing divergence described in chapter 8 between market-driven policies in England and a greater emphasis on public health in Wales and, to a lesser extent, Scotland. There is also the issue of PR for local government elections, with proposals for STV from the Sunderland Commission in Wales and the Kerley Committee in Scotland. Whether PR is introduced will depend on the bargaining power of the Liberal Democrats in any coalition negotiations in Scotland and Wales, where many Labour-led local authorities continue to be bitterly opposed.

Public policies may also converge, or come together round a new norm, as the devolved administrations learn from each others' experience. The best single example of that is the idea of a Children's Commissioner, first adopted in Wales, with proposals to copy it in Scotland and Northern Ireland. Others are free care for the elderly (first introduced in Scotland, partly copied in Wales); and abolition of student tuition fees, also first introduced in Scotland, partly copied in Wales, and now on the political agenda in England. Devolution is about difference, and it will be interesting to see whether in their second term the devolved assemblies continue to pioneer new policies, and whether other governments continue to follow them.

Part I

The Nations

2

From Corporate Body to Virtual Parliament

The Metamorphosis of the National Assembly for Wales

John Osmond

As the National Assembly neared the end of its first four-year term it increasingly took on the appearance of a virtual parliament. This was most obvious in the titles its various components awarded themselves: Ministers, not Assembly Secretaries; the Cabinet, not an Executive Committee; Presiding Office rather than Office of the Presiding Officer; the Executive Board of senior civil servants rather than Management Board; but most stridently, the Welsh Assembly Government in place of the corporate body that had been the kernel of devolved responsibility enshrined in the 1998 Government of Wales Act.[1]

Three years into Welsh devolution the Assembly Government emerged as a strong executive authority. It exerted increasing control over what were now renamed the Assembly-sponsored bodies (the old quangos such as the Welsh Development Agency); it developed more clearly defined and inevitably more controversial policy initiatives; and it established a stronger presence abroad for the Assembly Government in the form of self-styled embassies around the world.

Accompanying these trends were three further developments. The first was increasing concern about the ability of the wider Assembly to hold the Welsh Assembly Government to account. There was a de facto split in the civil service machine with the greater proportion out of a total complement of 4,000 becoming the exclusive preserve of the Assembly Government. The remainder, just 200 or so, are within the ambit of the Presiding Office. They service the committees and generally support the backbench element of the Assembly. This alerted some observers and participants to a danger that the

[1] Richard Rawlings, Professor of Law at the London School of Economics, reaches the same conclusion in his O'Donnell lecture, *Towards a Parliament: Three Faces of the National Assembly for Wales*, given at the University of Wales, Swansea, in February 2002. Much of the content of this chapter is derived from the IWA's quarterly reports monitoring the National Assembly, produced by the following team: Nia Richardson, the IWA's Research Officer; Jane Jones of the Department of Law, University of Wales, Swansea; Adrian Kay, of the University of Bristol; Alys Thomas and Gerald Taylor of the University of Glamorgan; and Mark S. Lang of the Welsh Governance Centre, Cardiff University. I am particularly grateful to Denis Balsom, Editor of the *Wales Yearbook*, for commenting on an early draft of this chapter.

Welsh Assembly Government could revert to the old pre-Assembly Welsh Office by another name, with the Assembly itself retreating to the status and impact of the Commons Welsh Affairs Committee.

Figure 2.1: Key events in the National Assembly's third year, 2001–02

5 September 2001	Education and Lifelong Learning Minister, Jane Davidson, unveils *The Learning Country*, her comprehensive policy statement on education and training in Wales for the next ten years.
30 October 2001	Tony Blair visits the National Assembly and delivers a speech on the Afghan war.
31 October 2001	An emerging consensus on the Assembly's year long procedural review breaks down when the opposition parties together with the Liberal Democrats refuse to endorse a draft final report because it lacks detailed and radical recommendations.
15 November 2001	A rift appears in the coalition over Labour's insistence on pushing through major structural changes to the organisation of the Welsh NHS against Liberal Democrat objections. Last-minute negotiations lead to a compromise, which keeps the Liberal Democrats on side.
16 November 2001	Assembly Administration endorses the Flanders Declaration by European regions with legislative powers seeking more influence within the institutions of the European Union.
27 November 2001	Rhodri Morgan declares that the Administration should in future be known as the 'Welsh Assembly Government'.
28 January 2002	Assembly Government launches *A Winning Wales*, its ten-year economic development strategy.
12 February 2002	Assembly Government introduces a new, means-tested, 'Learning Grant' for higher and further education students worth up to a maximum of £1,500 a year.
14 February 2002	Adjudicator's report on disputes between the Assembly and the architects of the new debating chamber, the Richard Rogers Partnership, rules that the Assembly owed Richard Rogers £432,000 in unpaid fees.
14 February 2002	Final report of the Assembly's procedural review is presented to plenary.
15 February 2002	Education and Lifelong Learning Committee publish their review into higher education.

26 February 2002	Cabinet mini reshuffle moves Andrew Davies from his position as Business Manager to take over the Economic Development portfolio, while Minister for Rural Development Carwyn Jones is given the additional role of Business Manager.
1 March 2002	Edwina Hart, Minister for Finance, Local Government and Communities launches *Freedom and Responsibility in Local Government* which sets out the Assembly Government's vision for the future of local government in Wales.
14 April 2002	The Assembly Government pulls out of its involvement with the Wales European Centre in Brussels, deciding instead to expand its direct representation in the European capital.
18 April 2002	Labour Peer Lord Richard of Ammanford appointed to chair the independent commission on the Assembly's powers.
25 April 2002	Assembly Government appoints an economic research advisory panel to recommend a rolling programme of economic research, monitoring and evaluation.
16 May 2002	Assembly vote unanimously to challenge Westminster to find the resources for free personal care for the elderly out of general taxation.
13 June 2002	Crown Prosecution Service clears Liberal Democrat leader Mike German of criminal charges relating to his time as Head of the European Unit at the Welsh Joint Education Committee.
17 June 2002	Mike German returns to the Cabinet as Deputy First Minister and Minister for Rural Development and Wales Abroad. Carwyn Jones gains a new responsibility for open government in addition to his continuing role as Business Manager.
27 June 2002	Culture and Education and Lifelong Learning Committees publish *Our Language: Its future*.
3 July 2002	The Sunderland Commission on Local Government Electoral Arrangements in Wales publishes report recommending the introduction of the Single Transferable Vote for local elections.
26 July 2002	Assembly Government launch *Bilingual Future*, a landmark policy statement on the Welsh language.
31 July 2002	Membership of the Richard Commission on the Assembly's powers announced.

The second development was an inclination for the Assembly Government to avoid debate in pushing ahead with controversial policy interventions. The outstanding example was its determination to pursue a radical restructuring of the health service, involving the abolition of the five health authorities and their replacement with 22 new local health boards. This was undertaken not only against the opposition of the Conservatives and Plaid Cymru, but by Labour ministers in defiance of their coalition Liberal Democrat partners. In the process effective scrutiny was avoided in Westminster as well as Cardiff Bay.

The third development was evidence that the Cardiff administration was distancing itself as far as it could from many of the policy edicts emanating from the Blair administration in Westminster. Most often this took the form of the Assembly Government not following, or retreating from, Westminster initiatives. So, for example, it abolished Key Stage One tests for seven-year-olds in primary schools, declared it would not be following experimentation with the comprehensive system, attacked the notion of university top-up fees, refused to explore the idea of foundation hospitals, and dragged its feet in pursuing the Private Finance Initiative. The result was a noticeable cooling in relations between the Assembly Government and the Wales Office in Whitehall, led for most of the first term by an increasingly devolution-sceptic Secretary of State for Wales, Paul Murphy. As a result of the Cabinet reshuffle in October 2002 Murphy was succeeded by Neath MP Peter Hain, previously Minister for Europe in the Foreign Office, and a long-standing devolution enthusiast. With Hain as an advocate in Whitehall this change may prove significant in pushing forward aspirations for the Assembly to acquire wider powers.

A CLASH OF PRIORITIES

A defining moment came in May 2002 when the Assembly voted unanimously to challenge the UK government to fund free personal care for the elderly. This event was significant, not so much because of the originality or the radicalism of the initiative — its provenance lay three years earlier with the Sutherland Royal Commission on Long Term Care — but because of Whitehall's reaction.[2] The notion that the Assembly should presume to encroach on Westminster territory was immediately dismissed as 'pathetic' and symptomatic of the Assembly's 'irresponsible approach to politics'.

These comments were made by Adrian McMenamin, political adviser to the Secretary of State for Wales, Paul Murphy, ostensibly the National Assembly's lead ally in Whitehall.[3] Notwithstanding that McMenamin left

---

[2] See Chapter 9 in this volume.

[3] They were reported by BBC Wales' political current affairs programme *Dragon's Eye*, 16 May 2002.

the Wales Office shortly afterwards, there is little doubt that his remarks reflected the sentiments, if not the diplomacy, of his boss.[4] Murphy tended to operate at arms length from the National Assembly, rarely visiting it and often issuing cautionary edicts.[5] On this occasion, another source from within the Wales Office, undoubtedly also close to Murphy, added:

> We do not think that it is a spending priority and this decision in the Assembly will have no impact on government policy. It is not clear to anyone what the thinking behind this is. There hasn't been a vote on this issue in the Assembly Labour group or at the Welsh Labour conference.[6]

In actual fact the Assembly did a great deal of 'thinking' on the issue before it went to a vote. It had launched a consultation on a *Strategy for Older People* more than a year earlier, in March 2001. At this point the Assembly Government was reluctant to open up the consultation since it was aware that it was only too likely to lead to a confrontation with Whitehall. Nevertheless, after some deliberation and pressure from outside bodies and AMs of all parties, the Assembly Government agreed to allow their expert panel on older people to look at the issue. After months of deliberation the panel insisted that their report to the Assembly should firmly endorse the recommendations of the Sutherland Commission. At the same time the panel acknowledged that primary legislation from Westminster would be necessary and that the funding of universal personal care would have to contend with other priorities. As the panel said: '. . . it would be difficult to accord [free personal care] higher priority than, for example, addressing the pressures of social services spending across the board'.[7] It therefore called upon the Assembly Government to: '. . . challenge the UK government to fund and implement free personal care in the context of UK taxation . . . as the Royal Commission had intended'.[8]

That such a considered policy process, backed by a unanimous vote of members across the parties, should be treated with dismissive contempt by the Assembly's notional champion in Whitehall, the Wales Office, was indeed a defining moment. Two matters were immediately highlighted:

[4] McMenamin had worked at the Wales Office since December 1999.

[5] Commenting on the role of the Secretary of State for Wales, the Presiding Officer, Lord Elis-Thomas, stated: 'There is a question mark over how this role has been developed as a constitutional role, to what extent it is seen as being a representative of the UK government at Cabinet level in Wales and to what extent it is seen as a conduit for the National Assembly at Cabinet level.' House of Lords Constitution Select Committee on the Constitution Session 2001–02 *Devolution: Inter-institutional relations in the United Kingdom* Evidence complete to 10 July 2002 HL Paper 147, p. 264.

[6] *Western Mail*, 17 May 2002.

[7] Assembly Government Advisory Group on Older People, *When I'm Sixty Four*. See report from Health Minister Jane Hutt to the Health and Social Services Committee, 1 May 2002.

[8] *Ibid.*

1. The contrasting position in Scotland and Northern Ireland where devolved institutions were moving forward on the same issue because they have primary legislative powers.

2. The financial implications for the Assembly's budget, which is dependent on block funding from Westminster. Independent research commissioned by the expert panel costed the policy at £87 million a year immediately, rising to £180 million by 2020.[9] This lay behind the recommendation that the UK government should be 'challenged' to fund free personal care for the elderly from general taxation. To find the necessary money from within the existing block would have obvious consequences for spending elsewhere.

These two matters could be replicated in almost every area where the Assembly wished to pursue a substantial policy initiative. The Assembly's frustrations in wishing to put in place free personal care for the elderly provide part of the background for the Commission, under Lord Richard of Ammanford, on its powers. This began work in September 2002 and will report towards the end of 2003. It also marks out one area of the battleground for the forthcoming Assembly general election in May 2003.

THE ASSEMBLY GOVERNMENT

The National Assembly's inaugural four-year term falls neatly into three parts. The first 18 months saw a new and unstable institution finding its feet and personality, a process that witnessed the vote of no-confidence in Alun Michael as First Secretary. This led directly to the formation of the majority Labour / Liberal Democrat coalition in October 2000 which provided a more coherent government and programme. The final year of the first term was inevitably dominated by the politics of the forthcoming Assembly election in May 2003. In between was a middle period of some 18 months during which the Assembly self-consciously paused for reflection. The mechanism was the Review of Procedures, which brought all four parties together under the chairmanship of the Presiding Officer. Its terms of reference expressly set aside any fundamental examination of the Assembly's powers. Nevertheless, this requirement was constantly in the background. The Review's four main themes were:

- Seeking to ensure that the National Assembly delivers for Wales
- Enhancing policy development
- Improving scrutiny
- Providing a greater focus for the Assembly's legislative role.[10]

---

[9] See the quarterly monitoring report, *Engaging with Europe*, Cardiff: IWA, June 2002, for a full account.

[10] For an account of the work of the Procedural Review see Osmond, J.,' Constitution Building on the Hoof' in *Building a Civic Culture: Institutional Change, Policy Development and Political Dynamics in the National Assembly for Wales* (Cardiff: IWA, 2002).

Getting to grips with these matters, and especially the last, led the Review to confront the many anomalies in the Assembly's constitution as established by the 1998 Government of Wales Act. The core difficulty is the Assembly's creation as a corporate body — 'a single legal personality' as the Counsel General, Winston Roddick, has it[11] — in which its legislative and executive functions are combined rather than separated, as is normal in parliamentary institutions. The constitutional history of the Assembly's opening period was dominated by an emphatic rejection of this mode of operation. Instead, the Assembly moved as far as it possibly could in the direction of separating its administrative and legislative roles. By October 2000 these two elements had developed highly distinctive personalities in the form of the majority coalition Administration on the one hand, and the independent office of the Presiding Officer on the other.

The main force driving the split in the first period of the Assembly's life was the Presiding Officer, Lord Dafydd Elis-Thomas.[12] However, by the middle period it was the Administration, led by the First Minister, that was most anxious to define and emphasise the difference. Part of the motivation was a widespread anxiety that the Administration's decisions and actions were being interpreted by the media as coming from the Assembly as a whole. Both government and opposition in the Assembly shared an interest in avoiding such confusion. The result was the emergence of the Welsh Assembly Government, determined to be the decisive hand in shaping the future of the country.

One indication was a transformation in the relations between the Assembly Government and its executive agencies. Pre-devolution, organisations such as the Welsh Development Agency, the Health Authorities, the Education Funding Councils, Arts Council and Wales Tourist Board led relatively autonomous lives. Apart from delivering annual reports and agreeing broad outline targets they were largely unmolested by the old Welsh Office, and only rarely interrogated by MPs at Westminster.

All this has changed. Instead of one Secretary of State for Wales there are now nine ministers and five deputy ministers who keep a constant watch on the activities of the assembly sponsored bodies, as the quangos have become known. They meet formally with the Administration at least quarterly, and their activities are also reviewed by the subject committees. There is a sense that they are being corralled and disciplined, becoming more like state departments along Whitehall lines than free-standing, arms length organisations. No longer do they project their own corporate image, separate from

---

[11] Winston Roddick QC, *Crossing the Road*, Law Society lecture, National Eisteddfod, Ynys Mon, August 1999.

[12] For an account see Osmond, J., 'In Search of Stability: Coalition Politics in the Second Year of the National Assembly' in A. Trench (ed) *The State of the Nations 2001: The Second Year of Devolution in the United Kingdom* (Exeter: Imprint Academic, 2001) pp. 26–31.

that of the Assembly Government, and their plans and strategies are ever more closely aligned with those of the Assembly Government. The new relationship was spelt out by the Permanent Secretary, Sir Jon Shortridge, responding to the House of Lords Committee on the Constitution during an oral evidence session at the National Assembly in May 2002:

> I think one of the features of the Assembly [Government] is that there is a greater intensity and proximity, politically driven throughout the relevant structures associated with the Assembly, and because of that there is a sharper edge to my relationship with the sponsored bodies.[13]

Developments in the administrative culture of the National Assembly have further underpinned the creation of a stronger executive machine, capable of developing policy and pushing it through. In this respect changes to the Cabinet secretariat made in the wake of the majority Coalition government had the biggest impact. The old civil service management board was replaced by a new executive board with a strengthened communications and policy role, emphasised by the inclusion of two political advisers as members. Its role was now to deliver on Assembly Government policies as well as dealing with management issues. The Permanent Secretary described its work in the following terms:

> The one thing I have done is establish an Executive Board which meets every Tuesday morning. I have as observers one special adviser from the Labour Party and one from the Liberal Democrats who sit on that Board and on a Tuesday morning what we are doing is looking at the issues of the day which are flowing through the Assembly. It meets on a Tuesday morning because the Cabinet has met on the Monday afternoon.[14]

Another expression of the new administrative culture was the Assembly Government's decision to pull out of its involvement with the Wales European Centre in Brussels and instead expand its direct representation in the European capital. The end result will be to increase the number of the Assembly Government Brussels staff from three to seven or eight and its funding from £330,000 to nearer £500,000 a year. The move, which follows the representation pattern established by the Scottish Executive, reflects a determination to be more firmly in control of policy development and decision-making. As the First Minister Rhodri Morgan declared:

> We need to establish a stronger presence and a clearer profile in European institutions in Brussels, Strasbourg, Luxembourg and elsewhere . . . We must now look forward with a view to what will happen after the next Assembly elections.

[13] House of Lords Constitution Select Committee on the Constitution Session 2001–02 *Devolution: Inter-institutional relations in the United Kingdom* Evidence complete to 10 July 2002 HL Paper 147, p. 280.

[14] *Ibid.* p. 279.

We have considered the nature of our representation in Brussels and the need to establish a clearer identity to answer the question of who speaks for Wales in Brussels more clearly than in the past. We concluded that strengthening our office must be a priority if we are to face up to the challenges and opportunities presented by a demanding European agenda and the increasing significance of that agenda for Wales, namely in the fields of governance, the White Paper on Governance, the future of Europe, structural funds, common agriculture policy reform, enlargement, regional policy, the European networks, the Committee of the Regions, and attendance at Council of Ministers meetings.[15]

The decision also provided another demonstration that the National Assembly is in practice — though not in a strictly legal sense — moving rapidly away from the corporate foundation on which it was established by the 1998 Wales Act. That is to say, the idea of an Assembly whose powers are legally shared by all elected Assembly members. Instead, in practice powers are exercised by the majority coalition Assembly Government. The National Assembly first joined the Wales European Centre in February 2000 as a result of a unanimous decision made in plenary session. The opposition party leaders were appointed Directors of the Centre alongside the leadership of the minority Administration at the time. In other words, it was the Corporate Body that voted to join the Wales European Centre. However, it was the Assembly Government that unilaterally took the decision to leave and set up a representative presence on its own account. Other 'embassies' will follow in New York, San Francisco, Sydney, Tokyo, and Singapore.

The emergence of a strong central authority represents a profound innovation in Welsh political life. The notion of Wales having a civic culture is novel to a society with such little experience of its own institutions. Before the onset of the National Assembly it could be fairly said that there was *a civil society in Wales* rather than a *Welsh civil society*. This was simply because there were was an under-developed civic infrastructure to which Welsh society could respond. We now see a civic culture beginning to develop and its clearest manifestation is the Assembly Government. However, unless there are substantial changes made to the operation and powers of the Assembly as a whole, there will inevitably be a diminution of accountability.

ACCOUNTABILITY

A special issue of their newsletter *Links Dolenni* floated across the desks of the 4,000 or so civil servants in Cathays Park and Cardiff Bay on St David's Day, 1 March 2002. It announced that the vast majority of them no longer served the National Assembly for Wales. Instead their new master was to be the Welsh Assembly Government, complete with a new logo. As the

[15] Assembly *Record*, 16 April 2002.

Permanent Secretary Sir Jon Shortridge put it: 'This new identity is aimed at making a clear distinction between the actions and decisions of the Cabinet and the work of Assembly members as a whole.'[16]

On first reading the constitutional implications were unclear. The change could be laying the foundations for the future development of the Assembly in extending its functions and acquiring primary law-making powers. On the other hand, the stage could be set for the bulk of the Welsh administration reverting to type, in effect reconstituting the old-style Welsh Office in Cathays Park. In this scenario the Assembly would be left as the smaller arm in the Bay, inconvenient at times but generally a forum in which ministers make pronouncements rather than being held to account.

'Who do I work for now?' was a question posed by one headline in the newsletter. So far as the strict legal position was concerned, the response was that civil servants 'are still bound by the Civil Service Code which requires us to be accountable to 'Assembly Secretaries and the National Assembly as a body'.' But, in practice, it continued: '. . . most civil servants except for those in the Presiding Office, work most of the time either for the Assembly Government or provide corporate services across the whole of the Assembly.'[17]

The newsletter is significant because it marked the point where the idea of the National Assembly as a corporate body was formally abandoned — *de facto* if not *de jure*, since the latter would require amendment to the 1998 Government of Wales Act. The stage is set for further development of a conventional parliamentary institution along Westminster lines, with the executive on one side, based in Cathays Park, clearly separated from the Assembly in Cardiff Bay on the other.

There is no doubt that the vast majority of politicians across the parties have welcomed this development. Greater clarity of function and clearer lines of accountability have ensued. As we have seen, the establishment of the independent Presiding Office with its own £23 million budget, together with the creation of the majority coalition between Labour and the Liberal Democrats, made it inevitable in any event.

However, a danger arises because of the disproportionate size of the two arms of the government of Wales. On the one side there is the Welsh Assembly Government, the Cabinet of nine ministers and five deputy ministers serviced by some 3,500 (full-time equivalent) civil servants (see Figure 2.2). On the other there are the backbench Assembly Members serviced by the Presiding Office. Although this has 229 civil servants working for it, in practice only around a quarter provide direct administrative services for the Assembly, including research and policy support for backbench members and the committees. Even comparing the respective libraries, the one in

---

[16] Welsh Assembly Government, *Links Dolenni*, 1 March 2002.
[17] *Ibid.*

Cathays Park, which is now part of the Assembly Government, has more staff than the one serving the Assembly in Cardiff Bay.

Figure 2.2: The Assembly Cabinet, August 2001 — July 2002

First Minister	Rt. Hon. Rhodri Morgan AM[18]
Deputy First Minister, Minister for Rural Development and Wales Abroad	Mike German AM[19]
Minister for Economic Development	Andrew Davies AM[20]
Minister for Finance, Local Government and Communities	Edwina Hart MBE AM
Minister for Open Government	Carwyn Jones AM[21]
Minister for Education and Lifelong Learning	Jane Davidson AM
Minister for Culture, Sports and the Welsh Language	Jenny Randerson AM
Minister for Environment	Sue Essex AM
Minister for Health and Social Services	Jane Hutt AM
Deputy Minister for Education and Lifelong Learning	Alun Pugh AM
Deputy Minister for Local Government	Peter Black AM
Deputy Minister for Health	Brian Gibbons AM
Deputy Minister for Rural Affairs, Culture and Environment	Delyth Evans AM
Deputy Minister for Economic Development	John Griffiths AM

In these circumstances the question arises whether the Assembly is equipped to hold the Welsh Assembly Government effectively to account. In the Wales Act it was envisaged that Assembly committees would have access to the full range of civil service support and back up. Under the new dispensation this is now simply not the case. The *Links Dolenni* newsletter suggests that in future officials in Cardiff Bay will be dealing with those in Cathays Park as though they are negotiating with a separate government department.

[18] Minister for Economic Development until 26 February 2002.
[19] From June 2002.
[20] Minister for Assembly Business until 26 February 2002.
[21] Minister for Assembly Business and Rural Affairs (26 February 2002 — 17 June 2002); Minister for Rural Affairs (until 26 February 2002).

To this it should be added that officials within the Presiding Office remain civil servants, answerable finally to the Permanent Secretary, Sir Jon Shortridge. This is in contrast with the position in Westminster and in the Scottish Parliament where parliamentary officials are entirely separate from the civil service with their own career structures. As the Presiding Officer has asked: how enthusiastically can officials in the Assembly's Presiding Office be expected to advise backbench members on opposing Welsh Assembly Government policies when they know that ultimately their promotion prospects lie on the other side of the fence?[22]

The year-long review of the Assembly's procedures recognised the force of these arguments and made a limited concession to the pressure for more resources. It recommended that an additional specialist member of staff be allocated to each of the seven subject committees, plus a pool of around three other specialists to serve any of the Committees as required. Significantly, one of the specialists would be a lawyer to monitor forthcoming Assembly Government, Westminster and European Union legislation. This was described by the Deputy Presiding Officer, John Marek, as 'probably our biggest advance.'[23]

However, the appointment in mid 2002 of just one legal adviser to service all the Committees as a result of the Procedural Review (an Assistant Counsel transferred from the Office of the Counsel General), merely highlights the scale of the problem. At this point the subject committees were just beginning to get to grips with their responsibilities for dealing with the flood of secondary legislation. The prospects were that they would be engulfed in the process, especially the health, education and agriculture committees.

These problems point to the need for the Presiding Office to have considerably more staff if it is to service members effectively, a need that would be that much greater if the Assembly were to extend its competence to primary legislation. The outstanding contrast is with the Scottish Parliament which, during the first term, dealt with some ten pieces of primary legislation a year. To deal with this, together with making the Parliament effective in holding the Scottish Executive to account, the Presiding Office has a staff of 463 with more than 100 directly supporting and advising its committees and backbenchers.

The Scottish figure should be placed against job advertisements placed by the Assembly's Presiding Office in July 2002 seeking a Deputy Clerk (salary between £70,000 and £90,000) and up to eleven researchers to service the committees, plus five extra staff for the Assembly library. This was an important step forward, but given the size of the task only a modest one.

---

[22] Lord Elis-Thomas, Evidence to the Richard Commission, December 2002.

[23] Assembly *Record*, 14 February 2002. For a full account of the Procedural Review see Osmond, J., 'Constitution Building on the Hoof'.

THE COALITION

Coalition government may have brought stability and policy coherence to the Assembly Government, but amongst some Labour backbenchers it was an ongoing irritant. For instance, Ron Davies, who announced that he was available as an alternative leader whenever Rhodri Morgan chose to step down, accused him of bouncing the party into the deal without consultation.[24] Another Labour backbencher, Peter Law, declared:

> Many sections of the Labour Party are very concerned about the way we're going now, we're going wider and wider away from the core membership with the leadership taking us down the road that nobody voted for in the Labour Party — to be with the Liberal Democrats.[25]

These were peripheral voices, however. A more serious ongoing problem for the coalition was the position of the Liberal Democrat leader, Mike German, who stepped down from his post as Deputy First Minister in July 2001 while a police investigation into his affairs continued. It had been expected that the investigation, into allegations concerning the Liberal Democrat leader's former role as Head of the European Unit at the Welsh Joint Education Committee, would have been completed by Christmas 2001. However, its continuation into the New Year forced the First Minister to make some changes to ward off criticism that economic development was failing to receive a minister's undivided attention. At the end of February 2002 Andrew Davies was moved from his position as Business Manager to take over the Economic Development portfolio, while Carwyn Jones became Business Manager, though continuing to hold on to his post as Minister for Rural Affairs. Some four months later German was finally cleared of criminal charges, allowing his immediate return to the Cabinet as Deputy First Minister and Minister for Rural Development and Wales Abroad. The 'Wales Abroad' title was a new portfolio which gave the Welsh Liberal Democrat leader responsibility for co-ordinating the promotion of Wales in the rest of the UK and overseas. The press immediately labelled him Wales's new Foreign Minister.[26]

While Rhodri Morgan's persistence in standing by his coalition partner throughout the year-long police investigation provoked frustration amongst the opposition and some of his own backbenchers, it reaped the dividend in terms of reciprocal loyalty from the Liberal Democrats. This was put to a large test in the latter half of 2001 over Labour's insistence on pushing through major structural changes in the organisation of the Welsh health service, against strong Liberal Democrat objections. Only top-level, last

[24] HTV Wales, 23 August 2002.
[25] *Dragon's Eye*, BBC Wales, 18 July 2002.
[26] *Western Mail*, 18 June 2002.

minute negotiations led to a compromise which kept the Liberal Democrats on side.

Radical proposals to abolish the five Welsh health authorities and replace them with 22 local health boards, coterminous with the 22 local authorities, were presented to the Cabinet in early July 2001 without prior consultation with the Liberal Democrats. This attempt to railroad the proposals through the coalition resulted in the Liberal Democrat group in the Assembly taking the extraordinary step of making its own response to the formal consultation process that ensued. In it the group called for substantial modifications to the coalition policy, specifically an all-Wales health authority to keep the administration of the Welsh health service at arms length from the Assembly.

The background to the row was a key health component of the partnership agreement that established the coalition between the Liberal Democrats and Labour in October 2000. This stated that the new Administration would: 'Seek a period of organisational stability within Health Services in Wales to allow staff to prioritise the delivery of better health care.'

In December 2000 Health Minister Jane Hutt sought the agreement of the Liberal Democrat health spokesperson Kirsty Williams, chair of the health committee, for this clause to be set aside. Her consent was given but not in anticipation of the radical proposals that subsequently emerged, and certainly not in the expectation that there would be no further consultation. The issue came to a head in mid November 2001 when a crisis meeting to thrash out a compromise was held between First Minister Rhodri Morgan, Health Minister Jane Hutt, the Deputy First Minister, Jenny Randerson (a Liberal Democrat), and the Liberal leader, Mike German. The Press Association quoted 'a senior Liberal Democrat source' as claiming the Health Minister had learned a lesson in partnership:

> We have been screaming blue murder about this for three weeks telling her she must stop and talk to us before going ahead. But she kept on going, digging herself deeper and deeper into it. There was no ideological split, it just comes down to practical solutions. There will be some bruised people on both sides after this, but we have always said partnership government is not comfortable or easy.[27]

Liberal Democrat caution over the changes was underlined eight months later when Jane Hutt revealed that, despite her initial claim that the reorganisation would be 'cost neutral',[28] it would in fact cost an estimated £15.5 million.[29] In October 2002 a leaked memorandum by the civil servant in charge of managing the restructuring process, revealed there were problems in meeting the 1 April 2003 deadline for making the change. These included

---

[27] Press Association report, 14 November 2001. For a full account of this episode see the monitoring report, *Coalition Creaks Over Health*, Cardiff: IWA, December 2001.

[28] Assembly *Record*, 27 November, 2001.

[29] *Western Mail*, 13 July, 2002.

major recruitment problems with only 12 of the 22 new health board chief executives appointed. None of the chief executives of the old five health authorities had applied, most of them taking up positions elsewhere in the UK.[30]

The Assembly Government's determination to drive through this policy, regardless of the opposition, also revealed a structural weakness in the process of achieving primary legislation for Wales. Without primary powers the Assembly has to rely on Westminster to legislate for major policy initiatives. Each year this entails the Assembly entering a competition with other Whitehall departments for consideration of its bills. A further difficulty is that the timetables of the Assembly and those of Westminster are invariably out of phase with one another. The upshot can mean that major proposals go through without effective scrutiny, either in the Assembly or at Westminster. This proved to be the case with the health service reorganisation. In June 2001 the Assembly Government announced that an NHS (Wales) Bill to implement the organisation would be included in the forthcoming Queen's Speech at Westminster. In a Press release Health Minister Jane Hutt made clear that the stand-alone Welsh Bill would allow greater debate: 'The intention is for the draft Bill to be published in the Autumn and the Assembly will have a strong voice in discussing and debating the proposals before they reach the House of Commons.'[31]

However, within a few weeks this was withdrawn and, instead, the proposals were incorporated within an England and Wales bill, due it was said to pressures on parliamentary time. This meant that the proposals went to Westminster in November before they were debated in plenary session in Cardiff. Not only that, details of the Assembly Government's consultation on the proposals, a document running to 500 pages, only arrived in the House of Commons library on the morning of the Second Reading debate. Former Welsh Office Health Minister Jon Owen Jones, Labour MP for Cardiff Central, revealed that in a few hours reading his researcher had found a good deal of concern amongst respondents to the consultation at the details of the proposed restructuring. This went against the Assembly Government's claim that there was widespread support for the changes. In his intervention Jon Owen Jones reflected on the constitutional position whereby the first controversial Welsh legislation to be considered by Parliament since the devolution settlement was being inadequately scrutinised:

> The debate is an opportunity to test whether the present constitutional settlement for Wales provides a means for adequate scrutiny of new Bills. The Welsh Assembly does not have primary legislation powers, but if Parliament simply acts as a rubber stamp for Welsh matters brought to the House, we should dispense

[30] BBC Wales, *Dragon's Eye*, 24 October 2002.
[31] Assembly Administration Press Release, 20 June 2001.

with the charade and move towards giving the Welsh Assembly primary legislation powers.[32]

POLICY DIVERGENCE

In his annual report to the Assembly in October 2002 First Minister Rhodri Morgan highlighted eight main achievements of the coalition's second year:

**Figure 2.3: Assembly Government achievements
August 2001– July 2002**

- Lower prescription charges than in England.
- Free local bus travel for pensioners and disabled people.
- Free entry to our eight national museums.
- No Key Stage 1 statutory testing in schools.
- Six weeks free home care.
- Assembly Learning Grants for people in higher and further education after the age of 18 on a means tested basis.
- Finance Wales set up as a user-friendly 'bank' for small and medium enterprises.
- Piloting the Welsh Baccalaureate for the 16–19 age group in 19 schools and colleges.

The Assembly Government's legislative aspirations for the 2002–03 parliamentary session are laid out in Figure 2.4.[33] Presenting these to a plenary debate in March 2002 the First Minister Rhodri Morgan noted that the Scottish Parliament had been passing about ten measures a year. He added that in its attempt to pursue primary legislation at Westminster the National Assembly was in a similar position to a Whitehall Department which might hope to achieve one or two measures per year:

> We must try to work out what is a reasonable share for us in terms of primary legislation. When there are 25 Bills in a typical Queen's Speech, should we be looking to include one or two Bills, or one major Bill and one small, tidying-up measure?[34]

He also drew attention to the two proposals in the list specific to Wales, the termination of the requirement to hold ballots on Sunday opening and management of common land. On the latter he remarked:

> It may not be a big issue, and it is certainly not a big issue in England, and will never be subject to legislation there. It is a much bigger issue in Wales. This is a

[32] HC Deb, 20 November 2001, col. 252.

[33] For a more detailed discussion of these measures see the IWA quarterly report, *Engaging with Europe: Monitoring the National Assembly March to June 2002*, p. 32–35.

[34] *Ibid.*

classic example of where we need the House of Commons' legislative facilities to pass a Bill on a specific Welsh problem, namely overgrazing on our commons. That does not seem to occur outside Wales to such a degree that would cause people to consider legislation necessary.[35]

By the Autumn of 2002, it was possible to identify four significant areas where significant policy innovation had occurred outwith the requirement for primary legislation to allow it to happen: education, the Communities First regeneration programme, the Welsh language, and European affairs.

Figure 2.4: The Assembly Government's eight priorities for Welsh legislation in the 2002–03 Westminster parliamentary session

1. **Common Land (Wales) Bill** to reform and strengthen the management of common land in Wales.

2. **Sunday Licensing (Wales) Bill** to remove the need for local authorities to hold polls on the opening of licensed premises on Sundays, where requested.

3. **St David's Day Bill** to provide for St David's Day to be a public holiday in Wales.

4. **Land Use Planning Bill** to implement proposals on changes to planning procedures designed to speed up the operation and clarity of the system. These are currently subject to consultation following a Green Paper in England. There are no financial impacts for the Assembly and potential cost savings for users of the planning system.

5. **Education Bill** to strengthen the Assembly's ability to implement proposals in the education paving document *The Learning Country.*

6. **Audit (Wales) Bill** to merge the functions of the Audit Commission in Wales and the Auditor General for Wales to create a single audit body for Wales (as already exist in Scotland and Northern Ireland).

7. **Housing Ombudsman (Wales) Bill** to extend the remit of the Local Government Ombudsman for Wales to cover registered social landlords.

8. **Passenger Transport Bill** to follow up the recommendations of a policy review of public transport, providing for organisational structures to support public transport planning and provision and giving the Assembly

Education

The Assembly Government's introduction of a 'Learning Grant' for students in February 2002 confirmed the emergence of a distinctive education system in Wales. It followed the elimination of league tables for school examination results, the commissioning of a pilot study for a new Welsh baccalaureate

---

[35] *Ibid.*

qualification, and the publication of a Welsh 'White Paper' *The Learning Country*, in September 2001, which separated Welsh from English education policy in a number of respects. In addition, during this period the education committee published a comprehensive report on the future of higher education in Wales. Taken together these changes mark a significant divergence of education policy in Wales.

The new 'Learning Grant', worth up to £1,500 per person a year, will provide financial support for students in higher education and, for the first time, students in further education. It was estimated that it would average around £700 to £800 and would be paid to some 43,000 students at a cost of £41 million during 2002–03. The announcement meant there were now three different arrangements for student support in Wales, Scotland, and England — providing one of the clearest examples of policy divergence due to devolution. As Education Minister Jane Davidson put it: 'Wales already has a better record than any other part of mainland UK when it comes to attracting youngsters from the lower attainment groups into higher education. We want to improve on that record.'[36] She added that the initiative was based on one of the key recommendations in a report she had commissioned the previous year from an independent investigation group into student hardship, chaired by Professor Teresa Rees of Cardiff University: 'The Rees report told us that our concerns that potential students are put off applying for courses because of student hardship — either real or perceived — were well-founded. We had to do something imaginative to tackle the problem.'[37] Her education White Paper, *The Learning Country* also differed from the provisions for England in other areas. In England the private sector will be encouraged to bid for proposals to build new schools. The Welsh document did not envisage such extensive private sector involvement. There was also no mention of the targets set for English Local Education Authorities to allocate 90 per cent of their resources straight to schools. England may have centrally controlled numeracy and literacy strategies but, according to *The Learning Country*, teachers in Wales would be allowed to decide on their own teaching methods. There was also no mention of city academies and specialist and faith schools, ideas that were strongly advocated in the English initiatives. Other provisions included:

- An end to testing at age seven
- A new foundation level for ages three to seven
- Closer links between primary and secondary schools to raise standards for children between ages 11–13
- An overhaul of special needs.

---

[36] Assembly Government Press Release, 12 February 2002.
[37] *Ibid.*

During the plenary debate on the England and Wales education bill, which embraced the provisions laid down in *The Learning Country*, Jane Davidson emphasised that it provided an exemplar of the way devolution should work:

> I reiterate that this Bill is an example of devolution working. In the 20 odd years that I have been involved in looking at Parliamentary Bills, I am not aware of any other where two countries have been able to go in two different directions, using the same piece of legislation, devised together before the legislation went for scrutiny through the various parliamentary stages.[38]

Communities First

Communities First is a major programme aimed at tackling Wales' relatively low GDP by addressing high economic inactivity in deprived areas, found largely within the Objective 1 region of west Wales and the south Wales Valleys. Involving expenditure of £83 million over the first three years (2002–05), the programme is targeting 142 of Wales' most disadvantaged communities.[39]

The programme, which has a lifespan of at least ten years, aims to have long-term effects through tackling the factors that cause or contribute to poverty. Communities themselves, in partnerships with statutory bodies, voluntary groups and the private sector, will identify their requirements and how to achieve them. Capacity building forms an important part of this strategy. As the Director of the Assembly Government's communities directorate, Norma Barry, put it:

> Because it is so difficult for people to break out of the cycle of poverty and deprivation the Assembly has gone to the experts — the people who live in our most deprived communities. It is from their experience that we are most likely to learn both about the problems being faced and the solutions which can be applied to them. This bottom-up approach is very different from measures adopted in the past. Finding ways of making it easier for individuals who are living in some of our most disadvantaged communities to improve their living conditions and personal circumstances in a way that suits them gives power and responsibility to people themselves. It puts communities first, itself the name of the Assembly's programme for tackling poverty and social disadvantage.[40]

'A Bilingual Wales'

At the end of July 2002, the Assembly Government published *Bilingual Future* and it was immediately labelled a landmark document. In it First Minister Rhodri Morgan and Culture Minister Jenny Randerson pledged that: 'The Welsh Assembly Government is wholly committed to revitalising

---

[38] Assembly *Record*, 10 January 2002.

[39] Assembly Government Communities Directorate, *Communities First Guidance*, September 2001. See also the Annual Report on Social Exclusion in Wales, March 2002.

[40] Norma Barry, 'Ten Years to Tackle Social Exclusion', *AGENDA*, IWA, Summer 2002.

the Welsh language and creating a bilingual Wales.'[41] This was highly significant since for the first time in the history of the Welsh language, a government was taking full responsibility for its future. The commitment also came
in the wake of an 18-month period in the life of the Assembly when, contrary to
expressed hopes at the outset, the language had become a matter of contentious
dispute between the parties, especially Labour and Plaid Cymru. *Bilingual
Future* agrees with the definition of what would constitute a 'bilingual Wales' as
set out at the head of the joint report of the Culture and Education committees'
policy review *Our Language: Its Future*, published a month earlier:

> In a truly bilingual Wales both Welsh and English will flourish and will be treated
> as equal. A bilingual Wales means a country where people can choose to live their
> lives through the medium of either or both languages; a country where the
> presence of two national languages and cultures is a source of pride and strength
> to us all.[42]

In their Foreword to *Bilingual Wales*, Rhodri Morgan and Jenny
Randerson continued:

> The Welsh language is an important part of our national identity and creativity,
> and awareness of the educational, cultural and social benefits of bilingualism is
> growing. Bilingual, and even multilingual cultures are the norm rather than the
> exception in much of Europe and across the world. That is why the Assembly
> Government believes that languages should be seen as providing opportunities
> and economic benefits for Wales . . .[43]

The policy statement commits to two significant strategic initiatives:

- The Assembly Government will ensure that the Welsh language is
  mainstreamed across Ministerial portfolios and within all Assembly sponsored public bodies. Each Assembly Government minister will take
  responsibility and ownership of the language within their own particular
  policy areas.
- The Assembly Government would publish an action plan for a bilingual
  Wales by the end of 2002. The plan would involve a blend of policies
  across the range of Assembly Government Ministerial portfolios, and
  would contain concrete measures in support of the language.[44]

Engaging with the European Union

In May 2002 First Minister Rhodri Morgan pronounced a 'first for Welsh
diplomacy in Europe' when he joined with nine other regional governments

---

[41] *Bilingual Future: A Policy Statement by the Welsh Assembly Government*, July 2002.
[42] *Our Language: Its Future*, joint report of the Culture and Education Committees, June 2002.
[43] *Bilingual Future: A Policy Statement by the Welsh Assembly Government*, July 2002.
[44] *Ibid.*

in promoting a declaration in response to the Commission White Paper on European governance. The declaration called for more involvement of the European regions in European policy formulation, with the European Commission consulting directly with regional governments rather than via member state governments.

The move was as much declaratory and symbolic as indicative of real political pressure being mounted on behalf of the regions. Nevertheless, it was a further indication of the First Minister's enthusiasm for promoting Welsh aspirations on as wide a stage as possible. Previously the Assembly Government has merely endorsed declarations emanating from other regions seeking greater influence within the councils of the European Union.[45] On this occasion the Press notice observed: 'This is the first time that the Welsh government has been an original signatory of a trans European declaration'.[46]

The other participating regional governments were: Emilia-Romagna, Marche, and Tuscany within Italy; Hesse within Germany; Flanders and Wallonia within Belgium; Skane within Sweden; Aquitaine within France; and Scotland. Rhodri Morgan judged that Wales' involvement marked a significant step:

> It shows great progress in our standing in Europe that other Regions want to work with us and share our experience. Just a couple of years ago it would have been impossible to imagine Wales being at the core of a group of this sort. This development shows that the concept of a 'Welsh diplomacy' in Europe is developing as a reality.[47]

A further indication of the Administration's determination to establish a firmer grip on the European dimension of policy making was revealed in two Cabinet papers prepared by the First Minister, *The Spanish Presidency of the European Union* and *An Analysis of Opportunities for Ministers to Influence Policy in the EU*, published in March 2002.[48] The former was the first occasion for a Cabinet paper to be prepared on the priorities of a member state holding the presidency of the European Union. It notes:

> In the context of the debate on EU reform, the EU's six-month rotating presidency has been facing increased criticism from all sides and could well be abolished in the future. Recently, Peter Hain, the UK's Minister for Europe, and José Maria Aznar, the Spanish Prime Minister and current EU President, both expressed their support for the abolition of the rotation.[49]

---

[45] See 'Wales joins EU Legislative Regions Lobby' in the quarterly monitoring report *Coalition Creaks Over Health*, Cardiff: IWA, December 2001, pp. 57–59.
[46] Assembly Government Press notice, 13 May 2002.
[47] *Ibid.*
[48] Assembly website: Cabinet minutes for 11 and 18 March 2002.
[49] *Ibid.*

The second Cabinet paper sets out a matrix for the European policy questions that Assembly Cabinet ministers should target, as shown in Figure 2.5.

Figure 2.5: Assembly Government target pressure points for influencing European Union policy

CABINET MINISTER	OPPORTUNITY TO INFLUENCE
Cohesion Policy: **First Minister** (future of economic & social cohesion, post–2006) & **Minister for Economic Development** (current Structural Funds programmes)	• Cohesion workshops in Brussels 27–28 May. Though ministerial presence has not yet been proposed by either the Commission or the UK lead department (DTI), we are pursuing the question of representation of Wales' interests at these workshops. • Visit of Commissioner Michel Barnier to Wales, mid–2002, date to be confirmed.
Review of Common Fisheries Program: Rural Affairs Minister (sensitivities as above)	• Minister at UK Fisheries Ministers meeting 18 April; Assembly officials involved in agreement on UK government position on CFP review.
Consistency with European Union Sustainable Development Strategy (again sensitivities as above) and **Impact Assessment methodology; Environment Minister**	• Minister sees papers on UK position in respect of the EU SDS in the run-up to Barcelona and Seville, and attended the European Environment Council on 4 March. • DEFRA are sponsoring a seminar on sustainability impact assessment in Brussels on 23 April to look at the experience of the Member States, international and regional bodies, and may be willing to feature the Integration Tool we are developing.
Transport Policy — First Minister or Environment Minister	• There is an opportunity to influence on integrated transport. Wales is a member of the Conference of the Peripheral Maritime Regions and we can put forward our ideas for integrated transport through this forum for peripheral regions of the EU. They hold meetings throughout the year and our FM has been invited to Spain in March.

THE RICHARD COMMISSION

The independent commission on the Assembly's powers, agreed as part of the coalition partnership, began work in September 2002. Rhodri Morgan described its chairman, the Labour peer Lord Ivor Richard, as:

> . . . halfway between being 100 per cent Labour Government loyalist, never departing from the party line, and an independent who is outside the party. He is the right kind of person in terms of having clout in Whitehall and Westminster ... Requesting transfers of functions or primary legislative powers means that someone must relinquish power and that someone else must gain it: power that Whitehall and Westminster give up is gained by the Assembly. Experience and clout in Whitehall and Westminster is needed as well as knowledge of Wales.[50]

The extent of Lord Richard's 'clout' in Whitehall remains to be tested, as does the relatively low profile and general lack of constitutional expertise of the other nine appointments to the commission.[51] Following publication of the Commission's report, towards the end of 2003, the timetable will be dictated by Westminster. As Rhodri Morgan judged:

> ... it will become part of the political process of drawing up manifestos for the general election in Westminster. If there were recommendations requiring primary legislation, they would have to appear in manifestos at the time of the next Westminster general election in 2005 or 2006.[52]

The commission is charged with making recommendations on the powers, size, funding and electoral arrangements of the National Assembly, based on the evidence of the Assembly's first term. During the Assembly debate on the establishment of the commission Rhodri Morgan drew attention to the coincidence of the timing of its deliberations with those under way on the future constitution of the European Union:

> A major revision of European treaties will take place at an inter-governmental conference in early 2004. The Laeken convention has been set up to cover the next 12 months, and the double subsidiarity question will be considered. What should Europe, member states and regional tier governments be doing? That was Tony Blair and Gerhard Schröder's deal at the Nice summit in 2001. That is why the Laeken convention is in full swing now, and is why any recommendations by the

[50] Assembly *Record*, 18 April 2002.

[51] The appointments were announced in August 2002. Four members were nominated by the political parties, and five public appointments were made following advertisement. The political appointments were former Merthyr MP Ted Rowlands (Labour); political lecturer Laura McAllister (Plaid); former MEP Peter Price (Liberal Democrat); and former Swansea councillor Paul Valerio (Conservative). The public appointments were Eira Davies, Managing Director of a Wrexham web publishing business; Vivienne Sugar, former Swansea Chief Executive; Sir Michael Wheeler-Booth, former Clerk of the Parliaments at Westminster; Tom Jones, a farmer from Powys and Chair of Wales Council for Voluntary Action; and Huw Vaughan Thomas, former Chief Executive of Denbighshire.

[52] Assembly *Record*, 18 April 2002

Richard commission would be relevant to the conclusions of the
inter-governmental conference in the first quarter of 2004.[53]

What Rhodri Morgan has in mind is that separate arguments made at the
Welsh and European Union levels will reinforce once another in helping
persuade a Westminster government to give ground on extending primary
legislative powers to the National Assembly some time beyond the next
general election. Written and oral evidence presented to the House of Lords
Committee on the Constitution by the Presiding Officer, Lord Elis-Thomas,
in May 2002, argued strongly that the 1998 Wales Act was fundamentally
flawed in failing to delineate the Assembly's powers in terms of subject
areas. Instead, as a memorandum, prepared by his legal adviser David
Lambert, put it, the Assembly:

> . . . exercises its functions by reference to an uncomfortable amalgam of general
> powers in the Government of Wales Act, of specific powers in the Transfer of
> Functions Orders made under section 22 of the Act, of specific powers given in a
> variety of ways in post-devolution legislation and by subject areas in derogation
> orders enabling it to implement Community Directives. Each legislative
> instrument which may give powers to the Assembly has to be carefully scrutinised
> page by page. There is no overall subject area competence and no general way of
> quickly and comprehensively finding whether an Act gives powers to the
> Assembly. Can the Assembly continue in this way with such fragmented powers,
> while seeking to make a significant contribution to the future well-being of
> Wales? This is one of the matters that will need to be considered by the [Richard]
> Commission . . .[54]

Meanwhile, practical experience of the Assembly wielding its existing
powers is already leading to some modification. The outstanding example
was the 2001 foot and mouth crisis. As a result the Animal Health Act 1981 is
to be amended to devolve operational control to the National Assembly in
line with the position in Scotland and Northern Ireland. This was made clear
by Carwyn Jones, former Minister for Rural Affairs and now Business
Manager, in oral evidence he gave to the House of Lords Constitution
Committee in May 2002. As he put it:

> Our viewpoint publicly, and the viewpoint that has been accepted in principle by
> the Department for the Environment, Food and Rural Affairs, is that we should
> have the powers over foot and mouth, the same powers that exist in Scotland and

---

[53] Assembly *Record*, 20 June 2002. He has made this point on a number of occasions during the
previous few years, for example in December 2000: see Osmond, J., 'In Search of Stability. Coalition
Politics in the Second Year of the National Assembly for Wales,' in, A. Trench (ed) *State of the Nations
2001: The Second Year of Devolution in the United Kingdom* (Exeter: Imprint Academic, 2001), p. 41.

[54] David Lambert, 'Statutory Functions: the Complications of Executive Devolution', House of
Lords Constitution Select Committee on the Constitution Session 2001–02 *Devolution:
Inter-institutional relations in the United Kingdom* Evidence complete to 10 July 2002 HL Paper 147, p.
268.

the same powers that exist in Northern Ireland, because we have the staff to enable the operation centres to be run.[55]

The fact that the powers are not devolved is a classic example of the arbitrary nature of the Government of Wales Act 1998. As indicated by the Presiding Officer's legal adviser, in the quotation above, this transferred functions to the National Assembly piece-meal, on the basis of the previous functions of the Welsh Office. In turn, these were derived from a complex array of specific ministerial functions, named in more than 300 separate pieces of Westminster primary and secondary legislation. In the case of foot and mouth Carwyn Jones described the problem in the following terms:

> The Assembly is a corporate body according to the Government of Wales Act but the fiction that it acts as one has in practice been abandoned, with a *de facto* Executive scrutinised by a legislature. Yet, Assembly Ministers are not Ministers according to law, and this means that whenever primary legislation talks of the 'Minister' it means the UK Minister unless the Assembly or previously the Secretary of State is specified in the legislation. The Animal Health Act 1981, which largely governs animal diseases, only mentions the 'Minister' and so animal health is not devolved.[56]

In his evidence to the House of Lords Constitution Committee Jones made the case for the Assembly's powers to be devolved in terms of subject areas, as with the Scotland Act that established the Scottish Parliament:

> Administrative devolution began in Scotland in Victorian times, in Wales in the 1960s, and the tendency has been for some powers in policy areas to be transferred rather than full responsibility to be transferred. This is something that we see further devolution settling. It means, of course, that agriculture is in the main as devolved as it can be, given the Common Agriculture Policy, but there are situations such as this [foot and mouth crisis] where the power was reserved to DEFRA but where experience and practice suggests that it would be best devolved to an institution that has the staff to be able to carry out policy. The difficulty that I faced personally was whilst from a strictly legal viewpoint I had no responsibility at all and could have turned around and said 'this is nothing to do with me' and done nothing, and that from a legal viewpoint is correct, but from a political and public viewpoint that would have been wholly unacceptable. The political accountability was seen as resting in this place whereas legally it did not and that is the circle that has to be squared next year.[57]

[55] House of Lords Constitution Select Committee on the Constitution Session 2001–02 *Devolution: Inter-institutional relations in the United Kingdom* Evidence complete to 10 July 2002 HL Paper 147, p. 270.

[56] Carwyn Jones, 'Responsibility Without Power', *AGENDA*, IWA, Autumn 2001.

[57] House of Lords Constitution Select Committee on the Constitution Session 2001–02 *Devolution: Inter-institutional relations in the United Kingdom* Evidence complete to 10 July 2002 HL Paper 147, p. 271.

FINANCE: A CORE CONCERN

In July 2002 Gordon Brown announced the results of the latest UK government's Comprehensive Spending Review, which determines almost all the financial resources that will be available to the Assembly over the next three years. The bare bones of the settlement are set out in Figure 2.6.

Figure 2.6: Comprehensive Spending Review for Wales, July 2002

£ million	2002–03	2003–04	2004–05	2005–06
Resource Budget	8,829	9,655	10,240	11,000
Capital Budget	801	830	919	999
Total Departmental Expenditure Limit[57]	9,424	10,275	10,941	11,774

Political reactions to these headline figures concentrated on three main issues:

1. The 'Barnett squeeze', that is the relative difference between increases in spending between England and Wales.
2. EU money and matched funding.
3. The link between financial transfers and the Assembly's powers.

The 'Barnett Squeeze'

Plaid Cymru demonstrated that, comparing like-for-like (that is, those items which correspond exactly to items in the budget of the Assembly) the English budget will rise from £131.87 billion to £171.38 billion between 2002–03 and 2005–06. However, the corresponding budget in Wales will only rise from £9.42 billion to £11.77 billion. This enabled the party to make the argument that: 'Allowing for inflation this means that the overall budget in England for the devolved matters will increase by 6.6 per cent per annum in real terms. The corresponding budget in Wales will rise by 5.2 per cent per annum.'[58]

This is the essence of what has become known as the 'Barnett squeeze', named after the Financial Secretary to the Treasury, Joel Barnett, who gave his name to the formula which calibrates the distribution of funding increases between England, Wales, Scotland and Northern Ireland. The actual increase in the budget in Wales is equivalent to about six per cent of the actual increase in the English budget. As a population-weighted formula this is what the Barnett formula predicts: six per cent is roughly the population of Wales as a proportion of the population of England. Consequently, the actual

---

[57] Full resource budgeting basis, net of depreciation

[58] Plaid Cymru Press Statement, *Dr Phil Williams AM responds to the CSR* 18 July 2002.

increase in expenditure per head in England and Wales is roughly the same. However, because existing levels of expenditure per head are higher in Wales than in England, the same actual increases when expressed as a percentage appear smaller.

This is a well-rehearsed argument in Welsh politics and is being used by Plaid and the Welsh Liberal Democrats to press for a reform of the Barnett formula to take account of the particular needs of Wales. The Assembly Government believes it would be unwise to press for change until it is absolutely clear that the outcome would be a larger share of public expenditure for Wales. As Finance Minister Edwina Hart queried in one debate: 'Can I guarantee that Wales will be better off?'[60] However, it is becoming harder to hold this line. In May 2002 the Liberal Democrats broke ranks with the coalition and sided with Plaid Cymru, arguing the case for change to a needs-based assessment. This view also gained ground amongst Labour backbenchers. Most notably, Ron Davies, the main architect of the Wales Act, put a strong case for change:

> We now need an act of political courage. We must say that the formula that determines how much we currently receive is outdated and must be brought up to date, not least because of the change in political circumstances. The days of Joel Barnett as Chief Secretary to the Treasury sitting in a Cabinet in London when the rules of collective Cabinet responsibility operated are long gone. We now have a new political settlement in this country and we need a new way of allocating financial resources which reflects that new political situation.[61]

Plaid Cymru argued that the Welsh needs position relative to the rest of the UK has worsened significantly since the Barnett formula was first established in the late 1970s. GDP per head in Wales had fallen from 88 per cent to 80 per cent of the UK average. In addition Wales' population of pensionable age was 15 per cent higher than could be predicted from the population under pensionable age — an equivalent of an extra 75,000 retired people. This resulted in quantifiable implications for the health and social services budget which were not covered by the Barnett formula. Using official figures Plaid Cymru calculated the amount to be equivalent to an extra health cost in Wales of about £200 million a year. It claimed that overall a fair needs assessment would benefit Wales by as much as £800 million a year.[62]

---

[60] Assembly Record, 7 May 2002. See the quarterly monitoring report, *Engaging with Europe*, June 2002, for an account of this debate.

[61] Assembly *Record*, 7 May 2002. Later in the year Ron Davies produced a detailed account of his view, arguing that Wales' relatively high spending on health distorted the operation of the formula: see his article 'Where Needs Must' in *Agenda*, IWA, Winter 2002/3.

[62] The figure is based on an assessment reached by Plaid's policy adviser on economic affairs, Professor Phil Williams AM, in a submission to the Treasury Select Committee's inquiry into regional spending across the UK, 'The Case for Replacing the Barnett Formula', April 2002. A Nuffield College, Oxford, paper submitted to the Committee in June 2002 estimated that a 'fair' allocation to Wales would result in an increase of £620 million a year.

EU Money and Matched Funding

The 2002 Comprehensive Spending Review allocates the Assembly money 'over and above' the Barnett formula to provide for EU expenditure in Wales, in particular the amount spent under the Objective 1 programme. So, in addition to the figures in Figure 2.6, Wales will receive an extra £492m between 2003–04 and 2005–06 (or £164 million per year) to 'cover' EU expenditure. However, these monies do not provide for match funding that the public sector in Wales must allocate to EU projects in order to access the EU funds.

The response of the Assembly Government to this criticism is simply that the large overall increases in public expenditure generally, and for economic development in particular, should provide sufficient extra resources for matched funding purposes. The counter-argument put by the opposition is that Wales should have been allocated extra money to take account of the need to match the European funds coming into Wales.

Financial Transfers and the Assembly's Powers

The mechanics of the Barnett formula are closely linked with the Assembly's powers. Following the 2002 Comprehensive Spending Review Plaid Cymru raised the question of the comparability percentages in the Barnett formula for public expenditure on railways. They noted that over the next decade the UK government plans to spend between £20 billion and £30 billion on railways. However, according to the present plans of the Strategic Rail Authority, only about £100 million will be spent in Wales. This is about 0.3 per cent of the total instead of a Barnett formula share of 6 per cent, which Plaid Cymru calculated would result in an extra £130 million a year coming to Wales.

In particular, Plaid argued that the Welsh budget has a zero per cent comparability figure for spending on railways. That is to say, there are no consequentials for the Welsh block for increases in Strategic Rail Authority expenditure. This is because powers over railways have not been devolved to the Assembly. However, these powers have been devolved to London, where London Regional Transport went from 0 per cent comparability in 1998 to 100 per cent in 2000; to Scotland which went up from 0 per cent to 100 per cent in this CSR; and to Northern Ireland which has remained at 100 per cent. As the Plaid Cymru paper put it:

> As the Government have already recognised the lack of investment in railways by the Strategic Rail Authority, a change in comparability to make Wales equal to Scotland and Northern Ireland would have been logical and justified. This was a wide-open door and the fact that Wales remains at 0 per cent is a clear indication of the feeble fight that Paul Murphy and Rhodri Morgan must have made.[63]

[63] Plaid Cymru Press Statement, *Dr Phil Williams AM responds to the CSR* 18 July 2002.

In this way financial issues in the Assembly are being increasingly inter-twined with constitutional debates about future increases in the Assembly's powers. No longer are they regarded as a separate issue that can be negotiated after the constitutional questions have been settled.

UNFINISHED BUSINESS

Funding debates such as these tend to obscure an important political reality. This is the not inconsiderable advantage that throughout the whole of its first term the Assembly has been able to live inside a comfort zone of an ever rising budget. Undoubtedly this central fact contributed more than anything else to the stability of the new institution and its relative harmony with West-minster and Whitehall. It more than counter-balanced the generally acknowl-edged inadequacies in the Government of Wales Act 1998, as articulated for example by the Assembly's procedural review, and frustrations that have constantly surfaced over the lack of clarity around the Assembly's powers. Another important stabilising influence has been the maintenance of Labour-dominated administrations in London and Cardiff, notwithstanding underlying tensions that have occasionally surfaced.

Imagine the difficulties that would have arisen if these circumstances were different, if say the Assembly had been established in the early 1980s. At that time there was a stridently right wing Conservative administration in West-minster, public expenditure was being cut, and major Welsh industries were being dismantled. In examining the lessons of the Assembly's first term, the Richard Commission should adjust its perspective to take account of these extremely benign circumstances. It needs to ask how the Assembly and its present constitutional arrangements would fare if the going became a good deal rougher. How would it manage a combination of falling UK public expenditure and party political competition between London and Cardiff?

There was, of course, no shortage of political melodrama during the Assembly's first term. Occasions that caught the headlines included the vote of no confidence in Alun Michael and his replacement by Rhodri Morgan as First Minister; the coalition between Labour and the Liberal Democrats; the resignation of Rod Richards as Conservative leader faced with a trial for allegedly causing bodily harm, from which he was acquitted; the ordeal of Liberal Democrat leader Mike German who stood aside as Deputy First Minister for a year until a police investigation cleared his name; and what was in effect a leadership coup against Plaid Cymru's President Dafydd Wigley and his replacement with Ieuan Wyn Jones.

Such incidents, involving leading personalities, undoubtedly caught the public's attention. BBC's *Wales Today* evening news bulletin achieved one of the highest recorded ratings for a Welsh television programme on the day Alun Michael resigned, in February 2000. About half the available audience, some 450,000 people, tuned in. In other respects, however, the Assembly has generally operated below the public radar screen, even when specifically Welsh initiatives have had a direct financial impact on the electorate. Free bus passes for the elderly, free entry to museums, free eye tests, and cheaper prescriptions have on the whole been taken for granted and certainly not attributed to the Assembly Government. One reason is that within Wales there has been no point of comparison for such benefits with the position elsewhere in the United Kingdom. Another is the relatively under-developed Welsh press when compared with, for example, the situation in Scotland.

The emergence of the Welsh Assembly Government as an institution separate from the wider National Assembly, in the way that Whitehall is from Westminster, has similarly been little noticed. Yet, as we have seen, this development has profound long-term consequences for the future of Welsh devolution. More generally, public attitudes to the effectiveness and impact of the National Assembly, as recorded by opinion polls, have been deeply discouraging for the politicians. The Institute of Welsh Politics at the University of Wales, Aberystwyth, has tracked attitudes at the key moments of the 1997 referendum, the 1999 Assembly election, and the 2001 Westminster general election.[64] Figure 2.7 provides depressing news for those who thought the Assembly would result in Welsh people believing they had more say in government.

**Figure 2.7: Assembly will give/has given
'ordinary people more say in government'**

Response	1997	1999	2001
More	57.3%	57.7%	35.1%
No Difference	38.0%	39.7%	61.5%
Less	4.6%	2.5%	3.4%

A similar picture is provided by Figure 2.8. This tracks perceptions of the impact the Assembly has had on education, a key policy area where, as we have noted, considerable initiative on a wide front was undertaken during the first term. Midway through 2001, nearly three-quarters of the respondents judged that 'no difference' had been made. Yet in 1997 a majority had believed the Assembly would improve education in Wales.

---

[64] The figures shown here are taken from the Institute's 1997 Welsh Referendum Survey: interviews with 686 respondents in the immediate aftermath of the event; the 1999 Assembly Election Survey: interviews with 1,251 respondents following the election; and the 2001 Welsh Electoral Survey: interviews with 1,085 respondents following the June general election.

Figure 2.8: Impact of the Assembly on education

Response	1997	1999	2001
Improve	54.9%	45.4%	25.0%
No Difference	39.7%	51.2%	71.4%
Reduce	5.4%	3.4%	3.5%

Such views might be expected to contribute to a general disillusionment with the devolution experiment, with many, perhaps a majority, deciding that the National Assembly should be abolished. It is significant, therefore, that the pollsters found the opposite. Rather than wanting less devolution, respondents opted for more. The sentiment appears to be: if we are to have an Assembly, let's make it work effectively. Figure 2.9 shows that since the referendum the number of those favouring a Parliament with law-making and tax raising powers along Scottish lines has nearly doubled, while the number of those opting for no elected body has fallen substantially. Devolution in Wales is unfinished business.

Figure 2.9: Constitutional preferences (%) in Wales, 1997, 1999 and 2001

Constitutional Preference	1997	1999	2001
Independence	14.1%	9.6%	12.3%
Parliament	19.6%	29.9%	38.8%
Assembly	26.8%	35.3%	25.5%
No elected body	39.5%	25.3%	24.0%

Whether the work of the Richard Commission results in the present, virtual Welsh Parliament progressing more or less rapidly to a fully-fledged, legally established institution, invested by the Westminster parliament with competences along Scottish lines, will depend, as ever, on political considerations. It is noteworthy, for instance, that the Welsh Labour Party has decided not to give evidence to the Richard Commission until after the May 2003 Assembly election. This has been prompted by two considerations. One is a desire, ahead of the election, to avoid exposing what are undeniably large differences of view amongst Labour's ranks on how far and how fast the Assembly should acquire further powers. But, secondly, Labour policy makers want to await the outcome of the election itself, so it can then judge what concessions it might have to make to its Liberal Democrat coalition partner, and what potential threat Plaid Cymru may continue to mount against its heartland seats.

That said, there is an undoubted caution within the leadership of Welsh Labour about making constitutional advances too soon. For instance, in early evidence to the Richard Commission, two Labour Ministers stated that they did not need further powers to implement their policies. Economic Development Minister Andrew Davies said that to give the Assembly primary law-making powers at this stage would be 'putting the cart before the horse'.[65] Health Minister Jane Hutt said her officials were already working 'flat out' building on secondary legislation, adding: 'We must walk before we can run and deliver what we can within our powers.'[66]

The 1999 election saw an upheaval in Welsh politics, what became known as a 'quiet earthquake', with Plaid Cymru emerging for the first time as a force to be reckoned with in all regions of Wales, and the main opposition party to Labour in the Assembly. In the Valleys there were extraordinary swings of between 25 and 35 per cent from Labour to Plaid Cymru, with the nationalists winning Islwyn, the Rhondda and Llanelli, and coming a close second elsewhere. Figure 2.10 gives these results, together with details of an NOP poll carried out in November 2002, the first to test voting intention in Wales since the 2001 general election. This suggests that there will be remarkably little change in the May 2003 Assembly election, and also indicates that differential voting between Westminster and Cardiff is now becoming firmly established. In particular, the Liberal Democrats appear to be benefiting more emphatically from proportional representation, with voters beginning to use their first-past-the post and regional list top-up votes more strategically. In fact, the poll suggests that, as has occurred in Scotland, the Liberal Democrats will inch ahead of the Conservatives to become the third strongest party in the National Assembly.

Figure 2.10: May 1999 National Assembly election compared with November 2002 NOP poll[67]

Constituency Results

	% Vote 1999 Election	Seats Won 1999 Election	% Vote Nov 2002 Poll	Predicted Seats Won May 2003
Labour	37.6	27	43	28
Plaid Cymru	28.4	9	27	8
Conservative	15.8	1	14	1
Liberal Democrats	13.5	3	13	3

[65] *Western Mail*, 8 November 2002.
[66] *Ibid.*
[67] Source: NOP for HTV Wales. A sample of 1,200 voters were questioned between 13 & 20 Nov. 2002.

Regional List Results

	% Vote 1999 Election	Seats Won 1999 Election	% Vote Nov 2002 Poll	Predicted Seats Won May 2003
Labour	35.5	1	32	1
Plaid Cymru	30.6	8	31	8
Conservative	16.5	8	15	6
Liberal Democrats	12.5	3	19	5

However, turn-out will undoubtedly be a key factor in the outcome of the election. It was only 46 per cent in 1999, and the November 2002 poll suggests this will drop even further, with only 37 per cent of the electorate saying they were certain to vote. Low turn-out favours those parties that can best motivate their core vote, a position that is generally recognised dispro-portionately benefits Plaid Cymru. Many commentators believe that Plaid Cymru is poised to fall back in Rhondda and Islwyn. Certainly, Labour is mobilising a vigorous campaign to regain both seats. The NOP poll suggests that Plaid Cymru might lose the Rhondda, but not Islwyn. On the List seats the poll suggests that the Liberal Democrats will gain a seat in South East Wales, at the expense of the Conservatives, and also in Mid and West Wales at the expense of Plaid Cymru. In South Wales Central, assuming Plaid Cymru loses the Rhondda, it should pick up a compensatory seat on the List, this time at the expense of the Conservatives. In all these contests, however, turn-out will be a decisive factor combined with the parties' effectiveness in mobilising their vote. Close contests generally produce higher turn outs.

The relative strength of the parties can be gauged in part by how much each will be spending. The new electoral rules, based on number of constitu-encies, allow a maximum of £600,000. It is estimated that Labour will spend in the region of £300,000, Plaid Cymru £150,000, and the Welsh Conserva-tives and Welsh Liberal Democrats around £100,000.

Other variables include general perceptions about how the Assembly is performing and, more specifically, the impact of the party leaders.[68] In this last respect Labour is undoubtedly in a strong position, given the salience of its leader, First Minister Rhodri Morgan. In contrast Plaid Cymru has been struggling to establish a stronger profile under the leadership of Ieuan Wyn Jones, who succeeded the more popular Dafydd Wigley.

---

[68] See Gerald Taylor, 'Mediating Between Levels of Government: The Role of the Political Parties' in J. Barry Jones and John Osmond (eds) *Building a Civic Culture* for a discussion of the performance of the parties in the Assembly during its first term.

Taking all these factors into account, proportional representation makes it likely that, following the May elections, Labour will still need the support of the Liberal Democrats to secure a majority. Even if Labour were to win a narrow majority, of say just one or two seats, Rhodri Morgan has made it clear that he might still seek a coalition rather than rely on backbench support from potentially dissident members on his own side.[69]

The major issues that will continue to preoccupy the Welsh Assembly Government will be improving the delivery of the health and education services, and addressing the relative poverty of Wales due to the high rates of economic inactivity concentrated in the Objective 1 region of west Wales and the Valleys. The Assembly Government's target of boosting Wales's GDP from the present 80 per cent to 90 per cent of the UK average by 2010 looks increasingly elusive. Constitutional change will do little to address such matters, certainly in the medium term. More resources would certainly help and a strong case has been made by Ron Davies and others for a change to the Barnett formula to reflect the need that exists for higher and sustained investment in Wales, especially in education and economic development.

A problem is that these are complex issues which inevitably inter-twine with constitutional questions. There is an ever-present danger that in confronting them politicians simply end up in a cul de sac where their arguments fail to connect with the wider public. This led to a great deal of frustration during the Assembly's first term which looks destined to continue into the second.

It may be that imaginative leadership, combined with unforeseen events, perhaps emanating from the European Union, will discover a lead through the Whitehall ice cap that presently blocks development in Welsh constitutional politics. In this respect Peter Hain's promotion to Welsh Secretary in the British Cabinet has at least established a convinced advocate for Wales in Whitehall. However, viewed from the perspective of the end of 2002, it looks more and more as though the decisive Assembly election will be in 2007.

BIBLIOGRAPHY

Official Documents

The Learning Country, Welsh Assembly Government, September 2001.

A Winning Wales: The National Economic Development Strategy, Welsh Assembly Government, January 2002.

National Assembly *Procedural Review*, Presiding Office, National Assembly for Wales, February 2002.

---

[69] Interviewed at the 2002 UK Labour Conference by the BBC Wales political programme, *Dragon's Eye*, 3 October 2002. Morgan said he had been impressed by the Irish Taoiseach, Bertie Ahern, coming to this conclusion following the Irish general election a few months earlier.

Skills and Employment Action Plan for Wales, Welsh Assembly Government, February 2001.

Reaching Higher: Higher Education and the Learning Country — a strategy for the higher education sector in Wales, Welsh Assembly Government, March 2002.

Freedom and Responsibility in Local Government, Welsh Assembly Government, March 2002.

Well Being in Wales, Welsh Assembly Government, 2002.

House of Lords Constitution Select Committee on the Constitution Session 2001–02 *Devolution: Inter-institutional relations in the United Kingdom* Evidence complete to 10 July 2002 HL Paper 147.

Our Language: Its Future, Education and Culture Committees, National Assembly for Wales, July 2002

Bilingual Wales, Welsh Assembly Government, July 2002.

Secondary Sources

Day, G., *Making Sense of Wales* (University of Wales Press: Cardiff, 2002).

Jones, J. B. and Osmond, J. (eds) *Building a Civic Culture, Institutional Change, Policy Development and Political Dynamics in the National Assembly for Wales* (Cardiff: IWA, March 2002).

Jones, I.W., *From Assembly to Parliament*, Annual Lecture, Institute of Welsh Politics, University of Wales, Aberystwyth, November 2001.

McAllister, L., *Plaid Cymru, The Emergence of a Political Party* (Bridgend: Seren, 2001).

Osmond, J., 'Nation Building: Implementing Devolution in the United Kingdom — the Welsh Experience', Working Paper 23, Institute for British-Irish Studies, University College Dublin, 2002.

Osmond, J., 'Welsh Civil Identity in the Twenty-first Century' in D. C. Harvey, R. Jones, N. McInroy, and C. Milligan (eds) *Celtic Geographies* (London: Routledge, 2002).

Osmond, J., *The Future of Welsh Devolution* (Cardiff: IWA, June 2002).

Osmond, J. (ed) *Coalition Creaks Over Health: Monitoring the National Assembly September to December 2001* (Cardiff: IWA, 2001).

Osmond, J. (ed) *Education Policy Breaks Loose: Monitoring the National Assembly December 2001 to March 2002* (Cardiff: IWA, 2002).

Osmond, J. (ed.) *Engaging With Europe: Monitoring the National Assembly March to June 2002* (Cardiff: IWA, 2002).

Osmond, J. (ed.) *A Bilingual Wales: Monitoring the National Assembly June to August 2002* (Cardiff, IWA).

Patchett, K., *Developing a Partnership Approach to Primary Legislation between Westminster and the National Assembly* (Cardiff: IWA, October 2002).

Rawlings, R., *Towards a Parliament: Three Faces of the National Assembly for Wales*, O'Donnell Lecture, University of Wales, Swansea, February 2002.

3

England Arisen?[1]

John Tomaney and Peter Hetherington

OVERVIEW

The constitutional ground in England began to shift noticeably in the year to August 2002. Few would have predicted that, in the space of a year, the government would have conceded the case for a referendum in at least one region, almost certainly the North East. English devolution, after all, never seemed a priority for a sceptical Prime Minister, well aware of potential criticism from the opponents of 'over government' and 'more bureaucracy'. Yet John Prescott, by May 2002, back in charge of local government and the regions (as well as housing, planning and regeneration) in a new Office of the Deputy Prime Minister (ODPM), had won the battle in Cabinet for the necessary legislation to trigger referendums after conceding ground to both Downing Street and other Whitehall departments, where doubts still remain about transferring power, however limited, to any Regional Assemblies.

Part of Mr Prescott's success can be attributed to a strengthening alliance with that other power base at the heart of government, Gordon Brown's Treasury. The Prescott-Brown axis cannot be underestimated in the campaign to establish the regional agenda within Whitehall — first by strengthening the eight Regional Development Agencies (RDAs) with increased budgets and more freedom over how to spend them, subject to Whitehall performance targets, then by arguing the case for what the Chancellor calls 'decentralisation' to the regions. While always circumspect in statements about devolution in England, Mr Brown has been persuaded that some regions, at least, should be given the choice of elected assemblies. Primarily though, he sees the RDAs as important in his drive to improve the economic performance of the weaker northern regions.

The Deputy Prime Minister (DPM), for practical purposes the head of the planning system, is crucial to the delivery of the Chancellor's vision of special business planning zones, where enterprise can be encouraged with a

[1] We would like to thank Lynne Humphrey, David Scott and Emma Pinkney for their work on the monitoring reports that underpin this chapter and help in producing this text. Special thanks to Lynne and Cath Flew for reading the text. Thanks also to Mark Sandford and Robert Hazell for advice. The section on the content of the White Paper draws on previous work by John Tomaney and John Adams, see Adams, J. and Tomaney, J., *Restoring the Balance. Strengthening the government's proposals for regional assemblies* (London: Institute for Public Policy Research, 2002).

string of incentives, without the need for what he sees as petty restrictions on development and expansion. The government published a Green Paper in December 2001, which proposed, among other things, transferring the current planning responsibilities from county councils to the regional level and the creation of new Regional Spatial Strategies to provide a new framework for planning in the English regions.[2] These though were presented within the context of a series of other measures designed to 'speed-up' the planning system. The link between proposed new planning legislation and John Prescott's devolution project became clear during 2002. Moreover, it was increasingly apparent that both of these controversial legislative proposals would be passing through Parliament simultaneously in late 2002/early 2003.

To achieve his goal of publishing a White Paper on regional governance, however, John Prescott had to concede Downing Street's case for a review of local government by the Boundary Committee of the Electoral Commission in regions chosen to hold a referendum; to avoid charges of extra bureaucracy. It was at the Prime Minister's insistence that electors should be told that approval of a devolution package would mean the creation of single-tier local government — raising questions about the future, say, of Northumberland and Durham County Councils. The title, *Your Region, Your Choice* was significant — devolution was proposed as an option not a compulsion.[3]

Despite these developments, by late 2002, regional government remained some way off. The ODPM was working on the assumption that, after the passage of legislation and a Boundary Committee review, a referendum would not be possible until the autumn of 2004. On that basis, and assuming approval from voters, the view was that elections to a first wave of regional assemblies — which, of course, will require further detailed legislation — would be unlikely before 2007, after the next general election, and with a lot of political water to pass under Westminster bridge before then.

For all that, it is remarkable how, in the space of a year, the English question moved from the academic to the practical and, in the context of inter-departmental argument within Whitehall, the intensely political. While the potential powers for elected assemblies, outlined in the White Paper, reflected the uneven gains and concessions made by John Prescott during at least 10 meetings of the Cabinet's Committee of Nations and Regions, spread over eight months, reports of rows between the Deputy Prime Minister and Downing Street, which appeared regularly in the press, were frequently exaggerated. On the contrary, the DPM appeared to have fought a subtle and patient campaign to extract his White Paper from a reluctant Whitehall.

[2] DTLR, *Planning: Delivering a Fundamental Change* (Planning Green Paper), Department of Transport Local and the Regions, 2001. (Available at: http://www.planning.odpm.gov.uk/consult/greenpap/pdf/greenpap.pdf).

[3] Cabinet Office/DTLR, *Your Region, Your Choice. Revitalising the English Regions*, Cm 5511 (Norwich: Stationary Office, 2002). (Available at: http://www.regions.odpm.gov.uk/governance/whitepaper/pdf/full_whitepaper.pdf).

Nevertheless, in late 2001, the prospect of progress for Mr Prescott was not favourable, largely because the outcome of the preceding general election threw up ambiguous implications for the governance of England's eight regions, with Whitehall reorganisation splitting responsibility for regional policy between three departments: Department of Trade and Industry (DTI), which assumed responsibility for the RDAs, the former Department of Transport, Local government and the Regions (DTLR), and the Cabinet Office.[4]

But fate dealt a kindly hand to Prescott. The departure of the unfortunate Stephen Byers from the DTLR, and its subsequent re-branding (minus transport) as the Office of the Deputy Prime Minister, has put the DPM back in charge (albeit of a much smaller department). And the Treasury's growing emergence as an economic ministry has, in many ways, sidelined the Department of Trade and Industry (where the Secretary of State, Patricia Hewitt, remained a devolution sceptic), with Gordon Brown effectively setting the agenda for the RDAs.

By early 2002, it became apparent that Downing Street had agreed the case for regional referendums, by extracting the price (from Mr Prescott) of a single tier of local government. Realising that old Labour grandees in northern counties would find a removal of their power bases difficult to stomach, ministers did a bit of simple arithmetic to prove their case. Why was it, they asked, that Birmingham with a population of over a million had 117 councillors (on a single authority) while two-tier Durham, with a population of 491,000, had 369 on eight councils.

Behind the scenes, other moves were taking place to prepare England for devolution, however relatively distant. A joint DTLR/Treasury research project, 'Identifying the Flow of Domestic and European Expenditure into English Regions', was seen to be particularly relevant, and may yet prove to be a pre-cursor to the long-awaited regional needs assessment study.[5]

The banner of administrative and political regionalism continued its slow progress up the flagstaff during 2002. Alongside this evolving process another significant development occurred: namely, a renewed concern with growing economic disparities between — particularly — London, the South East and East Anglia on the one hand and the rest of the country on the other. The Treasury published a major report on regional productivity alongside the 2001 pre-budget statement, which included a frank analysis of the scale of regional disparities and their potential impact on national productivity performance.[6] It contributed to a new political momentum with Stephen

---

[4] See Tomaney, J., 'Reshaping the English Regions', in A. Trench (ed) *The State of the Nations 2001: The Second Year of Devolution in the United Kingdom* (Exeter: Imprint Academic, 2001), pp. 117–148.

[5] See Tomaney, J., Hetherington, P. and Humphrey, L., *English Regions Monitoring Report, February 2002* (London: Constitution Unit, 2002). (Available at: http://www.ucl.ac.uk/constitution-unit/) for a fuller discussion.

[6] HM Treasury and DTI *Productivity in the UK: 3 – The Regional Dimension* (London: HM Treasury, 2001).

Byers, then the minister responsible for the regions, connecting the issue of tackling regional economic disparities to political devolution. At several public meetings he spoke of 'unacceptable' divisions between north and south, then, at a fringe meeting at Labour's local government conference in Cardiff on 2 February 2002 he noted: 'The most difficult thing for a Secretary of State to do is give up the powers we have. It is not easy for colleagues to give up powers, but we have to be prepared to do so'.[7]

The regional agenda, however, remained beset by conflicting signals from the centre. The Brown/Prescott strategy rests on giving the poorly performing northern regions the 'economic tools' to pull themselves up to the level of the better performing, like the South East and Eastern, with bigger RDA budgets and — eventually — more 'decentralisation' (in Brown's words) or 'devolution' (in the Prescott vocabulary). Indeed, the Spending Review 2002 gave additional resources and greater autonomy to RDAs (see pp. 362-64). According to its advocates, this 'new regional policy' seeks to find a way between the free-market approaches of the 1980s and the provision of large scale regional investment incentives in the 1960s and 1970s, by building up regional institutions capable of developing locally targeted policies.[8]

Alongside this, however, the Chancellor remained keen to underpin the economic importance of London, the South East and the bio-technology and IT 'clusters' of the greater-Cambridge sub region. In this context, in the aftermath of the 2002 Spending Review, John Prescott announced plans for 250,000 new houses in four new and expanding townships: Milton Keynes, Stansted, Thames Gateway from East London through to Kent, and Ashford (in Kent). The South East will also be the principal beneficiary of the government's emerging airport strategy, which appears to consign northern airports — particularly municipally-owned Manchester, the country's third largest — to a secondary role. Announcing plans for an unprecedented expansion of Britain's airport capacity, Alistair Darling, the new Transport Secretary, even floated the idea of a new international airport at Cliffe, in north Kent — prompting the (Conservative) leader of Kent County Council, Sandy Bruce-Lockhart, to call for extra capacity to be developed in the north to benefit flagging regions.[9]

Stirrings of discontent could also be heard from several other quarters — not only council leaders in the South East, but also senior planning professionals in the Town and Country Planning Association and the Royal Town

[7] Cited in Tomaney, J., Hetherington, P. and Humphrey, L., *English Regions Monitoring Report, February 2002* (London: Constitution Unit, 2002). (Available at: http://www.ucl.ac.uk/constitution-unit/), p. 3.

[8] Balls, E., 'Britain's new regional policy', in Balls, E. and Healey, J. (eds) *Towards a New Regional Policy* (London: The Smith Institute, 2000), see also Tomaney, J. and Mawson, J. (eds) *England: The State of the Regions* (Bristol: Policy Press, 2002).

[9] Tomaney, J., Hetherington, P. and Humphrey, L. *English Regions Monitoring Report, August 2002* (London: Constitution Unit, 2002). (Available at: http://www.ucl.ac.uk/constitution-unit/).

Planning Institute. In a series of interventions they expressed concern at what they regarded as the piecemeal, market-driven approach of both the Treasury and Downing Street. Their voices were added to calls for a 'planning framework' for England and, in the absence of any official moves on this front, were preparing to go it alone with an independent plan for the country. At the same time, backbench Labour MPs in the North were increasingly restless, viewing moves to strengthen the economy of the south as further undermining less-favoured regions.[10]

In short, the debate about regionalism in England was running increasingly on two parallel courses: first the case for regional government, with more emotional undertones tied to identity and a sense of place; and secondly, broader arguments about the absence of any clear, nationally determined regional policy, apart from a commitment to strengthen the economies of the better-performing regions while promising to give the poor performers a new set of tools to pull themselves up.[11] With some in Whitehall raising questions about the inconsistencies of these policies, and many outside — significantly, in some RDAs themselves — calling for a national debate on a 'framework for England', it remained unclear whether these courses would collide or reach a confluence in a much stronger force which could, conceivably, shake the foundations of the centre.

Figure 3.1: Key stages in the development of regional policy

November 2001	Publication of Planning Green Paper. Posits transfer of planning functions from counties to regions.
November 2001	Treasury study of 'Regional Productivity' published as part Chancellor's Pre-Budget Report.
2 May 2002	First seven mayoral elections in England.
9 May 2001	Publication of White Paper on regional governance, *Your Region, Your Choice*.
28 May 2002	Resignation of Stephen Byers as Secretary of State for Transport, Local Government and the Regions.
29 May 2002	Creation of Office of the Deputy Prime Minister (ODPM) with responsibility for regions, local government and planning.
15 July 2002	Spending Review 2002 assigns new responsibilities to Regional Development Agencies and increases 'single pot' to £2bn in 2005/6.

[10] *Ibid.*

[11] Morgan, K., 'The English Question: Regional Perspectives on a Fractured Nation', *Regional Perspectives on a Fractured Nation*, 36 (7), 2002, pp. 797–810.

'YOUR REGION, YOUR CHOICE': THE GOVERNMENT'S WHITE PAPER
ON REGIONAL GOVERNANCE, MAY 2002

The Battle for the White Paper

Ministers began to signal the scope of the proposed White Paper in a series of speeches in autumn 2001. In late 2001, the Regions Minister, Nick Raynsford, began to talk about a 'London-plus' model, small and strategic with powers over transport, land use planning, the environment, Regional Development Agencies and culture. The prospect was raised of some quangos with a regional presence being brought under the ambit of Regional Assemblies.

The policy's principal champion, the Deputy Prime Minister, John Prescott, spelled out his vision in a speech in his Hull constituency in October 2001. He acknowledged that no-one wanted 'a talking shop', but also suggested 'neither do people expect the equivalent of a Scottish Parliament for the English regions'.[12] The then Secretary of State, Stephen Byers, in a little reported speech to the annual meeting of the Coalfield Communities Campaign in South Shields on 10 September 2001, said:

> ...when we talk about regional government, what we must not be about is taking power away from local government. What regional government has got to be about is people like me giving up some of the powers I've got and devolving those powers down to regional level and also taking powers away from unelected bodies — the regional quangos we have still got in place, the regional government offices. The powers they've got, extensive powers, have to be moved to the regional elected level.[13]

But, speaking in Newcastle upon Tyne on 9 November, alongside John Prescott, Mr Byers cautioned:

> ...we have to be honest enough with ourselves to say that, at the moment, we need to do a lot more to raise awareness of the regional agenda...it is a challenge for us all to make sure that people are aware of the real opportunities that will come out of an elected regional body...it does have to make a difference. If we are to have a successful regional assembly, it has to have the powers, the responsibility, the authority, to make a difference...if we don't do that, it will be seen as a sham and it will fail.[14]

Support for devolution, especially of a radical kind, was difficult to find in some corners of Whitehall. Some departments, notably the Department for Trade and Industry (DTI) and the Department of Culture, Media and Sport (DCMS), remained lukewarm towards the regional agenda, apparently objecting even to a modest increase in the powers of the existing regional

[12] Prescott, J., 'Speech to Yorkshire Labour Party Regional Conference', Hull, 20 October 2001.

[13] Tomaney, J. and Hetherington, P., *English Regions Monitoring Report, November 2001* (London: Constitution Unit, 2001). (Available at: http://www.ucl.ac.uk/constitution-unit/).

[14] *Ibid.*

'chambers', as well as elected Regional Assemblies, in debates on the White Paper in the Cabinet's Nations and Regions Committee. The Secretaries of State at the DTI and the DCMS, Patricia Hewitt and Tessa Jowell respectively, fought hard in the Committee to retain central control over RDAs and regional arts funding. This classic inter-departmental Whitehall power struggle mirrored that which preceded the creation of RDAs at the beginning of the previous parliament.

As the debate about Regional Assemblies began to develop within Whitehall, the question of local government reform climbed up the agenda. Thus, while Tony Blair was conspicuously silent through most of the debate about the White Paper, never publicly opposing the concept of elected Regional Assemblies, he remained sensitive to arguments from business as well as from the opposition that another layer of administration, on top of two tiers of local government, could prove politically unsustainable. Indeed, in parliamentary debates, Opposition spokespersons presented any proposals for Regional Assemblies as precisely this, and, more specifically, as an attack on England's 'historic counties.' Downing Street's concerns were heightened in a context of apparently declining voter faith in the political class and declining voter turnouts in local and European elections. Privately, Downing Street advisers made such concerns clear. Consequently, it became increasingly evident during early 2002 that in any referendum(s) voters would be told that support for devolution would also require single tier local government.[15]

The Prime Minister's concerns about business reaction were borne out when, in January 2002, the CBI Director General, Digby Jones, claimed that business was 'deeply sceptical about government plans for elected Regional Assemblies.'[16] Mr Jones based his claims on a 'two-month consultation with business representatives in all the English regions'. Indeed, according to Mr Jones, in light of the experience of Scottish and Welsh devolution, firms were unimpressed with devolution in general, in terms of its benefits to business. He claimed that Assemblies would be:

> just another tier of bureaucracy on top of a plethora of decision-making bodies . . . We have little confidence that elected assemblies would be best able to tackle the problems of economic growth and job creation or that they would attract good enough people to make a real difference.

---

[15] Tomaney, J., Hetherington, P. and Humphrey, L., *English Regions Monitoring Report, February 2002* (London: Constitution Unit, 2002). (Available at: http://www.ucl.ac.uk/constitution-unit/).

[16] CBI Press Release, 'CBI Declares Scepticism on Regional Assemblies', 31 January 2002. Following the publication of the White Paper, the CBI reiterated its opposition to Regional Assemblies. In September 2002 the CBI claimed its grassroots had given a vote of 'no confidence' in the idea of regional assemblies, citing doubts about the quality of the political class in regions like the North East (CBI Press Release, 'Grassroots CBI gives "vote of no confidence" in government plans for English regions', 20 September 2002). Available: http://www.cbi.org.uk/news/index.html.

He urged Ministers not to get distracted 'by other energy-consuming initiatives that are of questionable value', but to concentrate instead on improving planning and training policies.

His views tended to be echoed, often in private, but occasionally in public, by RDA chairmen, who tended to be sceptical about the value of political devolution, relishing the freedom accorded to them as government appointed heads of 'business-led' organisations and its attendant status. Graham Hall, chairman of Yorkshire Forward, the development agency for Yorkshire and the Humber, said: 'People look to me now as — and I'm exaggerating for effect — the 'prime minister of Yorkshire'. There's an expectation now that Yorkshire Forward, and myself, provide this leadership role . . . people like it'.[17]

The Character of the White Paper
In the end, the publication of the White Paper on English Regional Assemblies, *Your Region, Your Choice* on 9 May 2002, was significant if only because it demonstrated that previous reports of the death of the devolution project had been greatly exaggerated.[18] Yet it was significant in other ways. The White Paper raised the prospect of referendums on regional government being held in at least some regions during Labour's second term. In his speech to the House of Commons, announcing the publication of the White Paper, Mr Prescott for the first time set out a timetable for achieving an elected Assembly in at least one English region. The strong expectation was that North East England was the region the government had in mind, although other northern regions were quick to stake a claim for inclusion in a first wave of referendums. The White Paper was replete with references to the North East and, while launch events were held in all regions of England, the Deputy Prime Minister and the then Secretary of State for Transport, Local Government and the Regions, chose to attend a launch in Newcastle upon Tyne. There both ministers made it explicit that the North East was the only region which would be expected to achieve support for a referendum in the medium term.

The government's proposals, if enacted, would change the landscape of the British constitution and the terrain of English politics. In one sense they are potentially more radical than the proposals for Scottish and Welsh

[17] Quoted in Tomaney, J. and Hetherington, P., *English Regions Monitoring Report, November 2001* (London: Constitution Unit, 2001). (Available at: http://www.ucl.ac.uk/constitution-unit/).

[18] See Cabinet Office/DTLR *Your Region, Your Choice. Revitalising the English Regions*, Cm 5511 (Norwich: Stationary Office, 2002). (Available at: http://www.regions.odpm.gov.uk/governance/whitepaper/pdf/full_whitepaper.pdf). For reviews and critiques of the White Paper see, among others, Adams, J. and Tomaney, J., *Restoring the Balance. Strengthening the government's proposals for regional assemblies* (London: Institute for Public Policy Research, 2002); Benneworth, P. and Dabinett, G. 'English devolution and regional development', *Local Work*, 46, November 2002; Newman, I. and Dungey, J., 'The government White Paper, *Your Region, Your Choice: Revitalising the English Regions*', *Local Economy*, 17 (3), 2002, pp. 253–255; and Sandford, M., *A Commentary on the Regional Government White Paper, Your Region Your Choice: Revitalising the English Regions* (London: Constitution Unit, 2002).

devolution, insofar as they represent a more fundamental challenge, albeit initially modest in scope, to the dominance of Whitehall over all aspects of English life. Scottish and Welsh devolution involved making separate departments accountable to an elected Parliament and Assembly respectively. In the longer run, English regional government suggests a re-evaluation of Whitehall and it was for this reason that departments struggled hard to resist the allocation of their functions to Regional Assemblies. The range of powers proposed for Assemblies reflects, then, the outcome of these Whitehall turf wars. However, in a conscious acknowledgement that devolution is 'a process and not an event', the government made it clear that the range of powers outlined in the White Paper was likely to evolve over time.

The White Paper proposed that Regional Assemblies would have full control over the budgets and activities of Regional Development Agencies (RDAs) and would appoint their boards. The planning powers proposed for Regional Assemblies also contained few surprises. The government had already signalled its intention to create new regional planning structures in its Green Paper on planning, published in early 2002. The government proposed that mandatory Regional Spatial Strategies should be produced in all regions and that Assemblies would have responsibility for these where they exist.

A further significant proposed power was control over European Structural Fund expenditure. Structural Fund expenditures, although likely to diminish in scale over time and disappear entirely with EU enlargement after 2006, remain an important element of regeneration funding, especially in the poorer regions such as Scotland, Wales and the northern regions of England. An Assembly would take these powers from regional Government Offices where they currently reside.

In some areas the proposed powers went beyond what was expected. For instance, the proposed housing powers exceeded most predictions, with Assemblies taking a central role in the allocation of housing investment. These are powers that the Mayor of London coveted but was denied by the Greater London Authority Act. The Mayor and his advisors subsequently argued that successful regeneration policy requires the integration of economic development and housing policies with the planning system. The creation of elected Regional Assemblies may, therefore, add further to the pressure for more devolution in London.

In other areas, though, the range of powers looked comparatively weak. The White Paper, for instance, made great play of the need for more regional action in the fields of skills and transport, but proposed only consultative powers for Regional Assemblies in both of these areas. In a meeting with the then junior Regions minister, Alan Whitehead MP, RDA chairmen expressed support for stronger powers in these two areas.

The government's proposals for Regional Assemblies to be accompanied by a move to a single tier of local government were well trailed prior to publication of the White Paper. However, the notion that this signalled 'the end of county councils', as prior speculation suggested, was not entirely borne out in the White Paper. Under the terms of the proposals it was possible that counties could survive in some places while districts disappeared. This issue was likely to prove more of a stumbling block in some regions than others. In the North East, for instance, some 70 per cent of the population already live in single tier local authority areas, whereas in the East of England the equivalent figure is nearer one in ten.

The White Paper made clear that Assemblies, comprising 25–35 elected members, would be elected by proportional representation (PR). The government proposed to adopt the same electoral system — Additional Member System — as used in Scotland and Wales. Even John Prescott, a noted supporter of first past the post, bowed to arguments for PR. Such proposals would have far-reaching consequences in Labour heartland regions. Labour does well under the first past the post in regions like the North East. But the mayoral elections there in May 2002 revealed that when new voting systems were introduced Labour came in for a shock, losing all three that took place in May 2002 (see pp. 70-74).

In some ways the financial powers of the proposed Regional Assemblies were stronger than those available to the other devolved institutions in the UK. The White Paper proposed to fund the core functions via a 'block grant', providing for substantially more financial flexibility than that available to the Greater London Authority, as, under the terms of the Greater London Authority Act, the Mayor is unable to switch funds between different budget heads. The White Paper also proposed significant borrowing powers for the purpose of investment by Regional Assemblies, another example of significant financial flexibility. Such powers were not made available to the Scottish Parliament or the National Assembly for Wales in their respective legislation, although these were given recently by the Chancellor to the Northern Ireland Assembly. The borrowing powers proposed for Regional Assemblies will be subject to a 'prudential' borrowing regime. Nevertheless, this would give the administrations of Regional Assemblies options to invest in their region's infrastructure.

The White Paper also proposed to grant revenue raising powers to Regional Assemblies, via a precept on the council tax, although it is unclear how much the proposed Assemblies will be able to raise through this method. The council tax precept is the means by which the Greater London Authority raises additional funds. Neither the Northern Ireland Assembly nor the Welsh Assembly were granted revenue raising powers when established, and the powers of the Scottish Parliament to raise revenue remained unused in its first term. Only the Greater London Authority was granted revenue-raising powers and had taken the opportunity to use them by 2002. Mayor Livingstone increased both the police precept and the transport precept — and used the money to fund increased numbers of police officers and to freeze London underground fares respectively. From 2003 the Mayor also proposed to introduce a congestion charge in central London, and to use the £150m per annum proceeds to invest in public transport. The proposed revenue raising powers of the proposed Assemblies would be limited and subject to a 'capping regime'. Nevertheless, the degree of fiscal flexibility proposed for Regional Assemblies clearly surprised most commentators and has potentially radical implications.

Perhaps the most surprising proposal contained in the White Paper was that each Assembly would be expected to agree a small number — perhaps six to ten — targets with the government. These targets would be relevant to an Assembly's responsibilities and would leave it open to the Assembly to establish how to achieve them. Some additional money would be available to reward those elected assemblies that achieved or exceeded the targets. Targets and rewards would be agreed between central government and each Assembly, along the lines of existing local public service agreements (PSAs).

The PSA target is not the only means by which the centre could restrict the autonomy of the Regional Assemblies. The government proposed that it would apply the principles of 'best value' to Assemblies, building on the lessons learned from local government, tailoring requirements to the particular circumstances of assemblies. Best value requires local authorities to seek continuous improvements in economy, efficiency and effectiveness, and to do this by reviewing services periodically in order to gauge whether they are still necessary, and whether current approaches to service delivery are the most appropriate. The government would doubtless 'tailor' the best value regime for Regional Assemblies in its own way, but the potential remained for this to be a centralising provision.

Unsurprisingly, the White Paper did not discuss the vexed issue of the Barnett Formula, although moves toward elected Assemblies are bound to be accompanied by increased interest in the issue. Significantly, though, the government commissioned a major study of the territorial flow of public expenditure in the UK in early 2002, linking it explicitly to the prospect of Regional Assemblies.

Overall the package of measures proposed in the White Paper for the English regions contained many surprises and, in some respects, went further than anticipated. But the proposals also bore the hand of a government reluctant to let go of the reins. As such they exhibited all the strengths and weaknesses of New Labour's approach to devolution.

The level of support for Regional Assemblies remains uneven at best (although see p. 75). Even under the most positive prognosis, there remained some regions which were likely to remain unpersuaded of the charms of devolution. The government's approach raised the likelihood that some regions would not proceed towards elected Regional Assemblies in the foreseeable future, and those regions which do would not see actual Assembly elections for some years. The White Paper therefore contained proposals to strengthen existing regional structures, even in regions where there is no appetite for elected Assemblies (see pp. 62-68).

Reactions to the White Paper

Regional campaigners welcomed the publication of the White Paper. Speaking for the Campaign for the English Regions (CFER), which had submitted its own proposals to the government on 9 November 2001, the Chair George Morran said:

> CFER believes the White Paper provides a starting point for the people in each region to express their views on the direction and pace at which they wish to move forward. We will use the time between now and any legislation to encourage as many people as possible to be involved in this consultation, and to lobby government to strengthen these proposals. We have no doubt that when referendums on devolution to the English regions are held they will be won.[19]

The media reaction was complex. The publication of the White Paper probably generated the greatest media coverage ever of the English regions. It was not all favourable. While the *Guardian, Economist* and *Financial Times* were generally supportive of the idea of devolution within England, the right-wing press were united in their hostility to the government's proposals. A theme in the coverage was that England's national identity would be undermined by the proposals. Richard Littlejohn, writing in *The Sun*, claimed that Regional Assemblies 'are specifically designed to break up England into administrative units in preparation for our absorption into a federal Europe. The Regional Assemblies correspond exactly with plans drawn-up by Brussels for the government of a fully integrated European Union'.[20] A similar theme was rehearsed in the *Daily Mail*, which reported the government's proposals under the headline 'Prescott's folly'. Its columnist, Simon Heffer, argued: 'You have to go back to the Dark Ages in England to find anything approaching regional identities . . . This has not prevented the government from arbitrarily, in consultation with Brussels, carving up England into "regions".'[21]

The regional press reaction varied significantly. Unsurprisingly, the regional press in the North East saw the proposals as historic and a

---

[19] CFER Press Release, 'Campaigners Welcome White Paper', 9 May 2002.

[20] Littlejohn, R., 'Carved up, stitched up . . . Labour's England', *The Sun*, 10 May 2002.

[21] *Daily Mail*, 10 May 2002.

vindication of their long support for the notion of 'home rule'. But, very quickly, local concerns began to emerge. For instance, the Middlesborough *Evening Gazette* gave space to the argument that a Regional Assembly could lead to 'Newcastle domination' of Teesside. In other regions, some of the media reaction was decidedly hostile. The *Yorkshire Post*, in an editorial, argued:

> If the government really wanted to address the democratic deficit, it would slash the number of quangos it has set up and return their powers and revenues to town and city halls. If voters were once again convinced that decisions taken locally could make a difference to the quality of their lives and their neighbourhoods, the numbers that turn out at local elections would show a marked increase. But the reinvigoration of local democracy is not going to be achieved through the creation of another layer of bureaucracy, further removed from the voters, which will, as likely as not, end up stuffed to the gills with former MPs and failed councillors.[22]

The reaction of local government was important because of the implications of the proposals for them. The publication of the White Paper has proved a challenge to the Local Government Association (LGA), with the emergence of a basic Labour–Conservative split, which has been difficult to disguise. The Leader of the LGA Conservative Group, Gordon Keymer, reacted in ways similar to Conservative MPs in the parliamentary debate on the White Paper:

> The myth of panacea that the likes of Prescott and Mandelson have peddled over regional assemblies must be expunged. Not one extra school will be built, social services will not improve and street cleanliness will not get better. Local services will suffer as regional assemblies suck power from those democratically elected institutions, the councils, that are best placed to serve the interests of local communities and people.[23]

Faced with these sentiments, the LGA leader, Sir Jeremy Beecham, a supporter of Regional Assemblies, was forced to acknowledge the publication of the White Paper in less than fulsome terms. 'The LGA is keen to ensure that regional assemblies have the backing of local people and that the process for establishing them does not divert councils from improving their services to local people.'[24]

In the North East, the initial reaction of local government was complex. In Northumberland, the leader of the county council, Michael Davey, speaking at the launch of the White Paper in Newcastle, argued that 'the issue of local government is too important to be lost in squabbles about local government'.[25] Meanwhile, in Durham, the county council made an early pitch to be

---

[22] *Yorkshire Post*, 9 May 2002.
[23] 'Reorganisation argument hots up', *Local Government Chronicle*, 17 May 2002.
[24] 'Reorganisation argument hots up', *Local Government Chronicle*, 17 May 2002.
[25] Source: authors' notes.

the unitary authority, claiming it already provides 85 per cent of services in the county, although it acknowledged the possibility of some job losses. The chief executive of Durham county council, Kingsley Smith, said: 'I can see this fantastic scenario with a regional assembly and very good, cost-effective delivery of services through one unitary authority in Durham. I would suggest 90 per cent of employees would automatically go into that authority.'[26]

The district councils in Durham offered a different scenario, where district mergers could take place, possibly leading to a south and north Durham council, calling the County Council proposals 'simply impractical'.[27] Given the nature of the White Paper's proposals, it was apparent that the local government debate would accompany — and possibly dominate — the regional government debate into 2003.

INSTITUTIONS OF REGIONAL GOVERNANCE

Figure 3.2: Key institutions in the English Regions

Government Offices for the Regions

Established in 1994, regional Government Offices are an office of central government which manage the work in the region of four departments:

- Department of Trade and Industry
- Department for Education and Skills
- Department for Transport, Local Government and the Regions
- Department for Environment, Food and Rural Affairs

Government Offices also contain staff representing the

- Department for Culture, Media and Sport,
- Home Office
- Department of Health

Regional Chambers/Assemblies

Established in 1999, Regional Assemblies comprise a membership of nominated local councillors (maximum 70 per cent of membership) and regional stakeholders, including business, trade unions, environmental and voluntary groups. They promote the economic, social and environmental well-being of their respective regions and scrutinise the relevant Regional Development Agency. Formally designated for these purposes by the Secretary of State, under the Regional Development Agencies Act 1998, Regional Chambers/Assemblies also act as Regional Planning Conferences for the preparation of Regional Planning Guidance.

[26] 'Job losses forecast if assembly elected', *Local Government Chronicle*, 17 May 2002.
[27] 'Town halls fight for their future', *The Journal* [Newcastle], 20 May 2002.

Regional Development Agencies

Established in 1999, RDAs brought together staff and functions of

* Government Offices
* Rural Development Commission
* English Partnerships
* Regional inward investment organisations

RDAs have five statutory purposes, set out in section 4 (1) of the Regional Development Agencies Act 1998. These are:

* To further the economic development and the regeneration of its region
* To promote business efficiency, investment and competitiveness in its area
* To promote employment in its area
* To enhance the application and development of skills relevant to employment in its area
* To contribute to the achievement of sustainable development in the United Kingdom where it is relevant to its area to do so.

RDAs prepare a Regional Economic Strategy to provide the framework for the economic development of their region.

Government Offices for the Regions

As well as proposals for elected Regional Assemblies, the White Paper also proposed strengthening the existing structure of regional governance. Chapter 2 of the White Paper proposed an enhanced role for regional Government Offices in 'joining up' the increasing number of regional strategies.[28] The government had already made plain its view that regional Government Offices were to be 'the key agents of government in the English regions'.[29] The range of functions acquired by Government Offices gradually increased after 1999, until, by 2002, they were being ascribed the role of 'strategic integrators' of public policy at the regional level.[30] These new tasks, irrespective of moves to elected Regional Assemblies, raised new challenges for Government Offices, which by the admission of senior civil servants within them, have traditionally lacked policy development capacities. The White Paper promised a 'strengthened role of the Government Offices by giving them responsibilities for new programmes and policies to complement the work of the Regional Development Agencies and regional chambers'. According to the White Paper, 'the value of Government Offices' role as the government's

[28] For an analysis of this problem see Tomaney, J. 'In what sense a regional problem? Sub-national governance in England', *Local Economy*, 17 (3), 2002, pp. 226–238.

[29] Cabinet Office, *Introducing the Government Offices*, 2001, p.1. (Available at: http://www.rcu.gov.uk/articles/gofactfile/IntroGOs.pdf).

[30] Tomaney, J., 'The evolution of English regional governance', *Regional Studies*, 36 (7), 2002, pp. 721–731.

'eyes and ears' in the regions has also been enhanced through greater use of their input to the design and implementation of policy and reviewing how programmes and initiatives are working in the region and locally'.[31]

Regional Development Agencies

The growing importance of RDAs as regional actors continued to develop during 2002, providing evidence of the existence of the Brown-Prescott axis noted above. Notably, the Spending Review 2002 signalled both new responsibilities and additional resources for RDAs.[32] Reflecting on the implications of the Spending Review for RDAs, the *Financial Times* suggested that 'they emerged yesterday as the main bodies trusted by the government with raising economic performance at the grass roots'. It went on to note:

> The bodies created three years ago by bringing together a disparate group of organisations, will also gain new responsibilities, such as promoting local tourism and contributing directly to planning and transport strategy. Their tentacles will also begin reaching out into vocational education and enterprise, with pilot schemes for the regional management of the Learning and Skills Council and the Small Business Service.[33]

The Spending Review argued that building the capacity and resources of RDAs was central to achieving the productivity goals of the Treasury. The regional aspects of the 'productivity problem' had been set out in a report published by the Treasury at the time of the 2001 Pre-Budget Report.[34] To this end, the Spending Review outlined a number of PSA targets, aimed at raising productivity and sustainable growth across the nations and regions.

In particular, the Spending Review signalled an increase in resources available to RDAs, providing an increase of £375 million to the RDAs' single pot by 2005–06. Together with the reduction in the Single Regeneration Budget (SRB), commitments over the Spending Review period, which were proposed to release an additional £535m by 2005–06, implied an increase in the uncommitted resources available in the single pot — the effective single pot — of £910m by 2005–06 compared to 2002–03. The single pot will be £2 billion in 2005–06 (see Figures 3.3 and 3.4).

---

[31] Cabinet Office/DTLR *Your Region, Your Choice. Revitalising the English Regions*, Cm 5511 (Norwich: Stationary Office, 2002). (Available at: http://www.regions.odpm.gov.uk/governance/whitepaper/pdf/full_whitepaper.pdf), Box 2.7.

[32] HM Treasury, *Opportunity and security for all: Investing in an enterprising, fairer Britain — 2002 Spending Review: New Public Spending Plans 2003–2006*, Cm 5570 (Norwich: The Stationery Office, 2002).

[33] *Financial Times*, July 16th 2002.

[34] See HM Treasury and DTI, *Productivity in the UK: 3 — The Regional Dimension* (London: HM Treasury, 2001).

Figure 3.3: Regional Development Agencies (RDAs) budgets[35]

	£ millions			
	2002–03	**2003–04**	**2004–05**	**2005–06**
Of which:				
Office of the Deputy Prime Minister	1,369	1,522	1,552	1,609
Department of Trade and Industry	172	191	236	296
Department for Education and Skills	42	42	42	42
Department for Environment, Food and Rural Affairs	42	41	46	51
Department for Culture, Media and Sport	0	2	2	2
Total	**1,625**	**1,798**	**1,878**	**2,000**

Figure 3.4: Increase in RDAs 'effective' single pot[36]

	£ millions		
	2003–04	**2004–05**	**2005–06**
Increase in RDAs single pot compared to 2002–03	173	253	375
Reduction in SRB commitment compared to 2002–03	214	414	535
Increase in 'effective' RDAs single pot compared to 2002–03	387	667	910

Tucked away in the Spending Review was an apparent proposal to create a new actor at the regional level in order to further the government's housing policy objectives. The Spending Review thus committed the government to:

establishing *strong regional housing bodies*, bringing together existing funding streams into a single non-ringfenced budget, so as to enable housing investment and

[35] Note: DTI figures include British Trade International and funding for Regional Selective Assistance.

[36] Note: SRB commitment figures are based on provisional ODPM estimates. This gives a baseline for the 'effective' RDA single pot of £850 million in 2002–03.

planning decisions to be better integrated with transport and economic development. This process will need to be supported by a more strategic approach to the regional distribution of funding, including a review of the funding formulae and systems.[37]

The Deputy Prime Minister expanded only briefly on these proposals in his statement to the Commons on the Spending Review. He announced two proposed institutional innovations: first, the establishment of a single housing inspectorate, incorporating the relevant activities of the Audit Commission and Housing Corporation; second, the intention 'to establish strong regional bodies, going with the grain of our proposals for regional governance. These will bring housing investment together into a single regional pot. And they will link that investment with planning, infrastructure and economic growth strategies'.[38] The proposals looked set to be fiercely resisted by the Housing Corporation.

Regional Chambers/Assemblies

The Regional Chambers came into being to scrutinise the Regional Development Agencies, and typically comprise the local government leaders in the region (comprising 70 per cent of the membership) and stakeholders: representatives of business, unions, the voluntary sector and other actors (30 per cent). Confusingly, all the Regional Chambers now call themselves Assemblies, although they are not directly elected.

In 2001 the government provided £15m for the eight existing Regional Assemblies to support their scrutiny role. The various Assemblies have used these resources in different ways. In the South West, for instance, the Assembly established two 'select committees' to consider the South West Regional Development Agency's (SWRDA) draft corporate plan. Hearings were held in public; evidence included written submissions from over 40 organisations and contributions from expert witnesses. The Regional Assembly's report made 23 recommendations for changes to the corporate plan, of which the majority were supported by SWRDA. By contrast, in Yorkshire and the Humber, the Assembly established 'Yorkshire Futures', a regional intelligence-gathering initiative, with Yorkshire Forward, the public health observatories, the Government Office, and other partners in the region. The intended outcomes included co-ordinated regional and inter-regional

---

[37] HM Treasury, *Opportunity and security for all: Investing in an enterprising, fairer Britain — 2002 Spending Review: New Public Spending Plans 2003–2006*, Cm 5570 (Norwich: The Stationery Office, 2002), para. 23.14 (emphasis added).

[38] Prescott, J., 'Sustainable Communities, Housing and Planning', Speech to the House of Commons on Spending Review 2002, 18th July, Office of the Deputy Prime Minister (http://www.odpm.gov.uk/about/ministers/speeches/prescott/180702.htm).

monitoring, better informed regional policy, and common standards of data collection and interpretation.[39]

Apart from acquiring a formal role as regional planning bodies, voluntary Regional Assemblies appeared to gain the least from changes announced in 2002, especially when compared to the Government Offices. The White Paper stated that Assemblies 'have a valuable role to play in the regions alongside the Regional Development Agencies and Government Offices',[40] although it did not enlarge on what that role might be. Most of the changes to the role of voluntary Assemblies suggested in the White Paper are already in place, and have been for some time: no further powers or responsibilities were offered.

Two pieces of research published in 2002 drew attention to the role of social and economic partners in the existing voluntary Regional Assemblies.[41] This research is noteworthy partly because the government's White Paper remained relatively open about the prospective arrangements for the inclusion of partners in future elected assemblies. The research revealed considerable progress has been made since the establishment of the voluntary Assemblies in 1998–99. In most cases social and economic partners had obtained full membership and voting rights on the regional assembly, and were treated as equal to the local authority members.

There was disquiet amongst some of the groups of regional partners that the White Paper was in practice proposing a downgrading of their role alongside the members of elected regional assemblies. This disquiet led to a first national meeting of partner groups, in Coventry in September 2002. The uncertainty of the government's position reflects the uncertainty about the purpose of regional partnership. It is not clear how the various options outlined in the White Paper — of a civic forum, non-voting assembly membership, co-option onto scrutiny committees or policy advice — relate to the hopes and expectations for the partners' role on the part of government.

By summer 2002 it was becoming clear that a Regional Assemblies (Preparations) Bill would be likely to be included in the Queen's Speech. This development posed a challenge for Regional Assemblies in those regions likely to be candidates for early referendums, with a lack of clarity about the legality of their capacity to get involved. In the North East, the region's only Conservative MP, Peter Atkinson, claimed that the North-East Assembly

---

[39] Cabinet Office/DTLR, *Your Region, Your Choice. Revitalising the English Regions*, Cm 5511 (Norwich: Stationary Office, 2002). (Available at: http://www.regions.odpm.gov.uk/governance/whitepaper/pdf/full_whitepaper.pdf).

[40] Cabinet Office/DTLR, *Your Region, Your Choice. Revitalising the English Regions*, Cm 5511 (Norwich: Stationary Office, 2002). (Available at: http://www.regions.odpm.gov.uk/governance/whitepaper/pdf/full_whitepaper.pdf), Box 2.5.

[41] Sandford, M., *Inclusiveness of Regional Chambers* (London: Constitution Unit, 2002); Shaw, K., Humphrey, L., O'Brien, P., Tomaney, J. *The Engagement of Economic and Social Partners in a Directly Elected Regional Assembly for the North East.* Report to the North East Assembly, 2002.

had used funds and staff time to promote the case for regional government, which was beyond its competence.[42] In the light of this charge the Regions' Minister, Nick Raynsford, responding to questions following his speech to the Campaign for the English Regions in Newcastle in August 2002, ruled out the use of Assembly monies for a 'yes' campaign.[43] This appeared enough to make the North East Assembly act with extreme caution, restricting itself to the provision of information. By contrast, the North West Regional Assembly appeared to be less constrained, lobbying hard on the issue and arguing that the North West was ready for a referendum.

Overall, the main institutions of regional governance saw modest gains in powers and resources, but within the context of enduring central controls, often in the form of targets. The growing dominance of the Treasury, as a target setter and as a shaper of the debate about the governance and economic development of England, was increasingly evident, especially in relation to the activities of RDAs.

PARLIAMENT

In the run-up to the publication of the White Paper the profile of the English regions increased noticeably in Parliament. In addition to the major debate on the occasion of the publication of the White Paper on 9 May, the preceding period saw a dramatic increase in the number of Parliamentary Questions (PQs) with an explicit regional focus. Many of these came from Labour MPs impatient with a lack of progress on the White Paper. However, PQs were also used by Conservative MPs, both before and after the publication of the White Paper, eager to draw attention to what they regard as an expensive and unpopular regionalisation agenda.

The Standing Committee on Regional Affairs met three times in the year to August 2002 to discuss 'Governance in England' (18 December 2001), 'Regional Development Agencies' (21 March 2002) and 'White Paper: *Your Region, Your Choice*' (17 July 2002). A particular feature of the year to August 2002 was the increasing use of Westminster Hall as a venue for debates about the English regions. Three debates with an explicit regional focus took place in Westminster Hall on 'Regional Government (South West)', proposed by Hugo Swire (East Devon), on 12 December 2001, the 'Barnett Formula', proposed by Derek Wyatt (Sittingbourne and Sheppey), on 18 December 2001 and 'Regional Government', proposed by Andrew George (St Ives) on 15 May 2002.

---

[42] 'Minister greeted by funding row', *The Journal* [Newcastle], 1 August 2002.
[43] *Northern Echo* [Darlington], 1 August 2002.

WHITEHALL

In the aftermath of the resignation of Stephen Byers as the Secretary of State for Transport, Local Government and the Regions, major changes were announced which led to the dismemberment of the Department for Transport, Local Government and the Regions (DTLR). On 29 May 2002, the Prime Minister created a separate Department for Transport 'to focus solely on transport issues', with Alistair Darling as Secretary of State. The remaining activities of DTLR were transferred to a new Office of the Deputy Prime Minister (ODPM), led by John Prescott.

A useful summary of the role of the ODPM was included in the 2002 Spending Review document:

> The ODPM brings together the Deputy Prime Minister's responsibilities for regional government and social exclusion with the local government, planning, housing and neighbourhood renewal responsibilities of the former Department for Transport, Local Government and the Regions. This new department at the centre of government will work with other departments to drive forward important priorities for the whole of the government, particularly neighbourhood renewal, social inclusion and regional prosperity. It will promote effective devolved decision making to regional and local levels. Its own programmes will be directed at raising the quality of life in urban areas and other communities and will deliver investment and reform of housing and the planning system.[44]

The creation of the ODPM went some way to meeting the criticism levelled at the departmental arrangements instituted by the Prime Minister in the aftermath of the General Election, which saw regional responsibilities split between three government departments.[45] The new arrangements also placed John Prescott back at the heart of the government's regional agenda and the department's name reflects his position. The new arrangements though are suggestive of a future 'Department of Local Government and the Regions'.[46]

---

[44] HM Treasury, *Opportunity and security for all: Investing in an enterprising, fairer Britain — 2002 Spending Review: New Public Spending Plans 2003–2006*, Cm 5570 (Norwich: The Stationery Office, 2002), para. 9.1.

[45] See Tomaney, J., 'Reshaping the English Regions', in A Trench (ed) *The State of the Nations 2001: The Second Year of Devolution in the United Kingdom* (Exeter: Imprint Academic, 2001), pp. 117–148.

[46] The following ministerial appointments were made to the ODPM: Rt. Hon Nick Raynsford MP retained his position as Minister of State (Local Government & Regions). Rt. Hon Lord Rooker was appointed Minister of State (Housing & Planning) while Barbara Roche MP retained her position as Minister of State (Social Exclusion) and Deputy Minister for Women. Dr Alan Whitehead left the government, while Tony McNulty MP and Christopher Leslie MP were appointed Parliamentary-under-Secretaries.

Figure 3.5: Mayoral referendums (to October 2002)

Council	Date	Result	For	Against	Turnout %	Ballot Type
Berwick-upon-Tweed	7 June 2001	No	3,617 (26%)	10,212 (74%)	64	In person (Held on the day of the General Election.)
Cheltenham	28 June 2001	No	8,083 (33%)	16,602 (69%)	31	All Postal
Gloucester	28 June 2001	No	7,731 (31%)	16,317 (69%)	30.80	All Postal
Watford	12 July 2001	Yes	7,636 (52%)	7,140 (48%)	24.50	All Postal
Doncaster	20 September 2001	Yes	35,453 (65%)	19,398 (35%)	25	All postal
Kirklees	4 October 2001	No	10,169 (27%)	27,977 (73%)	13	In Person
Sunderland	11 October 2001	No	9,593 (43%)	12,209 (57%)	10	In Person
Hartlepool	18 October 2001	Yes	10,667 (51%)	10,294 (49%)	31	All Postal
Lewisham	18 October 2001	Yes	16,822 (51%)	15,914 (49%)	18	All Postal
North Tyneside	18 October 2001	Yes	30,262 (58%)	22,296 (42%)	36	All Postal
Sedgefield	18 October 2001	No	10,628 (47%)	11,869 (53%)	33.3	All Postal
Middlesborough	18 October 2001	Yes	29,067 (84%)	5,422 (16%)	34	All Postal
Brighton & Hove	18 October 2001	No	22,724 (38%)	37,214 (62%)	31.6	All Postal
Redditch	8 November 2001	No	7,250 (44%)	9,198 (56%)	28.3	All Postal
Durham city	20 November 2001	No	8,327 (41%)	11,974 (59%)	28.5	All Postal

Harlow	24 January 2002	No	5,296 (**25%**)	15,490 (**75%**)	36.38	All Postal
Plymouth	24 January 2002	No	29,559 (**41%**)	42,811 (**59%**)	39.8	All Postal
Southwark	31 January 2002	No	6,054 (**31.4%**)	13,217 (**68.6%**)	11.2	In Person
Newham	31 January 2002	Yes	27,263 (**58.2%**)	12,687 (**31.8%**)	25.9	All Postal
West Devon	31 January 2002	No	3,555 (**22.6%**)	12,190 (**77.4%**)	41.8	All Postal
Shepway	31 January 2002	No	11,357 (**44%**)	14,435 (**56%**)	36.3	All Postal
Bedford	21 February 2002	Yes	11,316 (**67.2%**)	5,537 (**32.8%**)	15.5	In Person
Hackney	2 May 2002	Yes	24,697 (**58.94%**)	10,547 (**41.06%**)	31.85	All Postal
Mansfield	2 May 2002	Yes	8,973 (**54%**)	7,350 (**44%**)	21.04	In Person
Newcastle-under-Lyme	2 May 2002	No	12,912 (**44%**)	16,468 (**56%**)	31.5	In Person
Oxford	2 May 2002	No	14,692 (**44%**)	18,686 (**56%**)	33.8	In Person
Stoke-on-Trent	2 May 2002	Yes	28,601 (**58%**)	20,578 (**42%**)	27.8	In Person
Corby	1 October 2002	No	5,351 (**46%**)	6,239 (**53.64%**)	30.91	All Postal

Source: New Local Government Network (http://www.nlgn.org.uk/yourmayor/).

MAYORS

The year to 2002 may be known in future as the high tide mark of what was once regarded as New Labour's 'big idea' for the transformation of local government and its answer to the English Question, namely elected mayors. Some 29 referendums were held between June 2001 and October 2002. Of these, less than half (11) produced a 'yes' vote. Moreover, none of the 'yes' votes occurred in the big cities for which the office of elected mayor had been originally envisaged (See Figure 3.5).

Mayoral elections were held in May and October 2002. Some eleven elections took place in total (see Figure 3.6), producing a mixed bag of results. While Labour did well in London, winning all three Mayoral elections there, in the Labour heartlands Labour did poorly and independent candidates did well. As a consequence, five out of England's eleven mayors are independents. In the Labour heartlands mayoralties tended to be won by candidates strongly emphasising very local issues and, in some cases, employing a strong anti-political-party, as well as anti-incumbent, rhetoric.

The three results in North East England, all in May, are worth particular scrutiny because of the shock waves they sent through that region's one party state and because of the possible clues they might give to the pattern of results to a future elected Assembly. In North Tyneside, where Labour remained the largest party on the council and where all three MPs for the area, including Stephen Byers, were Labour, the new Conservative mayor, Chris Morgan, narrowly beat Labour's candidate, Eddie Darke, agent to Stephen Byers. In Hartlepool, the election of 'H'angus the monkey' — also known as Stuart Drummond, a credit controller in a local call centre and part-time monkey suited mascot for Hartlepool United FC — caught almost everyone by surprise, including the local MP Peter Mandelson. Like his Middlesborough neighbour, Ray Mallon, Mr Drummond promised an inclusive administration and appointed leading councillors to his Cabinet. But he made a virtue of being the anti-politician, with ties to no party. The Middlesborough story, in particular, demonstrated the opportunities presented by the Mayoral system for high profile populists. Ray Mallon's rise to prominence came as result of his suspension from his job as police

Figure 3.6: Mayoral Election Results May 2 2002

COUNCIL	ELECTORATE	TURNOUT	ELECTED MAYOR
Doncaster*	216,097	58,487 (27.07%)	Martin Winter (Labour)
Hartlepool*	67,903	19,544 (28.78%)	Stuart Drummond ('H'Angus the Monkey) (Independent)
Lewisham*	179,835	44,518 (24.75%)	Steve Bullock (Labour)
Middlesborough*	101,570	41,994 (41.34%)	Ray Mallon (Independent)
Newham*	157,505	40,147 (25.49%)	Sir Robin Wales (Labour)
North Tyneside*	143,804	60,865 (42.32%)	Chris Morgan (Conservative)
Watford*	61,359	22,170 (36.13%)	Dorothy Thornhill (Liberal Democrats)
Bedford**	109,318	27,715 (25.35%)	Frank Branston (Better Bedford Independent Party)
Hackney**	130,657	32,926 (25.20%)	Jules Pipe (Labour)
Mansfield**	78,371	14,043 (17.92%)	Tony Eggington (Independent)
Stoke-on-Trent**	183,225	43,994 (24.01%)	Mike Wolfe (Mayor 4 Stoke)

*   Held May 2nd 2002
** Held October 2002

Sources: New Local Government Network (http://www.nlgn.org.uk/yourmayor/) and SocietyGuardian.co.uk (http://www.societyguardian.co.uk/mayorquestion).

superintendent in the town, following disciplinary investigations of corruption and malpractice. Mallon shrugged off the accusations and presented himself as a local hero, who would drive crime off the streets of the town and shake up the political system — although he appointed several councillors to his Cabinet.

In the aftermath of this performance the Local Government Minister, Nick Raynsford, announced that the government would no longer compel referendums to be held in towns where consultations suggested that there might be an appetite for change.[47]

OUTLOOK

Perhaps the most thoughtful contribution to our understanding of the challenges surrounding the governance of England in 2002 came from a Welshman, Professor Kevin Morgan of Cardiff University and former leader of the campaign for a yes vote in the Welsh Assembly referendum, who suggested:

> Although New Labour has launched an impressive array of regional initiatives in England, . . . this new regional policy package should not conceal the most important fact of all — namely that in economic terms the north-south divide is actually growing . . . Given the profound southern-centric bias to economic development in the UK it is comical in the extreme to think that New Labour's modest regional policy package can in any way reverse the north-south divide.[48]

In view of the narrowness of Welsh support for devolution in the 1999 referendum, such a perspective is especially valuable to an awareness of the prospects for regionalism in England. Morgan noted how the argument for Regional Assemblies rests on claims about their abilities to address economic and democratic 'deficits', but that some of the assumptions upon which such claims rest can be challenged: Regional Assemblies can only ever be one part of the solution to regional inequalities and one element in an increasingly multi-level polity. These are subtle arguments to make in the heat of a referendum battle. When it is considered that government support for devolution in England remains lukewarm at best, and at worst completely offset by centralising tendencies, Morgan suggests that the challenges facing those who favour devolution within England remain formidable. Whether the pro-devolution forces, even in regions like the North East, are strong enough to overcome these obstacle still remains to be tested.

The government's proposals present a set of major challenges for the English regions. For those running existing regional institutions, even the modest changes proposed in the White Paper will require the rapid

---

[47] *HC Deb,* 25 Jun 2002, Cols: 812–813W.

[48] Morgan, K., 'The English Question: Regional Perspectives on a Fractured Nation', *Regional Studies,* 36 (7), 2002, p. 800.

development of new skills and capacities if they are to lead to improved policy outcomes. The regional campaigners face the task of enthusing the mass of population sufficiently to turn-out and vote in a referendum for regional government.

Regional campaigners took solace from a major BBC poll on attitudes to regional government in England, published in March 2002, which found that the most popular reason given by respondents for supporting regional government in England was to give a stronger voice to their area.[49] The poll appeared to show a high level of support in the regions of England for devolving power from Westminster to elected Regional Assemblies. Almost two-thirds of people interviewed (63 per cent) wanted regional government, according to the survey, with less than a quarter (23 per cent) opposed to the move, 8 per cent undecided and 6 per cent with no opinion.

The BBC's poll showed that enthusiasm varied between the regions:

- Support for the move was highest in the West Midlands (73 per cent), the North-East, North-West and Yorkshire and Humberside (all 72 per cent)
- The least support for a regional assembly came in those regions closest to London
- In the East 55 per cent were in favour and 49 per cent in the South-East — the only area where a majority did not favour the move
- In the South West 61 per cent backed Regional Assemblies, with 59 per cent in the East Midlands.

The depth of this support, however, remains questionable, even if it confirms trends identified in preceding polls. Even in regions like the North East, where the debate has a relatively high profile, campaigners face a major challenge to transform their successful pressure group tactics into mass support for regional government. It is difficult to disagree with Morgan's observation, made no doubt with the Welsh experience in mind, that:

> ... winning a referendum may be more difficult than pro-devolution campaigners realise, not least because it involves creating a new tier of politicians when this profession has plummeted in the public's esteem. Indeed, winning a referendum would seem to be the biggest barrier to the formation of regional government in England.[50]

On the other hand, should pro-devolution campaigners in the English regions find and deploy arguments that could overcome these barriers, the debate

---

[49] The BBC survey was conducted by Opinion Research Business, who interviewed by telephone a random sample of 2,646 people in every English region from 1–10 March. For more details see Tomaney, J., 'The evolution of English regional governance', *Regional Studies*, 36 (7), 2002, pp. 721–731.

[50] Morgan, K., 'The English Question: Regional Perspectives on a Fractured Nation', *Regional Studies*, 36 (7), 2002, p. 806.

about democracy in Britain would take a radical new turn and the English regions might yet find their voice.

BIBLIOGRAPHY

Official Documents

Cabinet Office, *Introducing the Government Offices*, 2001. (Available at: http://www.rcu.gov.uk/articles/gofactfile/IntroGOs.pdf).

Cabinet Office/DTLR, *Your Region, Your Choice. Revitalising the English Regions*, Cm 5511 (Norwich: Stationary Office, 2002). (Available at: http://www.regions.odpm.gov.uk/governance/whitepaper/pdf/full_whitepaper.pdf).

DTLR, *Planning: Delivering a Fundamental Change* (Planning Green Paper), Department of Transport Local and the Regions, 2001. (Available at: http://www.planning.odpm.gov.uk/consult/greenpap/pdf/greenpap.pdf).

HM Treasury and DTI, *Productivity in the UK: 3 — The Regional Dimension* (London: HM Treasury, 2001).

HM Treasury, *Opportunity and security for all: Investing in an enterprising, fairer Britain — 2002 Spending Review: New Public Spending Plans 2003–2006*, Cm 5570 (Norwich: The Stationery Office, 2002).

Prescott, J., 'Speech to Yorkshire Labour Party Regional Conference', Hull, 20 October 2001.

Prescott, J., 'Sustainable Communities, Housing and Planning', Speech to the House of Commons on Spending Review 2002, 18th July, Office of the Deputy Prime Minister (http://www.odpm.gov.uk/about/ministers/speeches/prescott/180702.htm).

Secondary Sources

Adams, J. and Tomaney, J., *Restoring the Balance. Strengthening the Government's proposals for regional assemblies* (London: Institute for Public Policy Research, 2002).

Balls, E., 'Britain's new regional policy', in Balls, E. and Healey, J., (eds) *Towards a New Regional Policy* (London: The Smith Institute, 2000).

Benneworth, P. and Dabinett, G. 'English devolution and regional development', *Local Work*, 46, November 2002.

Morgan, K., 'The English Question: Regional Perspectives on a Fractured Nation', *Regional Studies*, 36 (7), 2002 pp. 797–810.

Newman, I. and Dungey, J., 'The Government White Paper, *Your Region, Your Choice: Revitalising the English Regions*', *Local Economy*, 17 (3), 2002, pp. 253–255.

Sandford, M., *A Commentary on the Regional Government White Paper, Your Region Your Choice: Revitalising the English Regions* (London: Constitution Unit, 2002).

Sandford, M., *Inclusiveness of Regional Chambers* (London: Constitution Unit, 2002).

Shaw, K., Humphrey, L., O'Brien, P., Tomaney, J., *The Engagement of Economic and Social Partners in a Directly Elected Regional Assembly for the North East*, Report to the North East Assembly, 2002. (http://www.north-east assembly.gov.uk/ publications/CURDSecosocpart_research.doc).

Tomaney, J., 'Reshaping the English Regions', in A. Trench (ed), *The State of the Nations 2001: The Second Year of Devolution in the United Kingdom* (Exeter: Imprint Academic, 2001), pp. 117–148.

Tomaney, J., 'In what sense a regional problem? Sub-national governance in England', *Local Economy*, 17 (3), 2002, pp. 226–238.

Tomaney, J., 'The evolution of English regional governance', *Regional Studies*, 36 (7), 2002, pp. 721–731.

Tomaney, J. and Mawson, J. (eds), *England: The State of the Regions* (Bristol: Policy Press, 2002).

Tomaney, J. and Hetherington, P., *English Regions Monitoring Report, November 2001* (London: Constitution Unit, 2001). (Available at: http://www.ucl.ac.uk/ constitution-unit/).

Tomaney, J., Hetherington, P. and Humphrey, L., *English Regions Monitoring Report, February 2002* (London: Constitution Unit, 2002). (Available at: http://www.ucl.ac.uk/constitution-unit/).

Tomaney, J., Hetherington, P. and Humphrey, L., *English Regions Monitoring Report, May 2002* (London: Constitution Unit, 2002). (Available at: http://www.ucl.ac.uk/constitution-unit/).

Tomaney, J., Hetherington, P. and Humphrey, L. *English Regions Monitoring Report, August 2002* (London: Constitution Unit, 2002). (Available at: http://www.ucl.ac.uk/constitution-unit/).

4

Northern Ireland: Valedictory?[1]

Rick Wilford and Robin Wilson

INTRODUCTION

It is trite to say that Northern Ireland is 'different', but it is. (To complicate matters, the north of Ireland has also for centuries been somewhat different from the south.[2]) Devolution there has not been conceived by its principal ethnic parties or by Downing Street in the same manner as the project of democratically decentralising power to Scotland (and to Wales) inherited by Tony Blair from the former Labour leader, John Smith, and implemented by 'New Labour' after its assumption of power in 1997.

For one thing, opposition to devolution for Scotland and Wales was never matched, during the long Conservative era, by hostility to devolution for Northern Ireland. Quite the contrary: virtually the whole British political class has been united for decades on the desirability of offloading responsibility for that 'troubled' region to its inhabitants.[3] Nor were the new institutions in Edinburgh and Cardiff conditional on the support of the Republic of Ireland's electorate, nor were they linked to Stormont via a ministerial council — twice previously attempted by British governments in the last century — between north and south.[4] And, finally, while Labour was forced into coalition with the Liberal Democrats in Scotland and (eventually) in Wales, in Northern Ireland four mistrustful sectarian parties were thrust together in a consociational-style 'grand coalition' by application of the d'Hondt proportionality rule, to ensure not only non-majoritarian power-sharing but also that the ceasefires announced by the IRA in 1994 and 1997 would be underpinned and that there would no more bombs in London.

---

[1] A word about what this chapter does *not* address. Space does not permit us to rehearse the material in our quarterly devolution monitoring reports (http://www.ucl.ac.uk/constitution-unit/leverh/ monitoring.htm) on north-south and 'east-west' relations and the EU context, or on the media representation of events in Northern Ireland. But we are extremely grateful to all our fellow team members: John Coakley, Lizanne Dowds, Greg McLaughlin, Elizabeth Meehan and Duncan Morrow. Naturally, only we are responsible for the contents of this chapter.

[2] Foster, R., *Modern Ireland: 1660–1972* (London: Allen Lane, 1988), *passim*; Bardon, J., *A History of Ulster* (Belfast: Blackstaff Press, 1992).

[3] Bew, P., Patterson, H. and Teague, P., *Between War and Peace: The Political Future of Northern Ireland* (London: Lawrence and Wishart, 1997), p. 14.

[4] Even the weaker British-Irish Council was itself a product of the Belfast agreement.

For most people in Great Britain, Northern Ireland is 'really' Irish, whether members of its declining Protestant majority want to be or not, though the principle of consent is formally recognised. Meanwhile, most people in the republic want the north, eventually, to become part of their state but don't accept that the challenging arrangements enshrined in the Belfast agreement of 1998 — notably representation of the political wing of the IRA in government — should apply to them. Most Catholics in Northern Ireland see the leader of the republican movement, Gerry Adams (as Roosevelt said of the Nicaraguan dictator Somoza) as 'our son of a bitch' and insist his party be in devolved power; most Protestants, unmindful of the undemocratic character of the pre-1968 Stormont régime, believe this to be an affront to democracy while the IRA continues to exist. Many Catholics assume a united Ireland will come in the decades ahead, and hope this will be so; many Protestants agree, fearing they are right. Many Catholic supporters of the agreement, and its Protestant opponents, tend to see it as a stepping-stone to that unity; most Protestant supporters fervently hope it has copper-fastened partition instead.

In none of these highly contradictory considerations do good governance or the promotion of multi-ethnic politics in Northern Ireland figure prominently. It is thus unsurprising not only that the performance of devolution in Northern Ireland should have been sub-optimal but also, more seriously, that its trajectory should have been so fraught with difficulty.

Fitful Progress

While the First and Deputy First Ministers, David Trimble of the Ulster Unionist Party and Séamus Mallon of the SDLP, were elected in July 1998, a year before power was transferred to Scotland and Wales, Northern Ireland fell behind due to wrangling over the absence of arms decommissioning by the IRA (and the other paramilitaries). In anticipation of progress, devolution went live in December 1999 but with no movement taking place by February 2000 it had already been suspended.

Hopes of decommissioning led to renewed power-sharing in May 2000 but on 1 July 2001 David Trimble resigned as First Minister over allegedly broken promises by the IRA. It proved impossible to secure his re-election, and the (re-)election of a Deputy First Minister, within the six-week timescale allotted by the Northern Ireland Act 1998. Rather than precipitate fresh Assembly elections, the Northern Ireland Secretary, John Reid, announced two successive, one-day suspensions to buy time. At the third time of asking, in early November, despite some 'decommissioning' by the IRA, the crisis was only resolved by a bizarre change of political clothes by members of the non-sectarian Alliance Party. Mr Trimble and a new colleague, Mark Durkan, soon also to be leader of the SDLP, were duly elected.

This last period of devolution, from November 2001 to October 2002, was the longest phase of concerted implementation of the agreement, with its two other 'strands' — the north-south and 'east-west' relationships — also in working order. The legislative process was reformed, the legislative load increased significantly and Assembly members (MLAs) addressed the public finances in a more serious fashion. There was evidence of greater maturity on the part of the committees and — via the formation of executive sub-committees — of 'joined-up' government.

Yet the respite was not secure. At the end of the period under review, what in Northern Ireland parlance would be called 'a really serious crisis' developed. It was to lead that month to an indefinite suspension of the institutions.

Figure 4.1: Key events in Northern Ireland

20 August 2001	SDLP agrees to nominate members to Policing Board responsible for new Police Service of Northern Ireland.
17 September 2001	John Hume resigns as SDLP leader.
18 September 2001	Séamus Mallon, deputy SDLP leader, says he will not seek party leadership or re-election as Deputy First Minister, leaving field open to Mark Durkan, Finance Minister, in both cases.
20 September 2001	Executive Committee (minus demissioned First and Deputy First Ministers, David Trimble and Séamus Mallon respectively) agrees second draft Programme for Government and associated draft budget.
21 September 2001	For second time, Northern Ireland Secretary suspends devolved institutions for 24 hours, to allow further six weeks for (re-)election of First and Deputy First Ministers.
6 October 2001	David Ford becomes leader of Alliance Party, in succession to Sean Neeson.
12 October 2001	Northern Ireland Secretary, John Reid, declares Ulster Defence Association and Loyalist Volunteer Force ceasefires over.
18 October 2001	Five remaining unionist ministers (3 UUP, 2 DUP) resign.
23 October 2001	Independent International Commission on Decommissioning announces some IRA weapons have been put 'beyond use'; Mr Trimble announces UUP ministers will retake positions and DUP reluctantly follows suit.
3 November 2001	As midnight deadline looms for expiry of latest suspension, Alliance agrees three of its five MLAs will redesignate as 'unionists' to elect a First and Deputy First Minister.

4 November 2001	Royal Ulster Constabulary becomes Police Service of Northern Ireland.
6 November 2001	Alliance redesignation allows Messrs Trimble and Durkan to be elected First and Deputy First Minister respectively and institutions to be renewed, amid 'brawl in hall'; DUP calls for judicial review, claiming Northern Ireland Secretary should have announced new Assembly elections.
10 December 2001	Assembly endorses revised Programme for Government.
11 December 2001	Assembly endorses revised budget.
14 December 2001	Seán Farren replaces Mr Durkan as Finance Minister; Carmel Hanna replaces Dr Farren as Minister for Employment and Learning.
20 February 2002	Sam Foster retires as Environment Minister, being replaced by Dermot Nesbitt; he is in turn replaced by Hugh Leslie as junior minister in OFMDFM.
1 April 2002	Invest Northern Ireland, new single development agency for the region, comes into being.
8 April 2002	IRA announces second act of putting some arms 'beyond use'.
2 May 2002	Prime Minister, Tony Blair, and Chancellor, Gordon Brown, visit Belfast to launch Reinvestment and Reform Initiative, conferring a borrowing power on devolved administration.
17 May 2002	General election in republic sees big gains for Greens and SF, latter increasing its representation from one to five Dáil deputies.
17 July 2002	IRA issues apology for those 'non-combatants' it killed over preceding decades.
24 July 2002	Before Commons rises, Prime Minister, Mr Blair, and Northern Ireland Secretary, Mr Reid, issue 'yellow card' warnings to paramilitaries.
25 July 2002	Law Lords rule, on split vote, that election of First and Deputy First Minister in November 2001 was lawful.
21 September 2002	At specially convened Ulster Unionist Council, Mr Trimble announces he and fellow ministers will withdraw from executive on 18 January 2003, if republicans fail to demonstrate they have left violence behind for good.

4 October 2002	Police raid SF's offices at Parliament Buildings and the homes of SF officials, including party's head of Assembly administration, Denis Donaldson; four SF officials charged with possession of documents likely to be of use to terrorists.
11 October 2002	DUP's two executive ministers, Nigel Dodds and Peter Robinson, resign.
14 October 2002	Devolution suspended at midnight: two extra ministers drafted in to complement three-strong NIO ministerial team.
17 October 2002	Mr Blair, in flying visit to Belfast, effectively calls on IRA to disband to restore devolved institutions.
20 October 2002	IRA insists it is not a threat to 'peace process' but 'will not accept the imposition of unrealisable demands'.
24 October 2002	Paul Murphy, former Welsh Secretary and previously junior NIO minister, replaces John Reid as Northern Ireland Secretary when latter becomes Labour Party Chair.

Data on public attitudes had shown inexorably polarising opinion in 2001–02. Rising 'loyalist' paramilitary violence, at the expense of vulnerable Catholics, was its most nihilistic expression. But naked intercommunal hostility at Belfast interfaces evoked the 'sores' that 'suppurated and spread', as in John Hewitt's early 'troubles' poem, *The Coasters*.

Of greatest political import was a series of Macmillanite 'events' in Autumn 2002 involving apparently conspiratorial behaviour by the republican movement and the reaction of the UUP to them. Republicans blamed unionists for manufacturing the crisis; unionists blamed republicans for providing the raw materials. Fear of losing the 'blame game' appeared to keep Mr Trimble from walking out of government. But, eventually, the Northern Ireland Office stepped in to stop him doing just that.

The fundamental question avoided by the agreement finally demanded a definitive answer. Was it really feasible, contrary to the history of the Irish state — think of the parting of the ways with paramilitary *confrères* which had been required of Eamon de Valera, not to mention contemporary international experience where paramilitaries may find themselves before an international tribunal — to have a paramilitary organisation politically represented in a democratic government?

The Prime Minister, Tony Blair — apparently stung by reported private references to him in discovered republican documents as 'the naïve idiot' — came to Belfast to ask this very question. His answer appeared to be 'no'.

While the future remained uncertain at the time of writing, it was widely assumed that the Assembly elections timetabled for May 2003 would only go ahead if power-sharing was restored — otherwise, no one was predicting other than a lurch towards the ethno-nationalist extremes. Fear of a mauling at the polls had stimulated Mr Trimble to harden his position at a meeting of the Ulster Unionist Council in September, when he insisted his ministers would collapse the executive in mid-January unless the IRA had meanwhile disbanded.

Only the Democratic Unionist Party of Rev Ian Paisley, thundering as for three unmoving decades at the latest unionist 'betrayal', and Mr Adams' Sinn Féin — its supporters unmoved by further evidence of his ruthless behaviour during that period — could look forward to any elections with equanimity. And only the most naïve and wishful could envisage what one Trimble adviser dismissed as a 'Molotov-Ribbentrop pact' between those two parties, post-election, putting the institutional show back on the road, given the infinitesimal proportion of DUP supporters backing power-sharing with SF.

Part of the difficulty was the only limited evidence, as in Scotland and Wales, that the citizens of Northern Ireland had developed an instrumental commitment to devolution.[5] Particularly among Protestants, there was merely lukewarm affirmation of the devolved ministers' mantra-like claim to be 'making a difference'. Indeed, substantively, the record from December 1999 — however rationalised by suspensions — was limited. Free fares for the elderly and a rebalancing of student finance in favour of the less well off were the only major policy innovations in place before Mr Reid pulled down the shutters.

There were, moreover, egregious failures. The SF Health Minister, Bairbre de Brún, won the doubtful laurel of presiding over the longest hospital waiting lists in western Europe, as she remained bogged down in serial consultation, despite repeated cash injections. But the most glaring failure, for which Mr Trimble was particularly culpable, was the inability of the four-party Executive Committee, ensconced in the grandeur of Parliament Buildings, to agree a strategy on community relations — while, beneath it, Belfast was convulsed by ghetto wrath.

PUBLIC OPINION

We start our chapter this year with public attitudes because clear, and worrying, trends in opinion underpinned, and help us to comprehend, the flow of political events.

First, the good news. Positive attitudes to the *idea* of devolution emerged in the annual Northern Ireland Life and Times Survey data, based on polling

---

[5] Curtice, J., 'Devolution, the union and public opinion: report prepared for the House of Lords Committee on the Constitution inquiry into "Devolution: inter-institutional relations in the United Kingdom"' (Strathclyde: Strathclyde University, 2002).

in October 2001. While 51 per cent of respondents thought the UK government had the most influence over how Northern Ireland was run, as against only 28 per cent who felt the Assembly had most influence, when asked which institution *ought* to have most influence the ratio was reversed: 65 per cent favoured the Assembly, as against only 17 per cent Westminster.

As in all recent surveys — and belying the old nationalist rhetoric of 'no return to Stormont' — Catholics were more positive about devolution than Protestants. But only 24 per cent of the latter assumed what might be called a fundamentalist unionist stance.

Asked, however, whether the Assembly was giving 'ordinary people more say', while 40 per cent agreed, 44 per cent said it had made no difference and 8 per cent said 'less say'. Only 31 per cent of Protestants took the 'more say' position. Split views, and Protestant pessimism, also emerged in response to questions as to whether MLAs worked together to help solve Northern Ireland's problems and whether the Assembly represented value for money. Yet a large majority (57–27) favoured Scottish-style tax-varying powers.

Figure 4.2: From what you have seen and heard so far, do you think that having a Northern Ireland Assembly is giving ordinary people more say in how Northern Ireland is governed, less say, or is it making no difference?

| | % | | |
	Protestant	**Catholic**	**All**
More say	31	51	40
Less say	12	3	8
Making no difference	50	39	44
Don't know	7	7	8

Figure 4.3: How much would you say that members of the Northern Ireland Assembly from different parties work together to help solve Northern Ireland's problems?

| | % | | |
	Protestant	**Catholic**	**All**
A great deal	6	8	6
A fair amount	33	47	37
Not very much	36	32	35
Not at all	24	8	15
Don't know	4	6	6

On the big departments' devolved performance (both under SF ministers), the response was 'sickly' (health) and 'could try harder' (education): 39 per cent thought healthcare was worse under devolution (11 per cent thought better), while 24 per cent felt education had improved (as against 12 per cent worse).[6]

More disturbing were the findings on community relations. Converting these and prior Northern Ireland Social Attitudes Survey material into time series, Lizanne Dowds demonstrated a steady decline since the agreement in the proportion of respondents who felt that community relations were better than five years earlier, and a similar drop in the proportion who felt they would be better in five years time.

These two questions have been running since 1989 and this feel-good/ optimism quotient is falling worryingly close to its initial low base. The trend is reinforced by evidence that previously very high levels of support for cross-communal mixing, in residence and the workplace, are beginning to wane.[7]

The data were underpinned during the year by the findings of research by Pete Shirlow of the University of Ulster, on the attitudes and behaviour of residents of interface areas in Belfast. At the last count, there are now 27 barriers — 'peace walls' in the Orwellian language of the place — physically separating conflicting 'communities'.[8]

The research demonstrated deeply entrenched sectarianism — especially among young people with no other, more civic, memories — and deeply segregated patterns of use of public services (except, by necessity, the single genito-urinary clinic). The *Guardian* reported a research presentation under the banner 'PEACE BUT NO LOVE AS NORTHERN IRELAND DIVIDE GROWS EVER WIDER: Protestants and Catholics report more violence and less integration'.[9]

Violence in the region is often treated as if it were an independent variable, the 'cause' of its 'troubles'. Indeed the very idea of the 'peace process' was that by acting on violence division would be reduced. But violence is better seen as the dependent variable, predicated on underlying communal division. And, as division widened during the period, violence correspondingly worsened.

Police data indicated that while violent incidents had fallen to near zero in 1995, the calendar year 2001 saw more shootings than in any year since 1993 and more bombings than in any year since 1988.[10] The bulk of these attacks

---

[6] *Northern Ireland Life and Times Survey Research Update* 12, May 2002, available at http://www.ark.ac.uk/nilt/update12.PDF

[7] Dowds, L., *Northern Ireland Monitoring Report, August 2002* (London: The Constitution Unit, 2002), p. 24–25.

[8] Jarman, N., *Managing Disorder: Responding to Interface Violence in North Belfast* (Belfast: Office of the First Minister and Deputy First Minister (research branch) 2002), p. 23.

[9] *Guardian*, 4 January 2002.

[10] We are grateful to Tony Gallagher for his analysis of police statistics.

came from loyalists. Many were low-level (and so unreported outside the region). But the Prime Minister's refrain that the citizens of Northern Ireland should appreciate how much better things had become was wearing increasingly thin.

Figure 4.4: Shootings and bombings in Northern Ireland by year[11]

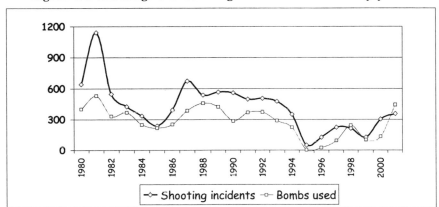

Anxiety in the Northern Ireland Office at the trends in opinion was evident during the year, notably in a speech in November by the Northern Ireland Secretary at the Institute of Irish Studies in Liverpool. Mr Reid warned nationalists not to let the region become a 'cold place for Protestants'.[12] He received little appreciation for his effort: nationalists claimed it was their 'community' that was under attack, whilst unionists twisted the speech to vindicate the claim that they were already frozen out.

In March 2002, Mr Reid told a Galway audience that nationalists should reassure unionists that a united Ireland was not 'inevitable'.[13] Yet the following weekend the UUP leader, Mr Trimble, was calling at his party's AGM for a border poll to accompany the Assembly elections (putatively) due in May 2003 — the NILTS evidence suggested the margin would be considerably closer than he appeared to think — and within weeks the SF President, Mr Adams, called on the Republic's government to produce a Green (in every sense) Paper on Irish unity.[14]

Most disturbing of all was the *Hearts and Minds* poll[15] taken in the two days following suspension in October 2002. It confirmed the continuing decline in Protestant support for the agreement since the 1998 referendum.

[11] Security incidents, 1980 to 2001 (source PSNI)

[12] available at http://www.nio.gov.uk/press/011121sos.htm

[13] *Irish Times*, 2 March 2002.

[14] *Belfast Telegraph*, 1 April 2002.

[15] Data available at http://news.bbc.co.uk/1/hi/northern_ireland/2335553.stm

Asked how they would vote if a referendum was held today, 33 per cent of 'unionists'[16] said they would support the agreement, while 67 per cent would vote against — compared with a 55 per cent 'yes' and a 45 per cent 'no' in 1998. A plurality of unionists (42 per cent) said direct rule was their preferred model of government.

While 82 per cent of 'nationalists' said they would vote 'yes' in a rerun of the referendum, this too showed a decline from the near unanimity (96 per cent support) achieved four years earlier. Among nationalists, a united Ireland vied with power-sharing as preferred alternative futures: each enjoyed 38 per cent backing.

Current antipathy among unionists to power-sharing is arresting: 58 per cent said they would not support sharing power with the SDLP and SF — more than double the proportion (26 per cent) that would. At face value, this appears to confirm the view often articulated by the SF leadership that 'unionists don't want a Fenian about the place' — though unionists would doubtless reply, in the now ritual discourse of antagonism, that republican behaviour had made this a self-fulfilling prophecy.

THE 'PEACE PROCESS'

Northern Ireland's school year, like its political season, opened in September 2001. And it saw some of the most dispiriting images of the region flashed around the globe since the days of mass bombings and endless funerals: (non-)working-class Protestants, their faces contorted with anger, confronting Catholic children, their faces traumatised and tearful. Republican propaganda equating the scenes with Little Rock and the deep south belied the fact that the children were attending a segregated school, not being denied access to an integrated one. But the visceral sectarian hatred directed at the pupils of Holy Cross genuinely shocked the world.

The dispute pitched a declining Protestant 'community' in north Belfast against an increasingly assertive Catholic neighbour. In so doing, it represented a microcosm of the worrying trend we identified in last year's chapter, with Protestants in general coming to believe that the agreement represented a nationalist 'victory' rather than a gain for both 'sides' and uneducated male Protestants in particular moving strongly against the deal.[17]

The latter, we pointed out — treating education as a proxy for class — represented just the constituency ripe for paramilitary recruitment. The largest loyalist organisation, the Ulster Defence Association, repositioned itself

---

[16] An infuriating aspect of post-agreement practice in Northern Ireland has been to treat its consociationalist categories as if they were real; thus some polls now use 'unionists' and 'nationalists' as sample sub-sets, as if they were interchangeable with 'Protestants' and 'Catholics'.

[17] Wilson, R. and Wilford, R., 'Northern Ireland: Endgame', in Trench, A. (ed.), *The State of the Nations: 2001: The Second Year of Devolution in the United Kingdom* (Exeter: Imprint Academic Press, 2001), p.101.

in the 'no' camp in July 2001,[18] subsequently disdaining its prior 'political' pretensions.[19] An amorphous and undisciplined body, the UDA perpetrated a barrage of attacks — in some cases fatal — against Catholics, particularly vulnerable individuals living or working in mainly Protestant areas.

Such assaults, often with 'pipe-bombs', perversely reinforced the determination of many Catholics to see the representatives of republican paramilitarism remain in government — what was all the fuss about SF and the IRA, many asked, when loyalists were responsible for the lion's share of violence? With evident reluctance, the Northern Ireland Office was forced to concede in October 2001 that the UDA's threadbare 'ceasefire' was over. The killing of a young Catholic postal worker in north Belfast in January excited the biggest peace demonstrations, spearheaded by the trade unions, that Northern Ireland had seen for years.

The establishment of the Policing Board was one of the year's success stories — though it was hard to dissociate that fact from the self-exclusion of SF from it. The board has 19 members, with 10 appointed by the Assembly parties on the d'Hondt-proportionality basis. Minus the two SF members, it went live on 7 November 2001. The board's early agreement[20] on an emblem for the new Police Service of Northern Ireland, growing out of but replacing the Royal Ulster Constabulary, was a feather in its cap.

But the intimidation of Catholic recruits to the PSNI by 'dissident' republicans, and the refusal by SF to condemn such attacks, created growing problems for the service as the year unfolded. The trouble was that the generous redundancy package for former RUC officers, the demoralisation of the service and consequent absenteeism and the requirement that there be one new Catholic recruit for every new Protestant (following the 1999 report of the former Hong Kong governor Chris Patten) combined to generate a manpower crisis.

This pressure on the police was unremitting, particularly as intercommunal violence spread in 2002 from north to east Belfast. Nightly pitched battles exhibiting the rawest sectarianism tied up huge numbers of officers. And apparent reluctance, post-Patten, to deploy plastic bullets in riot situations meant the police sustained injuries in large numbers as missiles rained down upon them — compounding the problems of absenteeism and morale. The first annual report of the Policing Board revealed that one in ten days were being lost through absenteeism and the detection rate had fallen to one in five crimes.[21]

While the Catholic perception of the source of most actual violence was the right one, so too, however, was the rather less sanguine Protestant view of

---

[18] *Irish Times*, 11 July 2001.

[19] *Irish News*, 28 November 2001.

[20] *Belfast Telegraph*, 13 December 2001.

[21] Northern Ireland Policing Board, *Annual Report 2001–2002* (Belfast: NIPB, 2002).

the republican movement's *capacity*. As the year progressed, scandal after scandal indicated that republicans were engaging in a 'dual strategy' in which, in Leninist fashion, democratic politics was being pursued simultaneously with undemocratic subversion.

In August 2001, three men were detained in Colombia, suspected of involvement with FARC *guerrillas* — a movement still attached to the 'armed struggle' almost the entire Latin American left had left behind. While the three faced trial at the end of the period and must be presumed innocent, evidence accumulated that the IRA-FARC connection was strong — including the use of IRA-type mortars in an audacious attack on the inauguration of the new, right-wing president, Alvaro Uribe, in August this year.[22] The SF President, Mr Adams, uncharacteristically declined invitations to the Oireachtas Foreign Affairs Committee in Dublin and a congressional committee in Washington to explain the links between the two organisations.

The First Minister, Mr Trimble, had already resigned on 1 July owing to the absence of arms decommissioning — which the agreement said should have been completed by May 2000 — on the part of the military wing of his governmental partner. His SDLP deputy, Mr Mallon, was simultaneously demissioned, as the agreement required them to be elected or depart within six weeks.

Due to what one 1998 talks participant claimed had been a drafting error in the Belfast agreement, the (re-)election required a majority in each of the 'unionist' and 'nationalist' blocs in the Assembly for success. With two of Mr Trimble's MLAs having drifted into the 'no' camp, he could only command 28 of the 58 'unionist' votes — the numbers didn't add up.

Talks convened by London and Dublin at Weston Park in July had proved inconclusive. In the hope that something might turn up, the Northern Ireland Secretary, Mr Reid, adopted the procedural device of two successive, one-day suspensions to reset the six-week clock, in mid-August and late September. As the next deadline loomed, the IRA eventually announced in late October that it had put some of its weapons 'beyond use', a claim verified by the Independent International Commission on Decommissioning. But with no indication as to the number or character of the items involved, or precisely what had happened to them, the confidence-building potential of the act among instinctively mistrustful Protestants was limited.

While it was enough for Mr Trimble to seek to return to government with Mr Adams, among others, it was not enough to change the political arithmetic in the Assembly. As the third six-week period came to a close the Alliance Party, its collective arm heavily twisted, agreed that three of its members, designated as 'others' under the Assembly registration system, would

---

[22] *Irish Times*, 9 August 2002.

redesignate as 'unionists', so that Mr Trimble could be re-elected.[23] He would now have a new partner, the Finance Minister, Mark Durkan, as Mr Mallon had indicated he would not be standing again.

From the Northern Ireland Office point of view, *Realpolitik* had prevailed — albeit (to borrow an epithet from a Dublin official) by 'Mickeyavellian' means. But there was no doubting the delegitimising effect of the affair on an agreement founded on the 'consociationalist' principle of mutual communal veto. And there were further destabilising events to come.

In January 2002, a west Belfast man pleaded guilty to making false statements while buying guns in Florida. He was reported to have sought to obtain hundreds of weapons, which evoked memories of an IRA gun-running operation in the state broken up by the FBI in 1999.[24]

In a remarkable development, on St Patrick's Day in March, a highly 'professional' raid took place on a room in Castlereagh police station in Belfast — once infamous to the IRA as an interrogation centre — which led to details being removed on some 250 Special Branch detectives. The nature of the attack led the then chief constable to speculate on an 'inside job'. But evidence accumulated — including, reportedly, from eavesdropping on telephone conversations between leading republicans — that, even if members of the intelligence services were involved in the raid, the material had indeed found its way to the IRA.[25] Concerned for their welfare, the government had to set aside some £30 million to relocate the detectives.

In April, it emerged that follow-up searches had discovered IRA intelligence files, including a list of senior Conservatives and details of army bases in Britain, which had recently been updated.[26] The following weekend it was reported, albeit on the basis of 'military intelligence' supplied to the *Sunday Telegraph*, that the IRA had secretly rearmed with powerful Russian assault rifles.[27]

More authoritatively, the *Irish Times'* security correspondent revealed that in 1999 police and republican sources had reported that the IRA leadership was telling its members it would only decommission as long as it could replace its arsenal.[28] A senior officer of the new Police Service of Northern Ireland told its first joint conference with the Garda Síochána that the IRA was 'very active' in training, recruiting, targeting and procurement.[29]

A second act of putting weapons 'beyond use' took place, again shrouded in mystery, in April. This was widely seen as timed to favour SF in the run-up

---

[23] The two Women's Coalition MLAs, originally self-defined 'others', had already re-designated: one, Jane Morrice, as a unionist, the other, Monica McWilliams, as a nationalist.

[24] *Irish Times*, 11 March 2002.

[25] *Observer* (Irish edition), 2 June 2002.

[26] *Belfast Telegraph*, 19 April 2002.

[27] *Sunday Telegraph*, 21 April 2002.

[28] *Irish Times*, 11 March 2002.

[29] *Irish Times*, 9 April 2002.

to the election in May to Dáil Eireann. The latter was to add a further twist to the spiral of mistrust.

The outgoing Taoiseach, Bertie Ahern, who once more failed to win an overall majority for his Fianna Fáil party, insisted there could be no question of going into government with a resurgent SF unless the IRA disbanded.[30] While this could be defended *stricto sensu* on the basis of the Republic's constitution — which allows of one army in the state — politically it smacked of double standards, given FF's insistence that SF had to be included in the northern administration at all costs.

Trimble Agitated

In this fetid atmosphere, even an unprecedented IRA statement of apology for the deaths of the 'non-combatants' — civilians — it had slaughtered in industrial quantities over the preceding three decades had little effect.[31] Facing the threat of yet another heave against him from within his ranks, Mr Trimble called on the Prime Minister to ensure that republicans implement a clear and unambiguous ceasefire or face expulsion from the executive.

At the conclusion of the parliamentary session, Mr Blair told the Commons that training, targeting, the acquisition of weapons and any preparations for a return to large-scale violence would feature in future ceasefire assessments. But he stopped short of indicating any measures that might follow a negative assessment.[32]

Mr Trimble's position correspondingly continued to weaken. A close supporter, asked in early September how he expected the next rendezvous between the leader and his party, a fortnight later, would go, replied that even members of Mr Trimble's 'praetorian guard' — the UUP Assembly group — were starting to 'drift'.

At the Ulster Unionist Council meeting on 21 September, a compromise was arrived at between the leader and his internal opponents, with which the latter were well pleased. This involved a pledge to withdraw from the executive, thereby precipitating its collapse, from 18 January 2003, unless the IRA disbanded in the interim period.

It looked, for all the world, as if Mr Trimble was about to lose the 'blame game' to his opponent, Mr Adams. But at the end of a week in which the IRA shot a Derry bus driver in front of his passengers and beat a student to a pulp, in an incredible turn of events — including spectacular TV footage of the (reformed) police raiding SF's offices in Parliament Buildings, following up dawn raids on republicans' homes in Belfast — it emerged that the IRA had been engaged in a huge spying operation, and that the NIO had known about it for over a year.

[30] *Irish News*, 20 May 2002.
[31] *Irish Times*, 17 July 2002.
[32] *Irish News*, 25 July 2002.

The operation had reportedly included gleaning personal details on up to 2,000 people, including the First Minister and other politicians, security chiefs, loyalist paramilitaries and even MI5 agents.[33] In a manner reminiscent of the Stalinist denial of all criticism as 'anti-Soviet', SF accused the police of pursuing an 'anti-peace process, anti-democracy and anti-Sinn Féin agenda'.[34]

The initial reaction on RTE of the leading 'peace processor' of the last decade and a half, the former special adviser to several FF Taoisigh, Martin Mansergh, was to compare the Stormont raid to events in Robert Mugabe's Zimbabwe. But when, a few days after the story broke, Mr Blair met Mr Ahern and apprised the latter of the seriousness of the security breach, Dublin rowed in behind the British position — as indeed did Washington. The Taoiseach later confirmed that transcripts of calls between Mr Blair and himself had been obtained by republicans.[35]

The only question now — and a question that was left for the moment unresolved — was whether the Assembly elections due in May 2003 would at some point go ahead. That there would be another suspension was not in doubt. Nor was it in any doubt where the onus would be held to lie in bringing the institutions back to life. In making the announcement on 14 October, followed by a joint statement by the two premiers, Mr Reid said he hoped the suspension would be 'short-lived'.[36]

The Prime Minister rammed the point home in a surprise visit to Belfast a few days later. Without a single politician in his invited audience, Mr Blair made it plain that 'four and a half years of hassle, frustration and messy compromise' had come to an end. He said: 'The fork in the road has finally come.' The IRA could not be 'half in, half out of this process'. Dismissing the rationalisations given by Dublin as to why SF could not be in government there while the IRA continued to exist, yet a different standard applied to the north, he said there had to be 'an end to tolerance of paramilitary activity in any form'.[37]

The speech was seen, and was no doubt intended, as 'putting it up' to the republican movement (there was no more complicity with the pretence that the latter comprised two distinct and separate organisations). But there was no overt threat of sanctions and, if this was an exercise of prime-ministerial virility, an unflattering comparison suggested itself.

Five years earlier, in his first major engagement outside London after the 1997 landslide, Mr Blair had come to Belfast, again out of the blue, to warn SF that the 'peace train' was moving off — with or without it. In 2002, the

---

[33] *Guardian*, 7 October 2002.
[34] *Times*, 5 October 2002.
[35] *Irish News*, 23 October 2002.
[36] Northern Ireland Information Service, 14 October 2002.
[37] available at http://www.number-10.gov.uk/output/Page6316.asp

Prime Minister rather sheepishly praised the parties of the moderate middle, roundly shafted by his focus on republicans in the intervening years. Now, for all the masculinist posturing, Mr Blair was in effect saying that the future of Northern Ireland lay in Mr Adams' considerably empowered hands.

The latter promised a 'considered' response from SF. He told a party meeting in Monaghan that he could envisage a future without the IRA — though he did not say how many months, years or decades ahead this might be — but he warned that the IRA would not disband in response to British or unionist demands.[38] The other key figure in the republican leadership, Martin McGuinness, meanwhile told BBC Northern Ireland that his 'war' was over.[39] The IRA's initial response[40] to Mr Blair's Belfast speech was to issue a statement on 20 October rejecting his disbandment call. Ten days later it announced that it had — and for the second time — suspended its 'engagement' with John De Chastelain's decommissioning commission, cushioned by the statement that it remained 'committed to the search for a just and lasting peace'.[41] The somewhat temperate response by the new Secretary of State to the IRA's withdrawal of co-operation was that it was 'regrettable and disappointing' but 'not surprising'.[42] As Mr Murphy begins his series of bilateral talks with local political leaders, any prospect of an early restoration of devolution is fast receding.

THE EXECUTIVE

During the period, concern emerged in the Assembly, and more widely, about the output of the Executive Committee. The frequency of executive meetings provides a rough-and-ready guide. The EC met only 21 times, if one charitably includes a meeting aborted by an alleged first-ministerial walk-out (see page 98), between July 2001 and mid October 2002, just once every three weeks. It was left to the small voice of the Alliance Party, the nearest thing to an opposition in the Assembly (with all the main parties in government), to protest about the executive's lacklustre performance. At the end of April, the latter did indeed signal a renewal of legislative momentum (see page 106ff).

The second Programme for Government,[43] agreed by the Assembly in December 2001, and the third draft programme,[44] promulgated by the exec-

---

[38] *Sunday Tribune*, 27 October 2002.

[39] *Irish News*, 30 October 2002.

[40] *Irish News*, 21 October 2002.

[41] *Irish News*, 31 October 2002.

[42] *Press Release*, Northern Ireland Information Service, 30 October 2002.

[43] Northern Ireland Executive, *Programme for Government: Making a Difference 2002–2005* (Belfast: Office of the First Minister and Deputy First Minister, 2001).

[44] Northern Ireland Executive, *Draft Programme for Government: Reinvestment and Reform* (Belfast: Office of the First Minister and Deputy First Minister, 2002).

utive in September 2002, betrayed like their initial predecessor[45] little ministerial input and had a correspondingly technocratic flavour. Relatedly, in the draft there was a drift towards an emphasis on the 'how' rather than the 'what' of government. As 'making a difference' was swapped for the slogan 'reinvestment and reform', the focus moved towards infrastructure investment and the mechanics of service delivery.

Figure 4.5: Executive Committee, at 10 October 2002

David Trimble (UUP):	First Minister
Mark Durkan (SDLP):	Deputy First Minister
Reg Empey (UUP):	Minister of Enterprise, Trade and Investment
Michael McGimpsey (UUP):	Minister of Culture, Arts and Leisure
Dermot Nesbitt (UUP):	Minister of Environment
Seán Farren (SDLP):	Minister of Finance and Personnel
Carmel Hanna (SDLP):	Minister for Employment and Learning
Bríd Rodgers (SDLP):	Minister of Agriculture and Rural Development
Nigel Dodds (DUP):	Minister for Social Development
Peter Robinson (DUP):	Minister for Regional Development
Bairbre de Brún (SF):	Minister of Health, Social Services & Public Safety
Martin McGuinness (SF):	Minister of Education

While many well-meaning individual actions were proposed in the second and (draft) third programmes, in the absence of a clear ministerial steer, there was little by way of big-picture reforms. And in as far as there were any underlying values, they were centrist or centre-right, as evidenced in the implicit preference for private finance (see page 105).

Nor did the Assembly have much impact on the matter. The only significant change to the draft of the second programme in the revised version was a (by the standards of the other administrations) belated commitment to introduce free 'nursing', but not 'personal', care in residential homes by October 2002 — and, even then, it turned out that 'free' wasn't entirely accurate.

---

[45] Northern Ireland Executive, *Programme for Government: Making a Difference 2001–2004* (Belfast: Office of the First Minister and Deputy First Minister, 2000).

When put to the vote, Alliance rejected the second programme as failing to 'tackle the deep divisions and inequalities in our society'.[46] It was by this standard, the party said, that the success, or failure, of the executive should be judged.

Reflecting on the NILTS data, a senior official close to the drafting of the third programme suggested bleakly that the key chapter headed 'Growing as a Community' — meant to address the twin challenges of sectarianism and social exclusion — should be retitled 'Withering as a Community'. Poignantly, the draft third programme had ministers declaring: 'We want the Executive to be a driving and unifying force for the whole community, working to address divisions and to promote good relations.'[47]

The official bemoaned the way individual departments saw the programme as a vehicle for their particular wish-lists. And the allocation of ministries by the d'Hondt rule clearly incentivised departmentalism, rather than a broader perspective.

This problem had been brought home to the Deputy First Minister, Mr Durkan, when, as Finance Minister, he was responsible for the distribution of the Executive Programme Funds, conceived as a way of using finance as an incentive for 'joined-up' government. Perversely, almost all the bids for the funds had come from single departments. And his answer was executive sub-committees.

Reorganisation of Government

The formation of sub-committees, when it came, represented the biggest single innovation in the working of the executive. The obstacles were obvious — the mistrust in the executive and the difficulty of delegating from a four-party structure.

But, like buses, after a long period when none was in sight, two came along at once. At its 16 May meeting, the executive decided to form a sub-committee on the Reinvestment and Reform Initiative (see page 105) and the review of public administration (which aimed to rationalise Northern Ireland's complicated and not unduly democratic sub-regional structures).[48]

The only other notable restructuring of government during the period — save, of course, the return of direct rule — was the establishment of Invest Northern Ireland, a single development agency replacing the previously fragmented industrial-development structure. But the minister, Sir Reg Empey (UUP), a small-c conservative, said the policies of the old agencies would not be significantly changed — even though INI's principal

---

[46] *Official Report*, 10 December 2001.

[47] Northern Ireland Executive, *Draft Programme for Government: Reinvestment and Reform* (Belfast: Office of the First Minister and Deputy First Minister, 2002), p. 28.

[48] Executive Information Service, 16 May 2002.

predecessor, the Industrial Development Board, had been severely criticised, including in a 'damning report' by the Northern Ireland Audit Office.[49]

The IDB's big problem was that it could not shake off the mindset that economic development was about handing large dollops of cash to individual clients, some dubious, in return for optimistic claims about job creation. Developing a regional 'agglomeration economy' is a more complex task, since it is about enhancing *inter*-firm networks and relationships between firms and higher-education and research institutions. These are weak in Northern Ireland.[50]

But Sir Reg believes in traditional 'pro-business' boosterism,[51] and got his fingers badly burned when he appointed six private-sector representatives to the seven-member INI board. With six suits and only one skirt around the table, Sir Reg then had to advertise for an additional seven members, to offset the glaring gender imbalance he had created. Inauspiciously, INI was launched on April Fool's Day.

There were some changes around the executive table during the year. The DUP took the opportunity to 'rotate' its two ministers once again when the institutions were restored in November 2001, Peter Robinson returning to Regional Development and Nigel Dodds to Social Development. The elevation of Mr Durkan to SDLP leader and Deputy First Minister left a vacancy at Finance and Personnel. Séan Farren moved from Employment and Learning and he was, in turn, replaced by his party colleague Carmel Hanna.

Later, ill-health forced the retirement of the UUP Environment Minister, Sam Foster, who had owed his unremarkable brief career in government to a shamelessly clientelistic appointment by Mr Trimble. Mr Foster was replaced by Dermot Nesbitt, whose place as joint junior minister in the office of First and Deputy First Minister was taken by James Leslie.

For the most part, ministers managed to do business. But the underlying raw nerves were exposed at a meeting on 19 March, the first following the AGM of the UUP. There the First Minister had, as party leader, engaged in an extraordinary attack on the allegedly 'sectarian, mono-ethnic, mono-cultural' character of the Republic, contrasted with the 'vibrant multi-ethnic, multi-national' UK.[52] Apart from the breathtaking hubris of unionists — whom most Britons see as conservative provincials — re-presenting themselves as in the van of anti-racist cosmopolitanism, the ideologically-driven picture Mr Trimble drew of the Republic, while true of de Valera's Ireland, was half a century out of date.[53]

[49] *Financial Times*, 29 October 1998.

[50] Roper, S., Hewitt-Dundas, N. and Savage, M, *Benchmarking Innovation in Ireland's Three NUTS2 Regions* (Belfast: Northern Ireland Economic Research Centre, 2002).

[51] *Irish Times*, 24 November 2000.

[52] *Irish Times*, 11 March 2002.

[53] Arguably, the best guides to today's Republic are the fiction of Dermot Bolger and Roddy Doyle (just as the best means to unpack Northern Ireland are the novels of Glenn Patterson and Robert McLiam

The SF Education Minister, Mr McGuinness, helpfully called the First Minister a 'twit'. What was reported as 'a heated and bitter exchange' ensued, before Mr Trimble left the executive room, allegedly for another engagement.[54]

Divisive Issues

A key — and hugely divisive — policy issue during the year was the future of selection in education. Sustained long after its abolition in Britain, the '11+' examination — strictly, the 'transfer test' — represents one of many ways in which Northern Ireland's ethnic divisions have militated against social development. Yet, and ironically, as in Britain all post-primary children study the same 'core' curriculum until the age of 16 whether or not their schools are religiously segregated, which most of them are.

Mr McGuinness, who had himself failed the '11+' and left school at 16, was determined to end the inequitable system. But, as so often with the republican movement, an abstract commitment to an 'equality agenda' was not reinforced by a positive policy portfolio. The Protestant middle class, principal beneficiary of the system over the decades, rallied in favour of selection and the minister's own IRA links only added to the sectarian imbroglio.

A survey of MLAs[55] indicated a strict polarisation around the transfer test — as on so much else. Most Catholics lined up behind the report of a review chaired by the former ombudsman Gerry Burns, which would keep existing post-primary schools (though encourage them to co-operate via area 'collegiates') but replace the test by 'informed parental preference' based on a 'pupil profile'.[56] Most Protestants backed academic selection, in some form.

But during the year a potential compromise intriguingly emerged. Opinion among the denominational providers in Northern Ireland's segregated system, the education and library boards (the region's LEAs), the SDLP and Alliance gravitated towards a radical suggestion emanating from within a quango — the Council on the Curriculum, Examinations and Assessment. The suggestion was that the core curriculum should only run to age 14 to favour greater individual choice thereafter, and that there should be election — rather than selection — of pupil trajectories at that age, dovetailed with the CCEA's innovative efforts to make the curriculum more competence- and less subject-based, with a new emphasis on citizenship and personal development. As it happened, this also neatly married the conventional Catholic emphasis on egalitarian collectivism with typical Protestant concern for individualism and diversity — hence its cross-sectarian appeal.

Wilson).

[54] *News Letter*, 20 March 2002.

[55] *Belfast Telegraph*, 15 January 2002.

[56] Department of Education, *Education for the 21ˢᵗ Century: Report by the Post Primary Review Body* (Bangor: DE, 2001).

Reading between the lines of remarks by Mr McGuinness, this was the 'emerging consensus' of which he detected 'strong signs' after the consultation around the Burns report.[57] But what was striking was that the impacted communal political system could not have thrown up such a proposition itself.

Mr McGuinness had given the consultation a populist twist by sending a questionnaire to every household, and he initially trumpeted the high response. But when it became clear that nearly two thirds of parents had endorsed selection, he decided that the response had been skewed towards the middle class. In a parting two-finger gesture at his unionist executive colleagues, he announced that the 11+ would be abolished from 2004; he did not indicate what would replace it.[58] In the shorter-run, designing and implementing an alternative may fall to Jane Kennedy, the NIO minister who has assumed responsibility for education matters with the return of direct rule (see page 103).

The most poignant deficiency of the executive was its inability to address *the* Northern Ireland issue — the fact that it is such a deeply divided society. Four years on, the perverse polarisation that has followed the agreement appears not as a temporary blip occasioned by the shock of the new but a deep re-entrenchment of the most visceral sectarian attitudes. It is hard not to conclude that this has taken place because of, rather than despite, the agreement to which London and Dublin remain dogmatically wedded.

Research on interface violence in north Belfast, published in the summer (with little fanfare) by the OFMDFM, raised troubling questions for the political class. The author, Neil Jarman, 'aghast' to discover from police statistics that there had been 2169 reported incidents in the area during 1996–99, concluded: 'In the not too recent past sectarian division many have been seen as something to be worked against, confronted and challenged, but it is increasingly seen as the inevitable basis for the political future of Northern Ireland, with the "two tribes" thesis copper fastened within the terms of the Agreement and within systems and structures of the Assembly.'[59] In this atmosphere of moral hazard, 'There is no agreement on the causes of the trouble and disorder, either long or short term[;] each side blames the other or excuses the actions of its members as justifiable or understandable retaliation.'[60]

The agreement was prepared with no regard to the wider intellectual debate between 'consociationalist' and 'integrationist' approaches to constitutional engineering in divided societies. By default, it followed a 'common-sense' consociationalism, without recognition of the latter's peculiarly dated

[57] Department of Education, *Review of Post-primary Education: Report on Responses to Consultation* (Bangor: DE, 2002), foreword.

[58] Executive Information Service, 8 October 2002.

[59] Jarman, 2002, p. 17.

[60] *ibid.*, p. 18.

anthropological assumptions about the 'primordial' nature of identity and its primary political pitfall — the entrenchment of communal division.

Four aspects of the agreement, it now appears with the benefit of hind-sight, have fostered rather than palliated division in this way.[61] The first two were uncritically carried over from the 1973–74 power-sharing scheme: the either/or constitutional choice of the United Kingdom or a United Ireland, belying more complex realities (including the effects of three decades of engagement with European integration), with a simple-majority decision mechanism between them; the use of (six-member) PR-STV as the electoral system, which arguably favours the election of candidates on small core votes rather than cross-communal vote-pooling,[62] though this is a matter of debate;[63] the requirement of communal registration in the Assembly, conse-quent upon failure to agree on a secular, numerically-based, weighted-major-ity arrangement for controversial votes; and the appointment of the executive by d'Hondt, uniquely in the world, with none of the centripetal effect of normal coalition formation by inter-party agreement and maintenance through collective responsibility.

From the outset, ministers had recognised they could not avoid the issue of intercommunal relations. So in their first programme,[64] as in other areas where they had no substantive answers to the region's problems, they said a 'strategy' would be developed — and they charged a retiring senior civil servant, Jeremy Harbison, with conducting a review.

After extensive discussions with interested parties, Dr Harbison produced his report in January 2002, fully expecting that, after consideration by minis-ters, it would be translated into an executive consultation paper in March. By the time of suspension, the paper had still not emerged.

From a number of sources, it became clear that the First Minister, Mr Trimble, envisaged a community-relations strategy as essentially reducible to 'fire-fighting' at local level, like the OFMDFM's (not particularly successful) intervention in north Belfast. This was reflected in the tenor of the actions suggested in the draft third programme.[65] It would dovetail with a broader (Protestant) middle-class definition of the challenge as confined to the *lumpenproletariat* and not implicating themselves — the 'coasters' of Hewitt's poem. With no agreed understanding of the problem — Catholic

[61] Wilson, R., 'War by other means: devolution and community division in Northern Ireland', paper presented to the American Political Science Association as part of a Constitution Unit panel, Boston, August 2001, available at http://apsaproceedings.cup.org/Site/papers/061/061002WilsonRobi.pdf

[62] Horowitz, D., 'The Northern Ireland agreement: consociationalist, maximalist, and risky', in McGarry, J. (ed.), *Northern Ireland and the Divided World* (Oxford: Oxford University Press, 2000).

[63] Reilly, B., *Democracy in Divided Societies: Electoral Engineering for Conflict Management* (Cambridge: Cambridge University Press, 2001).

[64] Northern Ireland Executive, *Programme for Government: Making a Difference 2001–2004* (Belfast: Office of the First Minister and Deputy First Minister, 2000), p. 26.

[65] Northern Ireland Executive, *Draft Programme for Government: Reinvestment and Renewal* (Belfast: Office of the First Minister and Deputy First Minister, 2002), p. 31.

nationalists portray their ethno-nationalism as benignly civic, while for republicans the issue is represented as one of unionist resistance to equality — it was unsurprising that the executive was unable itself to articulate a comprehensive solution.

The NIO became increasingly exasperated at the incapacity of the politicians to whom it had devolved power as tension mounted on the streets. The security minister, Des Browne, invited the parties to a meeting at Stormont before their long summer break to discuss the situation. The DUP rejected the invitation; the others came but could not agree a statement.[66] At the time of writing, initial indications from officials were that the direct-rule administration might show more expedition in this area.

Annual Report

Also before ministers took off with their buckets and spades (or Orange sashes), the executive launched its long-awaited first 'annual report' — it had, on and off, been in office for 31 months. In a wonderful mandarin understatement, the report declared: 'Last year we experienced some political difficulties . . .'[67]

The publication was thankfully shorn of the triumphalism that surrounded the first such New Labour report. And it alluded, fairly, to the 'key achievements' of the administration, notably the reform of student finance in order to widen access (effective from this academic year), free fares for senior citizens (effective from October 2001) and the establishment of a children's commissioner (in train at the end of the period).

But there was none of the humility, either, that Mr Blair has subsequently affected, with his 'A Lot Done, A Lot More to Do' election slogan of 2001 (bizarrely copied by Mr Ahern for this year's Dáil election, albeit with the second 'a lot' removed). The report claimed that 'good progress has been made across all the Executive's priorities'.[68]

The opinion evidence suggests less complacency would have been in order. The Alliance leader, David Ford, had mined a popular seam when he called in May for fellow MLAs to reject pay increases recommended by the Senior Salaries Review Board, as for MSPs and AMs. He said: 'While the Scottish Parliament and the Welsh Assembly have made significant impacts on the lives of their citizens, there is no doubt that, so far, the people of Northern Ireland have seen very little change brought about by the Assembly.'[69] A month later, MLAs duly voted to forgo the extra £5,000 per year.[70]

[66] *News Letter*, 1 August 2002.

[67] Northern Ireland Executive, *Annual Report 2001/02* (Belfast: Office of the First Minister and Deputy First Minister, 2002), p. 7.

[68] *ibid.*, p. 9.

[69] *Irish News*, 25 May 2002.

[70] *Irish News*, 26 June 2002.

A remarkable spat took place in the summer, when the Northern Ireland devolution monitoring project itself became the story. This followed the revelation in our August report that the number of officials in the OFMDFM was now greater than in Downing Street and the Taoiseach's Department put together — 424 to be precise.[71]

The story, which received wide publicity,[72] evoked raw anger at the highest levels of the civil service (though much *Schadenfreude* in the NIO). It was rebutted by the OFMDFM, which claimed that it was wrong to compare a department like itself with a private office such as that of the Prime Minister (though it didn't mention that the *Department* of the Taoiseach is just that). The 2000-strong Cabinet Office would be a better comparator, the OFMDFM said (though it took six days to hit upon that attractive suggestion).[73]

But the agreement and the enacting legislation (the Northern Ireland Act 1998) never envisaged the OFMDFM *being* a department — hence the odd, and rather messy, addition of the 'committee of the centre' to the statutory committees shadowing the departments when power was transferred in December 1999.[74] In May 2000, as the institutions were returning from their initial suspension, a senior OFMDFM official told the authors that when the office had reached full complement there would be 300 staff — that seemed dramatic but turned out to be an understatement. The number of officials in the Office of the Scottish First Minister — the obvious comparator as the Scottish Parliament has broadly similar powers to that at Stormont — is 18.[75]

This development had in fact to an extent been anticipated in our chapter in the first of these annual volumes. Discussing the unique construction of the Executive Committee by the d'Hondt rule, and the associated lack of any collective responsibility, we warned that the OFMDFM 'would grow like Topsy' in the absence of a co-ordinating political centre to hold such a centrifugal executive together.[76]

The evidence that a wider culture of soft-budget constraint (see finance section) may also have been to blame came when the story was picked up by David Walker of the *Guardian*.[77] He pointed out that Northern Ireland had about one civil servant for every 58 members of the population, as against one in 120 for the UK as a whole. And he estimated that MLAs' salaries and

---

[71] available at http://www.ucl.ac.uk/constitution-unit/files/leverhulme/ni_august_2002.pdf
[72] eg *Belfast Telegraph*, 8 August 2002.
[73] *Belfast Telegraph*, 14 August 2002.
[74] Wilford, R. and Wilson, R., 'A "bare knuckle ride": Northern Ireland', in Hazell, R. (ed), *The State and the Nations: The First Year of Devolution in the United Kingdom* (Exeter: Imprint Academic, 2000), p. 103.
[75] correspondence from the Scottish Executive, September 2002.
[76] Wilford and Wilson, 2000, p. 106.
[77] 'Trimble has twice as many civil servants as Blair', *Guardian* 21 September 2002.

allowances cost £10 per head of population, as against a UK figure for MPs of probably less than £2.

Direct Rule Ministers

It is unlikely that the new team in the Northern Ireland Office will wish to tackle the alleged over-staffing in OFMDFM — apart from anything else it would likely be interpreted as signalling that direct rule is here to stay for a considerable period. However, the fact that the UK government, unlike in February 2000 when the first suspension occurred, chose to increase the number of NIO ministers by two suggests that its perception is that resolving the current crisis is likely to be a protracted affair.

In addition to the Secretary of State — since 24 October, Paul Murphy, most immediately the Welsh Secretary and formerly in charge of political development in the NIO between 1997 and 1999 — and the existing ministers, Des Browne and Jane Kennedy, two assistant whips, Ian Pearson and Angela Smith, were drafted in to share the burdens of administering the previously devolved departments.

Mr Browne, Minister of State, retains his current NIO responsibilities (criminal justice, human rights and victims) and assumes responsibility for the Departments of Social Development and Health, Personal Social Services and Public Safety, together with the equality, human rights and community relations functions of OFMDFM. Ms Kennedy, the second Minister of State, retains her current responsibilities (security, policing and prisons), and assumes responsibility for the Departments of Education and Employment and Learning. Mr Pearson, Parliamentary Under Secretary, takes over at the Departments of Finance and Personnel, Enterprise, Trade and Investment and Agriculture and Rural Development and assumes responsibility for the economic policy unit and European affairs within OFMDFM. Finally, Ms Smith has been allocated responsibility for the Departments of the Environment, Regional Development and Culture, Arts and Leisure.

While Mr Murphy's predecessor had stated that the expanded team would not 'duck from the difficult issues'[78] they may not have the luxury of that choice. There is a raft of primary legislation confronting them (see page 106ff) and tricky issues are looming, including the generation of a budget, decisions on acute hospital service provision and the need to expedite the reinvestment and reform initiative. While some decisions can be 'put on the long finger', others are much more pressing — especially in relation to financial matters.

---

[78] John Reid, statement to the House of Commons, 15 October 2002, NIO *Press Release*.

FINANCE

'It's the public finances, stupid' might have been emblazoned over the offices of the executive during the year, as ministers grappled with three interweaving difficulties. First was their modest experience in the 'hard choices' of office, faced in particular with competing demands upon finite budgets and with only the regional rate to turn to as a source of additional revenue. Secondly, having only tangentially concerned themselves with the stuff of 'normal' politics in preceding decades, ministers became gnawingly ever more aware of the poverty of the public infrastructure bequeathed by the long Conservative era and New Labour's initial fiscal conservatism.

Thirdly, Gordon Brown's more recent largesse only threatened to make the 'Barnett squeeze' on Northern Ireland all the tighter, as the inherent tendency in the Barnett formula for *per capita* expenditure to converge with the UK average accelerated during rapid spending growth. While the comprehensive spending review released by the Chancellor in July 2002 envisaged an average annual increase in UK departmental expenditure limits of 5.2 per cent in the three years ahead, the corresponding rise for Northern Ireland was only 3.3 per cent.[79]

Ministers found two ways of avoiding this dilemma. The first was to blame Barnett's 'unfairness' to Northern Ireland. This was remarkably cavalier, given that the latest Treasury data had the region spending 36 per cent more per head than the rest of the UK — £6,424 in 2000–01, as against £4,709 for the state as a whole.[80] Part of this differential can be justified by higher expenditure on 'law and order', part also by Northern Ireland's high rates of social exclusion. But part reflects the long period of soft budgets — the numbers were always small by Treasury standards and the politics always overriding — and profligate duplication of services to assuage demands for local access from 'communities' balkanised by Northern Ireland's sectarian demography.

A sub-plot of the 'under-funding' claim was the Oliver-like behaviour of the Health Minister, Bairbre de Brún. Not only did SF MLAs delight in blaming 'the Brits' for their minister's plight, but she was not herself above pointing the finger at her executive colleagues — and in particular the successive SDLP Finance Ministers, Messrs Durkan and Farren — for denying her the resources she professed to need. Huge increases for her department — 8.9 per cent in the 2002–03 budget alone — were met with the same 'not enough' refrain. While keen to point to the mote in the eyes of others, she saw no beam in her own as she presided over the ever-escalating hospital waiting

[79] HM Treasury, *Opportunity and Security for All* (London: HM Treasury, 2002), p. 16.
[80] HM Treasury, *Public Expenditure Statistical Analysis (PESA) 2002–03* (London: HM Treasury, 2002).

lists — and continued to procrastinate over the hard choice of rationalising acute services.

The second response from ministers was to persuade themselves that private finance offered 'additional' money, over and above that available from the block grant.[81] The executive considered in April the report[82] of a working group set up by the OFMDFM, including the social partners, on public-private partnerships, and the following month it issued a consultation paper.[83]

Rehearsing the executive's commitment to a 'renewed infrastructure', the paper declared: 'It is clear that the level of resources routinely available to us would not be sufficient to achieve this outcome.' A key sentence made it into subsequent ministerial speeches: 'We are convinced that no single solution — be it borrowing, PPPs or more traditional public expenditure — is likely to meet our need.' Yet since borrowing and PPPs are funded over time by public expenditure, unless the costs of the project or service concerned are recouped through charging, this sentence was economically meaningless. The implication, that borrowing and PPPs somehow loosen the public-expenditure straitjacket, is erroneous.

Prudent borrowing, cognisant of the additional long-term liabilities incurred, is of course perfectly justifiable. And the Chancellor did announce in May, on a visit to the region accompanied by the Prime Minister, a borrowing facility for Northern Ireland, like that extended to English local government but denied to Scotland and Wales. This Reinvestment and Reform Initiative made available an initial £125 million, complemented by £75 million accrued from end-of-year flexibility monies and departmental underspend, and empowered the executive from 2004 to borrow, apparently, without limit.[84]

But this only reinforced the need for the executive to address the revenue side of the public-finance equation. The rating review[85] launched by the Finance Minister, Dr Farren, also in May, began this process. Northern Ireland consumers, unlike their counterparts in Britain, do not have to pay for their water — a point regularly rehearsed by the Treasury in response to additional funding demands — but the executive had yet to grasp the nettle of

---

[81] See, for example, the comments by the Education Minister, Martin McGuinness, at the opening of a PFI school in west Belfast, in Wilson, R., *Private Partners and the Public Good* (Belfast: Institute of Governance, Queen's University, 2002), p. 17.

[82] Office of the First Minister and Deputy First Minister, *Review of Opportunities for Public Private Partnerships in Northern Ireland: Working Group Report* (Belfast: OFMDFM, 2002).

[83] Northern Ireland Executive, 'Financing our future: initial response to report of working group on review of opportunities for public private partnerships in Northern Ireland' (Belfast: Executive Information Service, 2002).

[84] The Chancellor's speech is available at http://www.hm-treasury.gov.uk/newsroom_and_speeches/speeches/chancellorexchequer/speech_cx_020502.cfm

[85] Department of Finance and Personnel, *A Review of Rating Policy: A Consultation Paper* (Belfast: DFP, 2002).

water charges by the end of the period. When Dr Farren put his head over the parapet, the other parties roundly denounced the idea of a 'tap tax'.[86]

The public-finance debate again revealed the weaknesses in Northern Ireland's post-agreement political system. Constructed to embed the IRA ceasefire rather than to establish good governance arrangements for a divided society, its 'inclusive' executive allows of no alternation on any 'normal', left-right alignment (as, for instance, takes place in Belgium, where 50:50 cross-community but not inclusive coalitions are formed after elections). Parties do not compete by presenting to their supporters or potential supporters alternative values on the left-right spectrum, through which they can make sense of complex policy issues like PPPs, but on the prosecution of ethno-nationalist claims. And populist grandstanding is duly rewarded.

ASSEMBLY

As the Assembly ran into the sands of its fourth suspension in October 2002[87] it was, paradoxically, getting into its legislative stride. While earlier in the year the dearth of business had led to its meeting in plenary for just one, instead of the normal two, days for a total of six weeks, its legislative cup in the 2002–03 session threatened to run over. Some 28 primary bills were at various stages of the legislative process when direct rule was reimposed at midnight on 14 October, together with — and for the first time — four private members' bills and one committee bill.[88]

The weight of legislative business on the statutory committees — which, together with the committee of the centre, are required to take the committee stage of all bills — meant their agenda was even more highly structured by executive priorities than before. All other things being equal, the Assembly election remained scheduled for 1 May 2003 and the Bills Office had set a target date of the end of March to complete the passage of current legislative proposals — and the budget bill for 2003–04 / 2005–06, which had yet to be tabled.[89]

This was an ambitious target, not least because eight bills had been granted an extension of their committee stage before suspension, thereby threatening

---

[86] *Irish News*, 20 April 2002; *News Letter*, 22 April 2002.

[87] The three previous suspensions occurred between 11 February and 30 May 2000, on 10 August 2001 (for 24 hours) and on 22 September 2001 (24 hours).

[88] The full list of primary bills before the house in the 2002–03 session is available in Figure 4.6. The first of the private members' bills, Agriculture (Amendment) Bill (10/02), tabled by Billy Armstrong (UUP), received its first reading on 7 October 2002. The first committee bill, Assembly Ombudsman for Northern Ireland (Assembly Standards) Bill (25/01), was tabled by the standing standards and privileges committee and had reached its second stage on 10 September 2002.

[89] This was to have been the first budget to set out spending plans on a three-year basis. Thus one acute decision facing the NIO is whether to proceed on that basis — which would threaten to signal that direct rule is here for the long haul and tie the hands of the local ministers should devolution return — or opt for a budget for the next financial year only. The latter option would at least help to keep the metaphorical door to devolution open for the more immediate future.

Figure 4.6: Assembly legislation

Primary bills that had *received the royal assent* during the survey period (date of royal assent in brackets):

- Game Preservation (Amendment) Bill — NIA Bill 15/00 (13 February 2002)
- Social Security Fraud Bill — NIA Bill 16/00 (15 November 2001)
- Industrial Development Bill — NIA Bill 18/00 (7 February 2002)
- Local Government (Best Value) Bill — NIA Bill 19/00 (26 March 2002)
- Carers and Direct Payments Bill — NIA Bill 1/01 (2 May 2002)
- Budget Bill — NIA Bill 2/01 (20 March 2002)
- Railway Safety Bill — NIA Bill 3/01 (13 August 2002)
- Personal Social Services (Preserved Rights) Bill — NIA Bill 4/01 (26 March 2002)
- Budget (No. 2) Bill — NIA Bill 16/01 (12 August 2002)

Primary Bills that had *completed their final stage* at the date of suspension (date of final stage in brackets):

- Children (Leaving Care) Bill — NIA Bill 5/01 (7 October 2002)
- Limited Liability Partnerships Bill — NIA Bill 9/01 (8 October 2002)
- Open-Ended Investment Companies Bill — NIA Bill 10/01 (8 October 2002)
- Social Security Bill — NIA Bill 3/02 (23 September 2002)
- State Pension Credit Bill — NIA Bill 4/02 (30 September 2002)

Primary Bills at *other stages of the legislative process* at the date of suspension (stage and date in brackets):

- Local Government (Miscellaneous Provisions) Bill — NIA Bill 7/01 (committee stage extended to 17 October 2002: second stage completed 20 May 2002)
- Fur Farming (Prohibition) Bill — NIA Bill 8/01 (further consideration stage: consideration stage completed 7 October 2002)
- Employment Bill — NIA Bill 11/01 (further consideration stage: consideration stage completed 7 October 2002)
- Planning (Amendment) Bill — NIA Bill 12/01 (committee stage extended to 29 November 2002: second stage completed 24 June 2002)
- Local Air Quality Management Bill — NIA Bill 13/01 (committee stage extended to 29 November 2002: second stage completed 18 June 2002)
- Insolvency Bill — NIA Bill 14/01 (consideration stage: report stage completed 11 September 2002)
- Company Directors Disqualification Bill — NIA Bill 15/01 (final stage: further consideration stage completed 7 October 2002)
- Strategic Planning Bill — NIA Bill (committee stage extended to 25 November 2002: second stage completed 25 June 2002)

- Marriage Bill — NIA Bill 18/01 (committee stage extended to 4 November 2002: second stage completed 25 June 2002)

- Pollution and Prevention Control Bill — NIA Bill 19/01 (consideration stage: report stage completed 4 October 2002)

- Commissioner for Children and Young People Bill — NIA Bill 20/01 (committee stage extended to 22 November 2002: second stage completed 2 July 2002)

- Education and Libraries Bill — NIA Bill 21/01 (committee stage extended to 22 November 2002: second stage completed 2 July 2002)

- Protection of Children and Vulnerable Adults Bill — NIA Bill 22/01 (committee stage extended to 22 November 2002: second stage completed 3 July 2002)

- Housing Support Services Bill — NIA Bill 23/01 (committee stage extended to 13 December 2002: second stage completed 3 July 2002)

- Housing Bill — NIA Bill 24/01 (committee stage extended to 13 December 2002: second stage completed 3 July 2002)

- Family Law (Divorce etc) Bill — NIA Bill 1/02 (committee stage extended to 9 December 2002: second stage completed 17 September 2002)

- Areas of Special Scientific Interest Bill — NIA Bill 2/02 (committee stage: second stage completed 23 September 2002)

- Harbours Bill — NIA Bill 5/02 (second stage completed 30 September 2002)

- Audit and Accountability Bill — NIA Bill 6/02 (committee stage: second stage completed 1 October 2002)

- Health and Personal Social Services (Quality Improvement and Regulation) Bill — NIA Bill 7/02 (committee stage: second stage completed 1 October 2002)

- Strategic Investment and Regeneration of Sites Bill — NIA Bill 8/02 (second stage: first stage completed 30 September 2002)

- Energy Bill — NIA Bill 9/02 (committee stage: second stage completed 8 October 2002)

Private Members' Bills

- Children's Commissioner Bill — NIA Bill 14/00 (first stage completed 30 April 2001). Tabled by Jane Morrice (Women's Coalition) it has been superseded by the Commissioner for Children and Young People (NIA Bill 20/01), tabled by OFMDFM, which was at the committee stage at the time of suspension.

- Assembly Ombudsman for Northern Ireland (Assembly Standards) Bill — NIA Bill 25/01. This was tabled by the committee on standards and privileges, and is the Assembly's first committee bill. It completed its second stage on 10 September 2002 and was at the committee stage at the time of suspension.

- Agriculture (Amendment) Bill — Bill 10/02. Tabled by Billy Armstrong (UUP) it was at the second stage, having completed the first stage on 7 October 2002.

to frustrate their completion in advance of the planned election. The device of 'accelerated passage',[90] already applied in the case of two primary bills since September 2002, may have been the only — and unsatisfactory — means of expediting the legislative programme in time to meet the informal deadline. In addition, there was a raft of subordinate legislation to process and three *ad hoc* committees were sitting to examine three separate draft orders on reserved matters, referred to the Assembly by the former Northern Ireland Secretary.[91]

Suspension means that discrete, 'home-grown' bills would be placed indefinitely in cold storage, although 'parity' legislation would be taken forward by the (expanded) ministerial team in the NIO, as was the case in February-May 2000 when the institutions were first suspended. As then, the NIO would also assume responsibility for taking forward the budgetary proposals,[92] which existed only in draft at the time of writing. Announcing the distribution of devolved portfolios to the direct-rule ministers (see page 103) Mr Reid made clear that the latter would meet the 'suspended' ministers to establish their respective legislative priorities, so that at least some momentum would be sustained.

In all, 29 primary bills had received royal assent since powers were transferred on 2 December 1999 — a total that would have at least doubled by the end of the Assembly's first term, had things gone to plan. But the fitful outworking of devolution, characteristic of the process throughout, threatened (*pace* Ron Davies) to become an event.

The mutual trust and confidence essential to political progress in Northern Ireland, always at a premium, ebbed over the year. While the perfect should not be allowed to be the enemy of the good, in Northern Ireland's case the good-ish has fallen prey to mounting suspicion, chiefly among unionists, and the latter's perception that the republican movement is not committed to democracy and exclusively peaceful means of, if not resolving, at least managing this deeply divided society.

It was not only the streets that witnessed the deterioration of intercommunal relations over the year. Parliament Buildings itself provided the *mise en scène* for the unfolding political drama — and not just on the floor of the chamber.

---

[90] Accelerated passage — which was granted initially by leave of the House but since February 2002 has required a weighted majority following a change to standing orders — omits the committee stage of a bill. See standing order 40(2)(4). For the debate on this and other changes to the legislative process, see *Official Report*, 26 February 2002. The debate concerned the procedure committee's report *Review of the Legislative Process in the NI Assembly*, 1/10r, 16 January 2002.

[91] Disqualification Legislation, Access to Justice (Northern Ireland) and Firearms Orders — see the committee page of the Assembly's website.

[92] *Official Report*, 24 September 2002.

While the way was made clear by the IRA's weapons initiative in October for the joint election of Mr Trimble and Mr Durkan,[93] respectively as First and Deputy First Minister, the situation nevertheless remained highly charged: just before the IRA announcement, the remaining three UUP ministers, plus the party's one junior minister, had also resigned, closely followed by the DUP's two ministerial incumbents. Thus, for a short period the Executive Committee comprised only the three SDLP and two SF departmental ministers. With no 'acting' First Minister[94] the executive was, in effect, rendered inoperative until the fresh election was completed.

Evident disquiet within the UUP's Assembly group on the lack of information about the IRA initiative — and doubt that it signalled the beginning of a disarming process — led two of its number, Peter Weir and Pauline Armitage, to vote against the joint slate of Messrs Trimble and Durkan, thereby depriving them of the requirement for a 'unionist' majority to validate their election.[95] Despite some procedural ingenuity[96] enabling one member of the Women's Coalition to redesignate as a 'unionist' for the purpose of the vote — both WC members were originally designated as 'other' — when the result was declared, 29 unionists, including the WC's 'convert', had supported the joint candidacy, but 31 unionists had opposed, including Mr Weir and Ms Armitage. While all designated 'nationalists' supported the joint ticket — including the other WC MLA, Jane Morrice, who had so redesignated so as to sustain her own party's even-handedness in what was a highly fraught situation — it was to no avail under the parallel-consent rule.

---

[93] Mark Durkan had emerged as the SDLP's candidate following Séamus Mallon's decision to stand down as Deputy First Minister — and deputy leader of the SDLP — announced in the late summer. Mr Durkan, his party's unopposed candidate, also succeeded John Hume as party leader following his retirement from the post, while the Agriculture Minister, Bríd Rodgers, took over from Mr Mallon as deputy party leader. Mr Durkan also retained the finance portfolio in the devolved administration until the passage of the 2001–02 budget bill.

[94] Following Mr Trimble's resignation on 1 July 2001, Sir Reg Empey and Mr Mallon had carried out the functions of the First and Deputy First Minister, thereby enabling the Executive Committee to tick over until the crisis had been resolved.

[95] The election of the First and Deputy First Ministers, on a joint ticket, requires the achievement of 'parallel consent' — an overall majority of those present and voting in the chamber, including a majority of both 'unionist' and 'nationalist' members. This is the only test of cross-community support on a 'key decision' that is subject to the parallel-consent test alone: all others, such as the approval of the budget and standing orders, can alternatively be subject to the less stringent 'weighted-majority' test — 60 per cent of all present and voting, including 40 per cent of both unionists and nationalists. Had this second test been provided for in the Northern Ireland Act 1998 for the FM and DFM (re-)election, then the Trimble/Durkan dual 'premiership' would have been elected on 2 November 2001.

[96] Before the vote, the Assembly debated an amendment to standing orders whereby redesignation could take immediate effect, whereas initial standing orders required 30 days written notice to the speaker of a planned change. The amendment was carried by weighted majority (*Official Report*, 2 November 2001).

Figure 4.7: MLA changes

- Peter Weir ceased to be a member of the UUP with effect from 9 November 2001. He became a member of the DUP with effect from 30 April 2002.
- Pauline Armitage was suspended from the UUP with effect from 9 November 2001.
- Arthur Doherty, SDLP, resigned his seat with effect from 1 September 2001. He was replaced by Michael Coyle with effect from the same day.

The matter was not resolved until 6 November when three Alliance MLAs[97] redesignated as 'unionists' from their 'other' status, but only after the Assembly had approved, by weighted majority, a further amendment to standing orders enabling members to resume their original designation within seven days.[98] Thus, by means of some procedural inventiveness — or, as the anti-agreement unionist bloc preferred, 'fix' — the candidates were finally elected: all 38 nationalists in the chamber supported the joint ticket, while 31 unionists did so — including the four newly anointed members — and 29 voted against.

The matter was not to end there. While the newly elected duo were giving interviews to the media in the foyer of Parliament Buildings, a scuffle broke out alongside them among pro- and anti-agreement members, quickly dubbed the 'brawl in the hall'. While no one was hurt, though some pride was injured, it was an unedifying spectacle — and one that underscored the passion of the moment.

More significantly, the DUP embarked on a legal challenge arguing that, because the election had taken place beyond the six weeks allowed by the Northern Ireland Act (the period had expired at midnight on 3 November and the Northern Ireland Secretary had not introduced a third 24-hour suspension), Mr Reid was obliged to dissolve the Assembly and set an early date for an election. Eventually, the action reached the Lords and on 25 July 2002 the law lords upheld the Northern Ireland Secretary's decision, albeit by the narrowest of margins (3–2).

Among other things, the election of Messrs Trimble and Durkan enabled all three 'strands' of the agreement to operate concurrently for the first time

[97] David Ford, Eileen Bell and Sean Neeson.

[98] The Alliance Party had gone into conclave over the intervening weekend to discuss the matter of (temporary) redesignation and was to agree to do so having secured a commitment from the Northern Ireland Secretary, Mr Reid, to review the voting arrangements. The review did take place but Alliance's attempt to change the voting rules was to fail, not least because of stiff opposition from the SDLP. This means that on 'key decisions', votes cast by parties and/or individuals who are not designated as unionists or nationalists can be of no consequence: some votes, it might be said, are more equal than 'others''. There was no further occasion during the year when the issue of redesignation was to arise and thus no means of testing the readiness of Alliance members to 'save the agreement' a second time. Interestingly, the WC's two members retained their changed labels until the beginning of the 2002–03 session, when they reverted to 'otherness' (*Official Report*, 4 September 2002).

since October 2000.[99] Mr Trimble had refused thenceforth to endorse the attendance of SF's two ministers at meetings of the North/South Ministerial Council, in turn prompting SF to boycott meetings of the British-Irish Council. Indeed, SF had itself mounted a challenge against Mr Trimble's unilateral action, which it had won in the lower courts but which the First Minister had appealed and which was pending at the time 'normal service' was resumed in early November 2001. Since 'devolution day' on 2 December 1999, the three strands have operated simultaneously for just 20 months.

During the period since the previous chapter, there were 73 plenaries up to the time of suspension, including a special session[100] convened to enable members to express their condolences in the wake of 11 September. The temper of this session — anti-agreement unionists equating 'Sinn Féin/IRA' with those who had perpetrated the enormities of two days earlier — served as a measure of the wider mood.

MLAs' Temper

Hindsight is a cheap commodity but, nevertheless, the atmosphere in the chamber was so strained over the past year that the most recent suspension came as no surprise. The 2001 session of the Assembly began with a highly charged debate[101] on the events at Holy Cross school (see page 88). By early October, with as yet no sign of IRA decommissioning, two motions seeking the exclusion of SF from the executive were tabled — one by the UUP, the other by the DUP. The debate had been prefaced two weeks earlier by a DUP motion which deplored the participation in government of groups 'allegedly on ceasefire' and determined that it was 'inconsistent and intolerable that any party associated with active terrorism continues to hold Executive positions'.[102]

Predictably, the exclusion motions failed to secure the necessary cross-community consent — the SDLP has never supported an exclusion motion, on the ground that it contravenes the 'inclusiveness' of the agreement. And the DUP's earlier motion was amended by the SDLP to include the repudiation of violence by all paramilitary organisations and a plea that they begin decommissioning in earnest.

While the first IRA act generated some optimism, the fault line in the Assembly — deepened by the outcome of the 2001 general election, which

---

[99] That is, the institutions within Northern Ireland, those between Northern Ireland and the Republic of Ireland (north-south), and those between the island of Ireland and Britain (east-west).

[100] There was a second special session on 4 April 2002 to mark the death of the Queen Mother. SF members did not attend. On 14 May, as part of the golden jubilee roadshow, the queen visited Parliament Buildings and delivered a short address in the Great Hall that managed to offend no one. Again, SF members voted with their feet and, more significantly, there was no protest by republicans (or nationalists) over the visit.

[101] *Official Report*, 10 September 2001.

[102] *Official Report*, 18 September 2001 — the exclusion motions were debated on 4 October 2001.

had seen the DUP and SF advance — threatened to become unbridgeable. True, bills were passed, the budget was set, policy strategies launched (or sent out for consultation), and committee inquiries embarked upon. But the stresses were palpable. Even when there was virtual unanimity in the chamber, as over the demand for greater health expenditure, this was invariably used by unionist, 'other' and some SDLP members to question the competence of the minister, Ms de Brún, culminating in a call for her resignation.[103]

One other area of widespread agreement among members was the much reviled Barnett formula. Members took the opportunity repeatedly to berate the perceived inadequacies of the formula and found a sympathetic ear in the then Finance Minister, Mr Durkan. Presenting the draft 2001 budget to the chamber, Mr Durkan expressed the executive's determination 'to seek improvements to our position with regard to the formula'. But he reminded members of the higher *per capita* spend in Northern Ireland compared with the rest of the UK and warned that the Treasury was unlikely 'to see things from our perspective'.[104]

To strengthen its critique of Barnett, the executive had commissioned six 'needs and effectiveness' evaluations,[105] designed to assist the Finance Minister in his dealings with the Treasury by demonstrating the objective needs of Northern Ireland, as opposed to hand-wringing over the lack of available expenditure. The evaluations were scheduled to appear in May 2002 but these were much delayed and, while parts were leaked to the regional media in August, they had not entered the public domain before suspension and will now be swallowed up in the maw of the NIO.

General dissatisfaction with Barnett, coupled with an 'infrastructure deficit' in investment estimated by the administration to be £6 billion over ten years,[106] occasioned debates on the options for revenue-raising and alternative means of financing public-sector investment. The major foci of the debates were the rates, water charges and the Private Finance Initiative.

Predictably, increases in the rates for businesses and householders proved unpopular — not least because 60 MLAs were also district councillors — and the review of rating policy was still under way at the time of suspension. PFI proved almost equally unpopular — not least with the finance and personnel committee, whose chair, Francie Molloy (SF), understood it to mean 'private finance and profit making'[107] rather than partnership with the public sector.

[103] Duncan Shipley-Dalton (UUP), *Official Report*, 11 December 2001.

[104] *Official Report*, 25 September 2001 and 5 November 2001.

[105] Led by the Department of Finance and Personnel, these covered health and social care, education, training, housing, selective financial assistance and culture, arts and leisure — which, in aggregate, accounted for about three quarters of all public spending (*Official Report*, 4 March 2002).

[106] The figure was cited by the Finance Minister, Dr Farren, during a debate on public-private partnerships (*Official Report*, 21 May 2002).

[107] *Official Report* 1 October 2001.

Though the Reinvestment and Reform Initiative was welcomed, there was disquiet in the chamber about the means of repaying any loans and the likely impact such borrowing would exert on the rates. Dr Farren, who had succeeded Mr Durkan as Finance Minister on 14 December 2001, had an uncomfortable time in the chamber throughout the session. Budgetary pressures, the rates review, the loans facility, the comprehensive spending review, PPPs/PFI, public procurement policy and a total departmental underspend of £365 million in the 2001–02 financial year combined to make his brief a challenging one, to say the least.

With suspension, of course, a mass of unfinished financial business waited to be inherited by the NIO's ministerial team, including a new budget, and legislation[108] to give effect to the RRI by the creation of a new strategic investment body. The latter was scheduled for its second reading on 8 October 2002 but, with the press of wider events, the First and Deputy First Ministers requested that the second stage be postponed.[109] Like much else, the bill landed on the NIO's desk.

There were 54 committee reports[110] during the survey period, one third of which were committee-stage responses to primary bills or draft orders referred by the Northern Ireland Secretary. A further eight reports were 'executive-driven', so that a total of 26 were responses to matters placed on the agenda by ministers, individually or collectively. The volume of reports was testament to the industriousness of the committees, aided by a change to standing orders[111] that enabled them to establish sub-committees to expedite their business.

By the time of suspension, the committees were maturing and developing a more systematic approach to executive business. This was, in part, fostered by the informal liaison committee of chairs / deputy chairs, which discussed

[108] The Strategic Investment and Regeneration of Sites Bill received its first reading on 30 September 2002.

[109] The second stage was rescheduled for 14 October, the last sitting day before suspension, but at the request of the first and Deputy First Ministers it was again postponed. It emerged during exchanges with the speaker that a petition of concern had been tabled delaying a vote on the second stage for 24 hours and that a reasoned amendment — the Assembly's first — had been laid by Billy Hutchinson (Progressive Unionist Party) designed to alter the terms of the bill. Indeed, a number of MLAs remarked that in its present form the bill would not secure the support of the house. Mr Hutchinson requested that, as and when the bill was referred to the NIO, the relevant direct rule minister (Ian Pearson) be informed of the reasoned amendment and the extent (unquantified) of the opposition (*Official Report* 14 October 2002).

[110] The numbers of reports produced by committees, in descending order, were: public accounts 10; enterprise, trade and investment & environment 6 each; finance and personnel 5; health, social services and public safety & employment and learning 4 each; committee of the centre & social development & agriculture and rural development 3 each; education & regional development & standards and privileges 2 each; culture, arts and leisure & procedures 1 each. There were 2 *ad hoc* committee reports during the period.

[111] The amendment was moved by Conor Murphy (SF), chair of procedures, and, since standing orders are defined as 'key decisions', had to be endorsed by cross-community consent (*Official Report*, 9 October 2001).

how to effect a more efficient system. Co-ordination of committee responses to the budgetary process was the task of finance and personnel, which emerged as a persistent and constructive critic of the opportunities available to subject the executive's spending proposals to appropriate scrutiny. This committee led on the review of rating policy and the executive's proposals on PPPs. Each has been left in abeyance, but the battle lines between the committee and the executive had been clearly drawn by the time the curtain on direct rule had again been raised. Notwithstanding Mr Reid's seeming relish to grapple with such difficult issues, his successor may find the temptation to leave well alone is compelling.

The long delayed review of public administration, finally under way at the time of suspension, is likely to be a another potential source of conflict avoided by the NIO. Based in the OFMDFM, the review team would have been assured of close and critical scrutiny by the Committee of the Centre, whose members had already set in motion oversight of the process, including briefings on administrative reform during a visit to the US.[112]

The review — which excludes the institutions created by the agreement — is a major item of unfinished business, and one that is unlikely to make much headway until a fresh Assembly is elected, whenever that may be. But the make-up of the Assembly itself was the occasion for a relevant debate during the period.[113]

Sixty of the 108 MLAs (56 per cent) are district councillors,[114] a sizeable wedge of individuals who have an interest in relation to the review — and, indeed, on rates. The dual-mandate problem, which Jane Morrice of the WC unsuccessfully sought to challenge, was underlined by the frequent sight of members scurrying from committee rooms at around 4pm to attend meetings in their council chambers. This left some committees inquorate, causing embarrassment for committee clerks and discomfiture for witnesses.[115] The signal given was that some members had a less than compelling commitment to the work of the committees — and, by extension, the Assembly.

The public was largely unaware of the problem. But it was made aware of the relative lack of transparency of committee minutes,[116] assiduously

[112] Committee report, 03/01/r, 12 June 2002.

[113] *Official Report*, 28 May 2002.

[114] A dozen MLAs are also MPs, one is both an MEP and an MP, and two are peers, including the speaker, John Alderdice (who has indicated that he would not stand for re-election to the Assembly). A total of five MLAs hold three elected offices.

[115] The procedure committee was contemplating a change to standing orders such that the quorum for committees might be waived if, after the start of a meeting, members left, provided that it was quorate at the outset. The liaison committee also discussed reducing the quorum from five to four.

[116] The controversy stirred over the opaqueness of committee meetings was keenly felt by some chairs, including Esmond Birnie (UUP chair of employment and learning). On 27 June 2002 Mr Birnie issued a press release which noted that only one in four of all committee meetings had been held fully in public but described his committee as a 'star performer' since two thirds of its meetings (60 out of 94) had been fully open: 'no other committee did so well' (committee press release 45/01, 27 June 2002).

reported by the *Belfast Telegraph*, and the escalating running costs of the Assembly — especially when juxtaposed with reports of underspending by devolved departments.

CONCLUSION

London and Dublin face a massive task in resuscitating devolution. Yet, it was not the idea of devolution *per se* that was the casualty of the shift in popular opinion. Rather, lack of trust in the republican movement subverted Protestant support. The catalogue of perceived and actual breaches of the spirit (and letter) of the agreement by republicans can, in the views of the UK, Irish and US administrations, only be remedied by the effective disbandment of the IRA.

While inclusiveness, including in the executive, was and is a cardinal principle of the agreement's consociational philosophy, on Mr Blair's post-suspension visit to Belfast he issued a stricture to nationalists (*ie* the SDLP) that they must 'act if violence returns'. This implies that they should support an exclusion motion against SF, should the republican movement fail to 'make the commitment to exclusively peaceful means real, total and permanent'. Still reeling from being overtaken by SF at the 2001 general and local elections, the SDLP was already apprehensive about its electoral fortunes next May (*ceteris paribus*), which some in its ranks would calculate would be further diminished were it to be party to the conferral of pariah status on its rival.

Such is the juncture — a crossroads, the former Stormont premier Terence O'Neill called it, back in the late 60s — at which Northern Ireland stands. It is difficult to see how — short of what many republicans would regard as 'surrender' — devolution modelled on the 1998 agreement can be restored.

If it cannot, would it matter? To pose the question is to answer it: it would matter, very much indeed.

This is not to claim that the record of the Assembly has been glittering, nor that the public harboured vaulting ambitions about the differences a regional legislature would make to daily life.[117] The list of policy and legislative achievements is — with some exceptions — modest and has not been aided by the frustrations caused by three, now four, suspensions. While the Assembly has undertaken reform of the legislative process, and its committees have begun to develop a more effective and joined-up approach,[118] operational

[117] MacGinty, R. and Wilford, R., 'More knowing than knowledgeable: attitudes towards devolution', in Gray, A. M., *et al* (eds.), *Social Attitudes in Northern Ireland: The Eighth Report*, (London: Pluto Press, 2002), p. 5–21.

[118] Besides the closer co-operation that developed among and between committees in pursuing inquiries and expediting the legislative passage of primary legislation, outreach became a more evident practice. Committees were increasingly likely to hold off-site sessions and undertake visits both within and outwith Northern Ireland, including to their sister legislatures in Edinburgh and Cardiff. In

problems remain — not least those occasioned by the dual mandate and the resulting impression that some members have adopted a rather Corinthian attitude to the MLA role.

There are thinkable alternatives to devolution, including joint authority, independence, majority rule and, of course, the 'safety net' of direct rule, but to rehearse them is merely to line up a series of straw men — the last alternative being the obvious exception, for both the short and long term. Yet, both governments and the U.S. Bush administration, see the 1998 agreement as the template for the future — as do SF, the SDLP and the rump of pro-agreement unionists but only, currently, minorities of 'nationalist' and 'unionist' electors. For the purpose of impending negotiations, initially on a bilateral basis between the parties and the NIO, this means the restoration of the consociational-plus model bequeathed in 1998.

Power-sharing may not necessarily mean inclusiveness as dictated by the mechanistic d'Hondt principle. But straying from the 'inclusiveness' path would certainly alienate the republican movement and most likely offend the SDLP, whose support would be essential for its realisation. While some in the UUP will articulate a demand for the abandonment of regional government, in favour of revitalised local government, support for this would barely extend beyond the narrow confines of a section of the party.

Where next? The IRA's rejection of the Prime Minister's disbandment demand and its disengagement from the decommissioning commission underlined the gravity of the crisis confronting the political classes and their dependence on the wider republican movement. In the interim, direct rule rules again — if not okay.

The fact that London has, unlike in 2000, taken the decision to add two ministers to the NIO team is significant. The benign interpretation is that it frees up the hands of the Secretary of State to focus on prospective negotiations and bring the impasse to a speedier conclusion. The less sanguine view is that it signals the apprehension that direct rule is here to stay for the foreseeable future.

BIBLIOGRAPHY

Official documents

Department of Education, *Education for the 21st Century: Report by the Post Primary Review Body* (Bangor: DE, 2001).

Department of Education, *Review of Post-primary Education: Report on Responses to Consultation* (Bangor: DE, 2002).

Department of Finance and Personnel, *A Review of Rating Policy: A Consultation Paper* (Belfast: DFP, 2002).

September 2002 the Enterprise, Trade and Investment committee sponsored a conference on tourism in Omagh, Co Tyrone. This was regarded as a pilot of alternative means of gathering evidence for the purposes of an inquiry, instead of the routine sessions with witnesses in Parliament Buildings.

HM Treasury, *Public Expenditure Statistical Analysis (PESA) 2002–03* (London: HM Treasury, 2002).

Northern Ireland Assembly, *Official Report*.

Northern Ireland Executive, *Programme for Government: Making a Difference 2001–2004* (Belfast: Office of the First Minister and Deputy First Minister, 2000).

Northern Ireland Executive, *Programme for Government: Making a Difference 2002–2005* (Belfast: Office of the First Minister and Deputy First Minister, 2001).

Northern Ireland Executive, *Draft Programme for Government: Reinvestment and Reform* (Belfast: Office of the First Minister and Deputy First Minister, 2002).

Northern Ireland Executive, 'Financing our future: initial response to report of working group on review of opportunities for public private partnerships in Northern Ireland' (Belfast: Executive Information Service, 2002).

Northern Ireland Executive, *Annual Report 2001/02* (Belfast: Office of the First Minister and Deputy First Minister, 2002).

Northern Ireland Policing Board, *Annual Report 2001–2002* (Belfast: NIPB, 2002).

Office of the First Minister and Deputy First Minister, *Review of Opportunities for Public Private Partnerships in Northern Ireland: Working Group Report* (Belfast: OFMDFM, 2002).

Secondary sources

Jarman, N., *Managing Disorder: Responding to Interface Violence in North Belfast* (Belfast: Office of the First Minister and Deputy First Minister (research branch) 2002).

MacGinty, R. and Wilford, R., 'More knowing than knowledgeable: attitudes towards devolution', in Gray, A. M. *et al* (eds), *Social Attitudes in Northern Ireland: The Eighth Report*, (London: Pluto Press, 2002).

Wilford, R. and Wilson, R., 'A "Bare Knuckle Ride": Northern Ireland', in Hazell, R. (ed), *The State and the Nations: The First Year of Devolution in the United Kingdom* (Exeter: Imprint Academic, 2000).

Wilford, R. and Wilson, R., 'Northern Ireland: Endgame', in Trench, A. (ed), *The State of the Nations 2001: The Second Year of Devolution in the United Kingdom* (Exeter: Imprint Academic, 2001).

Wilson, R., *Private Partners and the Public Good* (Belfast: Institute of Governance, Queen's University, 2002).

5

Third Year, Third First Minister

James Mitchell and the Scottish Monitoring Team[1]

INTRODUCTION

The main event of the last year was the resignation of Henry McLeish as First Minister to be replaced by Jack McConnell. The extraordinary events surrounding the change appear to have done little damage to the Labour Party or devolution. After the turbulence of the period leading up to McLeish's resignation, McConnell attempted to provide stability and manage expectations. McLeish's flagship policy of care for the elderly was implemented but signs of problems emerged early in the financing of this policy, however McConnell had little choice but to implement this inherited policy. It was little surprise that he chose the slogan 'doing less better'. The Executive could not afford to make rash promises and build up expectations — especially as worries increased about the health of the economy.

THIRD YEAR, THIRD FIRST MINISTER

In early November 2001, Henry McLeish resigned as First Minister after mounting controversy surrounding the lease of his constituency office. It had been a fairly abstruse issue but McLeish's failure to provide a full and open account of the financial arrangements had undermined his authority and called his integrity into question. He had not had a successful period as First Minister since replacing Donald Dewar after the latter's death in October 2000 and did not have a reservoir of goodwill to draw upon when he needed it. He had narrowly defeated Jack McConnell for the leadership of the Scottish Labour Party with the support of Gordon Brown, a neighbouring Fife MP.

The assumption had been that McLeish would maintain Brown's firm grip on the Scottish Labour Party and ensure that relations between London and Edinburgh remained good, but the new First Minister did not prove to be the cautious, safe pair of hands anticipated. In two respects, policy and style — which were often conflated in media representations — McLeish proved independent, even idiosyncratic. First, McLeish had his own agenda which

---

[1] Barry Winetrobe, Neil McGarvey, John Curtice, Philip Schlesinger, David Bell, Mark Shephard, Alex Wright.

did not conform to London's and created friction. Second, he failed to provide firm leadership, contributing to a sense of incoherence in the Executive. Dewar had always been seen as transitional in the establishment of devolution, but the sense of a leadership in transition (and essentially Westminster-derived) remained even after McLeish became First Minister. The leadership contest that had simmered away from day one continued with McConnell and Wendy Alexander now being the main contenders.

The first intimation that McLeish would not be London's poodle, despite strong support from Gordon Brown for the post of First Minister, came in an interview in which he reversed the earlier policy on free care for the elderly. This created a running tension with London throughout his leadership, with London making it clear that it would not pick up the bill for a more generous policy in Scotland compared with that south of the border. Pressure from senior members of the London Cabinet made no impact on McLeish. When McLeish intimated his desire to change the official designation 'Scottish Executive' to 'Scottish Government' only three months after coming to office the reaction in London was unrestrained criticism. Many newspapers carried the comments of an unnamed senior Labour figure in London describing the First Minister as 'thick'. McLeish's base of support in London was crumbling, so when he ran into trouble over 'Officegate', he could not rely on erstwhile powerbrokers to come to his aid. McLeish had risen through the machine politics of the Fife Labour party and this only contributed to his downfall.

McLeish's poor performance as a speaker became an endless source of amusement for sketch-writers and commentators. The term 'McCliches' was invented for his verbal infelicities. But more serious was his inability to weld together his disputatious Cabinet colleagues. These tensions were not so much between Labour and Liberal Democrat members but amongst Labour members of the Cabinet. This problem had never been resolved by Dewar but after his death it became standard for unflattering comparisons to be made which were based on a rather mythical first holder of the office. But comparisons with his predecessor aside, McLeish was a weak leader.

Notably, McLeish's successor was another machine politician. Jack McConnell had been a former general secretary of the Labour Party in Scotland who narrowly became MSP for Motherwell and Wishaw, in a contest within Labour's Lanarkshire machine politics for the party's candidacy, and then became Finance Minister in Dewar's Cabinet. He had stood against McLeish after Dewar died and did better than anticipated and was believed to have out-polled McLeish amongst backbench Labour MSPs. McConnell's leadership bid had been blighted by 'Lobbygate', allegations of improper relations between his office and the lobbying firm he had worked for between standing down as general secretary of the Scottish Labour Party and

Figure 5.1: Diary of 'Officegate' and the fall of Henry McLeish[2]

April 1 2001	*Mail on Sunday* discloses that since 1998, Henry McLeish received £4,000 a year from Digby Brown, a firm of solicitors with strong Labour connections that sublet part of his constituency office in Glenrothes, Fife.
April 22	Elizabeth Filkin, House of Commons Parliamentary Commissioner for Standards, writes to McLeish in connection with sub-letting. Peter McMahon, McLeish's spin doctor, says: 'The matter has been dealt with. The income in question was not for Mr McLeish's personal use, it went straight into covering the costs of running the office.'
October 23	McLeish issues a statement saying that he has paid £9,000 to the Commons' Fees Office. McMahon says the matter should now be considered closed.
October 25	MSPs are barred from questioning the First Minister in the Scottish Parliament by Sir David Steel, Presiding Officer, who says it is a matter for Westminster.
October 28	Fife constabulary confirms that an investigation has begun after a complaint made against the First Minister.
October 29	The First Minister, while opening a hospital, refuses to answer reporters' questions.
November 1	McLeish publishes details of his expenses, saying he paid the money back out of his own pocket and that the £9,000 figure was arrived at in agreement with the Commons' Fees Office. Later, on BBC1's *Question Time*, he admits that he does not know the total sum received for various sublets at his constituency office but insists he has made no personal gain from the rental.
November 2	John Swinney, SNP leader, who had until then stood his distance from the affair, calls for McLeish to resign following his 'humiliating' performance on *Question Time*.
November 4	It emerges that McLeish has instructed his accountant to hand over information about the row to the Inland Revenue.
November 5	David McLetchie, Tory leader, who had been the lead Officegate inquisitor in the Parliament, says McLeish has three days to save his career before he faces a debate in the Scottish Parliament.
November 6	McLeish blames his troubles on an 'honest mistake'. He offers to pay back £27,000 to the Commons after it emerges that the total rental income from subletting since 1987 was £36,122.
November 7	First Minister cancels all engagements to prepare with his aides for the next day's debate on 'Officegate.'
November 8	Tom McCabe, Parliament Minister, announces the resignation of Henry McLeish as First Minister to the Scottish Parliament at 11am, prior to opening of debate.

[2] Source: *The Times*, 9 November 2001

becoming an MSP. This combined with a lack of support amongst Labour fixers at the top of the party to block his first bid for the leadership. He was given the education portfolio by McLeish and this had been seen as a poisoned chalice coming after the exams crisis that had recently afflicted Scottish education but a year later McConnell was deemed adept in this post largely because he was credited with preventing a repeat of the previous year's exams crisis.

McConnell's main rival for the leadership was Wendy Alexander but she had suffered, much as devolution generally, from having had high hopes invested in her on which she was unable to deliver. Alexander's reputation for political naivety, lack of contact with Labour's ordinary members and lack of any significant achievement as a minister (other than instigating the repeal of 'Section 28') placed her in a weaker position. The first two of these weaknesses were highlighted in how she handled herself after McLeish's resignation. Having initially led her supporters to believe that she would stand, resulting in statements of support as well as decisions not to stand on the part of others, she then decided not to stand after all, leaving her supporters exposed. McConnell was thereby given a free run at the leadership. However, rumours circulated about his private life and, accompanied by his wife, he held a press conference at which he admitted to having had an extra-marital affair with a former Scottish Labour Party employee. It was an altogether bizarre start to the third First Minister's term in office.

McConnell's support in the contest with McLeish had been drawn heavily from Labour backbenchers with little support from the front benches and it was no great surprise that he cleared out the old Cabinet, despite assurances that this would not happen. Only two former Cabinet ministers were offered jobs in his Cabinet. Susan Deacon declined the offer in part because she was expecting a baby, leaving Alexander as the only surviving Labour member of the Dewar-McLeish Cabinets other than McConnell himself. McConnell's 'day of the long knives', coming at the start of his leadership, was a signal of his determination to impose his authority on the Executive in a manner that neither of his predecessors had succeeded in doing. The nature of the coalition meant that the Liberal Democrats remained in post. Deputy First Minister Jim Wallace was asked to accept the enterprise portfolio after Alexander later stood down, but he declined this invitation.

Alexander was given a widened remit prompting commentators to refer to her as the 'Minister for Everything'. Transport was absorbed into her existing enterprise and lifelong learning portfolio. This was criticized on two counts by sectional interests. First, transport interests argued that it involved a downgrading of transport and, second, environmentalists criticised the association of transport with economic development instead of the environment. But more significant was the observation made throughout the media and by political opponents (both inside and outside her party) that this large remit would prove too much for one minister. Unlike the poisoned chalice McLeish had handed to McConnell, Alexander was unable to turn it to her advantage and resigned in May 2002. Sections of the business community expressed concern that this 'business friendly' minister had gone and that her successor, Iain Gray, had no business experience. In the event, commentary focussing on the impossible nature of the vast remit of the minister's responsibilities ended as a much lower-profile approach was adopted by Gray.

Figure 5.2: McConnell's Cabinet as announced on his coming to office

First Minister	Jack McConnell (Labour)
Deputy First Minister and Minister for Justice	Jim Wallace (Liberal Democrat)
Minister for Education and Young People	Cathy Jamieson (Lab)
Minister for Enterprise, Transport, and Lifelong Learning	Wendy Alexander (Lab)
Minister for Environment and Rural Development	Ross Finnie (Lib Dem)
Minister for Tourism, Culture and Sport	Mike Watson (Lab)
Minister for Social Justice	Iain Gray (Lab)
Minister for Finance and Public Services	Andy Kerr (Lab)
Minister for Health and Community Care	Malcolm Chisholm (Lab)
Minister for Parliamentary Business	Patricia Ferguson (Lab)
Deputy Minister for Justice	Richard Simpson (Lab)
Deputy Minister for Education and Young People	Nicol Stephen (Lib Dem)
Deputy Minister for Enterprise, Transport and Lifelong Learning	Lewis Macdonald (Lab)
Deputy Minister for Environment and Rural Affairs	Allan Wilson (Lab)
Deputy Minister for Tourism, Culture and Sport	Elaine Murray (Lab)
Deputy Minister for Social Justice	Margaret Curran (Lab)

Deputy Minister for Finance and Public Services	Peter Peacock (Lab)
Deputy Ministers for Health and Community Care	Hugh Henry (Lab) and Mary Mulligan (Lab)
Deputy Minister for Parliamentary Business	Euan Robson (Lib Dem)
Lord Advocate	Colin Boyd
Solicitor General	Elish Angiolini

Alexander explained the reason for her resignation in a private letter which was later leaked to the *Sun* and *Courier* newspapers in late September 2002 which confirmed for many Labour members that she was unfit for leadership of the Scottish Labour Party. The letter had been written to Jim Sillars, the *bête noire* of Scottish Labour. Sillars was a former Labour MP who had divided the party in the 1970s, defected to the SNP in the early 1980s and took the Glasgow Govan parliamentary seat for the Nationalists in a by-election in 1988. Even Margaret Thatcher did not provoke the same ill-feeling inside Scottish Labour. In her letter, Alexander complained that,

> perhaps one of the last times the Labour Movement in Scotland made a real intellectual contribution to the UK Labour Party was around the rapid growth of the ILP following the establishment of Forward newspaper in 1906. The way in which Tom Johnston and John Wheatley took a bunch of trade unionists and revolutionary socialists and turned it into a mass party of the working class which in the 20's won a victory, albeit one that was squandered, has a resonance a century later.

This was not well received by Labour members who believed the Scottish party's contribution to be significant across a range of public services during the twentieth century. She maintained that the SNP, more than Labour, had anticipated that the Scottish Parliament would lead to 'Scottish politics departing from the UK narrative'. One irony in this correspondence is that Sillars had been amongst the tiny band of SNP hardliners who had failed to appreciate this.[3] Writing such a letter to such a person with the possibility of it being leaked was at best risky and naïve.

THE SCOTTISH NARRATIVE

A distinct strategy had been discernible under McLeish though all too often obscured by his idiosyncratic style. McLeish appeared to be pushing the boundaries of devolution but no clear strategy has emerged which might be

---

[3] I am grateful to Andy Nicoll of the *Scottish Sun* for a copy of the letter.

associated with his successor. McConnell has proved more like the safe pair of hands willing to work in parallel with London that his predecessor was supposed to be. However, McConnell's personal mandate is attenuated as the third First Minister. His main contribution has been a reasonably successful attempt to produce stability. However, there are a few signs suggesting a change of approach. Borrowing the Santer European Commission slogan of 'doing less, better', he has set out to narrow the scope of devolutionary activity though he has continued/expanded the Executive's 'foreign policy' activities, which he had when Finance Minister. McConnell has been adept in the art of symbolic politics. Delivering public policy efficiently with an emphasis on welfare services has been a theme that has been criticised for playing down the importance of economic development. It reflects an appreciation that the hype surrounding devolution created unrealistic expectations that could only undermine the Executive and/or the Parliament. Lowering expectations, however, has proved difficult not least because opponents, inside his own party and beyond, portray this as lack of vision. The Scottish Council Foundation, for example, has accused the Executive of a 'poverty of ambition' i.e. acting in a managerial mode. In this respect, McConnell retains his 'New Labour' credentials. Managing expectations may prove the most challenging task before the First Minister as he moves towards and beyond the next elections.

The CBI (Confederation of British Industry) Scotland has been amongst those who have been most critical of the high expectations invested in devolution and, more recently, the emphasis placed on matters such as gay rights, smacking children under three years old and fox hunting. This culminated in a radio interview in September 2002 in which Iain MacMillan, the CBI's Scottish director accused the Parliament of being 'self-indulgent', urging it to 'grow up' and address important issues such as economic growth instead of insignificant issues such as foxhunting and breastfeeding. This provoked a response from Presiding Officer David Steel who accused MacMillan of 'ignorance', noting that in three years the Parliament had spent just nine hours and 48 minutes debating fox hunting, nine hours and 45 minutes discussing the repeal of Section 28 and 130 hours discussing issues relating to Scottish business.[4]

However, MacMillan's comments get us to the heart of devolution's purpose. Devolution's support in the 1997 referendum had been largely negative — preventing the perceived imposition of Thatcherite policies on Scotland in the future. Its positive appeal — improved democracy and improved services — was vague and not always informed by a detailed understanding of devolution's public policy potential. In part this was the result of campaigning, required in the context of a referendum, which tended

[4] *The Scotsman*, 3 October 2002.

to exaggerate benefits. However, significant differences in the understanding of devolution's public policy purpose have emerged amongst devolution's supporters since its establishment. Controversy has developed around what might loosely be categorised as devolution's economic management, public service delivery, and social regulation functions.

The issue of devolution's purpose has some intriguing aspects. Despite the tendency of business to argue for less state intervention and the CBI's historic opposition to devolution, largely due to the fear that devolution equated with increased state intervention, CBI Scotland has had, as noted above, high expectations of devolution. Its claim that the Parliament has placed emphasis on non-business matters sits uneasily with its past fears that it would spend too much time interfering in business matters. However, in common with sections of each of the two main parties, business has adopted the view since devolution that business should be given greater priority, at least that business supports political action when this gives benefits and advantages. Inside the Labour Party, Wendy Alexander has been most closely associated with the view highlighting devolution's role in economic development. After her resignation, Alf Young of the *Herald* reported that she had been frustrated at being unable to get the 'growth issue on the agenda.'[5] Within the SNP, Andrew Wilson (who had shadowed Alexander) and Jim Mather (SNP Treasurer and a spokesman on business) articulated a similar position though from the standpoint that the Parliament's powers were inadequate. The perceived emphasis on the 'social' rather than 'economic' agenda — a factor of the limits of devolution's powers — can give the impression of devolution being local government writ large rather than second-level national government.

Emphasis on public service delivery has been a hallmark of McConnell's leadership, with his emphasis noted in a number of speeches since becoming First Minister. Speaking to the Institute of Directors in September 2002, McConnell emphasised his aim to 'create stability within Scotland's devolved government' and he conceded that he had talked 'relentlessly about the priority of our key public services — health, education, crime, and transport.' He went on to maintain that 'Somewhere along the way though, there has been the impression that my fifth priority — jobs — has somehow been downgraded.' His speech went on to emphasise the importance of job creation, which McConnell tended to see as synonymous with economic growth.[6] Business commentators noted that McConnell's emphasis on 'jobs' was not the same as 'economic growth'.[7] Inside the SNP, a similar preference to emphasise the delivery of welfare services has emerged amongst another element of that party's leadership. Mirroring the leadership ambitions inside

[5] Young, A., 'Motives for quitting open floodgates of speculation', *The Herald*, 4 May 2002.

[6] McConnell, J., 'Speech by the First Minister Jack McConnell to the Institute of Directors',

[7] Young, A., 'Actions not words, if Jack is to build a real growth', *Herald*, 12 September 2002.

the Labour Party, those that might be seen as rivals to Andrew Wilson — most notably Nicola Sturgeon and Fiona Hyslop — can be identified with emphasizing public service delivery. This might partly reflect the portfolios of the politicians concerned but there appears more to this tension that cuts across Scotland's two main parties, as evidenced by the fact that each politician has ambitions beyond the particular responsibilities held in recent times and each has a wider remit within his or her respective parties which includes developing strategy and tactics into the next election.

The social regulation and related functions of devolution have also emerged strongly, particularly on the left/liberal side of Scottish politics. A number of initiatives have been launched attempting to place issues that might broadly come under that heading onto the agenda. Removal of 'Section 28' (prohibiting the promotion of homosexuality), corporal punishment for children under three years of age, outlawing of fox-hunting, encouraging breast feeding to improve long-term health, and improving healthy eating through the provision of free (healthy) school meals for all have all been pursued by individual MSPs. These were amongst the initiatives criticized by CBI Scotland but also by a number of Scotland's seasoned commentators. The criticisms range from hostility to the particular proposal to criticism of the priority attached to these. Those behind these initiatives have argued that these are relatively inexpensive proposals but with wide-ranging implications for the health of Scotland and in a number of cases with long-term benefits. Leaving aside whether these initiatives are desirable, they suggest a degree of imagination and innovation in making use of the powers available under devolved government. In most cases, however, the immediate impact is likely to be limited though the long-term and symbolic effect will be of greater significance.

POLICY DIVERGENCE AND POLICY CONVERGENCE

The extent of Scottish policy autonomy had been a central issue in past debates on constitutional reform and the extent to which there has been policy divergence post-devolution has been discussed at length in the Scottish media. There have been a number of high profile examples of Scotland diverging from London's policy line over the period since devolution and, based on past practice, there can be little doubt that this divergence has been more extensive than under the old Scottish Office system. Most notably, it would have been inconceivable for Scotland to have such a markedly different policy on care for the elderly as that which came into force in July 2002.[8] Equally, policy on university fees has differed — though not quite as much as

---

[8] See Chapter 9 in this volume.

Executive members would have us believe — but crucially has encouraged pressure for 'abolition' of tuition fees south of the border.

Under the old system, Scotland's scope for policy autonomy had been limited. The 'basic rule of the game [was] adherence to the principle of parliamentary sovereignty, under which unlimited authority is given to Parliament and thus, under normal circumstances, the party with a majority in the House of Commons'.[9] A distinction was drawn between 'policy autonomy' and 'policy leadership': the former referring to when a Whitehall department, including the Scottish Office, was allowed to proceed on its own, the latter referring to when one department takes the lead on a policy. The Scottish Office frequently had policy autonomy but rarely led on policy. Though this autonomy operated within strict limits, there was scope for a distinct Scottish line in a number of public policies. This was particularly notable where distinctiveness in a given policy area already existed. In addition, policy autonomy occurred where it had no or little spending implications or little or no likelihood of similar demands being provoked elsewhere in the UK. Any prospect of a Scottish policy involving additional spending would be unlikely unless there was substantial pressure for such coming from Scotland. The Scottish Office very rarely was a lead department but was rather a follower. Fisheries policy was one of the few policy areas where the Scottish Office sometimes took the lead. A tendency that emerged in the 1980s, especially with regard to local government reforms under the Thatcher Governments, was that of the Scottish Office engaging in policy experimenting whilst English departments waited to see the effects of the policy before committing themselves.[10]

Devolution has had a significant impact on the balance between policy autonomy and policy leadership. The Scottish Parliament has had greater scope for policy autonomy but, so far, there has been little change in terms of policy leadership, though policy autonomy in Scotland has led to pressure for change in England. In a number of areas, Scotland has set out on an autonomous route. In both urban and rural policy fields, significant changes are underway which might have been possible under devolution but would have been most unlikely other than from a party commanding substantial support in Scotland. And even then parliamentary time, and the role of the Lords in policy-making, would have made some changes unlikely. One effect of devolution has been the removal of the Lords' veto on policy.

Public sector housing transfer has been initiated and Glasgow City is in the process of losing its status as the largest landlord in Europe as stock transfer to Glasgow Housing Association takes place following a referendum of tenants in the city in April 2002. More tenants turned out to vote in this ballot

---

[9] Midwinter, A., Keating, M. and Mitchell, J. *Politics and Public Policy in Scotland* (Basingstoke: Macmillan, 1991), p. 73.
[10] *Ibid.*, p. 82.

than had bothered to vote in the general election. The implementation of the decision has proved much more complex than had been envisaged and initial timescales for the transfer have had to be pushed back. To some extent these changes mirror changes in England but the historically larger public sector in housing in Scotland, especially as concentrated in urban centres such as Glasgow, ensure that the changes in Scotland are potentially very significant. Land reform has also been underway. Once more, the different socio-economic conditions of Scotland ensures that these amount to quite distinct changes in Scotland.

Fisheries has remained a contentious area especially in terms of policy leadership. Fisheries policy is significant because it is affected by the EU's Common Fisheries Policy (CFP) and as such lies on the cusp between devolved and retained matters. It is also significant given controversies surrounding the CFP. Under devolution, there has been less scope for Scottish policy autonomy largely because of the controversial nature of CFP and because EU matters are reserved to Westminster, with the UK as the member state. That has not stopped Scottish ministers and MSPs being vocal in defence of an industry that is under considerable pressure. In other policy areas, there has been evidence of something similar to policy experimentation. In areas such as tuition fees and care for the elderly, policies pursued in Scotland are being closely watched in England and pressures from opposition parties and other groups for their implementation there have developed.

There have been criticisms that the Scottish Executive has slavishly followed London's line. This has taken two forms. One criticism was based on extensive analysis of policy statements issued by the Scottish Executive and Whitehall departments. There is little doubt that in a number of areas, Edinburgh has adopted the same language in presenting policies that have already been presented in England. In a study of health policy statements issued by the Scottish Executive and the Department of Health, McGarvey and Shephard concluded that the Scottish Executive was still following Whitehall's lead[11] though the authors are careful to emphasise that this finding is based only on an analysis of press releases on health policy and readily accept that in areas such as care for the elderly divergence has occurred. In essence, it appears that over a range of public policy matters, little has changed in terms of outputs following London's lead, but in a significant number of cases divergence has occurred.

A second criticism has focused more on the use of Sewel Motions. Sewel Motions (named after Lord Sewel, former Scottish Office Minister) were designed to allow the Scottish Parliament to allow devolved policy to be made at Westminster. Donald Dewar had stated that he did 'not anticipate or expect' that the theoretical power of the UK parliament legislating across

[11] McGarvey, N. and Shephard, M., 'Policy Outputs in Scotland: Devolution or Duplication?' paper presented to Political Studies Association annual conference, 5–7 April, 2002, p. 26.

devolved areas would be used[12] but, according to one commentator, Holyrood had become a 'copycat' parliament with 'tartanised Whitehall'.[13] However, such blunt criticisms all too often fail to account for a number of factors that lead to similar policies being pursued in London and Edinburgh: the Executive in Edinburgh and Government in London are ideologically broadly similar; pressures across a range of public policies are common across the UK; both operate within a European Union framework; and past practice is unlikely to change overnight. Many devolutionists had not anticipated the extent to which Sewel Motions would be used. This is partly explained by a conception of devolution as involving the creation of a 'layered cake' policy-making process in which discrete layered policy-making would take place, rather than the more appropriate 'marble cake' analogy.[14]

EXECUTIVE-PARLIAMENT RELATIONS

McConnell's relations as First Minister with the Parliament did not begin well. He had made his preference for the vacant office of Deputy Presiding Officer known to Labour MSPs shortly after assuming office. MSPs voted against his preference, supporting the election of Conservative member Murray Tosh over Cathy Peattie, resulting in there no longer being a Labour MSP Presiding Officer. The result of the secret ballot — 68 votes to 45 — strongly suggests that a number of Labour MSPs voted against McConnell's recommendation.

An innovation introduced by McConnell was the appointment of Ministerial Parliamentary Aides (similar to Parliamentary Private Secretaries at Westminster) which necessitated a revision of the Scottish Ministerial Code. As the revised code states, MPAs are explicitly not members of the Executive and are 'afforded as great a liberty of action as possible; but their close and confidential association with Ministers imposes certain obligations on them . . . their position as Ministerial Parliamentary Aides means that they must support the Executive on key policy issues'. The eight MPAs appointed (all attached to Labour Cabinet ministers) can be seen as potential future ministers and most likely to be loyal supporters of the Executive. However, proposals to close a number of Glasgow hospitals raised serious questions about the coherence of the Executive, including the position of MPAs. Mike Watson, Minister for Tourism, Culture and Sport and Janis Hughes, his MPA (both with constituencies in the South Glasgow NHS Trust area) aligned

[12] Dewar, D., HC Deb, 28 January 1998, col.402–3.

[13] Hassan, G., *The Herald*, 4 September 2002; for a sober analysis of Sewel Motion see Winetrobe, B., 'Counter-devolution? The Sewel Convention on devolved legislation at Westminster', *Scottish Law and Practice Quarterly* 6, 2001, pp. 286–92.

[14] Grodzins, M., 'The Federal System', in *Goals for Americans: Report of the President's Commission on National Goals and Chapters Submitted for the Consideration of the Commission*, Prentice-Hall, Spectrum, 1960.

themselves with opposition to Executive policy. Watson retained his position in McConnell's Cabinet despite attending meetings planning opposition to the hospitals' closures. Watson voted with the Executive while simultaneously being involved with the campaign against the policy. McConnell backed him despite calls for Watson's ministerial head from Susan Deacon, former Health Minister and Kerr Fraser, former Scottish Office Permanent Secretary. Hughes retained her position despite attending a rally against Executive policy and abstaining in the vote, while Ken Macintosh, another MPA, resigned and voted against the policy. This relaxation of collective ministerial responsibility was the cost McConnell had to pay to maintain unity within his Cabinet. The removal of a minister at such an early stage in his term as First Minister would have been damaging. This has been the most serious challenge to the notion that McConnell has imposed authority on the Cabinet.

Figure 5.3: Key events in Scotland

7 June 2001	General Election. End of dual mandate for those MSPs who had also been MPs.
20 June 2001	Irish Taoiseach Bertie Ahern visits Scotland after an earlier visit was postponed.
21 June 2001	Scottish Parliament approves another increase in funding for new Parliament building.
21 June 2001	Finance Minister Angus MacKay announces his 'bonfire of quangoes'.
28 June 2001	Finance Minister Angus MacKay announces Executive's spending plans which broadly followed priorities agreed in London for England.
10 August 2001	Nick Johnston, Conservative List MP for Mid-Scotland and Fife, resigns. Murdo Fraser, next Conservative on the regional list, becomes MSP.
9 September 2001	Social Justice Minister Jackie Baillie takes over responsibility for asylum seekers.
10 September 2001	Robin Cook MP, Leader of House of Commons, visits Scottish Parliament.
11 September 2001	Lord Williams, Leader of House of Lords, visits Scottish Parliament.
13 September 2001	Education Minister Jack McConnell announces changes in the management of the Scottish Qualifications Agency.

24 September 2001	Executive announces intention to implement free personal care for the elderly on April 2, 2002.
12 October 2001	London rejects request from Scottish Executive for financial assistance to implement free personal care for the elderly.
23 October 2001	McLeish issues a statement saying that he has paid £9,000 to the Commons' Fees Office.
5 November 2001	Peter Hain, MP, UK Minister for Europe, appears before the Scottish Parliament's European Committee.
6 November 2001	Secretary of State for Scotland Helen Liddell announces a formal consultation on the future number of MSPs.
8 November 2001	Henry McLeish resigns as First Minister following 'Officegate' scandal disclosures. Jim Wallace, Liberal Democrat Deputy First Minister, takes over as acting First Minister.
12 November 2001	Only one nominee — Jack McConnell — for Scottish Labour leadership at close of nominations.
20 November 2001	Jack McConnell confirms his support for reform of local election electoral system, promising a timetable by Christmas.
22 November 2001	Jack McConnell formally elected First Minister.
27 November 2001	Jack McConnell announces his new Ministerial team.
29 November 2001	Murray Tosh, Conservative MSP, elected Deputy Presiding Officer, replacing Patricia Ferguson who entered McConnell's Executive.
29 November 2001	Changes announced in the membership of Parliamentary committees following changes in membership of Scottish Executive.
2 December 2001	Cathy Jamieson, Minister for Education and Young People, hands over responsibility for schools and teachers to her deputy Liberal Democrat Nicol Stephen.
10 December 2001	Justice Minister Jim Wallace announces establishment of a Human Rights Commission for Scotland.

18 December 2001	Finance and Public Services Minister Andy Kerr announces plans for changing way local councils are elected, to be based on Kerley Report.
19 December 2001	Senior Salaries Review Body recommends that MSPs' pay be set at 87.5 per cent of MPs in Commons and Cabinet ministers' salaries remain unchanged.
15 January 2002	Minister for Health and Community Care announces three month delay in implementation of free personal care for the elderly in Scotland.
5 February 2002	Boundaries Commission for Scotland produced proposals for reducing number of Scottish MPs (with consequences for Scottish Parliament) from 72 to 59. Consultation period until 29 March announced.
26 February 2002	Jack McConnell announced appointment of new posts of Ministerial Parliamentary Aides (equivalent to Parliamentary Private Secretaries in House of Commons).
14 March 2002	Environment and Rural Affairs Minister Ross Finnie announced Executive approval of GM oilseed rape trials in three more sites.
21 March 2002	MSPs voted for a 13.5 per cent pay rise over two years.
27 March 2002	Finance and Public Services Minister Andy Kerr announces publication of White Paper on Kerley report covering electoral reform with 'sweetener' of increased remuneration for councillors.
28 March 2002	Environment and Rural Development Minister Ross Finnie announces that existing three water authorities to be merged into one company, Scottish Water.
5 April 2002	Glasgow council tenants vote in a referendum in favour of transferring housing stock to the non-profit making Glasgow Housing Association by 58% to 42% on a 64.4% response.
18 April 2002	Jack McConnell follows announcement on health spending made in London with commitment to do similarly in Scotland.
25 April 2002	Scotland and Republic of Ireland present joint bid to host 2008 European Football Championships.

2 May 2002	Dorothy Grace Elder resigns as member of SNP group in Parliament.
3 May 2002	Wendy Alexander resigns from Executive.
4 May 2002	Iain Gray takes responsibility for Wendy Alexander's ministerial brief.
30 May 2002	First Minister McConnell launches legislative programme for Scottish Parliament proposing another six pieces of legislation before the elections.
6 June 2002	First Minister McConnell proposes a new 'Subsidiarity Council' for EU at a meeting of Convention on the Future of Europe.
1 July 2002	Implementation of free personal care for the elderly.
9 July 2002	Dumfries and Galloway council tenants vote to transfer houses to a new housing association, Dumfries and Galloway Housing Partnership.
14 August 2002	Sir Muir Russell, Head civil servant in Scottish Executive announces his intention to leave his post in 2003 to become Principal of Glasgow University.

**Figure 5.4: Acts passed by the Scottish Parliament
(July 1999 — July 2002)[15]**

Executive Acts (36 in total)

1999

- Mental Health (Public Safety and Appeals) (Scotland) Act

2000

- Abolition of Feudal Tenure etc. (Scotland) Act
- Adults with Incapacity (Scotland) Act
- Bail, Judicial Appointments etc. (Scotland) Act
- Budget (Scotland) Act
- Education and Training (Scotland) Act
- Ethical Standards in Public Life etc. (Scotland) Act
- National Parks (Scotland) Act
- Public Finance and Accountability (Scotland) Act
- Regulation of Investigatory Powers (Scotland) Act

[15] Source: 'Acts of the Scottish Parliament', *The Scottish Parliament* http://www.scotland-legislation.hmso.gov.uk/legislation/scotland/s-acts.htm

2001

- Budget (Scotland) (No. 2) Act
- Convention Rights (Compliance) (Scotland) Act
- Criminal Procedure (Amendment) (Scotland) Act
- Education (Graduate Endowment and Student Support) (No. 2) (Scotland) Act
- Erskine Bridge Tolls Act
- Housing (Scotland) Act
- International Criminal Court (Scotland) Act
- Police and Fire Services (Finance) (Scotland) Act
- Regulation of Care (Scotland) Act
- Salmon Conservation (Scotland) Act
- Scottish Local Authorities (Tendering) Act
- Transport (Scotland) Act

2002

- Budget (Scotland) (No. 3) Act
- Community Care and Health (Scotland) Act
- Education (Disability Strategies and Pupils' Records) Act
- Freedom of Information (Scotland) Act
- Fur Farming (Prohibition) (Scotland) Act
- Marriage (Scotland) Act
- School Education (Amendment) Act
- Scottish Local Government (Elections) Act
- Scottish Public Services Ombudsman Act
- Scottish Qualifications Authority Act
- Sexual Offences (Procedures and Evidence) (Scotland) Act
- Water Industry (Scotland) Act

Members Bills (*Introduced by/Supported by*) (6 in total)

2000

- Sea Fisheries (Shellfish) Amendment (Scotland) Act (Tavish Scott)

2001

- Abolition of Poindings and Warrant Sales Act (Tommy Sheridan/Alex Neil, John McAllion)
- Leasehold Casualties (Scotland) Act (Adam Ingram/Pauline McNeill)
- Mortgage Rights (Scotland) Act (Cathie Craigie)

2002

- Protection of Wild Mammals (Scotland) Act (Mike Watson/Tricia Marwick)
- University of St. Andrews (Postgraduate Medical Degrees) Act (Iain Smith)

Committee Bills (*Introduced by/on behalf of the Committee*) (2 in total)

2001

- Protection from Abuse (Scotland) Act (Alasdair Morgan on behalf of the Justice 1 Committee)

2002

- Scottish Parliamentary Standards Commissioner Act (Mike Rumbles on behalf of the Standards Committee)

OPPOSITION POLITICS

The SNP continues to poll better when voters are asked their preference in elections to the Scottish Parliament rather than the House of Commons. But as it approaches the 2003 elections the SNP continues to lie behind the Labour Party in terms of the number of seats that are likely to be won, though the battle for first place on the regional lists remains more open. John Swinney's best hope appears to be that the SNP will beat Labour on the second (regional list) vote. However, the SNP is coming under pressure from the Scottish Socialist Party (SSP) on the regional list as the latter's share of the vote has remained remarkably stable with the real prospect of a few more SSP MSPs joining Tommy Sheridan next year. Swinney's tenure as leader has been marked by a greater concern for internal organisational matters, but to date the party's constitution, having evolved during years when the party's parliamentary contingent was less significant and more reliant on volunteers, remains fundamentally unchanged. The prospect of an initiative from the leader to reform the party constitution to make it more streamlined and centrally controlled is likely after next year's elections.

The main policy development that has continued over the last year has been associated with the work of Andrew Wilson and Jim Mather on fiscal autonomy and the economic policies that an SNP administration would pursue. Wilson and Mather have taken their message to business elites and board rooms rather than the public at large. The central change of emphasis that has occurred has been the shift of focus away from the debate on whether Scotland is currently a net fiscal contributor or recipient in the UK towards the policies that an SNP Administration would pursue in order to generate economic growth. To date, this has been the most significant change under John Swinney's leadership.

SUMMARY OF ACHIEVEMENTS OF DEVOLUTION IN THE FIRST TERM

The expectations built up around devolution were not realistic and it was inevitable that in settling down to business it would disappoint even some of its most ardent supporters. In addition, in repatriating Scottish politics, devolution has repatriated contempt for politics, politicians and parliament. In considering its achievements, the yardsticks against which it should be judged need to be considered. The *Scotsman* newspaper had been one of the leading supporters of a Scottish Parliament from the 1960s but a change in ownership and editorial control, which ironically all but coincided with the coming of devolution, has meant that this erstwhile devolutionist paper has become one of its most strident critics. Assessments of the Parliament's performance need to take account of the agendas of those engaged in making the assessment.

Some of the achievements of the Parliament can be relatively easily seen, even quantified. The amount of specifically Scottish legislation passed by the Parliament has been impressive compared with the pre-devolution period. Lack of Parliamentary time to deal with even non-controversial matters had been a persistent problem pre-devolution. Additionally, scrutiny of Scottish government has increased dramatically. Instead of infrequent Scottish Questions in the Commons, ministers in the Scottish Executive are questioned regularly and, though doubts may be raised as to the value of this form of scrutiny, there can be no doubt that ministers and civil servants are more directly accountable to elected representatives than in the past. In addition, the Scottish media's coverage of politics in Scotland has increased, with considerable resources channelled into covering devolution.

However, perhaps the most significant change that has occurred in Scottish politics is one that has gone largely unnoticed. In the years leading up to devolution, the legitimacy of Scottish government was increasingly called into question. The notion that the Scottish Office — its political head rather than its body of civil servants — had 'no mandate' had become a central issue on Scottish politics. There remains debate on Scotland's constitutional status, but this continues against a backdrop of regained legitimacy. No significant section of Scottish society today questions the democratic foundations of the constitutional order. The SNP and others may wish to move on to independence but they accept that the existing arrangements are legitimate. The removal of the legitimacy issue from Scottish politics has arguably been the most significant achievement of devolution.

Whilst the policy making process is authoritative, the policy outputs remain contentious, but that is a hallmark of liberal democracies. However, devolution's purpose beyond this legitimacy function remains uncertain. As noted above, its functions as set out in the White Paper preceding the 1997 referendum and in the rhetoric of its supporters raised expectations that it would be more than simply a body that allowed for an accentuated Scottish dimension to British policy making across the limited field of Scottish Office functions. In particular, its economic functions remain unclear. The Scottish Parliament's powers *vis à vis* the economy and economic growth in particular are limited, but demands that this should be prioritized have been difficult to resist for fear that ministers (or their shadows for that matter) are 'anti-business'. This has created tensions from the inception as ministers have been criticized for making little impact where, in fact, there is little scope for impact. It would be wrong to suggest that a debate has been taking place on the purpose of the Parliament, but differences of emphases have emerged, especially in the last year, with a tension around economic affairs

ISSUES IN ELECTIONS AND CHALLENGES FOR THE SECOND TERM

The most likely outcome of elections next year is the return of the Labour-Liberal Democrat coalition. Jim Wallace, Liberal Democrat leader, has indicated on a number of occasions that this is his expectation. He has, however, been careful to note that this is based on his view that the SNP is not making electoral progress and therefore is not in the running for office. As the election looms, the issue which seems set to present the greatest challenge to First Minister McConnell is that of Liberal Democrat demands for electoral reform in local government. Opposition to any change or at least support for a less radical measure of reform within his own party than that demanded by his coalition partners will demand to be handled with great skill. At the last elections, there was less difficulty in Labour and Liberal Democrats adopting independent positions and fighting out their differences once the election was over. Being in a coalition at the outset of the campaign is likely to create more tension.

In some respects this resembles the debate within the Constitutional Convention a decade ago on the electoral system to be adopted for the Scottish Parliament and it is conceivable that, in true coalition style, a compromise will be agreed. One added dimension that did not exist back then however, adds to McConnell's difficulties. There were no MSPs in existence then to lose out, but there are many Labour councillors and council leaders who are set to lose out under any change to the electoral system for local government. Buying off existing councillors looks set to be a price that will have to be paid for reform. However, more fundamentally, the electoral map of Scotland will be transformed at local level. One party dominance would end in parts of Scotland and Labour will face more opposition in council chambers. The stakes are high. It is unlikely that any other issue will cause as much as tension between the parties but each will be intent on emphasizing its differences from its coalition partner. However, this game is far from straightforward. Short-term gain by emphasizing differences creates longer-term problems in negotiations over the legislative programme of the Executive and the prospect that a party, most likely to be the Liberal Democrats, might lose out by being unable to deliver on a policy.

One change that has occurred over the last year and may become more evident has been the economic context in which devolution is played out. Good times make governing easier and the Executive has been fortunate that its budget has been set over the period since 1999 during a period of remarkably good economic health. If the economic context was to change that could create very different conditions against which the public would judge both the Executive and devolution. In difficult times, the Executive will be required to be more imaginative in its policy initiatives and may resort to 'playing the Scottish card' in its relations with London in order to convince voters that it is capable of standing up for Scotland when need be. Even without a change in the economic context, a more assertive First Minister is likely to emerge who will be less bound by past expectations, sectional group interests and erstwhile colleagues. Jack McConnell's period as First Minister has been one in which stability has been the priority. Post-election he will have the opportunity to move on from the combined pressures for caution that come with any administration as it approaches an election and from his own lack of personal mandate.

BIBLIOGRAPHY

Official Documents
Grodzins, M., 'The Federal System', in *Goals for Americans: Report of the President's Commission on National Goals and Chapters Submitted for the Consideration of the Commission* (Prentice-Hall: Spectrum, 1960).
McConnell, J., 'Speech by the First Minister Jack McConnell to the Institute of Directors', http://www.scottishlabour.org.uk/pressrel/pr2002911123123.html

Secondary Sources
Dewar, D., HC Deb, 28 January 1998, col.402–3.
Hassan, G., *The Herald*, 4 September 2002.
McGarvey, N. and Shephard, M. 'Policy Outputs in Scotland: Devolution or Duplication?' paper presented to Political Studies Association annual conference, 5–7 April, 2002.
Midwinter, A., Keating, M. and Mitchell, J. *Politics and Public Policy in Scotland* (Basingstoke: Macmillan, 1991).
Winetrobe, B., 'Counter-devolution? The Sewel Convention on devolved legislation at Westminster', *Scottish Law and Practice Quarterly* 6, 2001, pp. 286–92.
Young, A., 'Motives for quitting open floodgates of speculation', *The Herald*, 4 May.
Young, A., 'Actions not words, if Jack is to build a real growth', *The Herald*, 12 September.

Part II

The State

6

Intergovernmental Relations
Officialdom Still in Control?

Alan Trench

The second half of 2001 and the first part of 2002 saw few dramatic developments in intergovernmental relations (IGR). The pattern already established and discussed in previous editions of *The State of the Nations* continued.[1] The UK government remained clearly the dominant partner, its position underpinned by its control of finance. A high level of informality and reliance on finding consensus permeated the system. Legislation remained a key area of interaction between administrations. A great deal went on behind the public gaze, and much of the business was done by the civil service with ministers involved chiefly to deal with liaison at the political level and to broker difficult issues when those arose, while also playing a representative role. To a large degree, 2001–02 saw more of the same.

Some more interesting developments were apparent behind the scenes, however. As the May 2003 elections started to appear on the radar screen, the devolved administrations seemed to pay more attention to their records on which they would campaign. That led to a greater concern with making policy and delivering tangible changes to their electorates. The nature of this process is discussed in more detail in the chapters by Greer and Simeon elsewhere in this volume.[2] That divergence will start to have significant effects over the next few years. The real meaning of devolution started to become clearer, as the public policies pursued by the various administrations started to diverge in appreciable ways. The fact that the devolved administrations function within the framework of Westminster statutes which they lack the power to change started to become an issue for both Scotland and Wales. A period of relative calm in the Northern Ireland peace process meant that the British-Irish Council (BIC; sometimes known as 'the Council of the Isles') started to become more active, and the work of the North-South Ministerial Conference (NSMC) also became clearer. And the working of intergovernmental relations came under sustained scrutiny as the House of Lords Select

---

[1] See Hazell, R. 'Intergovernmental Relations: Whitehall rules OK?' in R. Hazell (ed) *The State and the Nations: The First Year of Devolution in the United Kingdom* (Exeter: Imprint Academic, 2000); Trench, A. 'Intergovernmental Relations: Whitehall still rules UK' in A. Trench (ed) *The State of the Nations 2001: the Second Year of Devolution in the United Kingdom* (Exeter: Imprint Academic, 2001).

[2] See chapters 8 and 9 in this volume.

Committee on the Constitution carried out an inquiry into *Devolution: Inter-institutional relations in the United Kingdom.*

Figure 6.1: Key events in intergovernmental relations, 2001–02

22 October 2001	Meeting of Joint Ministerial Committee (Health).
30 October 2001	Plenary meeting of JMC in Cardiff.
8 November 2001	Resignation of Henry McLeish MSP as Scottish First Minister.
	Meeting of JMC (Europe).
22 November 2001	Jack McConnell MSP elected as Scottish First Minister.
30 November 2001	British-Irish Council summit meeting.
	North-South Ministerial Council plenary meeting.
17 December 2001	North-South Ministerial Council institutional meeting.
25 February 2002	British-Irish Council sectoral meeting on the Environment.
27 February 2002	House of Lords Select Committee on the Constitution starts inquiry into Devolution: inter-institutional relations in the United Kingdom.
1 March 2002	Formal establishment of Welsh Assembly Government.
7 March 2002	Meeting of JMC (Europe).
22 March 2002	British-Irish Council sectoral meeting on Drugs.
29 May 2002	UK government ministerial reshuffle and re-organisation: Office of Deputy Prime Minister established as free-standing Department.
11 June 2002	Meeting of JMC (Europe).
14 June 2002	British-Irish Council summit meeting.
28 June 2002	North-South Ministerial Council plenary meeting.
Early July 2002	Meeting of JMC (Officials).
15 July 2002	Chancellor announces Comprehensive Spending Review.
18 September 2002	Meeting of JMC (Poverty).
27 September 2002	Meeting of JMC (Europe).
14 October 2002	Suspension of devolution to Northern Ireland.
22 October 2002	Plenary meeting of JMC in London.
	Meeting of JMC (Europe).
28 October 2002	UK ministerial reshuffle: change in Secretaries of State for Wales and Northern Ireland.

THE FORMAL PROCESS OF INTERACTION:
MEETINGS AND AGREEMENTS

The Joint Ministerial Committee and Concordats

As the four governments have become accustomed to working with each other, formal meetings and procedures have declined in general importance. That can be seen in the chronology. The 2001 annual plenary meeting of the Joint Ministerial Committee (JMC) was held on 30 October in Cardiff, and produced a very bland joint press statement. The main substantive points were

- Communication and consultation between UK government and devolved administrations had worked well
- More could be done to improve understanding and best practice
- Ministers themselves had a key part to play in this. Personal and bilateral contacts were at least as important as mechanisms for inter-ministerial contacts within or outside the JMC framework.[3]

Such a bland statement — giving little real idea of what was discussed — does few favours to the process of holding such meetings. In fact the meeting appears to have been nearly as boring as the statement suggests, one official observing it describing it as 'largely ceremonial'.[4] The meeting did not go into 'dispute resolution' mode. Contentious matters such as funding arrangements, in the light of the impending Comprehensive Spending Review and attempts by the Scottish Executive to improve its position after committing to pay for free care for the elderly (discussed in Chapter 9) were not raised. This may have been due to the preoccupation of the Prime Minister with other matters, notably the conflict in Afghanistan (which formed the main subject-matter of his speech to the National Assembly that afternoon), and by the fact that (due to a hiatus in the offices of First and Deputy First Minister) Northern Ireland was represented by two stand-ins, Sir Reg Empey and Mark Durkan.

The one item of substantive business that was transacted at the plenary JMC in 2001 was the adoption of a new version of the Memorandum of Understanding, published in December 2001 and superseding the version published in July 2000.[5] The only material change in this, however, was to alter references from the Welsh First Secretary to First Minister, and similarly for Assembly Secretaries. There appear to be no substantive differences between the two versions, despite a formal review of the Memorandum of Understanding undertaken after the September 2000 plenary JMC.

---

[3] Summarised from *Joint Press Statement, Joint Ministerial Committee, 30 October 2001 'Devolution is Delivering'*; available on the internet at http://www.devolution.odpm.gov.uk/jmc/index.htm#jmccom

[4] Interview with devolved administration official, July 2002.

[5] *Memorandum of Understanding and Supplementary Agreements between the United Kingdom Government, Scottish Ministers, the Cabinet of the National Assembly for Wales and the Northern Ireland Executive Committee* Cm 5240 (London: The Stationery Office, 2001).

Much the same story applies to the plenary JMC held on 22 October 2002. The suspension of devolution to Northern Ireland meant that a minister from the Northern Ireland Office was the only representative of the province present. Again, a bland press statement was issued, according to which the three administrations emphasised their common commitments to public service reform, compared their strategies for education, health, local government, transport and fighting crime, and reviewed the way intergovernmental communications had worked. The year's topical issue (the fire service dispute) was also discussed.[6] Despite the establishment of the Welsh Assembly Government, no further amendments to the Memorandum of Understanding appear to be planned.

Of the JMC meetings in 'functional' format there is a little more to say. The JMC for the Knowledge Economy has not met. No press statement was issued after the JMC (Health) meeting in October 2001, but this appears to have been an information-sharing exercise relating partly to developments in each health system over the previous twelve months as they implemented the modernisation agenda, and partly discussing recurrent issues such as planning for winter demands on the health system. The JMC for Poverty was revived in September 2002, after a long break. This was at the instance of the Chancellor of the Exchequer, and the press statement issued after the meeting commits the four administrations present to joint work on the comparative analysis of poverty and social exclusion and to look at support for pre-school children in deprived neighbourhoods. It also commits the parties to further meetings in January and June 2003. The scale of that agenda and the matters discussed suggest that the revival of the JMC (Poverty) is a means of delivering Gordon Brown's social agenda in areas where he lacks the direct influence on social policy that he has at UK level.[7]

JMC (Europe) meetings have been rather more frequent (five in all), largely reflecting the active agenda for constitutional reform at EU level. They have usually preceded European Council summit meetings, and have been two-way briefings, serving both to alert the devolved administrations about what is to be discussed and to obtain the devolved administrations' views about the issues on the agenda.[8] In that respect they have lived up to the Memorandum of Understanding's statement that they will 'operate as one of the principal mechanisms for consultation on UK positions on EU issues which affect devolved matters'.[9] Again, however, and despite Foreign and

---

[6] *Joint Ministerial Committee, 22 October 2002, Joint Press Statement 'Committed to Devolution'*; available on the internet at http://www.devolution.odpm.gov.uk/jmc/index.htm#jmccom.

[7] Joint Ministerial Committee on Poverty, 18 September 2002, press statement; available at http://www.devolution.odpm.gov.uk/jmc/index.htm#jmccom.

[8] See House of Lords Select Committee on the Constitution Session 2001–02 *Devolution: Inter-institutional relations in the United Kingdom* Evidence complete to 10 July 2002 HL Paper 147, evidence of Sir Stephen Wall KCMG, LVO and Mr Michael Roberts, 24 April 2002, Q. 237.

[9] *Memorandum of Understanding*, Agreement on the Joint Ministerial Committee, para. A1.9.

Commonwealth Office statements to the contrary, press statements even about the occurrence of such meetings seem to be a rarity in practice. The JMC for officials was revived in July 2002, apparently at the instance of Mavis MacDonald who was translated from being Permanent Secretary at the Cabinet Office to being Permanent Secretary of the newly-constituted Office of the Deputy Prime Minister (discussed in more detail below). This apparently discussed the process of plenary JMCs with a view to sharpening them up.[10] However, the blandness of the press statement issued after the October 2002 plenary JMC suggests that such plans had resulted in little change.

The most regular inter-ministerial meetings take place outside the JMC framework. These are meetings of agriculture ministers, which take place most months in preparation for forthcoming EU Council of Ministers meetings. There were nine such meetings in 2001, and each is preceded by several meetings of senior officials. While the agenda is driven by EU issues, it also deals with domestic matters concerning all four administrations. One quirk of the meetings – dating back to their start in 1999 – is that the UK government is represented by two ministers, with the Cabinet minister (now the Secretary of State for the Environment, Food and Rural Affairs) in the chair, and one of her department's Ministers of State (usually Lord Whitty) attending to speak for specifically English concerns. Sustained enquiries about why these meetings fall outside the JMC framework suggest that in fact the reason is to avoid embarrassing the Secretary of State. Although the devolved administrations disavow any co-ordination of their positions in advance of the meetings, in fact they usually agree with each other but disagree, often profoundly, with the UK government's line. In itself this is hardly surprising — agriculture is far more important for the economies of Scotland, Wales or Northern Ireland than it is for England, and agriculture in each devolved territory is more pastoral and less intensive than in England. What is surprising is that the devolved administrations appear to be the ones reluctant to make such meetings into JMC meetings, because they consider that would make the meetings more formal and paint the UK government into a corner in a way that might prove counter-productive to their interests in the longer term.[11]

So far as the framework of documents relating to devolution is concerned, there have been few changes in 2001–02. As well as the cosmetic changes to

---

[10] Interview with UK government official, October 2002.

[11] Interviews with devolved administration officials, April 2002. See also House of Lords Select Committee on the Constitution Session 2001–02 *Devolution: Inter-institutional relations in the United Kingdom* Evidence complete to 10 July 2002 HL Paper 147, Memorandum by Department of the Environment, Food and Rural Affairs, para. 6, p. 70; evidence of Andy Lebrecht and Jim Scudamore, 24 April 2002, QQ 249–51, 257–58; evidence of Ross Finnie MSP, 15 May 2002, QQ 405–06, 424–427; evidence of Carwyn Jones AM, 28 May 2002, QQ. 973, 977–78; evidence of Peter Small CB and Patrick Toal, 10 June 2002, QQ. 1165–70, 1172.

the Memorandum of Understanding, two new technical concordats were established involving the devolved administrations, and one existing one was revised (see Figure 6.2).

Figure 6.2: Concordats agreed in 2001–02

October 2001	Revised version of Memorandum of Understanding and Supplementary Agreements
April 2002	Specific Concordat between the British Cattle Movement Service and the Scottish Executive Rural Affairs Department
	Draft Concordat between Resource — the Council for Museums, Archives and Libraries — and the Welsh Assembly Government[12]
June 2002	Concordat between the Department of Work and Pensions and the Welsh Assembly Government

One interesting development of the year was the first formal visit by one set of devolved administration ministers to another devolved administration. This occurred in June 2002, when David Trimble and Mark Durkan visited the Scottish Executive.[13] Hitherto contacts have been limited and informal, occurring perhaps once a quarter, according to Rhodri Morgan. They have also often been haphazard and on the periphery of meetings with the UK government (or events such as the Queen Mother's funeral).[14] There has still been no formal meeting of all the devolved adminstrations together, but that may come in the course of next year. The three presiding officers of the devolved parliament and assemblies find the House of Lords (of which they all happen at present to be members) the best setting for contacts, and have urged that ways be found to ensure this continues.[15] That would probably involve a new Presiding Officer becoming a peer ex officio, and presumably without being vetted by the Appointments Commission (as is already done for some senior UK figures).

[12] This remains in draft as it is subject to the agreement of Resource's board.

[13] See Scottish Executive News Release SEFM 038/2002, 20 June 2002, 'Northern Ireland FM visits Scotland'; Northern Ireland Executive Office of the First Minister and Deputy First Minister News Release, 21 June 2002, 'Trimble and Durkan meet Scottish Executive'. See also House of Lords Select Committee on the Constitution Session 2001–02 *Devolution: Inter-institutional relations in the United Kingdom* Evidence complete to 10 July 2002 HL Paper 147, evidence of Rt Hon David Trimble MP MLA and Mark Durkan MLA, 10 June 2002, QQ 1138–42.

[14] House of Lords Select Committee on the Constitution Session 2001–02 *Devolution: Inter-institutional relations in the United Kingdom* Evidence complete to 10 July 2002 HL Paper 147, evidence of Rt Hon R. Morgan AM, 27 May 2002, Q. 867.

[15] House of Lords Select Committee on the Constitution Session 2001–02 *Devolution: Inter-institutional relations in the United Kingdom* Evidence complete to 10 July 2002 HL Paper 147, Joint Supplementary Memorandum by the Presiding Officer of the Scottish Parliament, the Speaker of the Northern Ireland Assembly and the Presiding Officer of the National Assembly for Wales, p. 356.

The British-Irish Council and the North-South Ministerial Conference

One slightly surprising consequence of the period of relative calm in the Northern Ireland peace process was the development of work through the British-Irish Council. One official has described that work as 'mushrooming'.[16] Some of this is reflected in the ministerial meetings and summit meetings listed in the chronology. That does not tell the whole story, however, as much work has gone on at official level, through meetings or conferences in particular sectors such as drugs or social inclusion. The BIC has also established an informative website.[17] While its role is largely still that of a talking shop it appears to be useful as such — if nothing else, it offers a wider setting for the sharing of experiences than the JMC framework does. The UK and Irish Governments hope that the BIC will continue its work despite the suspension of devolution to Northern Ireland and the broader problems of the peace process, but finding ways to do that will not be straightforward. As the fate of the BIC is in practice tied to the success of the Northern Ireland peace process, there has to be a question-mark over its future should that process fail.

A similar problem faces the North-South Ministerial Conference (NSMC). Like the BIC this has done a great deal of work over the course of the year, and like the BIC it has established a useful website.[18] Not all of this is apparent from the chronology, which only shows meetings of the NSMC in 'plenary' or 'institutional' formats. The NSMC also meets in a number of sectoral formats — not just the six areas originally agreed under the Belfast agreement and agreement between the UK and Republic of Ireland Governments establishing implementation bodies, but in five more added subsequently, as set out in figure 6.3.

Figure 6.3: Areas of North-South co-operation

Implementation bodies established under the UK-Ireland Agreement[19]
Waterways Ireland
Food Safety Promotion Board
Trade and Business Development Body (InterTradeIreland)
Special European Union Programmes Body
The Language Body/An Foras Teanga/North-South Body o Leid
Foyle, Carlingford and Irish Lights Commission (including aquaculture)

---

[16] Interview with devolved administration official, July 2002.

[17] http://www.british-irishcouncil.org

[18] http://www.northsouthministerialcouncil.org

[19] The Agreement forms Schedule 1 to the North-South Co-operation (Implementation Bodies) (Northern Ireland) Order 1999, SI 1999 no. 859.

Areas of co-operation added subsequently
Health (overlaps with Food Safety Promotion Body)
Agriculture
Education
Transport
Tourism (including Tourism Ireland Limited)[20]

Each of these has had regular ministerial meetings — at least two per sector between August 2001 and September 2002, in several cases three and in the case of agriculture four. Such meetings have not been straightforward to organise — two Northern Ireland ministers, one nationalist and one unionist, must attend each meeting, so at least one minister for whom the meeting is at best peripheral to his or her portfolio must attend, and be briefed to attend. Attendance by Sinn Féin ministers has been withheld for long periods by David Trimble as a consequence of slow progress in arms decommissioning. Attendance at a meeting also involves making a statement to the Assembly afterward and then answering questions for up to an hour.[21] The areas chosen for sectoral meetings are all areas where there are substantial matters of common ground between the two governments (although the Foyle, Carlingford and Irish Lights Commission has been beset by problems arising from the fact that navigation is reserved to the UK government). Co-operation is probably strongest in the areas of agriculture, and matters which are the responsibility of the Special EU Programmes body. The Special EU Programmes body is responsible for the EU Objective 1 'PEACE II' programme to promote cross-border co-operation (and has also had responsibility for other EU programmes such as INTERREG, now completed). While not large (some £300 million), this funding is substantial enough to mean that co-operation has a real and direct benefit. Agriculture is an obvious area of shared interests, especially for animal health. Although outside the original framework of north-south co-operation, meetings in this area are said to be strongly supported by ministers and politicians from all parties and traditions, including the Democratic Unionist Party, when they are able to show tangible benefits for people in Northern Ireland.[22] A further strength of the NSMC is that it has its own secretariat – unlike the BIC or JMC, it does not

---

[20] See http://www.northsouthministerialcouncil.org/ac.htm

[21] House of Lords Select Committee on the Constitution Session 2001–02 *Devolution: Inter-institutional relations in the United Kingdom* Evidence complete to 10 July 2002 HL Paper 147, evidence of Lord Alderdice MLA, 10 June 2002 Q 1239.

[22] Interviews with Northern Ireland officials, April 2002.

depend on a joint secretariat provided by its member bodies, whose staff have to juggle organising such meetings with giving advice or other tasks.

FINANCE: BARNETT PERSISTS BUT SO DO THE QUESTIONS

The Power of the Treasury: Paying for Sutherland and Objective 1 for Wales

As discussed by Simeon in Chapter 9, Scotland's adoption of a policy of providing free care for the elderly raised many issues. The extent to which policy in devolved fields inevitably affects, and is affected by, reserved matters was illustrated clearly by the financial pressures which the Scottish Executive faced following its commitment to adopting Sutherland. One, probably unintended, consequence of this policy was that recipients of the free care in Scotland would lose their eligibility for Attendance Allowance, which is only paid to those who need to pay for their personal care.

To try to cover these costs, the Scottish Executive approached the UK government with a request that the amount of Attendance Allowance saved by the Exchequer be transferred to it. As both finance and social security are reserved, it was little surprise that the Executive's request was turned down (formally by Alistair Darling, then Secretary of State for Work and Pensions, but in fact after consultations with the Treasury). More interesting is the fact that the issue was not taken to the plenary meeting of the JMC in October 2001, although later press stories suggested that the issue had been raised once again bilaterally. Perhaps the bitter pill for Scotland was sweetened by the Treasury's agreement to assume responsibility for interest payments on the debt relating to Glasgow's housing stock, to be transferred to a housing association in November 2002.[23]

In Wales, an inquiry by the Commons Welsh Affairs Select Committee into Objective 1 funding looked into how and why Wales gained additional funding for this in 2000. During an interesting evidence session on 21 January 2002 attended by the First Minister, the Secretary of State and officials from the Treasury, the DTI and the National Assembly, it became clear that the Treasury quite simply changed its mind.[24] While the reasons for that may have been good, the fact that the Treasury has such power raises major questions about the extent to which devolution in public finance matches the transfer of administrative or legal powers — especially as the Treasury's original failure to make such funds available helped bring down Alun Michael as First Secretary.[25]

---

[23] Interviews with Scottish Executive and UK government officials, July, November and December 2001.

[24] House of Commons Select Committee on Welsh Affairs Second Report Objective 1 European Funding for Wales HC 520 (London: The Stationery Office, 2002), Ev. 24–Ev 31.

[25] See Osmond, J., 'The First Year of the National Assembly for Wales: A Constitutional Convention by Other Means' in Hazell (ed) 2000.

The Comprehensive Spending Review

On 15 July 2002 the Chancellor of the Exchequer announced the outcome of the Comprehensive Spending Review and his new spending plans to 2006.[26] This resulted in large nominal increases in the resources made available to the devolved administrations over the period covered by the Review, calculated in accordance with the Barnett formula.

Figure 6.4: Spending under the 2002 Comprehensive Spending Review[27]

(Figures are the Department Expenditure Limit for each administration, in £million)

	2002–03	2003–04	2004–05	2005–06
Scotland	18,207	19,718	20,884	22,319
Wales	9,424	10,275	10,941	11,774
Northern Ireland	6,418	6,813	7,178	7,626

In nominal terms, that is an increase of 22.6 per cent over the four years for Scotland, 24.9 per cent for Wales and 18.8 per cent for Northern Ireland. Yet such big numbers do not reveal the extent to which the growth in resources is slowing, under the Barnett squeeze.[28] Following the Review, a new edition of the Statement of Funding Policy was issued, containing no apparent substantive change from earlier versions.[29]

One big difference from the 2000 Comprehensive Spending Review is that there were few 'sweeteners' in it. Wales was induced to accept the 2000 settlement by the provision of additional funding from the Treasury as a result of Wales being granted Objective 1 status under the EU Structural Funds by the European Commission. Northern Ireland was also cushioned by some additional money for PEACE II, one of its Objective 1 programmes. While the new settlement (and the figures shown above) include funds to cover those existing commitments, there was no new money in the package to compensate the poorer devolved administrations (Wales and Northern Ireland) for the limited extra funds being made available to them.

The two administrations had followed differing approaches to the Review. Welsh Assembly Government ministers had been conspicuously keen to avoid criticising the Barnett Formula or the powers of the Treasury to

[26] HM Treasury *2002 Spending review: New Public Spending Plans 2003–2006. Opportunity and security for all: Investing in an enterprising, fairer Britain* Cm 5570 (London: The Stationery Office, 2002).

[27] Reproduced from HM Treasury 2002, Table 22.1, p. 130.

[28] See Bell, D., and Christie, A., 'Finance – The Barnett Formula: Nobody's Child?' in Trench (ed) 2001.

[29] HM Treasury *Funding the Scottish Parliament, National Assembly for Wales and Northern Ireland Assembly: A Statement of Funding Policy* 3rd edition, 2002 (London: HM Treasury, 2002).

determine their funding, emphasising that a new needs assessment might not benefit Wales.[30] It may be a measure of their disappointment that the First Minister has now indicated his willingness to consider a review of the Formula. Northern Ireland, by contrast, had carried out a tacit campaign against the Formula, pointing out how the Formula did not take account of the true level of need in Northern Ireland and emphasising that these needs were not related to the Troubles but rather to demographic and geographic factors (notably a young population and a high level of rurality).[31] Northern Ireland has further problems, as the Executive's responsibilities include matters such as housing, education, and social services which are local not central government responsibilities in Britain (but which are caught by the DEL and by the constraints of resource accounting and budgeting). Its campaign included carrying out, but not publishing, a new needs assessment using the model from 1978, which apparently showed that there were significant needs which were not being covered by the Barnett Formula. Wales did not carry out such an assessment, by contrast.[32] This campaign was, by and large, unsuccessful. However, Northern Ireland did secure one important victory, although one that was formally outside the scope of the Comprehensive Spending Review. This was the grant to the Northern Ireland Executive of a borrowing power from 2004–05, in connection with its 'Reinvestment and Reform Initiative' to fund capital spending and renewal for the local government-type services provided by the Executive.[33]

While the Barnett Formula has survived for another three years, the questions about it have not gone away. If anything, they have intensified, and the academic debate about the Formula's working and alternatives to it have increased.[34] Treasury officials have themselves been on something of a

[30] For instance, see House of Lords Select Committee on the Constitution, *Devolution: Inter-institutional Relations in the United Kingdom* Evidence complete to 10 July 2002, HL Paper 147, Memorandum by the Minister for Finance, Local Government and Communities, National Assembly for Wales, pp. 243–45; evidence of Mrs Edwina Hart AM, 27 May 2002, QQ. 873–82, 890–903, 909–10.

[31] House of Lords Select Committee on the Constitution, *Devolution: Inter-institutional Relations in the United Kingdom* Evidence complete to 10 July 2002, HL Paper 147, Memorandum by the Northern Ireland Executive, paras. 22–28, pp. 318–19; evidence of David Trimble MP MLA and Mark Durkan MLA, 10 June 2002, QQ. 1129–31; evidence of Dr Andrew McCormick, 10 June 2002, QQ 1145–50, 1157.

[32] Interviews with Northern Ireland and National Assembly for Wales officials, April and July 2002.

[33] House of Lords Select Committee on the Constitution, *Devolution: Inter-institutional Relations in the United Kingdom* Evidence complete to 10 July 2002, HL Paper 147, Memorandum by the Northern Ireland Executive, paras. 23-24, p. 318.

[34] See for example Heald, D., and McLeod, A., 'Beyond Barnett? Financing Devolution' in J. Adams and P. Robinson (eds) *Devolution in Practice: public policy differences in the United Kingdom* (London: Institute for Public Policy Research, 2002); McLean, I. and McMillan A., *The Fiscal Crisis of the United Kingdom* Nuffield College Working Papers in Politics 2002 W10; Midwinter, A. 'Territorial resource allocation in the UK: a rejoinder on needs assessment' (2002) *Regional Studies* 36, pp. 563–567.

charm offensive, attending a wide range of academic conferences and emphasising their interest in academic thinking on the subject. Whatever the official denials, it is clear that alternatives to Barnett are the subject of a lot of hard thought.

THE CIVIL SERVICE

Room at the Top?

The Civil Service has had a year in the relative spotlight. Part of that derives from the row about special advisers in the Department of Transport, Local Government and Regions (the Jo Moore and Martin Sixsmith affair), but part relates to the broader role of the civil service in delivering the UK government's targets. Clearly the focus on delivery was a major reason for the choice of Sir Andrew Turnbull to succeed Sir Richard Wilson as Cabinet Secretary and head of the Home Civil Service. Sir Andrew's appointment was announced on 19 April 2002.[35] This was followed by a period during which he considered the future structure of the Cabinet Office and the priorities the civil service should adopt. He set these out in a paper to the Civil Service Management Board on 24 June 2002. The paper, entitled *Cabinet Office: Reform and Delivery in the Civil Service* deals with both the role of the Cabinet Office at the centre of government and objectives for the operation of the Civil Service as a whole.[36] It emphasises four major goals:

- respect for the Civil Service's capacity to deliver as much as for its policy skills,
- an enhanced capacity to think and operate strategically,
- the creation of public value, relating both to the capacity to deliver and such traditional values as integrity, impartiality, recruitment and advancement on merit and a make-up reflecting that of the society it serves,
- a service attractive to both young people and those successful in other walks of life.

These may be priorities for the UK government, but the Home Civil Service which Sir Andrew now heads is not just the civil service for the UK government; it is also the civil service for the Scottish Executive and National Assembly for Wales. The Constitution Unit has noted before the contradictions and anomalies to which the integrated civil service gives rise.[37] It

---

[35] Press notice, 19 April 2002; internet reference: www.number10.gov.uk/output/page4835.asp

[36] Available on the internet at www.pm.gov.uk/output/page5409.asp

[37] Hazell, R and Morris, R., 'Machinery of Government: Whitehall' in R. Hazell (ed.) *Constitutional Futures: a history of the next ten years* (Oxford: Oxford University Press, 1999); Hazell, 'Intergovernmental Relations', in Hazell (ed) 2000; Masterman, R., and Mitchell, J., 'Devolution and the Centre' in Trench (ed), 2001. See also Parry, R., 'Devolution, Integration and Modernisation in the United Kingdom's Civil Service' *Public Policy and Administration* 16 (3), pp. 53–67.

means that the Home Civil Service must at one and the same time be the disinterested servant of different administrations, which may pursue contradictory or conflicting policies, and retain the trust of their political masters. As it does so it will also be pursuing a programme of internal management change and reform that applies throughout the organisation. The unavoidable question is what would happen if elected politicians in the devolved administrations of Scotland or Wales did not embrace that agenda for change in the way their counterparts in the UK government did.[38] Moreover, the drive for such a programme comes from the Head of the Home Civil Service who is also the principal adviser to one of the administrations which it serves, under the political drive of the Minister for the Civil Service who remains the UK Prime Minister. While this arrangement has been robustly defended by those involved, such views have often seemed to reflect an instinctive reluctance to change rather than an understanding of the dynamics of a devolved United Kingdom.[39] The apparent disregard for the concerns and priorities of the devolved administrations is likely to create increasing tensions in the future, if the integrated civil service acts as a means for channelling the activities of the devolved administrations in directions desired by Westminster not by them, and if serious concerns arise about the lack of control and accountability over their officials that the devolved administrations have. Some such concerns have been voiced by backbench Assembly Members in Wales, as the establishment of the Welsh Assembly Government deprives them of access to officials outside the Presiding Office. They may also lie behind the decision of Sir Muir Russell to retire early as Permanent Secretary of the Scottish Executive in September 2003 in order to become Principal of Glasgow University — certainly, if speculation in the Scottish press was to be believed.[40]

The New Office of the Deputy Prime Minister

The other key development of the year, as far as the civil service is concerned, was the removal of the ODPM from the Cabinet Office to become a free-standing department with programme management functions. The ODPM was only established in June 2001 to support John Prescott in his various duties following his removal from a line department.[41] The May

---

[38] In fact the Scottish Executive and National Assembly for Wales have embraced that agenda, not resisted it; interviews with devolved administration officials, June–August 2001.

[39] See for example House of Lords Select Committee on the Constitution Session 2001–02 *Devolution: Inter-institutional relations in the United Kingdom* Evidence complete to 10 July 2002 HL Paper 147, Memorandum by Cabinet Office, paras. 68–71, p. 22; evidence of Sir Richard Wilson GCB, 26 June 2002, Q 1310–11, 1336–40, and letter from Sir R. Wilson, pp. 371–72.

[40] See Dinwoodie, R., 'McConnell backs down over Civil Service jobs' and 'Jack can hire, but only Tony can fire' *The Herald* 18 June 2002; 'Top civil servant quits after clashes' and 'Why the top civil servant said "goodbye First Minister"' *The Herald* 15 August 2002.

[41] See Masterman and Mitchell, 2001, pp. 193–95.

2002 changes were themselves triggered by the Moore/Sixsmith affair and the resignation of Stephen Byers as Secretary of State for Transport, Local Government and the Regions. Byers's former department was split up, with part under Alistair Darling running transport, and the rest – dealing with regional government and local government for England, planning and housing – being merged with the existing ODPM and becoming "a central department in its own right".[42] With the creation of the new ODPM, the team developing policy on the English regions were able to merge with their colleagues working on the topic within the former Department of Transport, Local Government and the Regions. The DPM retains his existing responsibilities in relation to devolution, including the chair of the Cabinet's Nations and Regions Committee (CNR), and his Office continues to house the small team specialising in devolution who formerly were part of the Constitution Secretariat and latterly the Central Policy Group within ODPM.

Although Masterman and Mitchell were optimistic last year about the prospects for Prescott as a central figure for devolution, such hopes are now hard to sustain.[43] A central department has the weight of influence, access to senior ministers and distance from day-to-day policy responsibilities that makes it quite different from the demands of running policy in particular programme areas. The changes of May 2002 mean that the attention of Prescott (and his junior ministers) is divided between devolution and other 'central' matters and the demands of running an important line department. This was graphically illustrated when Prescott missed the October 2002 plenary JMC because he was making a statement in the Commons about the fire service dispute. In addition, Prescott's own interest in devolution and knowledge of it (other than his pet cause of English regionalism) have to be questioned — for example, his evidence to the House of Lords Select Committee on the Constitution suggested strongly that he does not have regular hands-on involvement.[44] His officials have lost the advantages they formerly had of being at the centre of government. A parallel between the UK government's treatment of intergovernmental relations 'up' (with the EU) and 'down' (with the devolved administrations) has been broken, as the European Secretariat remains within the Cabinet Office proper. This is highly important symbolically, as it indicates that the UK government in general and the Prime Minister in particular does not regard devolution as a continuing high priority. The officials involved in intergovernmental relations may remain the same people, doing much the same work, and they claim that their work and standing have not changed. However, it is hard for

---

[42] Cabinet Office Press Notice CAB 058/02, 29 May 2002.

[43] Masterman and Mitchell, 2001, pp. 193–94.

[44] House of Lords Select Committee on the Constitution Session 2001–02 *Devolution: Inter-institutional relations in the United Kingdom* Evidence complete to 10 July 2002 HL Paper 147, evidence of Rt Hon J. Prescott MP, 27 February 2002, QQ 43–93.

outside observers to avoid concluding that their position has changed significantly and for the worse. Perhaps the change will prove to be a short-lived one. Certainly, it is unlikely to last when devolution proves to be a matter needing active political management.

One part of the machinery of government that remained unchanged in May 2002 was the position of the Scotland Office and Wales Office. Questions about the role of each office and its Secretary of State persist, however, and were resolved by neither ministerial reshuffle in 2002.[45] While there appears to be regular contact between the Secretary of State for Wales and the First Minister, on a daily or weekly basis, private information suggests that such contact is much less frequent and much less formal in the case of Scotland.[46] So do questions about the disparity in the size of the two Offices, although it appears that the Wales Office may acquire more staff following an external staff inspection in the spring.[47] That need manifests itself most acutely when it comes to legislation, which (as discussed on pages 158-59) is a major concern of the Wales Office.

The year's second ministerial reshuffle, triggered in October 2002 by the resignation of Estelle Morris as Education and Skills Secretary, changed some of the faces involved in intergovernmental relations. John Reid moved from Northern Ireland to become Labour Party Chairman. He was replaced at Hillsborough by Paul Murphy, who was in turn succeeded at the Wales Office by Peter Hain, the former Minister for Europe. All the new faces were well known in the territories to which they were sent. Paul Murphy had been Minister for Political Development at the Northern Ireland Office under Mo Mowlam, during the negotiation of the Good Friday agreement. Peter Hain is MP for Neath, and organised Alun Michael's campaign to be leader of Labour in Wales in 1999, against Rhodri Morgan. While one might suspect a residual degree of mutual antipathy as a result, both denied that on Hain's appointment.[48] Good personal relations will be important given the key role of the Wales Office in dealing with Westminster legislation for Wales, but the fact that Hain retains his role from the Foreign Office in the Convention for the Future of Europe implies something of a downgrading of the importance of the post of Secretary of State for Wales. It is perhaps ironic that William Hague's vision of a territorial Secretary of State also holding another portfolio seems to be coming to pass stealthily under New Labour.[49]

---

[45] See Trench, 2001, pp. 162–3, and Masterman and Mitchell, 2001, pp. 186–189.

[46] House of Lords Select Committee on the Constitution Session 2001–02 *Devolution: Inter-institutional relations in the United Kingdom* Evidence complete to 10 July 2002 HL Paper 147, evidence of Rt Hon P. Murphy MP, 10 April 2002, Q 161; Q 43–93.

[47] Interview with UK government official, July 2002.

[48] See for example Betts, C., 'Only smiles in the jungle of Welsh politics' *Western Mail* 26 October 2002.

[49] See Masterman and Mitchell 2001, p.188.

LEGISLATION AND THE LAW

Wales

Primary legislation for Wales has come to be a pivotal aspect of the devolution arrangements for Wales. The powers of the National Assembly depend on the powers conferred by primary legislation, whether directly (in primary legislation) or indirectly (by transfer of functions orders). Some of the problems related to this were canvassed in *The State of the Nations 2001*.[50] They have not diminished over the last year — rather they have increased. Wales received no Parliamentary time for separate Welsh legislation in the 2001–2002 Session, although it did receive approval for a bill for the reform of the NHS in Wales.

Figure 6.5. Reform of the NHS in Wales: legislating to confuse[51]

The National Assembly published its plan for reform of the NHS in Wales in January 2001 as *Improving Health in Wales: a plan for the NHS with its partners*. Implementing this was adopted as the National Assembly's top priority for legislation on 13 March 2001 and the Queen's speech in June 2001 provided that there would be a draft bill on the reform of the NHS in Wales. The National Assembly was satisfied with this, as draft legislation enables the Assembly as a whole to consider the bill — timing constraints would make this difficult or impossible to reconcile with the Parliamentary timetable. It also avoids potential political embarrassment for UK government ministers responsible for the bill, as they do not have to argue the case in Parliament for legislation for England when the same bill contains different, often contradictory, measures for Wales.

The legislation, when it emerged, in fact was split over two bills. Some provisions — relating to local health boards, and health and well-being strategies — were incorporated into the National Health Service Reform and Health Care Professions Bill. The rest were incorporated into the proposed draft bill, the NHS (Wales) Bill, which has been subject to pre-legislative scrutiny by the Commons Select Committee on Welsh Affairs and the National Assembly. This will be a further case where one package of reforms is split over two different pieces of legislation, as also happened with the Children's Commissioner for Wales (split between Part V of the Care Standards Act 2000 and the Children's Commissioner for Wales Act 2002). This is likely to confuse legislators, as well as those who will have to use the legislation.

---

[50] Trench 2001, pp. 163-66.

[51] Interviews with National Assembly and UK government officials, July 2002; Williams, J., 'The Legislative Process' in Osmond, J., *Wales Devolution Monitoring Report, August 2002* (www.ucl.ac.uk/constitution-unit/leverh/monitoring.htm), p. 38-44.

The opaque way in which Westminster legislation affecting the Assembly is made, and the immense variation there has been in the powers conferred on the Assembly and the ways these are presented and expressed, are the edge of a set of much broader concerns about the making of legislation for Wales.[52] The Assembly's own concerns about them led to a set of recommendations in the Final Report of the Assembly Review of Procedure, chaired by the Presiding Officer and adopted by the Assembly on 30 January 2002.[53] These recommendations incorporated a set of principles with which the National Assembly wished subsequent Westminster legislation to comply, dealing with such matters as the powers which should be given to the Secretary of State for Wales or other UK ministers, commencement arrangements and so-called 'Henry VIII' clauses (powers to repeal existing Westminster legislation to ease implementation of the new law), as well as the nature of the functions legislation should confer on the National Assembly. The principles had their origin in recommendations made by Professor Richard Rawlings of the London School of Economics, though they also bore some kinship to the points used by the Assembly internally before that to assess Westminster legislation.[54] There has been a resounding silence from the Assembly about the principles since their adoption, however. This is due to several factors, notably the fact that the Assembly itself sees the debate as having moved on since their adoption and, perhaps, the establishment of the Richard Commission to look at the Assembly's powers and structure.[55] Nonetheless, the failure of the Assembly to use the principles as a benchmark by which to audit Westminster legislation is puzzling if it were serious about ensuring compliance with them. Officials at the centre in Whitehall do not see this as their job and do not seek to apply the principles at all, or police their application by line departments.[56] The Commons Select Committee on Welsh Affairs may use them in its forthcoming inquiry into Welsh legislation, which was suspended after the start of the Assembly's own Review of Procedure but which was to resume in the autumn of 2002.

[52] For discussion of the problems and how they might be resolved, see Rawlings, R., 'Quasi-legislative devolution: powers and principles' (2001) *Northern Ireland Legal Quarterly* 52, p. 54–81, and Patchett, K., 'The Central Relationship: The Assembly's Engagement with Westminster and Whitehall' in J. Barry Jones and J. Osmond (eds) *Building a Civic Culture: institutional change, policy development and political dynamics in the National Assembly for Wales* (Cardiff: Institute of Welsh Affairs and Welsh Governance Centre, 2002).

[53] National Assembly for Wales. Assembly Review of Procedure Final Report, Chapter Four and Annex v, available on the internet at http://www.wales.gov.uk/subiassemblybusiness/procedures/assemblyreview.htm.

[54] See Rawlings, 2001, pp. 75–76; interview with National Assembly official, July 2002.

[55] Interview with National Assembly official, July 2002.

[56] Interviews with UK government officials, February, May and October 2002.

Scotland

Westminster has continued to legislate for devolved matters in Scotland since devolution. The Sewel Convention provides for this, and has been incorporated into the Memorandum of Understanding so that such legislation normally requires the consent of the devolved legislature involved.[57] Nine such motions, relating to seven Westminster bills, were passed by the Scottish Parliament between August 2001 and September 2002.

**Figure 6.6: Sewel motions in the Scottish Parliament,
August 2001– September 2002[58]**

Adoption and Children Bill	24 October 2001
Proceeds of Crime Bill	24 October 2001
Anti-terrorism, Crime and Security Bill	15 November 2001
NHS Reform and Health Care Professions Bill	22 November 2001
Adoption and Children Bill	30 January 2002
Police Reform Bill	30 January 2002
Enterprise Bill	17 April 2002
Private Hire Vehicles (Carriage of Guide Dogs etc) Bill	19 June 2002
Police Reform Bill	27 June 2002

Both the Adoption and Children Bill and Police Reform Bill were twice the subject of Sewel motions (the Adoption and Children Bill has actually been the subject of three, as it was approved by the Parliament first in April 2001 but then lost at Westminster when the 2001 UK general election was called). This was due to amendments being made at Westminster which further affected devolved matters – what one might call a 're-Sewelising' amendment.

---

[57] Memorandum of Understanding, para. 13. For a discussion, see Page, A., and Batey, A., 'Scotland's other Parliament: Westminster legislation about devolved matters in Scotland since devolution' [2002] *Public Law*, pp. 501–23; Winetrobe B., 'Counter-devolution? The Sewel Convention on devolved legislature at Westminster', *Scottish Law and Practice Quarterly*, 6, 2001, pp. 286-92.

[58] Abstracted from information supplied by Scottish Executive to House of Lords Select Committee on the Constitution: see House of Lords Select Committee on the Constitution Session 2001–02 *Devolution: Inter-institutional relations in the United Kingdom* Evidence complete to 10 July 2002 HL Paper 147, Supplementary Memorandum by the Scottish Executive, p. 138.

Again, behind the scenes such Westminster legislation occasions a huge amount of intergovernmental negotiation at official and often ministerial level. Liaison of this kind is considered good practice, and is strongly recommended in Whitehall for any bill that affects Scotland whether or not it deals with devolved matters — for example, if a bill dealing with reserved matters creates a new criminal offence.[59] While it can be seen as giving Scotland a second legislature, and making more time available at Holyrood for the purely Scottish priorities, the process does not always work that way. Once a Sewel motion is passed at Holyrood, the Bill passes wholly to Westminster and will only return if 're-Sewelising' amendments are made and a further Sewel motion needed. On a number of occasions, a Sewel motion has been passed only for the bill in question to fail altogether, or for some or all of the provisions that occasioned the Sewel motion to be withdrawn from the bill before it completes its Parliamentary passage. The former was the case with the first incarnation of the Adoption and Children Bill in the 2000–01 session. In any case, the negotiations around Westminster legislation often have the effect of passing control of the Scottish legislative agenda to the UK government and Parliament. The Anti-terrorism, Crime and Security Act 2001 was an example of this (see Figure 6.7).

Although in principle the Sewel Convention applies equally to Northern Ireland, no settled procedure exists for the Assembly to signify its consent, which (with two exceptions) has always been signified on the Assembly's behalf by the Executive Committee. Suspension makes that all the more unlikely to change.

---

[59] *Devolution Guidance Note 10: Post Devolution Primary Legislation affecting Scotland*, paras. 6 and 7; interviews with UK government officials, February and May 2002.

Figure 6.7: The Anti-terrorism, Crime and Security Act 2002[60]

> This legislation was brought forward by the UK government in response to the 11 September 2001 attacks on New York and Washington DC, to provide a legal basis for ensuring UK security and dealing with terrorist threats on UK soil. The bill dealt with a wide range of matters, including taking control of terrorist financial assets, the detention without charge of terrorist suspects, improving measures to protect nuclear and biological materials, and improving the protection of religious groups. Much of the legislation relates to matters which are not reserved to the UK Parliament and so are devolved.
>
> The negotiations about the legislation were complicated, involving not just the ministers and policy officials from the Home Office, Scottish Executive and Scotland Office but also their legal advisers. Three key points stand out:
>
> - the power to implement legislation made by the EU under the 'third pillar' (justice and home affairs) was conferred directly on Scottish ministers (section 112), in the same way as UK ministers, so far as that relates to devolved matters — a compromise described as 'satisfying honour on both sides' by one official involved.
> - Two parts of the Act expressly do not apply to Scotland. These relate to religious hatred and the aggravation of offences if committed for religious reasons (Part 5), and broadening the scope of offences related to bribery and corruption (Part 12). The Scottish Deputy Minister for Justice and Home Affairs made it clear in the debate on the Sewel motion that this agreement was conditional on Scotland bringing forward its own legislation on the subject in due course.
> - Further provisions regarding the removal of face coverings and other disguises (Part 10) were limited to England, Wales and Northern Ireland, and do not extend to Scotland.
>
> Yet the Act as a whole gives extensive powers to the Home Secretary for devolved matters as well as reserved ones, and where the Act does not extend to Scotland that has been on the basis that the provisions in question either will be replicated in a Scottish way, or are unnecessary in Scotland.

Devolution and the Courts

Last year Masterman and Mitchell noted the relative absence of devolution-related litigation in the courts and discussed whether this would continue.[61] What was then only a trickle of cases has been practically extinguished in the year since. There are two exceptions worthy of note.

---

[60] Scottish Parliament Official Report, 15 November 2001, col 3841 (Iain Gray MSP); *Sewel Memorandum: The Anti-Terrorism, Crime and Security Bill* (available on the internet at http://www.scotland.gov.uk/library3/law/sewel_memo.pdf; interviews with UK government officials, February and May 2002.

[61] Masterman and Mitchell, 2001, pp. 178–80. The first 'devolution issue' cases in the Judicial Committee are usefully surveyed in O'Neill, A., 'Judicial politics and the Judicial Committee: the devolution jurisprudence of the Privy Council' (2001) 64 *Modern Law Review* pp. 603–617.

In *Mills*, the Judicial Committee of the Privy Council was asked for the first time to fill what was in effect a lacuna in the devolution legislation.[62] The Scotland Act 1998 provides that any act of the Scottish Executive, including the bringing of a criminal prosecution, is subject to the safeguards of the 'Convention rights' — those rights set out in the European Convention on Human Rights protected under the Human Rights Act 1998. Any challenge to a prosecution on that basis requires the service of a notice formally raising the point as a 'devolution issue'. Various law officers including the Advocate-General for Scotland, the UK government's law officer for Scottish law issues, may intervene in the proceedings. The Human Rights Act 1998 also applies in Scotland but does not require the service of such a notice, and gives no rights to the Advocate-General to intervene. In *Mills* the Advocate-General sought to persuade the courts that any case brought in Scotland raising a human rights issue should be treated as one brought under the Scotland Act, regardless of whether that Act or the Human Rights Act was pleaded as the basis for the human rights challenge. What is interesting is that not only did the Advocate-General's attempt fail, but despite a sustained attempt to establish the point the Judicial Committee did not even touch on it in their judgment.

The second case of interest has yet to reach the Judicial Committee, or even be heard in the Court of Session in Scotland. That is the legal challenge, again on human rights grounds, to the Protection of Wild Mammals (Scotland) Act 2002, passed by the Scottish Parliament in February 2002 to outlaw fox-hunting and other forms of hunting with dogs.[63] As noted in *The State of the Nations 2001*, one Act of the Scottish Parliament has been challenged so far on these grounds; the Judicial Committee dismissed the challenge in October 2001 with little ado.[64] Whether this latest challenge will be any more successful is similarly open to doubt, as many of the points raised appear to be tenuous at best.

THE SCRUTINY OF INTERGOVERNMENTAL RELATIONS

The process of intergovernmental relations has started to come under rather greater scrutiny than it has had hitherto. This has taken two chief forms. First, the House of Lords Select Committee on the Constitution began an inquiry into *Devolution: Inter-institutional relations in the United Kingdom* in late

---

[62] *K.A.P. Mills. v. Her Majesty's Advocate and The Advocate General for Scotland*, Privy Council DR. No. 1 of 2002;, 22 July 2002; Jamieson, I., 'Relationship between the Scotland Act and the Human Rights Act' [2001] *Scottish Law Times* (News) pp. 43–48.

[63] P557/02 *Petition of T. Adams and others;* Lord Nimmo-Smith dismissed the application in the Outer House on 31 July 2002.

[64] The Mental Health (Public Safety and Appeals) (Scotland) Act 1999, challenged in *Anderson, Reid & Doherty v. Scottish Ministers and Advocate-General for Scotland* (DRA Nos. 9, 10 and 11 of 2000), 15 October 2001; see Masterman and Mitchell 2001, pp. 178–80; Winetrobe, B., 'Scottish devolved legislation and the courts', *Public Law*, (2002), pp. 31-35.

February. This is the first major inquiry undertaken by the Committee, which is chaired by Lord Norton of Louth (Professor Philip Norton of Hull University), and which has hitherto produced reports on *Reviewing the Constitution* and *Changing the Constitution*.[65] The Committee took evidence from UK government ministers and officials in Whitehall, Select Committee Chairmen from the Commons, and also from ministers, presiding officers, officials and academics in Edinburgh, Cardiff and Belfast. The Committee took oral evidence from a total of 62 witnesses, and received written evidence from a further 17 witnesses. Its inquiry has therefore been one of the largest investigations of intergovernmental relations yet undertaken.[66] The bulk of the evidence taken in the course of the inquiry was published in July 2002, and the Committee's report is expected to appear in late 2002.[67] That is likely to endorse the basic arrangements for intergovernmental relations but to call for the UK government to change the way it approaches them so as to make greater use of formal mechanisms.

One point considered by the Committee was the existing arrangements across the UK for the scrutiny of intergovernmental relations. The evidence suggests that these are scanty. Neither the Scottish Parliament nor National Assembly for Wales have a committee whose remit includes intergovernmental relations within the UK (although both have committees which do look at EU issues). Both expect IGR issues to be considered as and when they arise by particular subject committees. In plenary, questions are often addressed to the First Minister on IGR issues, but usually in order to raise party political points. These are often of the 'When did the First Minister last meet the Secretary of State to discuss . . . ' type, rather than something designed to illuminate an otherwise- obscure matter. Northern Ireland does have a Committee of the Centre whose remit covers many aspects of the work of the Office of the First Minister and Deputy First Minister, but which again does not extend to IGR. Proper scrutiny in the devolved assemblies and legislatures is therefore very limited, and lacks a focus on the overall relations between that territory and the UK government.

At Westminster the position is only a little better. There is limited time for questions to the Secretaries of State and again much of that is taken up by party-political posturing rather than genuine inquiry. The territorial select committees in the House of Commons do consider intergovernmental

---

[65] House of Lords Select Committee on the Constitution Session 2001–02 1ˢᵗ Report *Reviewing the Constitution: Terms of Reference and Method of Working* (London: The Stationery Office, 2002); 4ᵗʰ Report, *Changing the Constitution: The Process of Constitutional Change* (London: The Stationery Office, 2002).

[66] The author of this chapter must declare an interest, having served as Specialist Adviser to the Committee for the Inquiry.

[67] House of Lords Select Committee on the Constitution, *Devolution: Inter-institutional Relations in the United Kingdom* Evidence complete to 10 July 2002, HL Paper 147 (London: The Stationery Office, 2002).

relations, but only in the context of other inquiries which they undertake.[68] They do not periodically review the subject as a matter of routine. When they consider it, they can look only at matters relating to one territory and the UK government — they cannot look at the overall pattern of intergovernmental relations across the United Kingdom as a whole. Clearly there is a gap here that needs to be filled. This could be taken on by the Lords Constitution Committee or Public Administration Select Committee in the Commons, or perhaps by a specially constituted joint select committee of both Houses. If Westminster does not take a lead, it may find that the devolved administrations pursue the matter instead.

CONCLUSION

Much about the conduct of intergovernmental relations in the UK remains ad hoc and driven by process. On one level ministers tend to produce bland reassurances about how good relations are, dependent largely on the fact that they can usually reach agreement with party colleagues about matters they are asked to resolve. On another, civil servants toil in obscurity to resolve highly technical problems in ways few outsiders can understand. This has worked well so far, and is likely to continue to work well up to a point. That point will be reached when a devolved administration determines to do something that is materially different to what the UK government proposes that materially affects UK-level policy or its presentation, perhaps because the devolved administration does not share the outlook and approach of the UK government. The coming year may start to see the emergence of this. With the May 2003 elections, the devolved administrations may get new governments. Even if the parties in office remain the same, they will certainly get a new mandate, and one less reliant on UK issues and the support of the UK parties than before. (Given the funding problems the UK parties face, that support may be negligible in any event.)[69] There is therefore at least a prospect that internal party harmony may deteriorate as a result.

Whatever the effect of the 2003 elections, it is likely that intergovernmental relations will start to become more formal over the next year or two. This is increasingly in the interests of the devolved institutions, which sometimes admit privately that informality enables the UK government to take the

[68] For example, the Welsh Affairs Select Committee investigated Objective 1 funding for Wales, including the circumstances in which additional funding became available in 2000. House of Commons Select Committee on Welsh Affairs Second Report *Objective 1 European Funding for Wales* HC 520 (London: The Stationery Office, 2002); see also House of Commons Select Committee on Welsh Affairs Fourth Special Report *Objective 1 European Funding for Wales: Responses of the Government and the Welsh Assembly Government to the Second Report of the Committee of Session* 2001–2002 HC 1169 (London: The Stationery Office, 2002).

[69] See for example Watson, I., and Dillon, J., 'Labour "too poor" to contest Scottish and Welsh elections' *Independent on Sunday* 21 July 2002.

initiative to an excessive degree. Increased co-operation between devolved administrations may add to the impetus behind that change. Given the many levers that remain within the hands of the UK government, such a change will be little real sacrifice for Westminster, but may make life more comfortable for Edinburgh, Cardiff and perhaps Belfast.

BIBLIOGRAPHY

Official Documents

Cabinet Office *Devolution Guidance Note 10: Post Devolution Primary Legislation affecting Scotland.*

HM Treasury *2002 Spending review: New Public Spending Plans 2003–2006. Opportunity and security for all: Investing in an enterprising, fairer Britain* Cm 5570 (London; The Stationery Office, 2002).

HM Treasury *Funding the Scottish Parliament, National Assembly for Wales and Northern Ireland Assembly: a Statement of Funding Policy* 3rd edition, 2002 (London: HM Treasury, 2002).

House of Commons Select Committee on Welsh Affairs Second Report *Objective 1 European Funding for Wales* HC 520 (London: The Stationery Office, 2002)

House of Commons Select Committee on Welsh Affairs Fourth Special Report *Objective 1 European Funding for Wales: Responses of the Government and the Welsh Assembly Government to the Second Report of the Committee of Session 2001–2002* HC 1169 (London: The Stationery Office, 2002).

House of Lords Select Committee on the Constitution *Devolution: Inter-institutional Relations in the United Kingdom* Evidence complete to 10 July 2002, HL Paper 147 (London: The Stationery Office, 2002).

Memorandum of Understanding and Supplementary Agreements between the United Kingdom Government, Scottish Ministers, the Cabinet of the National Assembly for Wales and the Northern Ireland Executive Committee Cm 5240 (London: The Stationery Office, 2001).

National Assembly for Wales. *Assembly Review of Procedure Final Report.*

Secondary Sources

Bell, D., and Christie, A., 'Finance – The Barnett Formula: Nobody's Child?' in A. Trench (ed) *The State of the Nations 2001: the Second Year of Devolution in the United Kingdom* (Exeter: Imprint Academic, 2001).

Heald, D., and McLeod, A., 'Beyond Barnett? Financing Devolution' in J. Adams and P. Robinson (eds) *Devolution in Practice: public policy differences in the United Kingdom* (London: Institute for Public Policy Research, 2002).

Hazell, R. 'Intergovernmental Relations: Whitehall rules OK?' in R. Hazell (ed) *The State and the Nations: The First Year of Devolution in the United Kingdom* (Exeter: Imprint Academic, 2000).

Hazell, R and Morris, R., 'Machinery of Government: Whitehall' in R. Hazell (ed.) *Constitutional Futures: a history of the next ten years* (Oxford: Oxford University Press, 1999).

Jamieson, I., 'Relationship between the Scotland Act and the Human Rights Act' [2001] *Scottish Law Times* (News) 43.

McLean, I. and McMillan A., *The Fiscal Crisis of the United Kingdom* Nuffield College Working Papers in Politics 2002 W10.

Midwinter, A. 'Territorial resource allocation in the UK: a rejoinder on needs assessment' *Regional Studies* 2002 36, pp. 563–567.

Masterman, R. and Mitchell, J., 'Devolution and the Centre' in A. Trench (ed) *The State of the Nations 2001: the Second Year of Devolution in the United Kingdom* (Exeter: Imprint Academic, 2001).

O'Neill, A., 'Judicial politics and the Judicial Committee: the devolution jurisprudence of the Privy Council' (2001) 64 *Modern Law Review* pp. 603–617.

Osmond, J., 'The First Year of the National Assembly for Wales: A Constitutional Convention by Other Means' in R. Hazell (ed), *State and the Nations: the First Year of Devolution in the United Kingdom* (Exeter: Imprint Academic, 2000).

Page, A., and Batey, A., 'Scotland's other Parliament: Westminster legislation about devolved matters in Scotland since devolution' [2002] *Public Law*, pp. 501–23.

Parry, R., 'Devolution, Integration and Modernisation in the United Kingdom's Civil Service' *Public Policy and Administration* 200116 (3), pp. 53–67.

Patchett, K., 'The Central Relationship: The Assembly's Engagement with Westminster and Whitehall' in J. Barry Jones and J. Osmond (eds) *Building a Civic Culture: institutional change, policy development and political dynamics in the National Assembly for Wales* (Cardiff: Institute of Welsh Affairs and Welsh Governance Centre, 2002).

Rawlings, R., 'Quasi–legislative devolution: powers and principles' (2001) 52 *Northern Ireland Legal Quarterly*, pp. 54–81.

Trench, A. 'Intergovernmental Relations. Whitehall still rules UK' in A. Trench (ed) *The State of the Nations 2001: the Second Year of Devolution in the United Kingdom* (Exeter: Imprint Academic, 2001).

Williams, J., 'The Legislative Process' in Osmond, J., *Wales Devolution Monitoring Report, August 2002* (London: The Constitution Unit, 2002), p. 38–44.

Winetrobe B., 'Counter-devolution? The Sewel Convention on devolved legislature at Westminster', *Scottish Law and Practice Quarterly*, 6, 2001, pp. 286-92.

Winetrobe, B., 'Scottish devolved legislation and the courts', *Public Law*, (2002), pp. 31-35.

7

Evolution from Devolution

The Experience at Westminster

Oonagh Gay

INTRODUCTION — THE LIMITS OF MODERNISATION

The devolution settlement of 1998–9 was expected to result in changes in the conduct of parliamentary business at Westminster. As long ago as 1973, the Kilbrandon Royal Commission on the Constitution expected that devolution would lead to a reduction of legislative business at Westminster and consequent saving of time, to be spent on English issues. Constitutional analysts considered that the Commons would eventually move towards a quasi-federal structure, dealing with more purely English issues. This would lead to the development of an English chamber within the parameters of Westminster. Others predicted that Westminster would transform itself into a forum for regional interests, following the creation of regional assemblies.

In *Constitutional Futures* Hazell looked forward to a new Westminster which would adjust its work to allow more predominance to territorial considerations.[1] It was expected that there would be fewer questions to the territorial Secretaries of State, that the territorial committees would wither away, that departmental committees would divide into 'English' and 'non-English' subjects and that 'English' procedures would develop, for example allowing only English MPs to vote on legislation applying to England only.

Some of these changes were considered to be only a matter of time, since the Select Committees for Scotland, Wales and Northern Ireland would have their roles confined to the activities of the three Secretaries of State in relation to reserved matters. A similar fate was expected for the Scotland, Wales and Northern Ireland Grand Committees, which are composed of all the MPs for a territorial area. Their role had been extended by the Conservative government in the early 1990s, in an attempt to preempt demand for devolution, but the advent of the new parliaments/assemblies seemed to make them redundant as a forum for set-piece political debates on territorial issues.

A reformed House of Lords was considered likely to transform itself into a House of Nations and Regions, with representatives from the constituent

---

[1] Hazell, R., 'Westminster squeezed from above and below' in R. Hazell (ed) *Constitutional Futures: A History of the Next Ten Years* (Oxford: Oxford University Press, 1999), pp. 111–135.

parts of the UK, thus fulfilling the classic federal role of a second chamber.[2] The new members would both champion territorial interests and act as a unifying body in the post-devolution UK. There are echoes of this argument in the Wakeham report of January 2000, although the Royal Commission did not accept that the chief role of a new upper chamber would be to sustain the Union.[3]

In fact, none of these hypotheses have been sustained by events. The Commons Procedure Committee produced a series of recommendations in May 1999 which might have helped bring about this transformation. Its most important recommendation was that the Speaker (as a non-partisan figure) should certify when a bill related exclusively to one of the constituent parts of the UK, and that a standing committee to scrutinise the bill would be composed of a majority of MPs for the relevant area. It also recommended changes for the territorial committees, in particular that the Grand Committees for Scotland, Wales and Northern Ireland be suspended, at least for an interim period, and that the select committees for these areas deal solely with the responsibilities of the Secretary of State for that territorial area.

The Procedure Committee is composed of backbenchers, and so the government did not have to accept its recommendations. The only area where change was inevitable was reducing the scope of questions to the Secretaries of State, so that he/she was not expected to answer for the actions of the devolved administrations. There was a clear precedent for such limitation since similar rules had applied for the period of devolution to the Northern Ireland Parliament from 1921–1972. The Procedure Committee recommendations were brought into effect, in that the rules on questions were limited in a new resolution on 25 October 1999 and the duration of Scottish and Northern Irish questions was reduced to 30 minutes. The then Leader of the House, Margaret Beckett, did not favour more radical changes, and there was little pressure for her to do so. The government collectively had an interest in minimising the changes devolution brought, so as not to inadvertently upset the English voter, who had been given no special procedures or consideration. The opposition were initially enthusiastic for some kind of solution to the West Lothian Question, (which challenged the right of Scottish MPs to vote on legislation affecting English voters only). But the party was handicapped by the crushing defeat of 1997, which sapped morale. Its new leader realised that campaigning on constitutional issues did not engage the interest of the voter, so downplayed this aspect of Conservative policies in the June 2001 election, although a vague commitment to English

---

[2] See also Osmond, J., *Reforming the House of Lords and Changing Britain (Fabian Pamphlet 587)* 1998.

[3] See 'Giving a Voice to the Nations and Regions' in *A House for the Future* Cm 4534 January 2000. Background to Wakeham is given in Masterman, R. and Mitchell, J., 'Devolution and Westminster' in A. Trench (eds) *State of the Nations 2001: The Second Year of Devolution in the United Kingdom* (Exeter: Imprint Academic, 2001), pp. 197–224.

votes for English laws appeared in the manifesto.[4] This policy was based on proposals in the commission on the constitution chaired by the Conservative peer Lord Norton, but was hardly prominent in the campaign.'[5]

A basic problem faced by those who lobbied for a more federal Parliament is the overwhelming preponderance of the English within the UK — forming 85 per cent of the population. Another is the asymmetric form of devolution enacted in 1998. In practice there is almost no 'English-only' legislation at all — bills apply either to the UK, Great Britain or England and Wales together. As the Welsh Assembly has found, both Whitehall officials and parliamentary draftsmen are reluctant to separate out clauses affecting only that territory. Moreover the frequent use of 'Sewel motions' by the Scottish Executive and Parliament has meant the enactment of more legislation on a UK wide basis than initially expected under the devolution settlement.[6] The Scottish Executive is, in effect, waiving its right to seek enactment of its own version of the legislation, due to pressure of time from its own bills. The time gained from the reduction of Scottish business at Westminster is minimal — less than 100 hours was spent on exclusively Scots bills in the 1992–97 Parliament.[7]

Another aspect of the original hypothesis was the belief that Westminster would learn from the procedural innovations of the new devolved parliaments and assemblies, in terms of new methods of scrutiny and family- and media-friendly hours. The argument was that Westminster would show interest in new ways of working, as part of a culture of self-improvement. This approach neglected to appreciate the insular culture at Westminster and that procedural changes in the Commons are only achieved with the determined support of the government, since the Leader of the House — the minister in charge of both organising parliamentary business and running the Commons — is a Cabinet minister. The Leader of the House chairs the Modernisation Select Committee, which since 1997 has taken over the modernisation agenda from the more traditionally constituted Procedure Committee. The advantage of this arrangement is that the government is more likely to support the recommendations of the Modernisation Committee. The disadvantage of the Modernisation Committee being chaired by the Leader of the House is of course that the Leader is a Cabinet member and committed to the efficient processing of government business through the House. This is not

---

[4] For an analysis of the position of William Hague see Masterman, R. and Mitchell, J., in *State of the Nations 2001*.

[5] *The Commission to Strengthen Parliament* established by William Hague and chaired by Lord Norton, reported in July 2000 proposing far-reaching changes to legislative process, accommodating devolution. For details see Hazell, R., and Russell, M., 'Devolution and Westminster' in *State and the Nations: the First Year of Devolution in the United Kingdom* (Exeter: Imprint Academic, 2000), pp. 183–222.

[6] For background see Chapter 6 in this volume.

[7] Commons Journal Office figures suggest that a total of 98 hours in the Commons was spent on exclusively Scottish bills in the 1992–97 Parliament. Comparable figures are not available for the Lords.

always consistent with the interests of Parliament, in as far as it can be said to be a separate institution and not just an arena for government and opposition to interact.

Many of the innovations seen in Scotland and Wales were the product of 'outsider' working groups, keen to ensure their new legislatures were more in touch with their citizens. The Presiding Officers there had more independent power to introduce new working practices. The Speaker in the Commons acts more as a brake on innovation, making clear when government initiatives trespass too far on backbencher's rights or the autonomy of Parliament. The main thrust of modernisation since 1997 has been to smooth the passage of legislation, rather than offer increased autonomy to back-benchers, or allow them more control over the allocation of time. This advantage lies firmly in the hands of the government. Robin Cook achieved a rescheduling of Commons sitting hours in October 2001, based partially on the working hours established in Scotland, Wales and Northern Ireland. But the new timetable allows no more time for backbencher's debates and concerns to be aired.

The Commons is essentially a very conservative institution (with a small c) and there needs to be immediate political spin-offs for innovations to be considered, since inertia is likely to frustrate all but the most determined reformers. MPs are themselves creatures of habit and not particularly keen to reduce the number of forums in which they can appear, so the abolition of the Grand Committees, for example, was unlikely to excite much interest from those MPs from Scotland, Wales and Northern Ireland, who would be able to feed their local newspapers with their speeches. Criticism from nationalist MPs is muted due to the minimal size of their groupings within the UK as a whole, although they have tried to counter this by forming a single parliamentary group. MPs pay attention to their postbag and other forms of constituency pressure. Insofar as the public have taken note of devolution at all, and have views, it is in the area of the perceived injustices of the Barnett formula, and the overrepresentation of Scots in Parliament and the government rather than the scrutiny of legislation.[8]

The first session of the 2001 Parliament, the first Parliament to be elected post-devolution, ended in November 2002, with modernisation activity a strong focus in both Houses. This was due to the appointment of forceful leaders in both the Commons and the Lords with a strong reform mission. Yet adjusting the practices and procedures of the Commons to reflect the reality of devolution did not feature in the agenda. Although there have been reforms to the Select Committee structure, these do not amount to the type of radical initiatives in the Scottish Parliament, where the roles of scrutinising bills at committee stage are combined with the scrutiny of the administration of individual departments of the Executive, in what is in effect a combination

---

[8] This may be seen in reaction to the appointment of Alistair Darling as Transport Secretary, summarised by Lord Tebbit in the Lords on 27 June 2002. HL Deb c1501.

of select and standing committees.[9] What was not in the Modernisation Committee report of September 2002 was as important as what was in it, as it represented a manifesto for change for the whole of the 2001 Parliament.[10] There was a perceptible nod to Scottish practice in the changes in sitting hours, but no increase in time devoted to backbench concerns.

Inter-Parliamentary Relations

There has not been a marked interest in importing procedural change from the new devolved bodies, but there are clear developments in inter-parliamentary relations, often sponsored by the permanent staff of the institutions. The devolved parliaments/assemblies have joined the Commonwealth Parliamentary Association as well as the British-Irish Inter-Parliamentary Body, transformed since the Good Friday agreement to cover all UK parliamentary bodies, including the Channel Isles. This has enabled direct contact between MSPs and Dail members. But continued unionist opposition to the Body has inhibited progress. The three devolution bodies have developed bilateral and multi-lateral relations with the wider Commonwealth and European family of parties.

Examples of official contacts include:[11]

- Visits and meetings of Presiding Officers
- meetings between parliamentary standards clerks and advisers/commissioners
- meetings between committee staff
- meetings between staff on FOI issues common to parliaments
- the Common Interest Group of finance and administration staff
- the Interparliamentary Information Services Forum, of research, information, reporting and IT staff.

A number of these meetings have included representatives from the Dail, as a relatively small legislature with Westminster traditions. But the limited size of the staffs of the smaller devolved bodies will act as a constraint on the number of secondments and exchanges in future.

The Post-Devolution House of Commons

The pre-devolution structure of the Commons remains fairly intact, as in the last Parliament. There are three Grand Committees which are convened when the government wishes, as forms of mini chambers, to hear ministerial

---

[9] For a short summary of the different types of committee at Westminster see the House of Commons Information Office factsheets at the parliament website www.parliament.uk

[10] *Modernisation of the House of Commons: A Reform Programme* Session 2001–2 HC 1168.

[11] See House of Lords Constitution Select Committee on the constitution Session 2001–02 *Devolution: Inter-institutional relations in the United Kingdom* Evidence complete to 10 July 2002 HL Paper 147.

statements, to provide a forum for oral questions and to hear set-piece debates on broad policy topics. These have no permanent secretariat and are chaired by the appropriate member of the Chairmen's Panel — a group of senior members expected to act as impartial chairs. There are three Select Committees which look into rather restricted subject areas, but which still manage to cover topics touching on the responsibilities of devolved administrations, because of the rather blurred boundaries between devolved and reserved matters. Each piece of legislation, whether applicable to the UK, Great Britain or England and Wales is still voted on by every member of the Commons, regardless of territorial considerations. Select Committee membership is not determined by territorial considerations, and committees which have UK wide responsibilities, such as Home Affairs and Foreign Affairs, are appointed without overt concern for representation from all the constituent parts of the UK. One innovation, a mini-chamber held in Westminster Hall, was designed principally to take less important business away from the main chamber of the Commons, and only incidentally as a forum for debating issues of concern to the nations and regions.[12] As part of the Cook reforms it has become a permanent arrangement, but with no particular territorial bias.

Further major change is unlikely in this Parliament because there is little pressure both within and without. The modernisation agenda does not include the establishment of English structures at Westminster. Change is likely to be slow and incremental.

Of more immediate interest is the subtly changing role of the Scottish and Welsh MPs, who have to adjust their parliamentary roles to the reality of the new devolved institutions. As yet, there is little evidence of major developments there either, as discussed below. MPs from Northern Ireland face many of the same pressures, but the uncertain stability of devolution there and their paucity of numbers make them a special case to be considered elsewhere.

The House of Lords

Similar modernisation initiatives are underway in the Lords, designed to regularise sitting hours and streamline the scrutiny of legislation. The Lords has however recognised the reality of the devolution settlement through the establishment of the new Constitution Committee.[13] This was a recommendation of the Wakeham Commission. Its remit is 'keep under review the operation of the constitution'.[14] It is no accident that it is the House with no government majority which has taken the initiative in scrutinising constitutional developments. The Committee has just completed an inquiry into the inter-institutional arrangements of devolution.

---

[12] For background on Westminster Hall see Hazell, R. and Russell, M., in *State and the Nations*, 2000.

[13] See Hazell, R. and Masterman, R., in *State of the Nations 2001* for background to the establishment of the Committee.

[14] HL Deb, 8 February 2001 c1269.

Evidence presented to the Committee suggested that AMs, MSPs, MLAs and MPs were not making the most of the opportunities to interact. It is evident that discussion and negotiation on legislation is taking place at the inter-governmental rather than the inter-parliamentary level, and this is unsurprising, considering that backbenchers are rarely early participants in the policy-making process.

The main focus of the Committee was inter-governmental relations (although it commissioned a paper on inter-parliamentary links) and these are expected to form the major recommendations of the report, due by January 2003. Whatever the final recommendations, the Lords has established itself as the House which is prepared to acknowledge and examine in some detail the new constitutional arrangements post-devolution. Its regular reports on bills are also offering a high-quality assessment of any points of constitutional significance, comparable to the work of the Delegated Powers Scrutiny Committee.

Further reform of the Lords awaits some kind of political majority, and developments this year are summarised on pp. 190-91.

THE ROLE OF MPs FROM SCOTLAND AND WALES

The Constitution Committee took evidence on the need for procedural changes at Westminster to take account of devolution. But the lack of interest from the Leader of the House, Robin Cook, was plain. His evidence was essentially conservative, with no plans for innovation in procedures.

Overall the chairs of the three territorial select committees considered that their role as territorial members had not been much affected by devolution, undertaking legislative and departmental scrutiny in much the same way as before. In terms of constituency work, many MPs were of the same party as the local constituency MSP/AM, which lessened room for conflict. The long-term development of the constituency roles forms the focus for a major ESRC project, with Constitution Unit input, due to run until 2004 .

Evidence suggests that both Scots and Welsh MPs have been overshadowed in the media and the public mind by their counterparts in the relevant Parliament/Assembly.[15] There is greater potential for closer working than in the early devolution days, when members of devolved bodies were concerned to assert themselves over more experienced MPs, but formidable obstacles remain to effective joint scrutiny with tangible outputs. In practice, devolved parliaments/assemblies have different policy agendas and different work timetables from Westminster.

MPs from Scotland and Wales are still adapting to the post-devolution world. Although a minority has consciously sought a national role, focussing

[15] See for example evidence from John Osmond to House of Lords Constitution Select Committee on the constitution Session 2001–02 *Devolution: Inter-institutional relations in the United Kingdom* Evidence complete to 10 July 2002 HL Paper 147.

on UK-wide issues, this is not a path followed by the majority.[16] Conversely, Northern Irish MPs have traditionally concentrated on policy developments in their constituent part of the UK, whether devolution is in force or not. As yet, Scots and Welsh MPs do not seem to be retreating into a role which is solely territorial either. Most appear to value the wider Westminster focus. However, data on their participation in divisions indicates that Scots MPs are significantly less active in the division lobbies:

Figure 7.1: Average participation rates of MPs in House of Commons divisions, 1999–2001[17]

1999–2000 Session:	
Location of consituencies	**Average participation rate**
England	64.7%
Scotland	51.1%
Wales	59.7%
Northern Ireland	16.7%
UK	61.8%
2000–2001 Session:	
Location of constituencies	**Average participation rate**
England	62.5%
Scotland	47.9%
Wales	63.3%
Northern Ireland	19.9%
UK	60.0%

Data from pre-devolution sessions is not yet available, so it is impossible to indicate whether the differentiation is part of a long-term trend. Also, participation in divisions is hardly the only or indeed the main indicator of activity within the Commons, it is simply the only quantitative indicator yet available. Moreover Scottish MPs are most likely to be excused divisions by whips, because of travel considerations.

In the period 1997–2002 there has been a 'significant increase' in the total number of parliamentary questions asked.[18] This has not been the case,

---

[16] Examples include Archy Kirkwood on social security and Donald Anderson on foreign policy.

[17] House of Commons Library, unpublished data.

[18] Several reasons have been put forward for this increase in the number of questions asked. See: House of Commons Procedure Committee, Parliamentary Questions Report, HC 622, 2001–02 session.

however, in terms of the number of questions that have been put to the Secretaries of State for Scotland, Wales and Northern Ireland, where an opposite trend has occurred. Regarding oral questions, Irene Adams, Chair of the Scottish Select Committee, noted that the hour on Scottish questions pre-devolution had reduced to 30 minutes, and that only questions 2 or 3 were reached on the order paper; her views were echoed by Michael Mates, Chair of the Northern Ireland Select Committee, who noted that Northern Ireland questions had reduced from an hour to half an hour and that questions rarely reached number 3.[19] Since the suspension of devolution in Northern Ireland, David Trimble has called for Northern Ireland questions to be restored to one hour.[20] It is notable that the opposition maintain a significant presence in the number of oral and written questions tabled to the territorial offices.

So devolution has led to an overall reduction in the number of parliamentary questions put to the Secretaries of State for Scotland and Wales, as set out in the tables below.

Figure 7.2: Parliamentary questions to the Welsh Office and Wales Office, 1997–2002[21]

	1997/1998 (18 months)	1998/1999 (12 months)	1999/2000 (12 months)	2000/2001 (5 months)	2001/2002 (10 months)
Oral	370	204	264	79	153
Written	2147	1073	548	183	510

Figure 7.3: Parliamentary questions to the Scottish and Scotland Office, 1997–2002[22]

	1997/1998 (18 months)	1998/1999 (12 months)	1999/2000 (12 months)	2000/2001 (5 months)	2001/2002 (10 months)
Oral	492	252	127	70	115
Written	2377	1209	364	189	516

[19] House of Lords Constitution Select Committee on the constitution Session 2001–02 *Devolution: Inter-institutional relations in the United Kingdom* Evidence complete to 10 July 2002 HL Paper 147 para. 1402.

[20] *House Magazine* October 28 2002.

[21] Source: Parliamentary Online Information System (POLIS), Note: Figures for 1998/1999 refer to questions to either the Welsh Office or the Wales Office, since this is the session during which the National Assembly for Wales was established and the Wales Office replaced the Welsh Office at Westminster; Figures for 2001/2002 include the period up to May 2002 only; These figures vary slightly from those given in 'State and the Nations 2001,' this is due to the reconciliation of statistics by POLIS at the end of each session.

[22] Source: POLIS, Note: Figures for 1998/1999 refer to questions to either the Scottish Office or the Scotland Office, since this is the session during which the Scottish Parliament was established and the Scotland Office replaced the Scottish Office at Westminster; Figures for 2001/2002 include the period up to May 2002 only; These figures vary slightly from those given in 'State and the Nations 2001,' this is due to the reconciliation of statistics by POLIS at the end of each session.

The Departmental Select Committees

Some Departmental Select Committees cover topics which are reserved and therefore apply across the UK, some deal in subjects, such as transport, which of necessity take in devolved areas. Welsh and Scottish members are to be found within the ranks of these other types of select committees, and a minority, such as Archy Kirkwood (Work and Pensions), Martin O'Neill (Trade and Industry), John McFall (Treasury Committee), Jimmy Hood (European Scrutiny) and Alan Williams (Liaison Committee) are chairmen with a distinct focus on UK wide issues.

The initial hypothesis was that these committees would become differentiated between UK and English issues, with Scottish, Welsh and Northern Irish representation confined to the former type of committee. However it is difficult to categorise any but Foreign Affairs and International Development as exclusively dealing with reserved issues, as enquiries by committees cover a whole range of topics. Membership of the committees does not necessarily reflect the scope of enquiries (see figure 7.4).

In the House of Commons there are 529 members representing English constituencies, 72 representing Scotland, 40 representing Wales and 18 representing Northern Ireland.

It is therefore surprising that the Home Affairs committee, which deals mainly with matters affecting the whole of the UK, consists solely of English MPs. This is in a session when its main reports have been on anti-terrorism legislation (reserved), drugs policy (reserved) and the Police Reform bill (mainly but not entirely England and Wales). Another interesting point is the absence of a Scots MP on the Foreign Affairs Committee, the main committee whose focus could be considered entirely on reserved matters. The Treasury Committee, chaired by a Scot, John McFall, has been conducting an enquiry into regional spending, which is likely to provoke some interest when published.

The hypothesis did not take account of the fact that very few topics indeed are 'English' in nature, due to the particular form of Welsh devolution, but also due to the blurred boundary between devolved and reserved matters. The Transport, Local Government and Regions Committee[23] ought, under this hypothesis, to cover simply English interests but a number of its enquiries do not fall within this category. In 2001–2 it covered topics as diverse as the financing of air traffic control (reserved), European regeneration (mixed reserved/devolved) and ordnance survey (reserved) as well as more obviously devolved subjects such as planning, the bus industry and the draft local government bill for England and Wales. The Culture Media and Sport Committee covered gambling (reserved), the Manchester Commonwealth

---

[23] Now renamed the Committee for the Office of the Deputy Prime Minister, following the reorganisation of the summer of 2002.

games (devolved) and the Wembley National Stadium (devolved) in the same session. Although whips do pay some attention to balancing representation regionally, they did so pre-devolution to take account of party groupings.

Figure 7.4: Membership of House of Commons Select Committees, 2001–2, according to territory

Select Committee	England	Scotland	Wales	Northern Ireland	Total
Culture, Media and Sport	7	3	1	0	11
Defence	9	2	0	0	11
Education and Skills	11	0	0	0	11
Environment, Food and Rural Affairs	16	0	0	1	17
Foreign Affairs	10	0	1	0	11
Health	11	0	0	0	11
Home Affairs	11	0	0	0	11
International Development	9	2	0	0	11
Northern Ireland Affairs	7	1	1	4	13
Office of the Deputy Prime Minister	11	0	0	0	11
Scottish Affairs	1	10	0	0	11
Trade and Industry	8	2	1	0	11
Transport	9	1	0	1	11
Treasury	10	1	0	0	11
Welsh Affairs	2	0	9	0	11
Work and Pensions	8	3	0	0	11
TOTAL	140	25	13	6	184

Modernisation and the Select Committees

As a Scot, Mr Cook was hardly unaware of the procedural innovations of the Scottish Parliament and referred to the new institution, in his Constitution Unit sponsored State of the Nations lecture in December 2001, as providing food for thought for Westminster. But when his reforms of the committee system were unveiled in February 2002, they did not amount to a root and branch reform of the handling of parliamentary business akin to the Scottish Parliament's committee system.[24]

Not all the Committee's proposals were accepted when put to the vote on 14 May 2002. An amendment sponsored by the SNP, welcoming the Modernisation Committee proposals to increase committee size to 15 and thereby improve the number of seats available to the minority parties was defeated.[25] A move to a 15 strong membership is now left to each individual committee.[26]

Other reforms did survive. Select committees must now follow a series of core tasks and a new staffing unit within the clerks department will provide new resources for two rather neglected aspects of scrutiny — financial and pre-legislative. As yet, there are no signs that the extra resources to be devoted to pre-legislative scrutiny will be focused on the territorial aspects of bills, despite the need highlighted by the key territorial committee, that for Welsh Affairs.

The Work of Territorial Select Committees

The Welsh Affairs Committee's terms of reference encompass the relations of the Office of Secretary of State for Wales with the Assembly, enabling the Committee to examine the impact of UK government policy on Wales.[27] This has enabled the Committee to cover broader topics than its counterparts in Scotland and Northern Ireland. These include social exclusion, transport, EU Objective One funding and farming and food prices. Its ambitious examination of the way Welsh interests are reflected in primary legislation has begun again after a long hiatus.[28] The topic of enquiry was clearly influenced by pressure from the Assembly and evidence sessions have been held there in October 2002. The requirement for primary legislation to be taken at Westminster gives the Committee a potentially influential role. The Welsh Affairs Committee carried out a scrutiny of the first Wales only draft bill — the NHS (Wales) bill, which was then debated again in Welsh Grand.[29] It is difficult to argue that this is effective use of scarce scrutiny time at Westminster. The practice of printing Assembly responses to Welsh Affairs Committee reports seems, by contrast, an innovative development.[30]

---

[24] For full background see Winetrobe, B.K. *Realising the Vision: A Parliament with a Purpose: An Audit of the first year of the Scottish Parliament* (London: The Constitution Unit, 2001).

[25] HC Deb, 14 May 2002 c712.

[26] HC Deb, 14 May 2002 c658 where Mr Cook acknowledged the objections of the Liaison Committee to an increase, as tending to affect the cohesion of committees. Representation of minority parties did not therefore feature as a major factor in the decision.

[27] Standing Order 152.

[28] Welsh Affairs Committee Press Notice 24 July 2002.

[29] HC 959 2001–2, reporting on 10 July. The debate in the Welsh Grand was on 16 July 2002.

[30] See HC 604 2001–2 , response from National Assembly to Third Report of the Committee of Session 1999–2000 on Social Exclusion; and HC 311 2001–2 Response from National Assembly to First Report of the Committee 2000–2001 on Wales in the World.

Martyn Jones, chair of the Welsh Select Committee, was careful to promote his committee before the Constitution Committee, as a liaison route between Assembly and Westminster on matters of legislation. He called for greater resources to enable the committee to carry out this function, noting:

> At the moment we have had to drop everything to look at the draft NHS bill, and we have simply managed to do that. On top of that there are parts of other England and Wales legislation that are not being covered, understandably, by other departmental committees. At the moment we have the role, but we do not have the ability to look at each Bill as it goes through the House of Commons to identify the consequences for Wales.[31]

The Welsh Affairs Committee is particularly under-resourced, with only one clerk and an assistant. It ought to have a role in analysing all legislation with an impact on Wales, but will have an impossible role to fulfill unless its staff is augmented. One possibility is the new scrutiny unit to be set up under the general modernisation reforms instituted by Robin Cook, but there has been no indication as yet that it will have a focus on territorial issues. This is one area where the Richard Commission might have some impact.

In the post-devolution Commons, the territorial Select Committees continue to function with some significant differences in roles. The Scottish Affairs Committee has undertaken a broad range of enquiries involving some overlap with devolved matters, such as Poverty in Scotland. It has already invited ministers from the Scottish Executive to give evidence.[32] Its major work in 2001–2 was a series of short, focused enquiries on post-devolution news and current affairs broadcasting, the customs service and employment around the Clyde — all reserved topics dealing with the work of UK departments. The former was the only one to excite attention at Holyrood, where interest in broadcasting matters is intense. Some indication of the rivalry between MPs and MSPs is given in the following extract from the report:

> A habit of some news and current affairs broadcasters in Scotland, which to our mind is a symptom of editorial laziness, is the tendency to interview MSPs, no matter what the subject in question.[33]

There was suspicion in Holyrood that the decision to choose this topic was prompted by a desire to see the media focus on MPs, rather than MSPs.

The Northern Ireland Affairs Select Committee's remit covers the Northern Ireland Office when devolution is in operation. If suspension continues

---

[31] House of Lords Constitution Select Committee on the constitution Session 2001–02 *Devolution: Inter-institutional relations in the United Kingdom* Evidence complete to 10 July 2002 HL Paper 147 para. 1365.

[32] Minister for the Communities gave evidence on 22 March 2000 on poverty; the Deputy Minister for Environment and Rural Development gave evidence on 31 October 2001 on the drinks industry in Scotland.

[33] *Post Devolution News and Current Affairs Broadcasting in Scotland* HC 549 2001–2.

for more than a month, its standing orders may need to be revised to cover the whole of Northern Ireland's administration. It chose a detailed policy area for its first enquiry in the new Parliament — the operation of the aggregates levy and this resulted in a temporary and partial concession on the levy in Northern Ireland.[34] The Committee launched a further report on cross-border fuel-price differentials, again choosing a discrete topic, which was over-looked in a UK context.

The Northern Ireland Select Committee has more of a concentration of minority party members than its equivalents in Scotland and Wales, where Labour forms the dominant party and provides the chair. This illustrates the separate party system there. Northern Irish MPs are rarely involved in departmental committee scrutinies on English or British matters.[35]

Joint Committee Meetings

Although there have been some meetings, effective joint working has proved elusive, due to other factors. Contacts between the Scottish Affairs Commit-tee and the Convenors' Liaison Group occurred over the possibility of joint working on 14 February 2002 and there is regular contact between clerks. But Irene Adams noted in the evidence to the Constitution Committee how the operation of privilege prevented joint working and that ground rules needed to be established to cover anything other than routine joint meetings. There seems little evidence that the Scottish Parliament has great interest in the workings of Westminster. Pressures of time and resources appear to make joint working difficult, and the devolved bodies seem be putting more effort into links with each other than with Westminster.

The Welsh Affairs Committee has regular meetings with the panel of chairs at the Assembly. It has given and received evidence to and from the Assembly, and its chair, Martyn Jones, has indicated that it has reached an informal concordat in asking the Assembly for issues to be taken up by the Committee. A major instance is the Committee's enquiry into the legislative process in Wales.[36] Difficulties with timetables cause problems, since the Welsh Affairs Committee tends to conduct business in Wales on Mondays, when Assembly members are in their constituencies or regions.[37] John Marek, Deputy Presiding Officer, noted the difficulties in arranging joint meetings in any detailed way given the onerous responsibilities of both types

---

[34] House of Lords Constitution Select Committee on the constitution Session 2001–02 *Devolution: Inter-institutional relations in the United Kingdom* Evidence complete to 10 July 2002 HL Paper 147, evidence from Michael Mates, Chairman of the Northern Ireland Select Committee, referring to HC 333 2001–2 para. 19.

[35] *Ibid.,* evidence from Michael Mates, para. 1367.

[36] *Ibid.,* evidence from Martyn Jones, para. 1378.

[37] *Ibid.,* paras 21–22. This gives examples where Committee members taken evidence to Assembly committees.

of member.[38] Timetables in the Assembly are set well in advance, making it difficult for committees to arrange joint sessions.

The Assembly Review of Procedure's support for an annual meeting between AMs and the Welsh Grand and Welsh Select Committee was endorsed by the Welsh Affairs Committee.[39] But it is difficult in practice to achieve joint work which has real added value.

The Scottish Parliament has launched the EC-UK network, consisting of chairs of relevant European committees in the Lords and the Commons, the Scottish Parliament, the Northern Ireland Assembly and the Scottish Parliament. It meets twice a year.[40]

Irene Adams called for a role for select committees in scrutinising inter-governmental outputs, such as Joint Ministerial Committees, commenting on the lack of transparency in her evidence to the Constitution Committee.[41] This appears to be an area where territorial select committees could make a real impact, since IGR remains seriously under-scrutinised, but lack of staff resources inhibits their further development.

The Grand Committees

It was expected that these committees would not long survive the advent of devolution, as they were designed in a pre-devolution era to offer some kind of territorial expression to MPs in Scotland, Wales and Northern Ireland. Nevertheless, there is no sign of their imminent demise. Grand Committees encompass all the members of a particular constituent part of the UK. They are standing committees with very little life from meeting to meeting, and chaired by the appropriate member of the chairman's panel. They have no forward work-plans. They offer an additional forum for debate on territorial issues, but the discourse rarely rises above partisan point scoring. There appears to be support still for their existence, however, with English Conservatives registering only a bare majority for their abolition. A majority of English Labour MPs support their continuance.[42]

Professor Keith Patchett has considered the survival of the Grand Committee would depend on its undertaking a legislative role.[43] On 10 July 2002, the draft NHS Wales bill was referred to the Welsh Grand for consideration, following scrutiny by the Welsh Affairs Committee. This at least keeps

---

[38] *Ibid.,* evidence from Lord Elis-Thomas, para. 943.

[39] *Ibid.,* evidence from Lord Elis-Thomas, para. 7.

[40] *Ibid.,* evidence from Lord Steel, Annex B para. 18.

[41] *Ibid.,* evidence from Irene Adams, para. 1358–60.

[42] Initial data from survey of English MPs carried out by Constitution Unit in summer of 2002. The Constitution Unit expects to publish some substantial research shortly on the results of surveys and interviews with MPs in 2000 and 2002.

[43] House of Lords Constitution Select Committee on the constitution Session 2001–02 *Devolution: Inter-institutional relations in the United Kingdom,* evidence complete to 10 July 2002 HL Paper 147, evidence to Constitution Committee from Keith Patchett para 34–36.

alive its role in the scrutiny of legislation. But the debate consisted mainly of party points. The big question for the survival of the Grand's legislative role will be whether the Welsh Grand takes the bill when actually introduced into Parliament.

The Standing Committee on the English Regions was once seen as a potentially important innovation, allowing the expression of regional interests.[44] But the format in which the committee has been established considerably limits its powers. It suffers from the same disadvantage as the Grand Committees, because it is also a standing committee. Confusingly this means that it has no permanent secretariat, and the frequency of its meetings is controlled by the government through the usual channels. It will not be able to develop into a forum offering a real representational role to English MPs until it achieves a different procedural form and establishes some autonomy for itself, akin to a Select Committee which decides its own agenda.

The Modernisation Committee report of September 2002 was silent about the continued existence of the Scottish, Northern Irish and Welsh Grand Committees and the Territorial Select Committees, whose functions differ markedly in scope from a standard Departmental Select Committee. Nor did opposition disapproval of modernisation stem from concerns to speed the pace of post-devolution procedures.[45]

Figure 7.5: Meetings of the Scottish Grand Committee, 2001–2

Date	Subject of Debate
28 November 2001	Scotland in the World a New Perspective
13 February 2001	Scottish Energy in the 21st Century
5 March 2002	Defence in Scotland
8 May 2002	North Sea Oil and Gas Industry
10 July 2002	Social Inclusion

Figure 7.6: Meetings of the Welsh Grand Committee, 2001–2

Date	Subject of Debate
3 July 2001	Legislative Programme
28 November 2001	Pre-Budget Statement (Implications for Wales)
24 April 2002	Budget Statement
16 July 2002	Draft National Health Service (Wales) Bill

---

[44] See Masterman, R. and Hazell, R., in *State of the Nations 2001* for the development of the Committee.

[45] Conservatives raised no concerns about the treatment of territorial issues during the debate on the Modernisation Committee report on 29 October 2002.

Figure 7.7: Meetings of the Northern Ireland Grand Committee, 2001–2

Date	Subject of Debate
13 December 2001	Draft Criminal Injuries Compensation (Northern Ireland) Order 2001
27 June 2002	Scope for a Bill of Rights
24 October	Draft Access to Justice (Northern Ireland) Order

Figure 7.8: Meetings of the Standing Committee on Regional Affairs, 2001–2

Date	Subject of Debate
18 December 2001	Governance in England
12 March 2002	Regional Development Agencies
17 July 2002	White Paper, Your Region, Your Choice: Revitalising the English Regions'

SCRUTINY OF LEGISLATION

The scrutiny of legislation has not changed in its essentials since pre-devolution days. There are no special procedures in use for the consideration of legislation which has a particular impact on individual nations and regions. The procedures which are technically available in the standing orders of the House, such as the potential for the Grand Committees to take the consideration of bills in committee, are not used. The government has no real incentive to allow it, and the opposition would fiercely resist, since its representation in the Grand Committees is minimal and it would lose all chance of amendment. Ordinary backbenchers do not have the power to achieve the referral of legislation to Grand Committees.

The carry-over procedures for bills, elements of which the Modernisation Committee report has initiated are intended to reflect elements of the Scottish practice. There was also a nod towards the Scottish Parliamentary Bureau role in allocating business in the recommendation for collective consultations with other parties on the broad shape of the legislative year, but plans to establish a Business Committee in the Commons never even reached the Commons since they were never formally published, having apparently foundered in Cabinet.

The original Cook memorandum, presented to the Modernisation Committee in December 2001, referred to a possible process of pre-legislative scrutiny for Wales – only bills, enabling the legislation to be examined in parallel in Westminster and in the Assembly.[46] Lord

---

[46] *Modernisation of the House of Commons: A Reform Programme for Consultation* HC 440 2001–2.

Elis-Thomas has called for a much more radical extension of the proposal to all clauses applying to Wales, which would be grouped separately. He pointed out that Wales-only bills are very rare, with two since 1997. The final Modernisation Committee report made no allusion to either of these proposals for the scrutiny of Welsh legislation.

Legislation — The West Lothian Question

We have seen how the Procedure Committee proposals of 1998–9 for territorial treatment of bills were ignored by the Government, and the so-called West Lothian Question put on one side.[47] The issue has now died away, with no private members' bills on the topic in this new Parliament so far. It is noticeable that Iain Duncan Smith's Shadow Cabinet has had very little to say on this. The more outspoken supporters for a solution to the Question in the previous Parliament, Eric Forth and David Maclean, have accepted the inhibitions of front-bench office but more importantly the new Conservative leader is determined to keep his party from highlighting constitutional issues. Labour members show little interest, pointing to the decades of Conservative votes determining policies for Scotland and Wales, and the Liberal Democrat leader is himself a Scot, but with an inevitable UK focus. But expected legislation on maintaining the current numbers of MSPs at Holyrood may provoke some comment on the revised role of the reduced number of Scots MPs at Westminster.

The West Lothian Question was taken seriously only by the Presiding Officers in their evidence to the Constitution Committee. Lord Elis-Thomas noted that he had never yet voted 'on a devolved matter which would be controversial [in Wales] and I would not do that. For example, fox-hunting, upon which I voted with relish, was not a devolved matter [in Wales] and therefore the way I voted on it was entirely non-controversial!'[48] Lord Steel also indicated that he voted sparingly in the Lords: 'If you look at my voting record in the Lords, it is appalling, because I deliberately do not vote on anything that might even be remotely connected — whether it is the same subject that is being debated in the Parliament or something that might come to the Parliament. I am very careful. I am really a non-participating member of the House of Lords'.[49] Some of their reticence may also be attributed to their impartial role in the Chair. The Constitution Committee showed very little interest in the whole Question in evidence so far published.

There may be a minor revival of the issue, should there be a bill on banning fox-hunting next session, given the separate legislation in the Scottish

[47] For background, see *Constitutional Futures* and *The State and the Nations 2000.*

[48] House of Lords Constitution Select Committee on the constitution Session 2001–02 *Devolution: Inter-insitutional relations in the United Kingdom* Evidence complete to 10 July 2002 HL Paper 147, evidence to the Constitution Committee para. 935.

[49] *Ibid.*, evidence Lord Steel, para. 773.

Parliament. Tam Dalyell has indicated that he would not vote on an England and Wales bill.[50]

In the absence of the type of radical reforms suggested by the Procedure Committee, the following sections look at some developments in the treatment of legislation in the territorial areas apart from England.

Legislation for Northern Ireland

The political volatility of Northern Ireland ensures a steady stream of legislation applicable only to that part of the UK. Since the 2001 general election there have already been three statutes, and in the parliamentary debates there has been no suggestion that only Northern Ireland members should vote on the legislation. The statutes are:

- Electoral Fraud (Northern Ireland) Act
- Justice (Northern Ireland) Act
- Northern Ireland Arms Decommissioning Act[51]

The Northern Ireland Grand Committee has considered proposals for draft Orders in Council since 1999, and this gives the Committee a definite role at Westminster.[52] Section 85 of the Northern Ireland Act 1998 provided for consultation by both the Assembly and Parliament on legislation relating to reserved matters and this appears to work well.

The Sewel procedure exists in principle in Northern Ireland, but has not been exercised in practice. Parity legislation can be seen as 'Sewel in reverse' since it refers to legislation which the Assembly feels obliged to pass to keep in step with the rest of the UK. This is particularly relevant for social security benefits. There is scope for further development of relations between Assembly Committees and Westminster when or if devolution returns.

Legislation for Wales

Following from the Principles which it wished to see adopted in Government bills affecting the Assembly, set out in the Assembly Review of Procedure, the Presiding Officer made a series of demands, which were echoed by other commentators on Wales giving evidence to the Lords Constitution Committee:

- More formal procedures to allow direct co-operation between Welsh MPs and AMs in the scrutiny of legislation affecting Wales. The model was formally constituted joint meetings to consider both draft bills and legislation formally introduced to Parliament.

---

[50] The stance of the government was rehearsed by the then Home Secretary Jack Straw in a debate on the Hunting Bill 2000–2001 on 20 December 2000 HC Deb c380–381.

[51] This was UK wide in extent to allow for decommissioning of paramilitary arms in other parts of the UK.

[52] Life Sentences Order and Financial Investigations Order 22 March 2001; draft Criminal Injuries Compensation Order 13 December 2001.

- Welsh provisions in a bill to be separately considered by a Lords committee which would have power to take evidence from Assembly members.
- A drafting presumption towards a specific Welsh section within every England and Wales bill.

These principles will be very difficult to realise in practice, but they are likely to be endorsed by the Welsh Affairs Committee enquiry into the legislative process. A number of bills with powers separately given to the Assembly were passed in 2001–2, including:

- NHS Reform and Health Care Professions Act 2002
- Education Act 2002
- Homelessness Act 2002
- International Development Act 2002
- Travel Concessions (Eligibility) Act 2002

The first contained measures significantly affecting the organisation of the NHS in Wales, which were originally planned for a Wales-only bill.

An illustration of the difficulties faced by Welsh MPs in participating in the legislation affecting Wales is given in the NHS bill in November 2001, when on the morning of second reading Jon Owen Jones sent his researcher to examine consultation responses only just lodged in the House of Commons Library. An analysis of responses illustrated that the consensus on change described by the Welsh administration did not exist. He made an intervention in the debate, noting that the proposals had not been debated in the Assembly and were being dealt with only perfunctorily at Westminster.[53] A major difficulty in co-operative working is that the timetables of the Assembly and of Westminster are out of synchronisation.[54] It is very difficult for the subject committees to make their views known before the relevant debate is held in Parliament.[55] The development of pre-legislative scrutiny would offer a more realistic timetable for the Assembly.

Legislation for Scotland
The following bills were passed since the 2001 general election with Sewel motions, which signified the Scottish Parliament's assent to Westminster legislation on matters devolved to Scotland;

---

[53] HC Deb 20 November 2001 c252. See evidence from John Osmond to House of Lords Constitution Select Committee on the constitution Session 2001–02 *Devolution: Inter-institutional relations in the United Kingdom* Evidence complete to 10 July 2002 HL Paper 147, para. 792.

[54] Supplementary evidence from John Osmond para. 57. House of Lords Constitution Select Committee on the constitution Session 2001–02 *Devolution: Inter-institutional relations in the United Kingdom* Evidence complete to 10 July 2002 HL Paper 147.

[55] House of Lords Constitution Select Committee on the constitution Session 2001–02 *Devolution: Inter-institutional relations in the United Kingdom* Evidence complete to 10 July 2002 HL Paper 147, evidence from Keith Patchett, Supplementary memo para. 9.

- Adoption and Children Bill
- Anti-Terrorism, Crime and Security Act 2001
- Enterprise Bill (RA expected October 2002)
- NHS reform and Care Professions Act 2002
- Police Reform Act 2002
- Proceeds of Crime Act 2002

There is no formal role for the Scottish Affairs Select Committee in scrutinising Sewel motion bills.[56] A number of witnesses to the Constitution Committee considered that Scottish members should develop such a role, particularly as subsequent amendments at Westminster are not routinely referred back to Holyrood. So far, MPs for Scotland do not appear to have adopted this role on a coherent basis. This is illustrated by studying the debates on the Proceeds of Crime Bill — a Sewel motion bill where SNP and Conservative members combined to illustrate policies perceived as detrimental to Scottish interests.[57] The Procedures Committee at Holyrood has begun to examine the operation of Sewel motions, which with SNP pressure may have some impact on Westminster in the current Parliament.

RELATIONSHIPS BETWEEN MPs AND MEMBERS OF
THE DEVOLVED PARLIAMENTS / ASSEMBLIES

This remains the trickiest aspect of post-devolution life for Scots and Welsh MPs. Lord Elis-Thomas indicated some difficulties in the relationships between AMs and MPs, with a feeling from the latter that they were being overshadowed. Although a working group established by Lord Steel set out the 'Reid principles' for dealing with relationships between constituency and list MSPs, it did not go on to establish similar principles for relationships between MSPs and MPs.[58] Responses from Westminster MPs to a survey conducted by the Constitution Unit in summer 2002 indicate difficult relationships in at least a minority of cases. Further surveys are planned in 2004. There is guidance from the Cabinet Office on how government departments should respond to constituency correspondence involving devolved matters, but this cannot govern the actions of MPs.[59]

Helen Liddell launched a review of the requirement in the Scotland Act 1998 to reduce the number of MSPs, in line with the reduction in the number of Scottish MPs upon completion of the current parliamentary boundary

[56] *Ibid.*, evidence from Irene Adams, para. 1376.

[57] Cited in evidence from Professor Alan Page to the Constitution Committee para 727, and see Winetrobe, B.K. 'Counter Devolution? The Sewel Convention on Devolved Legislation at Westminster' (2001) 6 *Scottish Law and Practice Quarterly* 286–92 and Page, A. and Batey, A., 'Scotland's other Parliament: Westminster legislation about devolved matters in Scotland since devolution' [2002] *Public Law*, pp. 501–23.

[58] For background see Winetrobe, B. K., 2001, pp. 27–38.

[59] *Guidance on handling correspondence under devolution* Devolution Guidance Note 2 1999.

reviews in 2005–6. Surprisingly, the consultation paper included some review of inter-member relations, but it remains to be seen whether that sensitive topic features in the conclusions, due in late 2002. The Boundary Commission for Scotland published its Fifth Periodical Review on 7 February 2002 recommending the reduction of Westminster constituencies in Scotland from 72 to 59. If the number of MSPs is to remain constant at 129 it will no longer be possible to maintain coterminous constituencies for MSPs and MPs.[60]

THE ROLE OF THE HOUSE OF LORDS

The role of the Lords as the House with a special interest in the constitution was a particular theme in the continuing saga of Lords reform post Wakeham.[61] At present, the House lacks any explicit territorial aspect. The White Paper issued on 7 November 2001 accepted only parts of the Wakeham Commission proposals, but weakened areas seen as essential to maintaining the independent and non-partisan nature of the House. It did not envisage a House of Nations and Regions, formed of indirectly elected members of the devolved parliaments/assemblies. The supporting documents stated: 'in the present state of the devolution settlement, it would not be right to ask the House of Lords to develop a special relationship with the devolved institutions'.[62] The 20 per cent elected element would be drawn from multi-member constituencies co-terminus with those used for the European Parliament. Scotland, Wales and Northern Ireland form single electoral regions for the European Parliament elections.

Public and political attention was caught by the decision to promote only a 20 per cent elected House (within the Wakeham range of 12–35 per cent). An immediate groundswell began for at least a 50:50 proportion between elected and appointed members, astutely channelled by the Public Administration Committee, whose chair, Tony Wright, stepped into the parliamentary vacuum. Dislike of a House predominantly composed of placemen was the major factor in the unpopularity of the White Paper.

Although Robin Cook floated the concept of indirect elections from the devolved parliaments/assemblies, the Committee did not endorse the suggestion, considering the Constitution Committee might canvass any demand from devolved bodies which might develop once elected assemblies existed in England. The evidence of the most recent Constitution Committee report did not touch on this matter and there is every indication of a lack of demand from existing AMs and MSPs. There is one major exception — the

---

[60] *The Size of the Scottish Parliament: A Consultation* published by the Scotland Office in December 2001.

[61] *A House for the Future* The Royal Commission on the Reform of the House of Lords Cmd 4534 January 2000.

[62] *Completing the Reforms* Support Documents December 2001 Chapter 3, para. 19.

position of the three Presiding Officers, all currently members of the Lords, more by accident than design. The three submitted a supplementary memorandum to the Constitution Committee setting out the advantages of their joint membership, which facilitated contacts between the devolved institutions and Westminster. It stated: 'very significantly, it has also allowed us to keep up-to-date with the thinking and actions of the UK Parliament. One of the key advantages in this has been to put us into the position of being able to contribute to the thinking of matters that are before the House of specific interest to Wales, Scotland and Northern Ireland'. They called for automatic membership of the Lords for their successor Presiding Officers — since both Lord Steel and Lord Alderdice will not be standing for the 2003 elections.

The Public Administration Committee did however consider a role for the parliaments/assemblies as nominating bodies for independent appointed members from their nations and regions.[63] Further thought is necessary about the constitution of the Appointments Commission, which might take on a federal model, rather as the Electoral Commission has Commissioners with separate responsibilities for the constituent parts of the UK.

Lord Irvine and Robin Cook made a simultaneous announcement of a joint committee of both Houses on 13 May 2002, to consider the next stage of Lords Reform. The first report of the Joint Committee, which has no Scottish MPs, is expected before Christmas.

CONCLUSION

Four years after devolution, the formal procedures of the Commons and the Lords show little sign of alteration. Both front benches remain resistant to suggestions for a more radical review of the operation of scrutiny post-devolution. There does not appear to be sufficient demand from the back-benches for real change. Scots and Welsh MPs have an interest in retaining specific forums, not least so that they can demonstrate to constituents how hard they are working for their local area. English MPs may feel the occasional resentment about the survival of pre-devolution structures, but these structures do not have a major impact on the operation of the House. Overt calls for English votes only on English legislation have fallen away since the passage of the devolution legislation, now that there is a greater appreciation of the complexity of the territorial extent of legislation.

There is a lack of understanding in the wider public of the conduct of business at Westminster, and the devolved assemblies/parliaments are absorbed with their own processes and structures.

The one major area where some kind of reform is likely remains the question of the treatment of legislation extending to Wales. Even if the power to initiate primary legislation is transferred to the Assembly, there is no realistic

[63] *The Second Chamber: Continuing the Reform* HC 494 2001–2 para. 148.

prospect of this occurring until after the next general election. There remain some years in which Parliament might attempt to offer a better scrutiny service for legislation which extends to Wales. The Commons is unusually preoccupied with modernisation of the legislative process at present, but the Assembly will need to develop more bargaining power than it yet possesses to ensure that any change is beneficial to Welsh interests.

BIBLIOGRAPHY

Official Documents
House of Commons Modernisation Committee *Modernisation of the House of Commons: A Reform Programme* HC 1168 Session 2001–2.
House of Commons Public Administration Committee *Ministerial Accountability and Parliamentary Questions* HC 1086 Session 2001–2.
House of Commons Scottish Affairs Committee *Post Devolution News and Current Affairs Broadcasting in Scotland* HC 549 Session 2001–2.
House of Commons Welsh Affairs Committee *Response from National Assembly to Third Report of the Committee of Session 1999–2000 on Social Exclusion* HC 604 Session 2001–2.
House of Commons Welsh Affairs Committee *Response from National Assembly to First Report of the Committee 2000–2001 on Wales in the World* HC 311 Session 2001–2.
House of Lords Constitution Select Committee on the constitution Session 2001–02 *Devolution: Inter-institutional relations in the United Kingdom* Evidence complete to 10 July 2002 HL Paper 147.

Secondary Sources
Hazell, R., 'Westminster: Squeezed from above' in R. Hazell (ed) *Constitutional Futures: A History of the Next Ten Years* (Oxford: Oxford University Press, 1999), pp. 111–135.
Hazell, R. and Masterman, R., 'Devolution and Westminster' in A. Trench (ed) *State of the Nations 2001: The Second Year of Devolution in the United Kingdom* (Exeter: Imprint Academic, 2001), pp. 197–224.
Hazell, R. and Russell, M., 'Devolution and Westminster: Tentative Steps Towards a More Federal Parliament' in R. Hazell (ed) *State and the Nations: the First Year of Devolution in the United Kingdom* (Exeter: Imprint Academic, 2000), pp. 183–222.
Osmond, J., *Reforming the House of Lords and Changing Britain,* Fabian Pamphlet 587, 1998.
Page, A. and Batey, A., 'Scotland's other Parliament: Westminster legislation about devolved matters in Scotland since devolution' [2002] *Public Law,* pp. 501–23.
Winetrobe B.K., *Realising the Vision: A Parliament with a Purpose An Audit of the first year of the Scottish Parliament* (London: The Constitution Unit, 2001).

Part III

Public Policy Divergence

8

Policy Divergence
Will it Change Something in Greenock?

Scott Greer

What explains policy divergence with devolution?

This is an important issue. Much of the justification for devolution was that there should be divergence — positive (giving all four countries their chance to experiment) and negative (making sure Northern Ireland, Scotland, and Wales would never again be subject to 'English' policies such as the poll tax). Great care went into designing the three devolved assemblies to ensure that they would be more democratic and accountable. Great care equally went into lobbyists' preparations to besiege the new bodies. If we want to find out what it all meant, there is hardly a better place to tell than health. It is one of the most devolved policy areas (the UK, almost uniquely, has no formal restrictions on social welfare variations; see the chapter 9 in this volume); it is one of the two most expensive things the governments do (education is the other big policy field for all of them and, for Westminster, social transfers and armed forces are its only other rivals); it affects the whole population; it is complicated and filled with strong professionals who often resent politicians' interference; its sunk costs are staggering; and it is made for media attention. If there is one mistake in a million in the UK health services, that means some government has a potential media explosion every twelve or fourteen hours.

The most common response is that it is too soon to tell if there has been meaningful divergence or what devolution will mean. Certainly, it is 'early days' both in the lives of the new political systems and in terms of the time-frames of health services (where little happens in less than five years), but we know that the formative moments of any political system shape it for its future and that disruptions on the scale of devolution shape organisations far more than the intentional efforts of later leaders. The first few years of devolution will almost certainly leave their mark on politics and the public services for decades to come. Given the extent of variation already — in structures, in policies, in long-term contracts, in bricks and mortar, in values, in personnel and in atmosphere — we can expect that the four UK systems will continue to diverge.

The first, short, section of this chapter presents a sketch framework for understanding devolved public and health policy. It stresses that devolved countries are sites for UK-wide, if not global, policy ideas to struggle; people interested in promoting markets, or new public health,[1] fight their corner wherever they are, regardless of whether that is in Scotland, England, or Manitoba. The bulk of the chapter touches on three important policy fields of health care: the organisation of health services; attention to new public health (i.e. socio-economic determinants of health and ill health); and the role of the private sector in a heretofore state-run system. In each case the different political systems vary according to the power of different advocates and their fit with the politics of the dominant party.

The data is primarily interview-based; the Devolution and Health project has conducted over 90 interviews in England, Northern Ireland, Scotland, and Wales as well as surveys and reviews of press and government documents. Working papers, monitoring reports, publications, and updated links to press and key government documents (including much of what is cited here) are available online at www.ucl.ac.uk/constitution-unit/d&h.

UNDERSTANDING DEVOLVED HEALTH POLICYMAKING

Policy outcomes are hardly random or exclusively the result of any one minister's ideas. They have advocates, they have people who work out the details, they have people who make the case and persuade others so that one idea, and not another, comes to prominence. There are broad — UK-wide, or increasingly global — coalitions of policy advocates hawking their wares to governments on every level.[2] These coalitions might advocate private-sector participation, wider forms of public health, markets, hierarchies, primary care, or any one of a range of ideas. Thus, Margaret Thatcher and Bill Clinton both tried reforming their different health systems in the early 1990s with ideas borrowed from a Stanford University economist, and now almost every country in Europe and North America is pursuing technology assessment schemes born in Oxford and Boston. For them, politics is a way to get policies enacted, and they pursue it where they live and where they can have the most impact (each health system has some high-level actors who chose to move there because they could pursue activities they wanted to pursue). Thus, when a new political arena appears on the map they will set about trying to shape its policies to the ends in which they believe.

The first factor determining their wins and losses is their institutional strength. Different policy advocacy coalitions have their roots in different institutions. Those who seek to standardise and improve medicine, and focus

---

[1] New Public Health is a movement dedicated to improving health via changes in economic and social conditions.

[2] Jenkins-Smith, H.C. and Sabatier, P.A. 'Evaluating the Advocacy Coalition Approach' in *Journal of Public Policy* 14 (2), 1994, pp. 175-203.

it on services, are based in universities, teaching hospitals, and Royal Colleges, and those are dense in some areas (England, Scotland) and almost invisible in others (Northern Ireland, Wales). Those who believe in markets are found where there are doctors and managers converted by their experience, a strong private sector, and right-wing think tanks — in England, but not the rest of the UK. The civil service in Wales and in England tends to have a different attitude towards health services versus public health. The key point is that these ideas are not best seen as the products of self-contained political systems, or as variations on a theme. They are options selected off menus, and the menus are set by advocacy coalitions and policy debates taking place around the world and strong in social institutions.

Thus, in each country there is an existing set of institutions with occupants who generally belong to consistent policy coalitions, and their balances vary greatly. Groups (such as pro-market advocates) that before devolution depended on winning their battles in London suddenly find that their lack of support on the ground in Northern Ireland, Scotland, and Wales has frozen them out of policy, while groups that rarely won in London but were strong in a devolved country suddenly can revel in their strength.

Policy advocates' influence comes from feeding up ideas, influencing debates, seconding advisors, or other influence. But the second factor political system also matters. There are two aspects of each political system that then determine any systematic variation in the results. The first, and in the UK the most important one, is the party system. A party is not just the creature of its activists and members; it is also shaped by the other parties in the system and they are in turn shaped by the basic cleavages in the society. The key point is that this means Labour cannot be the same party across England, Scotland, and Wales. In England, it is the centre-left and left party, facing a centre-right and right official opposition party. In Scotland and Wales, it is quite different — Labour is a centre-left unionist party with left, nationalist, opponents. In Scotland and Wales Labour fights on its left flank; in England it fights on its right flank. That means that Labour in England will often have strong reasons to move to the right when its Scottish and Welsh peers have cause to move left.

The other factor is the institutional framework of each polity. The key factor is the electoral system. England continues to be wholly governed by the Westminster system with its first-past-the-post votes and consequent tendency to exaggerated government majorities (and immense power for the executive). Scotland and Wales, however, have proportional representation. These work in ways that are good for small parties and bad for big parties. In both, Labour was denied a majority that it would have won under first-past-the-post. As a result it had to join a coalition with the Liberal Democrats. In addition, the nationalist opposition parties that had suffered under Westminster rules gained, and small parties that had not been able to muster a single MP won seats, bringing the Scottish Socialists, the Greens, and the Conservatives into Scottish political life. Finally, there are other institutional effects; these mostly amount to veto points, or points at which interested parties may stop a policy. Westminster famously has next to none (although judicial review might change that); Scotland and Wales, with their coalitions governing with small majorities, have a few more in committees and external constraints. In Northern Ireland the proportional representation system, an inclusive Executive, and a veto-ridden legislative structure represents all four major parties not just in the Assembly (where there are others as well) but also in the Executive, where they are under no effective obligation to consult with each other, pursue agreed policies, or fulfil ministerial obligations.

WHAT HAS HAPPENED?

This chapter discusses three aspects of health policy, each one crucial to health services. The first is the organisation of health services — the mechanisms that allocate resources and determine priorities. The question is whether governments try to allocate priorities and resources by market mechanisms or by planning, and to whose benefit they try to skew the system. The second is the 'new public health' agenda — the extent to which the health services focus on the causes of ill health rather than its treatment. The question is whether the focus of health policy should be providing health services as against emphasising prevention. The third is the relationship between public and private — the extent to which gsovernments try to keep the health services in the public sector, provided by the state, versus introducing the private sector as contractors or providers. Here, the question is whether the government tries to contract outsiders through PFI, or direct service contracts, or keep the service directly publicly provided.

Each system has taken a distinct path from the 1991 baseline of Margaret Thatcher's 'internal market.' England is the most market-based; the Labour government has pursued market-based service organisation and private participation and focused on service provision rather than new public health. Scotland is its near-opposite, rebuilding the unitary NHS with strong planning and service integration and a buyout of Scotland's most prominent private hospital as well as a small but meaningful commitment to new public health. Wales diverges not only in its reluctance to work with the private sector and its strong commitment to new public health but also in the way that commitment shapes its service organisation. Northern Ireland has changed little, retaining the 1991 internal market for want of a political structure able to change; it has thus combined a meaningful commitment to new public health and scepticism about the private sector with a market model derived from England. In each case the explanation has been the fit between the strongest advocacy coalitions in the country and the politicians' strategic positions; unless there is a good party reason not to, the politicians in charge tend to adopt the preferences of the strongest advocacy coalitions.

Organisation

Organisational charts are not, in themselves, interesting, but they are extremely important. They tell us what groups will determine the priorities for the health system — where new money will go, what day to day goals will be, what activities are rewarded, and how organisations such as hospitals will function. Primary care and hospital managers, hospital consultants, GPs, local government, and civil servants can all make good cases for their supremacy in the system; the organisational chart reflects their various victories or losses and can shape the system's priorities more than any ministerial directive.[3]

Health services organisation in the UK is roughly arranged along a continuum from market to hierarchy.[4] Market mechanisms, as adopted in England (and, earlier, by Thatcher), emphasise the power of purchasers and the beneficial effects of a *process* that responds to purchasers' demands. This model is based on the thesis that actual demand will be the best guide to the requirements of the system; opponents respond that it is wasteful and rarely exercises any competitive discipline. Hierarchical models, by contrast, integrate health services into large organisations that can allocate resources based on their long-range goals; the NHS was such an organisation before Margaret Thatcher, and Scotland is the model closest to it now. Its critics respond that it is bureaucratic and centralist (although the extent to which a central organisation can ever control professionals is in doubt). Where market mechanisms expect the process to produce the best health service outcomes, hierarchical systems expect good-quality regional *planning* to make sure that priorities and the structure of services are appropriate.

England

In England, the market had more supporters before devolution, in the policy circles in London, and it sank deeper roots between its implementation in 1991 and the arrival of Labour in 1997. As a consequence there were more advocates of market-based solutions — among policy intellectuals in close touch with their American equivalents, among GPs that enjoyed the clout of being customers, and among the management of the big hospitals that

---

[3] For a more detailed review of policy in this area up to mid-2001, see Greer, S. *Divergence and Devolution* (London: The Nuffield Trust, 2001) available at www.ucl.ac.uk/constitution-unit/d&h.

[4] For more on this logic and other possible models, see Tuohy, C. *Accidental Logics: The Dynamics of Change in the Health Care Arena in the United States, Britain, and Canada* (Oxford: Oxford University Press, 1999), chapter 1 (the degree to which market and hierarchy systems can avoid professional dominance is actually unclear).

enjoyed their new autonomy and positions at the centre of the health system. The result was that there was a strong set of policy advocates arguing the thesis that market mechanisms would produce Labour's desired outcomes of more efficiently delivered services. They were accustomed to formulating policy and advising government, and the hospitable right-wing press and Conservative party gave them ways to keep their ideas in play. The freedom of a Westminster government with a large majority, meanwhile, allowed the government to reshape public policy at will, magnifying the consequences of the pro-marketeers' victory. The party system finally gave Labour a different mission in England: defenders of the government argued that unless the public services were made to work, the main opposition party, the Conservatives, would take power and eliminate much of the welfare state. In short, the advice Labour received as it sought a 'modern' NHS was about the virtues of market logics and management while the competing ideas were mostly even further right.

The result is a system based on market logics: Primary Care Trusts, organisations responsible for population health in a given area, either provide services directly or contract for more advanced hospital and other care. They are the chosen clients in the system to whom sellers (hospitals, clinics, and specialists) must respond. Labour finished this pseudo-market by establishing a range of regulatory bodies designed to assure quality control.[5] Since then, Labour has further moved to wipe out many of the intermediate bodies that had been engaged in planning (such as NHS regions and, crucially, health authorities) and begun to experiment with 'foundation hospitals' that cut against the principle of equal treatment and instead try to give the best hospitals more freedom to work as providers in competitive marketplaces.

Scotland

In Scotland, on the other hand, advocates of the internal market had always been weaker and professional elites stronger. Thatcher's internal market won little support from GPs or most managers, and the powerful clinical elites and professionals of Scotland, as well as the public sector more generally, were suspicious of or opposed to horizontal market mechanisms. The Scottish party system, meanwhile, gave little advantage to right or centre-right solutions that smacked of the private sector or even differences in quality. The advice advocates gave was mostly pro-professional and pro-planning, and Labour was happy to hear it.

---

[5] The shape of the system is in Department of Health, *The New NHS: Modern-Dependable,* (London: HMSO, 1997) and then in Department of Health, *The NHS Plan: A plan for investment, a plan for reform* (London: HMSO, 2000). For changes since then, see the collection of documents titled 'Shifting the Balance' and for the key speech by Secretary of State Alan Milburn introducing the general idea (to general surprise), see 'Shifting the Balance of Power in the NHS' a speech given at the launch of the NHS Modernisation Agency, 25 April 2001.

Thus, from the 1997 elections onwards, Scottish policy eroded the autonomy of trusts and the importance of commissioning. Instead, the centre of gravity shifted back towards large regional health boards.[6] In the Scottish Health Plan,[7] the boards clearly became the centre — symbolically, the various NHS facilities in each region were given common identities based on their boards, replacing the multiplicity of trust names with the constant use of 'NHS Glasgow' and 'NHS Forth Valley.' This is a planning-oriented model, in which regional management is responsible for allocating resources and determining priorities. It allows priorities to enter the system that are not requested by the chosen purchasers — if England's PCTs do not want to purchase a service, the English system in theory makes it hard to offer it. In Scotland, the boards' preferences shape priorities and the boards are closely connected to the minister. The result is a system largely dominated by professionals and staff, under the intermittent control of the politicians and a small number of top managers.

Wales

Wales adopted a market system formally similar to that of England, but for different reasons and probably with different effects. In Wales, neither pro-market managers nor pro-hierarchy clinical elites are particularly strong; the internal market never won over a large contingent in Wales while its small number of teaching hospitals and lack of strong professional organisations mean professional elites are thin on the ground. Instead, local government and primary care loomed larger in Welsh health policy. Meanwhile, like Scotland, the Welsh opposition is to the left of Labour; Labour would expose its left flank to Plaid Cymru room to breathe if it were to move its commissioning model rightward alongside England (and Welsh Labour is uninterested in doing that anyway).

Their influence created a system in which Local Health Boards (LHBs) advise on the commissioning of care; this showed even in 1997-1998, when the Welsh system showed the strong influence of English ideas, and has since diverged as the Welsh pushed it away from English competitive, service-oriented models.[8] The principle is that accountability and distributive justice require that health be local, integrated, and close to the consumer, or central and accountable. As with England, the idea is that the centre of gravity will be the local area, but there is a key difference. While the English stacked commissioning in favour of service provision, the Welsh stacked it in favour

---

[6] This began with the last Scottish Office administration; see Scottish Office, *Designed to Care: Renewing the National Health Service in Scotland* (Edinburgh: HMSO, 1997).

[7] Scottish Executive Health Department, *Our National Health: a Plan for Action, a Plan for Change* (Edinburgh: HMSO, 2000).

[8] Welsh Office, *NHS Wales: Putting Patients First* (Cardiff: HMSO, 1998) and for post-devolution activity, Government of the National Assembly for Wales, *Improving Health in Wales: A plan for the NHS with its partners*, 2001.

of local health outcomes. They primarily did this by giving the commissioning powers to Local Health Boards, or LHBs. LHBs are descendants of the old Local Health Groups that inherited the powers of Health Authorities. The scheme tries to create a local focus by retaining a fragmented organisation that gives LHBs the same borders as local government, and by giving local government excellent representation on the boards (and encouraging some areas to go further, by, for example, merging the acute care trust, LHB, and local government link into one organisation).

The Welsh reorganisation has been deeply troubled, in large part for lack of adequate pre-planning; organisational structures between the local level and the Wales level, a problem everywhere, are particularly fuzzy and ill-thought-out in Wales. This reflects some hasty political decisions but also, and more fundamentally, the Welsh lack of policy capacity. The Welsh Office before devolution developed little capacity on its own and was ill-prepared to take on post-devolution tasks such as the redesign of a complicated health system. The Scottish Office and Northern Ireland Civil Service were both more adept at modifying policy, and the insistence of the Welsh Assembly Government that its running costs not increase has led to overwork and delay in the centre.

Northern Ireland

Northern Ireland is moving excruciatingly slowly — despite the general agreement that its health service is ill-organised and in crisis. This does not reflect its lack of policy capacity so much as the flaws of Northern Irish society. The Troubles, and the strange political and social environment of the Stormont years, have a gravitational pull that little can escape. The most prominent victims are the political parties and political arena in general; neither recruitment, nor advancement, nor electoral outcomes are determined by party stances on policy, and parties accordingly are ill-prepared to discuss policy and must learn a great deal. Another prominent victim is the structure of devolved government, which is designed to induce parties to take office rather than to produce responsibility for policy. As a result, health policy is a distraction as well as a vote-loser, and the Sinn Féin minister accordingly tried to avoid reorganisation. There is latent demand in the Service for reorganisation and in the population for a different system; the problem is that the parties are unable to translate it into effective demand while the political institutions and small policy communities have difficulty supplying new ideas.

Labour had bequeathed Green Papers suggesting different options, ranging roughly from the Scottish to the English.[9] When the devolved govern-

---

[9] Northern Ireland Department of Health and Social Services, *Fit For the Future: A consultation document on the Government's proposals for the future of the Health and Personal Social Services in Northern Ireland* (Belfast: HMSO, 1998).

ment started up, the minister proposed the version closest to the English. She put it forward largely because the Northern Ireland Civil Service (NICS) was both the only group capable of putting forward policy ideas and the group most likely to borrow ideas from their larger and better organised English counterparts in the Department of Health. The relevant Committee in the Northern Ireland Assembly turned the plan down and extended fundholding on the grounds (helpfully supplied by the BMA) that the plan was ill-thought-out. A year later, she returned with much the same plan, because that was what the NICS had supplied. It passed, since something beats nothing. The rest of the pending organisational issues, such as acute care restructuring and reduction in the number of organisations (strewn across Northern Ireland by implementation of the internal market), would have to wait. Sinn Féin had little incentive to pursue hard public policy choices and the crisis-ridden political system discouraged strong legislative action.

New Public Health

New Public Health is a movement dedicated to improving health (and overall wellbeing) by trying to change the economic and social conditions of people rather than by focusing on their medical treatment.[10] Previously, public health had been focused on the older agenda of controlling communicable diseases (vaccinations, food safety) and combined NHS and local government work. In the 1980s a 'lifestyle' focus also emerged that focused on individual choices that made for ill health (such as smoking or unsafe sex); these focused on persuading individuals to change, or maybe just hectoring them, and often had little effect. However, from the 1980s onward a coalition appeared that argued problems such as excessive alcohol consumption were often due to social deprivation and that the answer would be shaping public policies to promote healthier lives and inclusion. When new public health advocates win victories, they influence and integrate other public policies to the end of improving health and focus on the way other public policies can improve health. Its rivals, given the weakness of libertarian opposition, are primarily those focused on health services — those who would rather spend the funds on hospitals or clinics. They, not advocates of the new public health, have been the dominant force in twentieth-century medicine.[11] Public health also bases its case on long-term outcomes, while politicians are far more interested in near-term outcomes and the media everywhere puts its emphasis not on health outcomes but on waiting lists and scandals (each of

[10] For more comprehensive introductions, see Baggott, R., *Public Health: Policy and Politics* (Basingstoke: Macmillan, 2000); for the link to territorial politics, see Greer, S. and Sandford, M. *Regions and Public Health* (London: The Constitution Unit, 2001) and Greer, S. *Strategic Regionalism: Policy Advocacy and Regional Activism in England and Wales*, available at www.ucl.ac.uk/constitution-unit/d&h.

[11] Fox, D. *Health Policies, Health Politics: The British and American Experience, 1911-1965.* (Princeton: Princeton University Press, 1986).

the four ministers is regularly under attack for waiting lists, scandal, and dirt; given the size of each health system, statistics alone suggest there will always be such problems).

Since the arrival of Labour in 1997, the language of new public health has been ubiquitous. It has been far more visible and visibly supported than before. Phrases such as 'joined-up government', 'social inclusion', and 'community action' are so often used in all four countries as to be targets of ridicule. Nevertheless, there are important differences in the extent to which the four systems focus on new public health goals. As with other outcomes, they respond to the strength of the different advocacy coalitions and the form of party competition. The outcomes are visible in the amount of money, staffing, and explicit policy governments devote to increasing the health impact of public policy and spending on public health outside traditional health services and environmental health.

Wales

The country most signed up to the new public health agenda is Wales. Wales had for some time been more interested in the new public health agenda than the rest of the UK; under the Conservatives it stealthily built and used more planning capacity and links with other areas of social policy than the other UK health departments.[12] This reflected both the particular leadership of the Welsh health service and the weakness of health service elites (hospital-based professionals and managers) and the lack of ideological resonance of service-focused Conservative policies. After 1997, and above all with the arrival of the National Assembly, the new public health agenda gained importance. In addition to the existing influence of new public health advocates in the management and clinical services of the NHS Wales who were able to take advantage of the shakeup, the Assembly created a more left-wing political debate and (if nothing else by its recruitment) dramatically improved the connection between local authorities and the centre.

As a consequence, new public health agendas such as Health Impact Assessment (which evaluates public policies in areas such as transport and housing for their health costs and benefits) gained prominence.[13] There is more staffing and money available, both in public health budgets and in a large fund dedicated to reducing inequalities (and efforts to get around the weak capacity inherited from the Welsh Office led to the integration into the National Assembly of the whole of the old Health Promotion Wales). Even the Welsh health plan used a different conceptual structure than the others: it

[12] Interviews; see also Welsh Office/ Health Promotion Wales *Review of Health Promotion Arrangements in Wales* (Cardiff: HMSO, 1998).

[13] Welsh Assembly Government, *Well Being in Wales: Consultation document* (HMSO: Cardiff, 2002). For Health Impact Assessment, Breeze, C. and Hall, R. *Health Impact Assessment in Government Policy-Making: Developments in Wales* (Brussels/Copenhagen: European Centre for Health Policy- Brussels/ WHO, 2002).

focused on using the NHS Wales, as well as local government and other parts of the Welsh Assembly Government, to produce population health outcomes.[14] To do this, in a progressively localising health system, it is developing a unified, Wales-wide, public health service. Finally, one odd indicator is available. Wales, due to its weak inherited policy capacity, tends to be slow in working out policy. New public health work has moved most quickly of any of Welsh policy fields.

Scotland

The next most interested is Scotland. Scotland is hardly short of clinical elites — its three Royal Colleges, four medical schools (bearers of the second-oldest tradition of Western medical education in the world), and elite hospitals all guarantee that advocates of new public health will face stiff competition from the demands of these traditional summits of medical prestige and expense. There is a substantial reservoir of new public health expertise, both in Scottish institutions that have traditionally been stronger and more interventionist in public health, and in Scotland's strong academic infrastructure and public health professional associations. However, the main reason for Scotland's progress is that the political structure of the country gives new opportunities to advocates of the new public health. The Labour coalition with the Liberal Democrats is an alliance of two centre left parties with a left opposition, and the structure of Scottish politics means it is electorally relatively comfortable and can expect to be in office for years. Thus, it is more able to pursue a broadly left agenda that fits well with new public health work. That is hobbled, however, by a focus on health services that is in large part a consequence of its powerful and well-established clinical specialists and hospital advocates, who point out the great needs of a worthwhile health services system.

The result is an advance on the previous new public health work of Labour in 1997-1998,[15] but less impressive than in Wales. The key reason is that in Scotland the strength of health services advocates is such as to make their renewal and improvement the key priority. Thus, the bulk of Scottish health work (and the first Health Minister's attention) was on the patient's journey in health rather than wider determinants. But it takes little to make new public health practitioners feel better, and Scotland has made those moves: there is dedicated funding for them, there is rhetorical cover, and there is soft money available for community and other work. A visit from the minister once every few months, asking health service and local government leaders what they have done to promote new public health work, is powerful

[14] *Improving Health in Wales.*
[15] Scottish Office, *Toward a Healthier Scotland* (Edinburgh: HMSO, 1998) for the pre-devolution Labour strategy and *Our National Health* for developments since; see also the tables in *Divergence and Devolution.*

compared to what came before. Even if it is hardly the minister's priority, it has an impact and strengthens new public health.

Northern Ireland

The next most interested in new public health work is Northern Ireland. Here, the legacy of the Troubles explains the outcome. Even if Northern Irish politicians and society are unable to formulate cogent demands on most points and there is not a sophisticated enough policy community to force issues onto the agenda, there is a powerful and entrenched insider constituency left over from direct rule that can do new public health work within largely unchanged policy parameters. The Troubles created the strong new public health coalition for two reasons. First, they gave governments a keen appreciation of the importance of social exclusion in fuelling violence — the most badly damaged parts of Northern Irish society, such as North and West Belfast, are also the ones with some of the most entrenched deprivation and unemployment. Thus, governments of all stripes invested in housing, health, and even a large number of public leisure centres in Belfast; in 1986, *The Guardian* dubbed it 'The independent Keynesian Republic of Northern Ireland.'[16] Second, the massive distrust between the population (including many loyalists) and the state, which impeded social services work, meant that the government often funded social services and ameliorative work in the voluntary sector in the hope of delivering services better and diminishing tension. This created a large and expert voluntary sector, and since the Belfast agreement international assistance has further expanded it. Such groups are both key participants in new public health projects and important members of such advocacy coalitions. Against this is the immense number of veto points in the Northern Ireland Assembly (including regular vetoes by key players of the whole thing, leading to the suspensions of devolution) and the entrenched insider politics that evolved under Stormont and direct rule and resist changing priorities or resources. Running a big institution or being a high-level professional or civil servant both meant one probably was already an insider and was enough to make one an insider, and that meant that professions and big institutions were very well represented in consultations and debates.

The result is an excellent environment for new public health advocates on the ground to have an impact, but little movement able to change the priorities of those who are not interested. There are funds available for voluntary sector and health service organisations in specific areas that want to develop joint working. There is also, held over from direct rule and reinforced since, a willingness to accept such work. Despite the flood of orders (often issued in a curious, imperial, style) from the minister and the department, demanding

[16] Bardon, J. and Burnet, D., *Belfast: A Pocket History* (Belfast: Blackstaff, 1996), p. 146.

greater throughput from the services, many civil servants and NHS adminis-
trators are used to and look kindly on engagement in social and economic
affairs. The help of civil servants also explains why the agreed *Programme
for Government* includes extensive new public health commitments, many of
them in transport and environmental health and geared directly to improving
health outcomes.[17] Nevertheless, there is little push for new public health
from the centre; rather, to the extent that it appears to have a priority, it is
managing the health services to lower waiting lists. In other words, Northern
Ireland's general lack of democratic accountability has made it impossible
for its distracted and not particularly well-prepared minister to change the
culture of the organisations she commands, and the result is that the environment is still good for those who wish to do new public health.

England

England has a unique party system among the component parts of the UK:
the key divide is between a centre-left and a centre-right party. Its government has an affection for market-like solutions and specialisation that is not
shared throughout the rest of the UK; much of that is linked by its defenders
to the need to make the case for having an extensive welfare state at all.
Given that an opposition victory would be by the Conservatives, a party with
many leaders who have mulled over abolishing the NHS, this means that the
English government faces significantly different challenges. They respond
to it with far more intense efforts to make the NHS perform better, both with
extensive managerial change and with more money. In this environment, the
pressure to 'deliver' on health services is immense. Furthermore, in responding to this pressure, the government faces strong policy advocates interested
primarily in health services, while policy advocates of new public health
have weaker institutional and other bases.

The government has provided intellectual weight to new public health
goals with its white paper *Our Healthier Nation*[18] and the goals surrounding
its various soft money funds. However, of the vast new funds flowing into the
NHS, very little has gone into public health staffing or grants, while administrative reorganisation has confused public health responsibilities. Much
public health work, let alone new public health work, is to be done by PCTs
but there is little incentive or capacity on that level of organisation.[19] Public
health professionals and advocates in England, in interviews, appreciate the
verbal support and the plethora of competitive public health grants, but are

---

[17] Northern Ireland Executive *Programme for Government*. 2001.

[18] Department of Health, *Our Healthier Nation* (London: HMSO, 1998).

[19] See the lucid and mostly ignored March 28 2001 second report on public health of the House of
Commons Select Committee on Health, which the government met with speeches from a junior minister
reminding PCTs to pursue public health (not necessarily new public health) activities.

scathing about the disregard for them that they see in the reorganisation.[20] In short, England is the most purely verbal commitment of any of the four systems.

Public and Private

The issue at stake here is whether the NHS should directly own and operate all the facilities and directly employ or individually contract with the staff it needs to do its work; or whether there are virtues to contracting with the private sector. The policy advocacy coalition advocating more work with the private sector largely argues that health care can best be provided through a diversity of forms, rather than directly; it is part of the broader coalition, so influential in Britain, dedicated to a 'new public administration' based on contracts rather than direct provision.[21] Its arguments — all of which are contestable — say working with the private sector will produce higher quality, offloaded risk, lower labour costs, and valuable experimentation.[22] The most common form is a Private Finance Initiative (PFI) to provide building and support services; this typically is a 'build–own–transfer' in which the private consortium builds and operates a public facility where publicly hired professionals work, and after a fixed period transfers it. There are more elaborate options, all falling under the category of 'public-private partnerships' or PPPs. They also carry all the charms of 'reform,' with its simple promises of streamlined organisations pursuing consistent goals. In opposition are those who advocate a single NHS; this includes most doctors and many consultants, who see both a violation of their principles and a direct power play by managers (the greater the managerial autonomy of a subunit, the more power its managers have) as well as, crucially, unions that resist the transfer of staff to the private sector where they will bear much of the burden of cost savings. Throughout the UK this has been hotly contested; press coverage is enormous and remarkably unenlightening (see the Devolution and Health website; most of this section, reflecting this, is based on interviews).

England

England is the most important site for PFI and its advocates. It is the only place where the government appears to see private sector involvement as an end, rather than a means. This is not primarily because of the partisan constraint England's government faces (opposition from a right, not a left,

---

[20] Greer, S. *The Real Regional Health Agenda: Networks, Soft Money, and Health in the East Midlands* (London: The Constitution Unit, 2001), available at www.ucl.ac.uk/constitution-unit/d&h

[21] An excellent presentation of New Public Management, particularly attuned to its consequences for the British state and constitution, is Drewry, G. 'The New Public Management,' in J. Jowell, and D. Oliver (ed.) *The Changing Constitution*, 4th ed, (Oxford: Oxford University Press, 2000), pp.167-189.

[22] For a summary of the case against PFI, see Pollock, A. M., Shaoul, J., Rowland, D., Player, S., *Public services and the private sector: a response to the IPPR Commission* (London: Catalyst, 2001).

party); it also reflects the victory of the pro-private-sector and pro-market policy advocacy coalition in England. Advocates of the internal market remain, as does an extensive management cadre fond of organisational autonomy, while public policy circles in London contain many advocates of new public management in general — to the point that the view is embedded in parts of the civil service. Making the case for direct NHS provision is difficult for a government largely interested in new ways of providing care that is under electoral pressure from the right (if from anywhere) and that is surrounded by advocates of new public management in general.

The outcomes are legion, and (unlike in the other countries) affect the fundamental structure of the health services. Most important is PFI, with some new hospitals contracts involving everything but professionals engaged in clinical services (doctors, nurses). It is almost impossible to have the central government approve spending for a new facility without doing it as a PFI. The bulk of new NHS construction, from the largest to the smallest facilities, will not be directly run by the NHS. Beyond that are plans to ease the NHS away from being a single giant organisation to being a largely contracted body, with foundation hospitals having commercial freedoms. There is also direct use of the private sector) in the form of a 'Concordat' that promises to use their capacity and assistance (this is not really much of an addition, since the private sector hires from the pool of NHS professional labour in a zero-sum game). There have regularly been discussions in the press of NHS plans to rely on private sector provision to fill gaps in NHS provision, and some trusts regularly now contract with the private sector when there are waiting list problems.

Scotland

Scotland's government, unwon by private sector advocates, pursues PFI for less ideological reasons, and it shows. The promise of a classic PFI (build–own–transfer) is that it gives the government more facilities quicker for less capital expenditure and less liability on a government's annual budget (exchanged for greater liability further on, charged to running costs). This looks like something for nothing, and that is intensely appealing to any politician. It is more appealing for centre-left politicians elected on the promise of new and better hospitals and schools. However, embracing the prospect of off-balance-sheet capital expenditures through PFIs is nothing like embracing the prospect of a diverse NHS contracting with the private sector as an end in itself. This is because unions, professionals, and Scotland's opposition (the SNP) are all deeply suspicious of the private sector — above all because staff and their activities are the main costs that the private sector seeks to reduce. Scots will also point out that their private sector is smaller — that is slightly beside the point, since what capacity is available they do not contract, and the promise of long-term profitable contracts could attract private-sector providers (as they do in England). What it does suggest is the depth of clinical, party, and union dislike of private sector activities in Scotland.

Rather, Scotland's most dramatic action with regards to the private sector was to purchase the jewel in the private sector crown — the HCI hospital in Clydebank, an ill-fated economic development project subsidised by the Conservatives but an excellent facility with good staff.[23] Buying it expanded NHS Scotland capacity and expressed a clear policy choice, since it would also have been possible to contract with it if the Scottish Executive had wanted to make a point about diverse provision. Likewise, there is no discussion of foundation hospitals or contracting with large companies such as Boots to work in the Scottish NHS, while there is in England. There is, however, extensive PFI activity to be found from Edinburgh to Lochgilphead. The root cause is that this produces the hospitals (and other public sector facilities) rapidly and displaces their costs away from a single year's capital budget; the opportunity to provide new facilities is very attractive. However, union resistance is building (although settling the issue of staff transfers, as in Wales, could reduce it). PFI has developed a bad reputation with professionals and the public, in large part due to the efforts of the anti coalition, which has won over the BMJ, the SNP, and many Scottish journalists. This creates a strong likelihood that politicians will be convinced by the pressure from Scotland's largely anti-market dominant coalitions, even before any of the bills critics promise come due.

Northern Ireland

A switch to large-scale private sector provision requires more new provision and more new policy than is visible in Northern Ireland (and more private sector providers, which is also a problem since small projects are not very appealing and political instability scares them away). The appeal of new facilities for little current expense is as strong as elsewhere and Sinn Féin Minister of Education Martin McGuinness was an advocate of PFI for schools, so there is little objection on that level.[24] However, the sluggishness of care planning and organisational change means that Northern Ireland is missing the health building boom going on elsewhere (there is a consensus that there should be a new hospital in Tyrone and Fermanagh, but the debate is still focused on its site rather than the way to build it). Interview evidence suggests that private sector involvement will be used insofar as it produces new hospitals. Certainly Northern Ireland's changes to primary care, which

---

[23] Thursday, 20 June, 2002, Private hospital bought for NHS (BBC online; link via the news and documents section of www.ucl.ac.uk/constitution-unit/d&h).

[24] Ward, S. 'Celtic Catch-Up' in *Public Finance*, 4 May 2001.

moved away from the market, abolished fundholding, and eliminated a successful group of fundholders in Belfast, suggests that there is little sympathy for markets or the private sector in the government. The composition of insiders, with unions, professionals, and a conservative civil service all strong, suggests the same, and if the Assembly is restarted with the same Sinn Féin minister, that party's self-description as 'democratic socialist' suggests that the private sector can expect little attention.

Wales

Like the rest of the UK, the Welsh health system professes pragmatism towards PFI; like the other devolved countries, it restricts its interest to PFI and speaks warmly of the public sector ethos, and like Northern Ireland it is too small to have many valuable PFI contracts to offer. Part of the Welsh way in PFI — i.e. cautious movement — is Wales' simple inability to lure contractors from the richer and more easily accessible mountain of projects commissioned in England: a PFI for a small Welsh hospital takes staff time for firms that could be spent on a far larger and more profitable project in England. However, Wales, like Scotland, is a victory for anti-private-sector coalitions led by unions and professionals that focus on direct provision in organisations with professional rather than managerial values dominant.[25] There is very little private sector capacity in Wales, and the NHS Wales has little to do with it, while there is no interest in private-sector solutions.

Fundamentally, advocacy coalitions interested in new public management, the private sector, and PPP were strongest in England where they now appear to dominate government policy. They were weaker in Scotland and Wales (and exiguous in Northern Ireland). Thus, Scottish and Welsh outcomes are similar — use of PFI to get more buildings built than otherwise, even if it incurs expenses later. Wales then marks out a position to the left of Scotland by having stiffer criteria for staff transfer; even porters, laundry and catering, which are always the easiest parts of a facility to privatise, are considered part of the NHS and will not be transferred to the private sector. Without the ability to lower those wage costs, private sector operators are largely reduced to build–own–transfer contracts and the economic case is not so good (in essence, the big cost savings from PPPs to date, when there have been any, come from paying unskilled workers less, so if the unskilled workers stay in the NHS the PFI turns into a combination of construction and maintenance contract in which there is little private sector advantage or

---

[25] 'Hutt promises public ownership of NHS' icwales.co.uk, Mar 23 2002 and 'Hart announces 'Welsh way' for PFI' icwales.co.uk Dec 13 2001. The latter report was sparked by a ministerial statement that purported to open the door for PFI and instead effectively restricted it to building and maintenance. Link to both via www.ucl.ac.uk/constitution-unit/d&h

profit). Add in the small size of Welsh projects and the result is that Wales is nearly free of new private sector involvement and shows no signs of pursuing any more.

SUMMARY OF OUTCOMES

In the short time since devolution there has been surprising policy divergence and even greater divergence in the values and 'mood music' of the four systems. Even the shibboleths now vary: England speaks of 'modernisation,' Wales of 'inequalities' and even (quietly) 'socialism', Scotland of 'partnership'. Furthermore, many studies of political institutions across the literature highlight path dependency — the dominant coalitions, institutions, and practices that develop in the first years of an organisation shape it for a long time to come — and thus suggest that the four countries will continue to become more distinct. Change is easier now than it will be, and the works of the first devolved governments will constrain their successors.

There are in most issues two poles: Scotland and England, with the former running a health service for patients and the latter running one for consumers. England is by far the most radical, out of line with the others, and in policy terms unstable. This is due to its pluralist policy communities, left–right cleavage, Westminster government system, and the ongoing victories of pro-market, pro-management, pro-health-services groups. Scotland is the most traditionalist, rediscovering the virtues of the pre-Thatcher NHS with its focus on planning, its forays into new public health, and its reluctance to experiment with private provision of public services. Where England has in spirit and in policy opted for a market-based set of solutions, Scotland is opting for dominance by the professionals who work in the system (or at least their leaders, which is not the same thing).

Wales is, as usual, radical in its own underreported way. It has most clearly pushed hospital services away from the centre (and its leaders would like to do that more) and replaced them with a focus on primary care and the wider determinants of health. Public health advocates, unions, and primary care professionals' ideas dominate this system, which means that it is close to the reverse of the others. Wales is in many ways one of the only places in the Western world to take the global agenda of new public health and primary care dominance seriously; if it continues, it will deserve to be a health policy case study. Northern Ireland, meanwhile, has delivered a sad reminder of its political pathologies. The Belfast agreement, when it was more or less operating, was riddled with veto points seemingly designed to prevent policies, but that was not the core of the problem (indeed, the Programme for Government was full of agreed health policies, and the Minister's power in the Department reduced her accountability to anyone). The core of the problem was the legacy of the Troubles — an easygoing, conservative, insider- dominated policy system surrounded by an angry society aware of its problems but so dominated by constitutional and sectarian politics as to be unable to formulate demands. Perhaps the Belfast agreement would prevent change, but right now the problem in Northern Ireland is that there is neither enough supply of ideas nor demand for new policy.

What does this mean for ordinary people? Right now, not much. Health politics takes time to feed through. A meaningful expansion of capacity takes seven to ten years, while medical students become doctors, complicated projects like hospitals come to fruition, and managers settle down (assuming the politicians ever let them settle down). We are now seeing the first serious consequences of the actions of the first Labour government; the real payoff for patients of any policy enacted since 1998 is years away.

What we can say is that the four health systems of the UK will look very different in a few years. Each of them is taking its direction for long-term reasons explained by social cleavages, political institutions, and the structure of medicine (i.e. the power of different interest groups). That means that even if the details change — and politicians around the UK, if not everywhere, like to leave their marks by reorganising things — they will continue to move in different directions. And in ten years, if English patients go to a clinic operated by Boots and Welsh patients to a joint local government-NHS clinic, they will be treated differently by professional staff who are themselves treated differently. It does bear noting that England is the most erratic; when we speak of divergence, the likely diverger is England. For better or for worse, England is the only country trying explicitly to reinvent its health services, and is certainly the only one that might reinvent the NHS out of existence. That alone might strike people in Northern Ireland, Scotland, and Wales as a reason for devolution.

England, Scotland, and Wales are not run by the same people, they are not listening to the same people, and their leaders need not run against the same people. The result is that each health system's selections from the menu are different, and the internal coherence of each system is the product of its own political difference.

BIBLIOGRAPHY

Official Documents

Department of Health, *The New NHS: Modern-Dependable* (London: HMSO, 1997).

Department of Health, *The NHS Plan: A Plan for Investment, a Plan for Reform.* (London: HMSO, 2000).

Department of Health, *Our Healthier Nation* (London: HMSO, 1998).

Government of the National Assembly for Wales, *Improving Health in Wales: A Plan for the NHS With Its Partners* (Cardiff: HMSO, 2001).

Northern Ireland Department of Health and Social Services *Fit For the Future: A consultation document on the Government's proposals for the future of the Health and Personal Social Services in Northern Ireland* (Belfast: HMSO, 1998).

Northern Ireland Executive, *Programme for Government* (Belfast, 2001).

Scottish Executive Health Department, *Our National Health: A Plan for Action, a Plan for Change.* (Edinburgh: HMSO, 2000).

Scottish Office, *Designed to Care: Renewing the National Health Service in Scotland* (Edinburgh: HMSO, 1997).

Scottish Office, *Toward a Healthier Scotland* (Edinburgh: HMSO, 1998).

Welsh Assembly Government *Well Being in Wales: Consultation document* (HMSO: Cardiff, 2002).

Welsh Office, *NHS Wales: Putting Patients First* (Cardiff: HMSO, 1998).

Welsh Office/ Health Promotion Wales *Review of Health Promotion Arrangements in Wales* (Cardiff: HMSO, 1998).

Secondary Sources

Baggott, R. *Public Health: Policy and Politics* (Basingstoke: Macmillan, 2000).

Bardon, J. and Burnet, D., *Belfast: A Pocket History.* (Belfast: Blackstaff, 1996).

Breeze, C. and Hall, R., *Health Impact Assessment in Government Policy-Making: Developments in Wales* (Brussels/Copenhagen: European Centre for Health Policy-Brussels/ WHO, 2002).

Drewry, G., 'The New Public Management' in J. Jowell and D, Oliver (eds), *The Changing Constitution* 4th ed. (Oxford: Oxford University Press, 2000).

Fox, D., *Health Policies, Health Politics: The British and American Experience, 1911-1965* (Princeton: Princeton University Press, 1986).

Greer, S., *Divergence and Devolution* (London: The Nuffield Trust, 2001).

Greer, S., *The Real Regional Health Agenda: Networks, Soft Money, and Health in the East Midlands* (London: The Constitution Unit, 2001).

Greer, S., 'Strategic Regionalism: Policy Advocacy and Regional Activism in England' (working paper, London, the Constitution Unit, 2002).

Greer, S. and Sandford, M., *Regions and Public Health* (London: The Constitution Unit, 2001).

Jenkins-Smith, H.C. and Sabatier, P.A., 'Evaluating the Advocacy Coalition Approach' in *Journal of Public Policy* 14 (2), 1994, pp.175-203.

Milburn, A., 'Shifting the Balance of Power in the NHS' speech given at the launch of the NHS Modernisation Agency, 25 April 2001.

Pollock, A.M., Shaoul, J., Rowland, D., and Player, S., *Public services and the private sector: a response to the IPPR Commission* (London: Catalyst, 2001).

Tuohy, C., *Accidental Logics: The Dynamics of Change in the Health Care Arena in the United States, Britain, and Canada.* (Oxford: Oxford University Press, 1999).

Ward, S. 'Celtic Catch-Up' in *Public Finance* (4 May 2001).

9

Free Personal Care
Policy Divergence and Social Citizenship

Rachel Simeon

INTRODUCTION

On 1 July 2002 Scotland's policy of providing free personal care for the elderly was launched. Despite a public commitment made by then First Minister of Scotland, Henry McLeish, in November 2000, many observers doubted it would ever come into being. After almost two years and a change of First Minister, Scotland's initiative is seen as a victory by the elderly lobby and has been endorsed by Lord Sutherland, the Chair of the Royal Commission that recommended it. It is also seen as a victory for the Scottish Parliament and for devolution.

In a reversal of the usual confrontational dynamic of Westminster-style politics, all the major parties in the Scottish Parliament take credit for the policy. In fact, the only key players opposing it were Labour members of the Cabinet. However, on the day of the launch, even the Labour First Minister, Jack McConnell, was keen to take credit: 'free personal and nursing care is happening today because it is a promise we made to Scotland's older people and because we believe that it is the right thing to do.'[1] Moreover, he used the launch as an opportunity to float additional spending ideas, such as free or subsidised travel for young people,[2] which could see the range of social benefits available in Scotland diverge even further from that in the rest of the United Kingdom.

As a case study of policy divergence in the UK, the issue of free personal care for the elderly is interesting precisely because so many people did not think it could be achieved. The twists and turns it took in the Scottish Parliament and the debate it engendered in both Scotland and England brought into stark relief many of the tensions and issues around divergence that affect policy outcomes in the new and complex world of devolved governance.[3]

---

[1] Scottish Executive Press Release, 'Free personal care now on stream', 1 July 2002.

[2] Scott, D., 'McConnell Puts Families First', *The Scotsman* 2 July 2002.

[3] This chapter is based on work conducted for a Master's dissertation at the School of Public Policy at University College London. Material for this case study comes primarily from interviews with people involved in the Scottish policy process. These included Scottish parliamentarians from each of the four major political parties, as well as representatives of the Scottish civil service and the elderly lobby.

The debate over free personal care also touches at the heart of the tension, which is inherent to all multi-level polities, between what Keith Banting calls 'the logic of social citizenship and the logic of federalism.'[4] The logic of federalism is that of regional diversity: democratically elected governments respond to the needs and priorities of their electorates in ways that may or may not reflect those chosen by other governments. Where the logic of federalism leads to policy divergence, the logic of social citizenship suggests policy uniformity and national standards. It implies that citizens have a right to a common set of welfare state programmes and services by virtue of their citizenship in the larger polity. By making access dependent on where a person lives, divergence challenges that right. When Help the Aged (England) claimed that the difference in policy over personal care for the elderly results in an unjust 'post-code lottery', they were invoking the logic of social citizenship. Alternatively, using the logic of federalism, the difference was defended by the Secretary of State for Scotland as the legitimate consequence of two separate democratic processes.[5]

Although it is not put in these terms, much of the literature on devolution in the UK reveals a profound ambivalence toward the trade-off between these values. Authors like Robert Hazell argue that devolution ultimately will be judged in terms of the ability of the new administrations to adopt policies that diverge from London.[6] However, much of the literature focuses on barriers to divergence such as the continued use of the Barnett Formula, and the reluctance of London Labour to relinquish control.[7] Kevin Woods argues that a 'UK government wishing to see political devolution succeed has to accept that it may unleash demands for greater diversity in the level and organisation of health services that are funded from a UK tax system.' The

---

[4] Banting, K., 'Social Citizenship and Canadian Federalism: the Old and New Politics of Health Care' (draft paper prepared for the Workshop on Federalism and the Welfare State, University of Bremen, May 2002), p. 2.

[5] BBC Radio 4, 30 June 2002.

[6] Hazell, R., 'Conclusion: The State of the Nations after Two Years of Devolution' in A. Trench (ed) *State of the Nations 2001: The Second Year of Devolution in the United Kingdom* (Exeter: Imprint Academic, 2001), pp. 225–272.

[7] There is extensive literature on the impact of the fiscal arrangements of devolution. For example, see Cowley, P., 'Legislatures and Assemblies', in P. Dunleavy, A. Gamble, I. Holliday and G. Peele (eds) *Developments in British Politics 6* (Basingstoke: Palgrave, 2000); Trench, A., 'Introduction' (pp. 1-10), and Bell, D. and Christie, A., 'Finance — The Barnett Formula: Nobody's Child?' in *State of the Nations 2001*, pp. 135–152. Hazell, R., and Cornes, R., 'Financing Devolution: the Centre Retains Control', in R. Hazell (ed) *Constitutional Futures: A History of the Next Ten Years* (Oxford: Oxford University Press, 1999) pp. 196–212; Bradbury, J. and Mitchell, J., 'Devolution: New Politics or Old?' *Parliamentary Affairs* (April 2001) 45 (2), pp. 257–275; and Ward, A., 'Devolution: Labour's Strange Constitutional 'Design'', in J. Jowell and D. Oliver (eds) *The Changing Constitution 4th ed* (Oxford: Oxford University Press: 2000). David Trimble has already challenged the government on the effect of the Barnett formula claiming it does not operate 'fairly.' (May 2001 question to the Secretary of State for Northern Ireland, quoted in Hazell, R., 'Conclusion', *State of the Nations 2001*, p. 259.)

ambivalence is revealed when he also asks 'at what point does such diversity become reinterpreted as inequality?'[8]

The primary purpose of this chapter is to explain why Scotland chose to implement free personal care for the elderly, particularly in the face of London's rejection of Lord Sutherland's recommendation. This requires that we understand first what room exists for policy divergence between Scotland and the rest of the UK, and second, why Scotland used that room as it did to expand the provisions of the welfare state.

The secondary purpose of this chapter is to use the case to provide some wider thoughts about the relationship between the logics of social citizenship and regional diversity in the UK. The way in which the space for policy is organised and used can be seen as a reflection of how a country balances social citizenship with diversity in a particular policy field.[9] The implication is that the existence of central co-ordinating structures to constrain divergence reflects a balance in favour of social citizenship. In the UK, there are relatively few constraints on divergence in healthcare. However this seems to be at odds with public expectations reflecting a commitment to common social citizenship. Moreover, the analysis of the case of free personal care suggests that the relationship between these values need not necessarily be such a straightforward trade-off. Sometimes policy divergence can enhance rather than reduce the full scope of social citizenship.

FREE PERSONAL CARE AND THE SUTHERLAND REPORT

Most journalistic accounts of the development of free personal care for the elderly focus on Henry McLeish and the cut-throat manoeuvrings of parties in the Scottish Parliament. It is indeed the stuff of good political story telling. As Woods notes 'it will take some years and several political memoirs to unravel all that took place and why.'[10]

[8] K. Woods, 'Health Policy and the NHS in the UK 1997–2002', in J. Adams and P. Robinson (eds) *Devolution in Practice: Public Policy Differences within the UK* (London: IPPR, 2002), p. 28. Regarding London Labour's attitude, see A. Wright (ed) *Scotland: the Challenge of Devolution* (Aldershot: Ashgate Publishers, 2000).

[9] This is the premise behind the model developed by Banting and Corbett to understand divergence in access to health care services across federal countries. See Banting, K., and Corbett, S., "Health Policy and Federalism: 'An Introduction'", in K. Banting and S. Corbett (eds) *Health Policy and Federalism: a comparative perspective on multi-level governance* (Kingston: Queens-McGill Press, 2001). The model, which focuses on (1) the central policy framework for health care and (2) the interregional equalization system of transfers, is used as the framework for analysing the case of free personal care in this chapter. Although there are many studies of the effect of federalism on policy outcomes, this is the first model to explicitly address the question of how countries with multi-level systems of government balance the competing values of social citizenship and regional diversity. According to Banting, 'the dominant conclusion' from the literature on federalism is 'that federalism and/or decentralization constrain an expansive and redistributive welfare state' (p. 6). Studies also suggest that it tends to slow the speed of policy change.

[10] Woods, p. 43.

The story begins with the creation of the UK Royal Commission on long term care for the elderly in 1997, chaired by Lord Sutherland. The Commission was asked: 'to examine the short and longer term options for sustainable systems of funding of Long Term Care for elderly people, both in their own homes and in other settings, and within 12 months, to recommend how, and in what circumstances, the cost of such care should be apportioned between public funds and individuals.'[11]

The Commission issued its final report in March 1999. Attracting the most media attention was the recommendation that 'personal care should be available after an assessment, according to need and paid for from general taxation.'[12] The recommendation was rooted in a belief in the efficiency of single-risk pooling through general taxation as well as concerns over equity. As Lord Sutherland stated in his evidence to the Scottish Health and Community Care Committee:

> If a person ruins their liver with too much alcohol; if they abuse tobacco and get an illness as a result or if they get any of the many illnesses to which people fall prey, their treatment and care is free. If a person has dementia or Alzheimer's however, they are means tested. No one can understand why there is a gap or what the justification is for it, apart from the fact that care of such cases amounts to a significant bill.[13]

Joel Joffe and David Lipsey, two of the 12 members of the Commission, took issue with the recommendation for free personal care and authored a 'Note of Dissent' that was released as part of the final report. The Note claims that increased demand will push costs far higher than those anticipated in the majority report. It also grounds its position in 'Third Way' philosophy, arguing that benefits should be targeted at those most in need and that 'provision should neither be universally public nor universally private.'[14]

The UK government adopted the position of the minority report, but committed itself to implementing almost all the other recommendations made by the Commission, including paying for nursing care through the National Health Service (NHS). In October 2000, Susan Duncan, then Scotland's health minister, announced the Scottish Executive's response to the Sutherland Report making clear that it shared London's view regarding free

[11] Sutherland, Lord S., 'Chairman's Introduction', in *With Respect to Old Age: Long Term Care — Rights and Responsibilities*, (final report by The Royal Commission on Long-Term Care, 1999), para. 1.

[12] Sutherland, Lord S, (Chair), 'Executive Summary and Summary of Recommendations', *With Respect to Old Age: Long Term Care — Rights and Responsibilities*. Other recommendations included the establishment of a National Commission, support for carers, changes to budgeting procedures, further research and a focus on prevention and rehabilitation.

[13] Quoted in the Scottish Parliament Information Centre Research Note, 'Royal Commission on Long Term Care (Sutherland Report)', 26 Sept. 2000 (RN 00/78), p. 7.

[14] Joffe, Lord J. and Lipsey, Lord D., 'Note of Dissent' *With Respect to Old Age: Long Term Care — Rights and Responsibilities*, para. 15, 17.

personal care.[15] However, in November, in a move that surprised even his closest advisors, Henry McLeish announced that his government would reconsider its position on the issue given that there were ' . . . very strong feelings on the subject in Scotland.'[16] This was widely interpreted as endorsing free personal care. According to Peter McMahon, press secretary to Henry McLeish, the following months witnessed a confusion of pressure from London to back away from the commitment and from the Liberal Democratic members of the coalition government to confirm it.[17]

At the end of November, the Scottish all-party Health and Community Care Committee issued a unanimous report endorsing free personal care for the elderly, estimating it would cost £110 million, the figure given in the Sutherland Report.[18] On 25 January 2001 the Scottish National Party (SNP) proposed a motion demanding 'an unequivocal commitment' to free personal care in response to Executive proposals announced the previous day which had continued to avoid a clear statement on the issue. Minutes before the final vote, the prospect of losing the support of their Liberal Democrat coalition partners forced the Executive to concede: 'I can . . . assure the parliament that the executive will bring forward . . . proposals for the implementation of free personal care.'[19]

Despite this assurance however, doubt over the government's commitment to free personal care continued. This was fuelled in part by news that the Scottish Executive had failed in its attempts to secure a transfer from the UK Department of Work and Pension (DWP) for the Attendance Allowance payments normally made to low-income people to help cover the cost of personal care. According to DWP rules, a person loses eligibility for the Allowance if the costs of their care are paid for by another source.[20] This meant that Scottish pensioners living in care homes would loose their Allowance because of the new policy. Alistair Darling, then Secretary of State for DWP, refused either to change the rules or to transfer the savings to Scotland to help fund their policy. It is rumoured he acted on the direction of Chancellor Gordon Brown. McLeish's failure in London added £21.7 million to the costs of implementation.

In the meantime, debate over the merits of free personal care for the elderly also continued. Lord Lipsey warned in the press that 'populist

---

[15] For a chronology of events see Woods; Mitchell, J. and the Constitution Unit's Scottish Monitoring team, 'Scotland: Maturing Devolution', in *State of the Nations 2001*, pp. 45–76; Age Concern Scotland Briefing Note 'Long Term Care Funding Update''November 2001; and Help the Aged Scottish Policy Briefing 'Free Personal Care' June 2002.

[16] Quoted in McMahon, P., 'How McLeish made up his policies on the hoof', *The Scotsman* 26 Jan. 2002.s

[17] *Ibid.*

[18] Age Concern Briefing Note, 'Long Term Care Funding Update', November 2001.

[19] *Ibid.*

[20] Bell, C., and Christie, A., 'Finance — The Barnett Formula: Nobody's Child' in *State of the Nations 2001*, pp. 135-152.

wheezes like Sutherland' would cause a rush of elderly residents of England across the border to take advantage of Scotland's generosity.'[21] The replacement of Henry McLeish by Jack McConnell as First Minister cast further doubt. McConnell was known to have originally opposed the plan. Despite all these obstacles, however, on 1 July 2002 (after a further three month delay preparing local councils for implementation), Scotland's free personal care initiative for the elderly was finally launched.

The policy provides up to £145 per week to individuals for personal care and an additional £65 for nursing care as well as a total of £50 million for improving home care services.[22] To be sure, some media coverage has pointed out that 'free care is nothing of the sort' because funding is capped[23] however the policy has generally been well received by those who advocated it, as well as by all of the major parties in the Scottish Parliament.[24]

Whatever one's views on the subject, it is clear from the amount of press coverage that the Sutherland Report and the issue of free personal care for the elderly caught the public's attention and raised questions about fairness in the context of devolution. Although calculating the actual net benefit for elderly people living on one side of the border versus the other is complicated by a much larger set of programmes and policies that affect old age care,[25] the public perception is that, thanks to this move by the Scottish Parliament, Scottish pensioners are now better off than their peers in England, Wales and Northern Ireland.

---

[21] Lipsey, Lord D., 'Free Care? Don't make me laugh', *Evening News (Edinburgh)* 18 Sept. 2001. According to Mitchell *et al*, Lord Lipsey was sent by London to Edinburgh to oppose the policy.

[22] Help the Aged Scottish Policy Briefing, 'Free Personal Care', June 2002. Also see Scottish Executive press releases 'Free Personal Care' and 'Free personal care now on stream' 1 July, 2002. These figures apply to people living in residential or care homes who will loose their entitlement to Attendance Allowances as a result of the policy.

[23] Amongst the many articles making this point, see Luckhurst, T., 'Why we really shouldn't buy 'free care' spin', *Daily Mail* 1 July 2002; and 'Free(ish) care for the elderly has arrived' *The Scotsman*, 1 July 2002.

[24] Age Concern Scotland, which had fought hard for free personal care, gave only muted criticism of the details of the policy. Age Concern's comments focused on the potential for care homes to raise prices, eating into savings that were supposed to result from the policy, and the potential for uneven implementation due to lack of clarity in the guidelines issued to Local Councils. See Age Concern Scotland, Briefing Note, 'Free Personal and Nursing Care' June 2002.

[25] For instance, in 'The Great Illusion of Free Care for Elderly', *The Scotsman* 24 Sept. 2001, F. Nelson points out that the nursing care allowance in England is £110/week as compared to £65 in Scotland. When combined with the Attendance Allowance, low-income people could receive £10/week more south of the border. Another example cited by one of the interviewees is the fact that Scotland did not draw-up regulations to implement a DWP change in policy raising the capital allowance for hotel costs. This results in savings for Scottish local councils while people in Scotland miss out on what would have been savings worth about £50 a year.

Figure 9.1: Key events leading up to the launch of the Scottish policy on free personal care[26]

December 1997	Creation of UK Royal Commission on Long Term Care (Sutherland Commission).
March 1999	Commission releases final report: *With Respect to Old Age: Long Term Care — Rights and Responsibilities.*
July 2000	UK government rejects recommendation on free personal care for the elderly.[27]
5 October 2000	Scottish Health Minister, Susan Deacon, announces Scottish Executive's response to the report, rejecting free personal care.
5 November 2000	Scottish First Minister, Henry McLeish, suggests U-turn on free personal care in a newspaper interview.
28 November 2000	Scottish Parliament's Health and Community Care Committee publishes a report calling for the full implementation of Sutherland including free personal care.
24 January 2001	Susan Deacon announces the creation of an Expert Development Group, under Malcolm Chisholm, Deputy Minister of Health and Community Care, to study the costs and report in August 2001. Her statement avoids a clear commitment to free personal care.[28]
25 January 2001	Scottish National Party motion demanding 'an unequivocal commitment' to free personal care forces the Executive to adopt the policy.
29 January 2001	Statement by Henry McLeish: 'We are embracing the principles of Sutherland in full . . . I don't want any doubts to remain in your mind as to which direction we are taking.'[29]
17 September 2001	Release of report by Expert Development Group recommending existing charges for personal and nursing care end by April 2002.[30]
23 November 2001	Jack McConnell replaces Henry McLeish as First Minister of Scotland.
1 July 2002	Launch of Scottish policy on free personal care.

[26] Unless otherwise cited, the source is Mitchell *et al*, 2001.
[27] Age Concern Briefing Note, 'Long Term Care Funding Update, November 2001'
[28] Woods, 44.
[29] *Ibid.*
[30] *Ibid.*

As Woods has argued, 'no other health issue has demonstrated the power and consequences of political devolution [more] than the issue of free personal care for the elderly.'[31] Implementing free personal care meant diverging from London on a high profile and directly comparable policy issue. It also meant finding a substantial investment from within a budget almost entirely fixed by London. So, why did Scotland do it and what can this case tell us about future policy divergence in the UK?

Divergence over free personal care is by no means the only significant example of divergence in the field of health policy in the UK since devolution.[32] However, it is the most high profile instance to call into question the similarity in the overall package of services delivered through the NHS. Differences in the organisational structure of the NHS in England and Scotland can be justified, as they were by some interviewees, in terms of differences in the organisational requirements of a population of just over 5 million in Scotland as compared to almost 50 million in England. It is not so obvious, however, that free personal care is a solution to a problem that is uniquely Scottish.[33] Political or democratic imperatives, rather than any impartial judgement of a particularly Scottish need, formed the basis for this significant case of policy divergence. Understanding what made it possible for Scotland to diverge in this way, and why it chose to use that policy space as it did, sheds light on the relationship between social citizenship and regional diversity in the UK.

ANALYSING THE CASE

Central Policy Framework

According to Banting and Corbett, the first key structural feature determining the capacity for policy divergence within a particular policy field, such as health care, in a multi-level governed state, is the central policy framework. The specificity of the framework defines the boundaries of allowable divergence by articulating the core features of health policy that must apply to all the regions of a devolved state. [34]

---

[31] Woods, p. 43.

[32] As a number of authors point out, there has been considerable divergence in terms of the organizational structure of the NHS and the role played by the private sector and market mechanisms. This process started with the 1997 White Papers: *The New NHS: Modern-Dependable* (UK Department of Health) and *Designed to Care* (Scottish Office), and has continued since without causing any significant rifts between Edinburgh and London. See Woods; and S. Greer, *Divergence and Devolution* (London: The Nuffield Trust: 2001). See also chapter 8 in this volume.

[33] In practice, care for the elderly falls under a complex array of policies and programs. There are programs, such as the fuel programme, which address a concrete difference in circumstances faced by people in Scotland (the cost of fuel is 45 per cent higher in Northern Scotland according to Help the Aged Scotland). However, the basic argument over the principle of free personal care applies on both sides of the border.

[34] Banting and Corbett, p. 22.

To anyone familiar with the 1998 Scotland Act and accompanying documents, it will be obvious that there is no central policy framework guiding
the development of the NHS in the UK. With few exceptions, the official
devolution documents, including the Act, concordats and 'devolution guidance notes', emphasise over-arching issues of co-ordination between
governments and how devolution will work rather than substantive questions
of policy. There is a concordat between the Department of Health and the
Scottish Executive Health Department; however it focuses on process issues
such as protocols for advance notice and dispute resolution. Moreover, the
concordat was written not to ensure any measure of policy similarity in the
name of UK-wide standards, but rather because 'without close co-operation
between all four UK administrations there is the risk that developments in
one administration may inadvertently constrain or put pressure on policy or
finances for the other administrations.'[35]

Nowhere in any of these documents has anyone seen the need to write
down a framework to safeguard the overarching principles of the NHS.
Hence, there is no policy impediment to dramatic divergence in terms of
access to health services. Viewed from the perspective of the long history of
administrative devolution, the absence of a central policy framework may
not have seemed significant. Responsibility for health care in Scotland has
been separated from the other countries of the UK since long before the
creation of the Scottish Parliament. Where both ministers' responsible sat in
the same Cabinet, there was no need to articulate a framework to guide overall policy. However, now that the ministers responsible for health care
belong to separate governments and answer to different Parliaments, the lack
of an agreed upon statement of, at least, general guiding principles for the
NHS may be at odds with the wide-spread presumption that there are high
expectations of equity across the UK.[36]

The reason the UK lacks a central framework may be that the shared
commitment to the NHS was thought to be so ingrained that no one perceived
devolution as a threat to its core principles. Indeed, the fact that there are four
national health services in the UK instead of one would still take many by
surprise. However, as more divergence occurs, particularly in terms of
access to health services, the commitment to a common social citizenship
may begin to weaken. To avoid that happening, it could be important to make
the institutional arrangements fit with the current balance of values. As far
back as 1999, Hazell warned: 'it may be that we will also need to develop a
baseline statement of social and economic rights, to give expression to our
deeply felt expectations of equity.'[37]

[35] Department of Health and Scottish Executive, 'Concordat on Health and Social Care.'
[36] Hazell, R. and O'Leary, B., 'A Rolling Programme of Devolution: Slippery Slope or Safeguard
of the Union? ' in *Constitutional Futures*, pp. 21-46.
[37] *Ibid.*

Inter-regional Equalisation

Just as the UK lacks a central policy framework for the NHS, so too, it is without a proper equalisation system of intergovernmental transfers. Whereas the nature of the central framework defines the degree to which a country requires common benefits in all regions, the interregional transfer system determines the degree to which a country makes it possible. The purpose of an interregional transfer system is to equalise the ability of regions of different economic means to provide a similar standard of services at a similar level of taxation. The implication is that a country which places a high value on common standards will have a robust equalisation system so that all governments can provide similar levels of service.[38]

The effect of the current financial arrangements in the UK is that Scotland can afford to be more generous in its social programmes than other parts of the Union.[39] Free personal care, like the decision on teacher's pay, can be seen as an example of Scotland making use of its budget flexibility. However, it is important to remember that Scotland's relative fiscal capacity does not derive from strong economic performance. Rather, according to Heald and McLeod, 'perceptions of different need played some part [along with political bargaining] in shaping the public expenditure allocation before the 1978 establishment of the Barnett Formula.' These authors also suggest that the Barnett formula was originally seen as a 'transitional arrangement', although no formal system of regular needs assessments was ever introduced.[40] Given the lack of data, it is the 'best guess' of experts that a new needs assessment would lower Scotland's allocation relative to the other administrations.[41] In a sense, Scotland's budget is over-equalised. Thus, one cannot conclude that the value of regional diversity prevailed in the design of the devolution fiscal arrangements. In fact, the opposite is probably true.

The UK Treasury has considerable control over the devolved administrations' budgets, and thus over the capacity for policy divergence. With the exception of the 3 per cent 'Tartan Tax' (which many argue will become more difficult to use the longer it is left untouched), there is almost no independent revenue source for Scotland. In other words, Scotland's capacity for divergence is not guaranteed.

[38] Banting and Corbett, p. 21.

[39] Woods, p. 26.

[40] Heald and McLeod McLeod 'Beyond Barnett? Funding Devolution' in *Devolution in Practice*, p. 150. The more formal system, which never got under way, would have involved regular needs assessments (every four years) to re-negotiate the allocation formula.

[41] D. Heald, N. Geaughan and C. Robb, 'Financial Arrangements for UK Devolution', in M. Keating and H. Elcock (eds) *Remaking the Union* (Londong: Frank Cass, 1998), pp. 25-59. These authors speculate that the Scottish Office's marked indifference toward a new needs assessment since 1979 reflects an awareness that Scotland's share would most certainly fall as a result. For a fuller discussion of the problems surrounding data availability, see Heald and McLeod 'Beyond Barnett? Funding Devolution' in *Devolution in Practice*.

According to Bell and Christie, the financial arrangements for devolution reflect the 'Treasury's determination' to manage the 'key macroeconomic variables in the UK economy' as well as to 'micro-manage the UK fiscal stance.'[42] Indeed, there is a widely held perception that the Treasury tries to interfere with Scottish affairs. Although not all interviewees could confirm the means of Treasury intervention, most agreed that 'off-the-record brief-ings' or other kinds of less formal 'pressure' are common events in Edin-burgh and that they were likely to have occurred with respect to free personal care. One interviewee who denied Treasury interference nonetheless admit-ted to conversations with London in which there was pressure to reverse the position over free personal care.

London's decision not to transfer the DWP Attendance Allowance savings can also be seen in this light. Although some interviewees argued it was a matter of constitutional principle, the alternative view is that London's refusal was political. It wanted to block McLeish and make matters difficult for Scotland. As one interviewee put it: 'it was about not co-operating with a policy they thought was stupid and inconvenient.' Both the officials inter-viewed felt that 'if they were sympathetic, they would have found a way of helping.' Instead, London 'wasn't looking for a neat solution.'

Most observers predicted that the fiscal arrangements of devolution would prohibit significant divergence. In fact, the generosity of Gordon Brown's recent budgets and Spending Reviews has created the unexpected situation where 'Barnett consequentials' have provided considerable flexibility in the budgets of the devolved administrations.[43] The irony is that the higher spend-ing by London, which makes policy innovation in Scotland possible now, also speeds up the process of convergence.[44] This will make innovation in the future more difficult.

In the end, this raises questions about the sustainability of Scotland's free personal care policy and the capacity for further divergence in the future. In the meantime, however, it is clear that two conditions necessary for Scot-land's policy to diverge currently exist: there is no central policy framework requiring common health care services, and Scotland has the fiscal capacity to offer a more generous set of welfare programmes than do the other coun-tries of the UK. Determining that the policy room existed for Edinburgh to

[42] Bell and Christie, p. 137. An example of the extent of Treasury control is the provision in *Scotland's Parliament* for the Treasury to oversee the way the Scottish Parliament manages local council finances: 'If growth relative to England were excessive and were such as to threaten targets set for public expenditure as part of the management of the UK economy and the Scottish Parliament nevertheless chose not to exercise its powers, it would be open to the UK government to take the excess into account in considering the level of their support for expenditure in Scotland' (para. 7.24).

[43] MacKenzie, K., 'Great Expectations: — The Scottish Experience' (notes for speech at PSA Conference, 2002, Aberdeen, Scotland).

[44] Heald, D., 'Memorandum by Professor Heald: Funding Devolution', submission to House of Lords Constitution Select Committee on the Constitution Session 2001–02 *Devolution: Inter-institutional relations in the United Kingdom* Evidence complete to 10 July 2002 HL Paper 147.

diverge from Westminster over the issue of free personal care is one issue. Understanding why Scotland chose to use it in the way that it did is another.

Political and Cultural Differences

Strong political and cultural differences between regions in a state with multilevel governance are often used to explain policy divergence[45] and could be expected to account for Scotland's decision regarding free personal care. In fact, public opinion surveys indicate that views on old age care in particular, and the appropriate role of government in general, do not appear sufficiently different on either side of the Scotland/England border to explain this case.

Data reported in *Research Volume I* from the Sutherland commission showed that there was strong support for government funding for long-term care across all of Great Britain. Seventy one per cent of respondents agree that 'the taxpayer should provide for the needs of all people who need care.'[46] Unfortunately these data were not broken down by country. On a similar note, funding of long-term care for the elderly was ranked as the fourth highest priority in a survey commissioned by the BBC.[47] This shows that even in England, where the government opted not to fund personal care for the elderly, there was significant public support for the proposal. Indeed, concerns about the Scottish tail wagging the British dog over free personal care can be seen as further evidence of support for free personal care on both sides of the border.[48] Otherwise, there would have been no pressure on England to follow Scotland's lead.

While it may be difficult to show a strong difference of opinion on long-term care specifically, some authors have found evidence of political and cultural differences between Scotland and the rest of the UK, which could have indirectly influenced the outcome over free personal care. Using data from the 1997 British Election Survey, the authors of *The Scottish*

[45] Banting and Corbett point to political and cultural differences, along with the relative strength of stakeholders (see page 228 below,) as an explanation of why governments choose to pursue different policies. p. 22.

[46] *With Respect to Old Age — Research Volume I*, Royal Commission on Long Term Care, p. 245. Data source: Swiss Re UK Insurance Report, 1997. Data is nationally representative of Great Britain; unfortunately, it is not broken down between England, Wales and Scotland. The bulk of the data in the report pertains to only England and Wales.

[47] " 'Get your priorities right — tackle waiting lists', says poll for BBC's YOUR NHS Day", BBC Press Release 20 Feb. 2002. The sample for the BBC poll was of English respondents, however the results were 'weighted to the profile of all adults in Great Britain.' Applying English responses to all of the UK implies that the authors of the poll at least believe there are not substantive differences between English and Scottish views.

[48] Articles in English, Welsh and Northern Irish newspapers all argued that their governments should follow the example set by Scotland. Jonathan Ellis, health policy officer at Help the Aged England was widely quoted urging 'Westminster to swallow its pride' and follow Scotland's lead. Among the many articles that covered Mr. Ellis' remarks, see Prosser, D., 'Anger as Scots Pick Up Better Care Payments' *Sunday Express*, 30 June, 2002.

Electorate claim that 'Scotland is different from the rest of Great Britain . . . being more socialist, more liberal and less British nationalist.'[49] Moreover, they claim that 'there is in fact relatively little regional variation [within Scotland] in these value scales.'[50]

The pervasive belief that Scotland is more to the 'left' than England is also reflected in the idea, raised by almost everyone interviewed, that it is 'Old' rather than 'New' Labour which dominates in Scotland. This distinction, however, was disputed by one interviewee. While he agreed that the party organisation has not changed in Scotland, he nonetheless argued that many who prefer to call themselves 'Old' Labour have, in fact, adopted 'New' policies so the differences are not as strong as many like to believe.

Although they conclude that Scotland's identity does have 'an important political dimension',[51] the authors of *How Scotland Votes* agree that the picture is more complicated. Using 1992 data, they claim that, although Scots in general are more likely to favour government intervention over a range of issues, once the results are broken down according to respondents' economic prosperity, it appears that it is the less-well off among Scottish voters who form a distinct group, rather than Scottish people overall.[52]

Using the 1999 Scottish Parliamentary Election Survey and the 1999 British Attitudes Survey, Paterson *et al* go even further to dispel the belief that Scottish and English policy preferences are significantly different. They found a 'broad similarity of views' on a range of questions regarding public welfare and the appropriate role for government. For instance, 89 per cent in Scotland and 84 per cent in England agreed that 'the government is mainly responsible for residential care of elderly people.' Similarly, even when reminded of the possible tax implications, 70 per cent in Scotland and 71 per cent in England felt that there should be more government spending on retired people.[53]

Although England may be large enough to resist pressure to adopt policies chosen by the devolved administrations, policy competition is acknowledged as an important factor determining Scottish policy. Westminster is too large a presence for Scotland to ignore. One interviewee stated that 'it is like being in bed with an elephant.' Similarly, in evidence it submitted to the

---

[49] Brown, A., McCrone, D., Paterson, L. and Surridge, P., *The Scottish Electorate* (London: MacMillan, 1999), p. 76.

[50] Brown *et al*, p. 78.

[51] Bennie, L., Brand, J. and Mitchell, J., *How Scotland Votes* (Manchester: Manchester University Press, 1997), p. 141.

[52] *Ibid*, p. 126. Data comes from the 1992 Scottish Election Study. For instance, 57 per cent of Scottish and 55 per cent of English respondents whose prosperity had risen strongly agreed that 'government should put more money into the NHS.' The comparable figures for those whose prosperity had fallen is 84 per cent in Scotland and 70 per cent in England.

[53] Paterson, L., Brown, A., Curtice, J., Hinds, K., McCrone, D., Park, A., Sproston, K. and Surridge, P., *New Scotland, New Politics?* (Edinburgh: Polygon, 2001), pp. 124–5.

Finance Committee as part of the Budget Process 2003–04, the Health and Community Care Committee of the Scottish Parliament acknowledged that:

> A major question to be addressed is the extent to which developments in Scotland should reflect the developments south of the border. . . . In principle, the Scottish Executive could choose a different course from that in England but clearly there will be major implications for the Scottish NHS through changes in public expectations and demands.[54]

One MSP interviewed claimed that public pressure to follow similar policies is much greater than he had anticipated. He believed it 'results from the publicity that attaches to different decisions in the different jurisdictions.'

Public pressure to follow policies adopted elsewhere in the UK suggests that, despite the strength of the Scottish press, there is a common debate over public policy across the UK. Similarly, it suggests that policy preferences share much common ground. Thus, despite the salience of Scottish identity, it appears that political or cultural differences are insufficient to explain the outcome over free personal care.

Relative Strength of Stake-holders

Differences in the relative strength of stakeholders in each region may also make policy divergence more likely and so help to explain why Scotland chose to implement free personal care. Indeed it does appear that the interests advocating in support of Lord Sutherland's recommendation were more influential in Edinburgh than London. When asked if they felt they had influenced the outcome over free personal care, a representative of one advocacy group claimed: 'I think we should take a lot of credit for it; we kept up the pressure.' Another claimed it was their evidence to the Health and Community Care Committee which ensured that a statement of the principle of free personal care was added to the Community Care and Health (Scotland) Act.

According to an official interviewed, 'pressure groups have, and expect to have, free access to Ministers' in Scotland. A number of interviewees felt advocacy groups are influential simply because the Parliament is so new. One argued that ministers do not yet have the 'firmness of purpose' to stand up to interest groups or media attention. Another said this was particularly true of Henry McLeish. From this perspective, one might expect that, as ministers gain confidence and experience, the influence of interest groups will fall. On the other hand, it is interesting that both of the organisations interviewed stressed their connections to the Parliament rather than to ministers. Both organisations provide co-secretaries to the cross-party group in the Scottish Parliament on Older People, Age and Aging. One noted the importance of this group for building relationships and identifying allies. Both

---

[54] Health and Community Care Committee, Scottish Parliament, 'Budget Process 2003–04 Stage 1 Submission to the Finance Committee', 16 May, 2002, p. 1.

groups have also provided evidence to the Health and Community Care Committee on a number of issues, including free personal care, and were pleased their relations with committee members were strong enough for them to 'be available to call.'

Where 'insider status' usually relates to influence over ministers and government officials, these groups were satisfied that their efforts targeted at the Parliament rather than the Executive had been effective in securing a commitment to free personal care. In other words, one reason for the difference in the strength of stakeholders is the institutional arrangements of the Scottish Parliament.

STRUCTURAL EXPLANATIONS FOR THE USE OF POLICY SPACE

To understand why Scotland implemented Lord Sutherland's recommendation on personal care for the elderly, two additional sets of structural factors must also be considered: the design of the Scottish Parliament and electoral system, and the division of responsibilities.

Design of the Scottish Parliament and Electoral System

In significant ways, Scottish devolution was explicitly designed to give greater power to the Scottish Parliament *vis à vis* the Executive than that enjoyed by the Westminster Parliament *vis à vis* the Cabinet. It was also designed to make the process of governance in Scotland more inclusive and democratic. As a result, societal factors will be translated into political decisions in a different manner. The additional member system and the design of parliamentary committees were two important features designed to change the shape of political debate. All interviewees were asked the extent to which these factors affected the decision over free personal care.

The representatives of the elderly lobby felt that the Health and Community Care Committee was important, not least because it provided a means of access to the political system. However, while the parliamentarians agreed that small changes can be made to legislation at the committee stage, they nonetheless argued that the impact of committees was less significant than intended because, on key votes, some parties require members to vote according to party line.

Unlike their mixed reaction to committees, all interviewees were adamant that the electoral system has a major impact on Scottish politics and was crucial to the outcome on free personal care. Although the Liberal Democrats' are only the fourth largest party in the Scotland Parliament, as minority members of the coalition government, their position is pivotal. Their willingness to turn against Scottish Labour over issues such as tuition fees and free personal care has clearly demonstrated their power. On the crucial vote over the principle of free personal care, the Cabinet was forced do a last-minute U-turn because of the Liberal Democrat threat to vote against the government.

In addition to raising the influence of the Liberal Democrats, coalition government has also altered the strategies of opposition parties. Although the Liberal Democrats are pleased to take credit for the decision over free personal care, the party had, in fact, voted against the policy on previous occasions and had not insisted that a commitment to free personal care be included in the coalition agreement it signed with Labour. It was an SNP motion which forced the U-turn by the government. Similarly, both the SNP and the Scottish Conservative and Unionist Party supported the principle and had raised the subject repeatedly in the house.

Although undoubtedly many individual MSPs were motivated by commitment to the principle of free personal care, it is equally clear that both parties saw a strategic advantage in challenging the government on issues it knew to be contentious for the Liberal Democrats. A Conservative MSP interviewed admitted that the opposition strategy in the Parliament is to compare the Liberal Democrat election manifesto with the coalition agreement and then raise for debate all those items which the Liberal Democrats had been forced to abandon in order to reach agreement with Labour.

If Labour and the Liberal Democrats continue to form a coalition government after the next election, and if the SNP and Conservatives continue to adopt this strategy in Parliament, then issues traditionally associated with the 'left' (such as social spending) will continue to dominate Scottish politics. This increases the likelihood of future divergence.

The Division of Responsibilities

Hazell has noted that the 'policy departures [of the devolved administrations] mostly involve additional public expenditure.'[55] In addition to the effects of coalition of government, the division of responsibilities between Westminster and the Scottish Parliament helps to contribute to this trend in at least two ways. First, the separation of expenditure and revenue raising responsibilities changes the shape of political debate in Scotland making it more likely to generate spending proposals such as free personal care. Second, the asymmetric character of devolution means that Westminster is poorly placed to serve as guardian of the welfare state. Instead, the devolved administrations, with spending proposals like free personal care, seem to be taking on that role.

The SNP generally sits to the left of the political spectrum so its strategy of supporting Liberal Democrat positions such as free personal care is easy to understand. It is harder to understand, however, why the Conservative Party would raise issues which were presumably too far to the left to have been

---

[55] Hazell, 'Conclusion', *State of the Nations 2001*, p. 259.

accepted by Labour. With respect to free personal care, a number of explanations, including the need to overcome the legacy of the Thatcher government and define the party as 'Scottish', almost certainly played a role.[56] An additional, structural, explanation is that the Conservative's traditional platform of fiscal restraint is undermined by the lack of fiscal autonomy for the Scottish Parliament. Without any significant responsibility for raising revenue or lowering taxes, there is no political capital to be gained for a party by arguing for smaller government. The result is that debate is biased toward spending initiatives rather than a cost-cutting agenda.

The devolution White Paper explicitly sets out responsibility for 'the stability of the UK's fiscal, economic and monetary system' as a reserved matter.[57] Thus, political debate at Westminster, as for most governments, involves a trade-off between spending and borrowing or taxation. In Scotland, there is a budget constraint (the limit of the transfer from London), but it is determined outside the Scottish political process. There is no internal debate over the appropriate level of government spending. Hence, the trade-off which characterises normal politics can be more easily ignored. When asked if his party would have been as likely to support free personal care if Scotland had more fiscal autonomy, a Conservative MSP conceded: 'if you have a spending commitment that would impact on your borrowing as a treasury, I suppose that would impact on everything else. We just simply have to say we know that for the next 20 years we're going to get a block so we'll just devote that much to it. So in that, it is easier.'

Where the focus of Scottish debate is likely to centre on spending priorities, the same is not true of Westminster. The dynamic set up by coalition government and the separation of expenditure and revenue raising responsibilities is accentuated by the asymmetric character of devolution. Banting and Corbett assume that social rights to citizenship in federal countries must be safeguarded by rules that are co-ordinated, if not enforced, by the central government.[58] By tying commitment to social citizenship to central co-ordinating structures, they imply that, in their absence, regional governments, in the name of diversity, will eat away at the provisions of the welfare state. Yet free personal care is an example of Scotland expanding the welfare state. Indeed, all the most likely scenarios for policy divergence in the UK involve either expansion of welfare state programmes by the devolved administrations or retrenchment by London. Central co-ordinating instruments can only safeguard a minimum level of access. London would only

---

[56] For a fuller discussion of the effect of Scottish valence issues on the Scottish Conservative and Unionist Party, see, Seawright, D., "The Scottish Conservative and Unionist Party: 'the lesser spotted Tory'?" (paper presented at the Annual Conference of the Political Studies Association, University of Aberdeen, 5–7 April 2002).

[57] Scottish Office, *Scotland's Parliament*, para 3.3.

[58] Banting and Corbett, p. 22.

ever agree to a policy framework that was consistent with its own more narrow definition of social citizenship.

The common assumption that regional governments seek to minimise the scope of the welfare state is plausible. Much of the research on the effects of federalism has shown that inter-regional competition commonly generates a 'race to the bottom' in government spending as sub-governments try to attract capital and investment.[59] Sitting apart from this dynamic, the central government in a federal state is, in theory, able to defend social citizenship by ensuring that an agreed upon level of services is provided across the country.[60]

The position of Westminster *vis á vis* the devolved administrations, however, is not the same as that found in a full-fledged federation. In addition to exercising reserved functions on behalf of all of the UK, Westminster acts as the unitary government for England. Thus, it is simultaneously the central government and the largest, most powerful regional government. As a result, it does not sit outside the competitive dynamic often attributed to regional governments in federal states. Moreover, unlike many federal governments, it has little scope for issuing unfunded mandates or off-loading to lower levels of government because it would in effect be off-loading to itself. Westminster is unlikely to recklessly champion social issues that could create expensive new demands on its own budget. All this means that Westminster may pose a greater threat to welfare state programmes in the UK than any of the devolved administrations.

In this context, policy variation doesn't necessarily indicate a lack of commitment to common standards. Rather, it may reveal a conflict over the appropriate boundaries of social citizenship, with the devolved administrations defining it more broadly than London. After all, free personal care was defended as the fulfilment of the NHS principle of universal access from cradle to grave, free at the point of delivery. It was not defended in the name of a uniquely Scottish need. As a result, so long as Scotland can afford it, central co-ordinating structures such as a central policy statement would not stand in the way of the kind of policy divergence that is most likely to occur.

CONCLUSION

If the battle over free personal care was a battle over the legitimate scope of the NHS, does that mean that making it free only in Scotland *is* an example of

---

[59] Banting.

[60] Antonia Maioni makes this point with respect to Canada. Against proposals for provinces to collectively agree and enforce principles of health policy in Canada, she argues that a federal role is essential because provinces will not live up to their commitments in the complete absence of federal coercion. See Maioni, A., 'Decentralization in health policy: Comments on the ACCESS Proposals', in R. Young, (ed) *Stretching the Federation: The Art of the State in Canada* (Kingston: Institute of Intergovernmental Relations, 1999).

a 'post-code lottery'? Not necessarily. There will always voices calling for it to be extended to the rest of the UK just as there will always be those who argue it was a bad policy even for Scotland. The creation of the devolved parliaments has given new weapons to those engaged in the UK-wide debate over the appropriate role of government. At the same time, it has made it possible for differing conceptions of the proper role to co-exist in the different countries of the UK, however uneasy the relationship between them might be. In this way, regional diversity can contribute to an ongoing debate over the appropriate scope of social citizenship. Policy competition and the spread of innovation from one region across to others are the creative expressions of the tension between social citizenship and regional diversity. Intergovernmental conflict and deadlock are its more destructive manifestations. The case of free personal care embodies both.

Free personal care for the elderly clearly illustrates the potential for policy divergence in the devolved UK. There are no structures in place to dictate the shape of health policy in any of the countries of the UK, and, under the current fiscal conditions at least, the centralised control over the budgets of the devolved administrations hasn't created any serious impediment to divergence. Although the financial situation creating Scotland's current budgetary flexibility may not last, it is clear that the arrangements of Scottish devolution will continue to lead to divergent trends in the policy agendas of Scotland and Westminster. These arrangements include the electoral system and committee structure which give a stronger voice to opposition parties and advocates, as well as the division of powers and the asymmetrical position of Westminster *vis à vis* the devolved administrations, which make the calculation of the trade-offs involved in particular policy proposals very different for each order of government.

Given these dynamics, a central policy framework probably would not have stopped Scotland from expanding on NHS services through the provision of free personal care. At the same time however, the lack of an agreed upon minimum level of health care service or set of guiding principles for the NHS does make it possible for future governments, including the Westminster government, to seriously challenge the fundamental nature of the NHS. Those who believe the commitment to equity across the UK should be reinforced, as well as those who support the current shape of the NHS, might be wise to argue for an articulation of the Union-wide principles of the NHS now, while commitment to it in all regions remains strong.

BIBLIOGRAPHY

Official Documents
Department of Health and Scottish Executive Health Department, 'Concordat on Health and Social Care.'

Health and Community Care Committee, Scottish Parliament, 'Budget Process 2003–04 Stage 1 Submission to the Finance Committee.' 16 May 2002.

Scottish Executive press release, 'Free personal care now on stream', 1 July 2002.

Scottish Executive press release, 'Free Personal Care', 1 July, 2002.

Scottish Office, *Scotland's Parliament*. 1997.

Scottish Parliament Information Centre, Research Note, 'Royal Commission on Long Term Care (Sutherland Report)' (RN 00/78), 26 Sept. 2000

Royal Commission on Long-Term Care, Lord S. Sutherland Chair, *With Respect to Old Age: Long Term Care — Rights and Responsibilities*, 1999.

Royal Commission on Long Term Care, Lord S. Sutherland Chair, *With Respect to Old Age — Research Volume I*, 1999.

Secondary Sources

Adams, J. and Robinson P. (eds), *Devolution in Practice: Public Policy Differences within the UK* (London: IPPR, 2002).

Age Concern Scotland Briefing Note, 'Long Term Care Funding Update', November 2001.

Age Concern Scotland Briefing Note, 'Free Personal and Nursing Care', June 2002.

Banting, K., 'Social citizenship and Canadian Federalism: the Old and New Politics of Health Care.' Draft paper prepared for the Workshop on Federalism and the Welfare State, University of Bremen, May 2002.

Banting, K. and Corbett, S., 'Health Policy and Federalism: An Introduction', *Health Policy and Federalism: a comparative perspective on multi-level governance*, K. Banting and S. Corbett (eds) (Kingston: Queens-McGill Press, 2001), pp. 1–38.

Bennie, L., Brand, J. and Mitchell, J., *How Scotland Votes* (Manchester: Manchester University Press, 1997).

Bradbury J. and Mitchell, J., 'Devolution: New Politics or Old?' *Parliamentary Affairs* (April 2001) 45 (2), pp. 257– 275.

Braun, D. (ed) *Public Policy and Federalism* (Aldershot: Ashgate, 2000).

Brown, A., McCrone, D., Paterson, L. and Surridge, P., *The Scottish Electorate*. (London: MacMillan, 1999).

Dunleavy, P., Gamble, A., Holliday, I. and Peele, G. (eds), *Developments in British Politics 6* (Basingstoke: Palgrave, 2000).

Greer, S. *Divergence and Devolution* (London: The Constitution Unit, 2001).

Hazell, R., (ed), *Constitutional Futures: A History of the Next Ten Years* (Oxford: Oxford University Press, 1999).

Heald, D. 'Memorandum by Professor Heald: Funding Devolution.' Submission to House of Lords Constitution Select Committee on the Constitution Session 2001–02 *Devolution: Inter-institutional relations in the United Kingdom* Evidence complete to 10 July 2002 HL Paper 147, CC/01–02/66.

Heald, D, Geaughan, N., Robb, C., 'Financial Arrangements for UK Devolution', in *Remaking the Union* M. Keating and H. Elcock (eds) (London: Frank Cass, 1998), pp. 23–51.

Help the Aged Scottish Policy Briefing 'Free Personal Care', June 2002.

MacKenzie, K. 'Great Expectations: — The Scottish Experience'. Notes for speech at Political Studies Association Conference 2002, Aberdeen, Scotland.

McMahon, P. 'How McLeish made up his policies on the hoof', *The Scotsman* 26 Jan. 2002.

Maioni, A., 'Decentralization in health Policy: Comments on the ACCESS Proposals', in R. Young (ed), S*tretching the Federation: The Art of the State in Canada* (Kingston: Institute of Intergovernmental Relations, 1999), pp. 97–121.

Paterson, L., Brown, A., Curtice, J., Hinds, K., McCrone, D., Park, A., Sproston, K. and Surridge, P., *New Scotland, New Politics?* (Edinburgh: Polygon, 2001).

Seawright, D. 'The Scottish Conservative and Unionist Party: 'the lesser spotted Tory'?' Paper presented at the Annual Conference of the Political Studies Association, University of Aberdeen, 5–7 April 2002. (Due for Publication in Hassan, G. and Warhurst, C. *Tomorrow's Scotland*, Forthcoming.)

Trench, A. (ed), *State of the Nations 2001: The Second Year of Devolution in the United Kingdom* (Exeter: Imprint Academic, 2001).

Ward, A., 'Devolution: Labour's Strange Constitutional 'Design',' *The Changing Constitution 4th ed.* J. Jowell and D. Oliver (eds) (Oxford: Oxford University Press, 2000).

Wright, A. (ed), *Scotland: the Challenge of Devolution* (Aldershot: Ashgate Publishers, 2000).

Part IV

The 2003 Elections, and issues in the second term

10

Elections in Multi-Level Systems
Lessons for the UK from Abroad

Dan Hough and Charlie Jeffery

INTRODUCTION

The devolution of powers to the Scottish Parliament and the National Assembly for Wales seems to have introduced a new dimension to British electoral politics. Figure 10.1 sets out the Scottish and Welsh results in the two Westminster elections of 1997 and 2001 and in the devolved elections which took place roughly at the Westminster midpoint in 1999. The outcomes for Westminster were fairly stable; the devolved election results looked, though, rather different. Most strikingly Labour lost out quite dramatically in Scotland and Wales, while the Scottish National Party (SNP) and especially its Welsh counterpart Plaid Cymru (PC) made remarkable advances.

Figure 10.1: Election results in 1997, 1999 and 2001 in Scotland and Wales

	1997 General Election		1999 Devolved Elections		2001 General Election	
	Scotland	Wales	Scotland	Wales	Scotland	Wales
Labour	45.6	54.7	33.6	35.5	43.9	48.6
Conservatives	17.5	19.6	15.4	16.5	15.6	21.0
Lib Dems	13.0	12.4	12.4	12.5	16.4	13.8
SNP	22.1	-	27.3	-	20.1	-
Plaid Cymru	-	10.0	-	30.6	-	14.3
Others	1.8	3.3	11.3	4.9	4.0	2.3

The parties' interpretations of the 1999 and 2001 results were interesting. The unexpected success of PC in Wales in 1999 was viewed as a massive 'swing' from Labour to PC amounting to an electoral 'earthquake'.[1] And the PC result for Westminster in 2001 was seen as a halt to the party's 'forward

---

[1] So said the then PC leader Dafydd Wigley. See Tristan, D. and Wyn Jones, R., 'A Quiet Electoral Earthquake', *Agenda:. Journal of the Institute of Welsh Affairs*, Summer 1999, www.iwa.org.uk

march' and as a resumption of 'normal service' for Labour.[2] The responses in Labour and the SNP in Scotland were similar. All these are most likely misconceived views. They interpret all election results, Westminster and devolved, through a Westminster lens. Devolution means, though, that voters in Scotland and Wales now vote in elections to new bodies with a significant scope of decision-making authority separate from that of Westminster.[3] The Scottish Parliament has the power to make its own laws across most fields of domestic policy. The Welsh Assembly, though dependent on a Westminster legislative framework, has the power to diverge from the Westminster norm in implementing and fleshing out legislation in Wales.

The assumption that this chapter will explore is that the new context of devolution will lead Scottish and Welsh voters to act differently in devolved elections as compared to Westminster elections. One of the mantras of the devolution campaigns in Scotland was that it would allow for 'Scottish answers to Scottish questions'.[4] The implication was that there was a distinctive Scottish political will straining to get off the Westminster leash. There was a similar, perhaps less strong feeling that devolution would better enable Welsh citizens to have an influence on the decisions that directly affect them.[5] Again the implication was that they would want things done differently. Devolution, in this view, will lead voters to respond to cues different to those that shape their decisions for Westminster.

This is of course not an uncontested view. The alternative — reflected in the party responses recounted above — would be that, despite devolution, Westminster will remain the main reference point for the expression of views about politics and political parties in all elections in all parts of the UK. Voters' decisions in Scottish and Welsh devolved elections will really be about their views on the parties in Westminster and the political issues which play out across the UK, irrespective of internal territorial boundaries. There was perhaps some circumstantial support for this view in the 2001 Westminster election, when the manifestos of the Britain-wide parties — Labour, Conservative and Liberal Democrat — each made promises which extended into the remits of the devolved bodies and beyond that formally in the hands of Westminster.[6] Are the distinctions between Westminster powers and

---

[2] Wyn Jones, R. and Scully, R., 'Devolution Five Years On: the Case of Wales', paper presented to the 2002 Annual Conference of the Elections, Public Opinion and Parties Specialist Group of the Political Studies Association of the UK, 13–15 September, p. 7.

[3] And, of course, in principle in Northern Ireland. However, because of the unique pattern of the party system in Northern Ireland and the uncertainty surrounding the devolution process after the Northern Ireland Assembly was suspended for the fifth time in October 2002, we do not discuss Northern Ireland in this contribution.

[4] Paterson, L. et al, *New Scotland, New Politics?* (Edinburgh: Polygon, 2001), p. 29.

[5] Osmond, J., 'Introduction', in Osmond, J. (ed) *The National Assembly Agenda* (Cardiff: Institute of Welsh Affairs, 1998), pp. 1–3.

[6] Trench, A., *Devolution and the 2001 General Election. Devolution Commitments of the Major Parties* (London: Constitution Unit, 2001).

devolved powers going to be understood by voters if the political parties fail to recognise them?

It is, of course, a little early to tell which view is the most accurate. Scottish and Welsh voters are still novices in working through the implications of what we have termed 'multi-level electoral competition'.[7] There will need to be a much fuller dataset of devolved and post-devolution Westminster elections before any firm conclusions can be drawn as to whether those voters will indeed vote according to different criteria for Holyrood and Cardiff Bay than for Westminster.

In the interim we can though look for pointers on how multi-level electoral competition works by looking at other countries that have regional elections and by identifying how far they present analogies relevant to the UK. What is the relationship between regional and national elections? Are regional elections subordinated to the dynamics of national politics?[8] Or are there circumstances in which regional elections can become uncoupled from the national electoral process and follow a region-specific dynamic?

In this chapter we present an overview of relevant models that may help us unpack the relationship between regional and national electoral arenas. In the first section we build on ideas about 'first' and 'second order' elections to explore the question of whether regional elections are dominated by national factors. We find that often they are not, so we then look at ways of capturing the scale of regional differentiation of voting behaviour from the nation-wide norm. At each stage we draw on illustrative data from three states:

- Germany, where a fairly predictable relationship between regional and national elections has existed and where strong regional differentiation of voting behaviour has been the exception.
- Spain, where the relationship of regional to national elections is complicated by distinctive sets of regional electoral dynamics in the historic 'nationalities' of Catalonia, the Basque Country and Galicia.
- Canada, where the sheer size of the country and the divide between a mainly Francophone Quebec and a mainly Anglophone rest-of-Canada has led to regional and national electoral dynamics becoming more or less completely uncoupled from one another.

The range of possibilities illustrated by these three states allows us in the third section to interpret the limited data we have on the Scottish and Welsh cases so far from election results, opinion poll data and survey analysis. On

---

[7] Work for this paper was carried out as part of the research project on 'Multi-Level Electoral Competition' which forms part of the Research Programme 'Nations and Regions: The Dynamics of Devolution' run by the Constitution Unit, University College London and funded by the Leverhulme Trust.

[8] The terminology of 'regions' may be controversial when applied to some territorial units, including the 'nations' of Scotland and Wales. However, it is the standard term and a necessary semantic simplification in comparative analysis, and will therefore be used here.

this basis we suggest in conclusion that Scottish and Welsh voters will indeed make different kinds of judgment at the ballot box for future devolved elections — starting in May 2003 — as compared to Westminster.

ARE REGIONAL ELECTIONS 'SECOND ORDER' ELECTIONS?

Oddly, relatively little work has been done on the relationship of regional to national elections. Most of the cues for understanding that relationship have to be drawn from work on the interrelationships of other electoral arenas. Ideas developed about the relationship of presidential to mid-term congressional elections in the USA and of both European Parliament and local elections to national elections in western Europe provide a useful starting point. In particular they point to the apparent existence of an 'electoral cycle' which reveals swings in support for the party or parties in power in national government in the results of elections to *other* bodies.[9]

The typical cycle works as follows: National government parties enjoy an (often painfully short) honeymoon period shortly after their election victory. In that period levels of support may even increase. But the honeymoon is followed by an (often rapid) drop in support which continues until roughly the middle of the legislative period, when it 'bottoms out'. At the same time support for the main opposition party rises. Only in the period immediately before the next national election do the governing parties begin to recover.

Among the earliest analyses of this cycle were those of Goodhart and Bhansali, then Miller and Mackie in the early 1970s on Great Britain.[10] Their analyses of opinion poll data clearly revealed a 'typical' cyclical pattern of government and opposition support, though they differed as to what best explained the cycle. Goodhart and Bhansali proposed a correlation with economic performance. In other words, governments tend to take unpopular economic policy decisions early in their period in office, and then try to engineer an economic 'feel-good' factor later on as the next election approaches. Miller and Mackie proposed a more general 'anti-government effect' based on the tendency of the party of government to lose by-elections in mid-term.

Tufte, Stimson and Erikson all applied a similar logic to the American case. The pattern they identified was (and is) unmistakable: 'In midterm elections, the president's party almost always suffers a decline in its share of

---

[9] A large body of research now exists on electoral cycles and their respective national manifestations. For a succinct overview see Soldatos, G., 'The electoral cycle: a brief survey of literature', in *Revue d'économie Politique*, 104 (4), 1994, pp. 571–587.

[10] Goodhart, C. and Bhansali, R.: 'Political Economy' in *Political Studies*, (1970), 18, pp. 43–106; Miller, W. and Mackie, M., 'The Electoral Cycle and the Asymmetry of Government and Opposition Popularity: An Alternative Model of the Relationship Between Economic Conditions and Political Popularity', in *Political Studies*, 21, 1973, pp. 263–279.

the congressional vote and a net loss of House seats'.[11] This phenomenon is 'an almost invariable historical regularity', with only two instances of mid-term *gain* by the presidential party — in 1926 and 1998 — through the twentieth century.[12] Tufte saw mid-term loss as a 'referendum' on the performance of the President, in particular on any failure to deliver on the pledges made in the election campaign, and on the tendency (as per Goodhart and Bhansali) for the economic cycle to become synchronised with the electoral timetable.[13] Stimson, meanwhile, downplayed the emphasis on economic performance variables and honed in on the 'problem' of holding the Presidency. As he put it, there was a 'suspicion that presidential approval may be almost wholly independent of the President's behaviour in office, a function largely of inevitable forces associated with time'.[14] Erikson called this the 'presidential penalty', where 'midterm electorates punish the presidential party' 'regardless of the quality of its performance or its standing in the electorate'.[15] Whatever the exact reason, 'at every midterm, the electorate turns against the presidential party' simply *'for being the party in power'*.[16]

First and Second Order Elections

Ideas on electoral cycles returned to western Europe in the late 1970s but in the form of a newly coined terminology of 'orders' of elections. The initial focus was the direct elections to the European Parliament (EP) held for the first time in 1979. These revealed a pattern in which, broadly speaking, the parties currently in national government under-performed 'in Europe' — much as the US President's party seemed to do in congressional elections in the USA. Two German political scientists, Karlheinz Reif and Hermann Schmitt, developed a conceptual framework to explain this European version of mid-term loss.[17] Writing in the immediate aftermath of the 1979 EP elections, they proposed that these elections should be viewed not as *European* elections, but rather as 'second-order' *national* elections, which presented voters with little extra stimulus or incentive than that with which they were already confronted in 'first order' national elections, where national governments are elected and seats in the national legislature are at stake. For Reif and Schmitt all other elections, including 'by-elections, municipal elections,

[11] Tufte, E., 'Determinants of the Outcomes of Midterm Congressional Elections', *American Political Science Review*, (1975), 69 (3) pp. 812–826; Stimson, J., 'Public Support for American Presidents: A Cyclical Model', in *Public Opinion Quarterly*, 40, 1976, p. 1–21; Erikson, R. 'The Puzzle of Mid-Term Loss', *Journal of Politics*, 50 (4), 1998, pp. 1011–1029.

[12] Erikson, 1988, p. 1011.

[13] Tufte, 1975, pp. 824–6.

[14] Stimson, 1976, p. 3.

[15] Erikson, 1988, pp. 1013–14.

[16] Erikson, 1988, p. 1028. Our emphasis.

[17] Reif, K. and Schmitt, H., 'Nine Second-Order National Elections: A Conceptual Framework for the Analysis of European Election Results', *European Journal of Political Research*, 8 (1), 1980, pp. 3–44.

various sorts of regional elections, those to a second chamber and the like', have 'less at stake' and are therefore to be regarded as 'second-order'.[18]

As Reif and Schmitt put it in 1980: 'Many voters cast their votes in these elections not only as a result of conditions obtaining within the specific context of the second-order arena, but also on the basis of factors in the main political arena of the nation'.[19] Reif went further after the next set of EP elections in 1984: 'what is important is the political situation of the first-order arena at the moment when the second-order election is being held'.[20] Building on insights from the US electoral cycles literature, Reif and Schmitt were able to set out the following key propositions about second order elections:

- With less at stake than in first order elections turnout will be lower.
- Crucially, where less is at stake, the government parties in the first order arena are likely to lose support at midterm, and opposition parties to gain support.
- Because less is at stake, voters may 'experiment' with smaller or new parties close to their preferences, but for which votes would be 'wasted' in the first order arena.

Reif and Schmitt therefore propose a European-style 'penalty effect' that punishes national government incumbency in the same way as the 'Presidential penalty' in the US. The only real deviation from the US case concerns the method of punishment, which in the more complex west European party systems can benefit not just the major opposition party but also small and/or new parties. Reduced turnout can also make it easier for small parties to 'flash' into prominence (as did for example the Greens and the UK Independence Party in the 1999 European Parliament elections in the UK by winning 6.2 and 7 per cent respectively of the vote when turnout fell to just 24 per cent of the electorate).

The notion of first/second order elections is now firmly established in the analysis of European election results. What is a little surprising is how few applications of the first/second order framework have been made to the other kinds of second order election Reif and Schmitt set out. One exception is a series of articles comparing British local government and EP elctions during the 1990s. These are notable both for confirming the general thrust of Reif and Schmitt's propositions, but also for differentiating between the 'rank order' of local and EP elections. 'Some second order elections are more second order than others', as McLean *et al.* put it in comparing 1994

---

[18] Reif and Schmitt, 1980, p. 8.
[19] Reif and Schmitt, 1980, p. 7.
[20] Reif, K., 'Ten Second-Order Elections' in Reif, K. (ed) *Ten Second-Order Elections* (Aldershot: Gower, 1985), p.8, our emphasis.

local and EP elections.[21] Heath *et al.* were more precise five years later: 'If the elections to the European Parliament are to be regarded as second-order, then we might think of elections to local councils as "one and three quarters order"'.[22] These differences had to do with the *amount* at stake. Voters evidently felt that more was at stake in local than EP elections — for example services provided by local government — and this was reflected in higher turnout, a higher degree of concern about who won, and a lesser likelihood to vote in accordance with national, first order issues.[23]

The Heath/McLean notion of 'partial second-order-ness' has immediate relevance for regional elections. Although the competencies of regional parliaments vary considerably from state to state, they typically possess significant legislative powers in key areas such as education, culture, public order and regional development. In short, there is normally quite a lot 'at stake', certainly much more than in British local elections. So just how 'second order' are regional elections? How far do Reif and Schmitt's assumptions about the penalisation of the incumbent parties at the national level and the mid-term success of non-government parties play out in regional elections?

Germany

In the German case, the picture was a relatively clear one, though it was complicated by German unification in 1990. The parties that are in power in Berlin (and beforehand in Bonn) have traditionally suffered losses in regional, or *Land* elections. One way of illustrating this in a broad brush way is to follow the approach of Rainer Dinkel in calculating the vote share a party might 'expect' in a Land election based on its performance in the preceding and succeeding national election in that Land.[24] If, for example, a party scored 52 per cent in Bavaria in the 1998 national election and 48 per cent in the 2002 national election, it might 'expect' 50 per cent in an intervening Bavarian Land election. This is obviously a fairly crude measure, but nonetheless provides a basic indicator of how national and regional voting behaviour are linked.

And the data for Germany, prior to unification in 1990 at least, are fairly clear cut (we look separately at the post-unification situation below). In 101

[21] McLean, I., Heath A. and Taylor, B., 'Were the 1994 Euro- and Local Elections in Britain Really Second-Order? Evidence from the British Election Panel Study', in Farrell, D. M., Broughton, D., Denver, D. and Fisher, J. (eds) *British Elections and Parties Yearbook 1996* (London: Frank Cass, 1996), p. 4.

[22] Heath, A., McLean, I., Taylor, B. and Curtice, J., 'Between First and Second Order: A Comparison of Voting Behaviour in European and Local Elections in Britain', *European Journal of Political Research*, 35 (3), 1999, p. 391.

[23] McLean et al, 1996, p. 18; Heath et al, 1999, p. 406.

[24] Dinkel, R., 'Der Zusammenhang zwischen Bundes- und Landtagswahlergebnissen', *Politische Vierteljahresschrift*, 18, 1977, pp. 348–360.

of 103 Land elections between 1949 and 1990, the parties of the national governing coalition polled less than their 'expected' percentage of the vote.[25] Dinkel understood the regularity of this phenomenon as a 'governmental penalty': 'in Land elections many people cast their vote based on the performance of the federal government'.[26] Land elections were therefore 'subordinate elections' that were 'systematically influenced by the national political environment.'[27]

There is a converse to this pattern, which was left implicit in Dinkel's work but which is clear in Reif and Schmitt's understanding: if national government parties typically perform poorly in regional elections, then the national opposition parties should, typically, do well. Indeed, if we use 'expected' vote as a benchmark, the main national opposition party has typically done better in Land elections between national elections than the national government parties. However, this is not a simple mirror image, with the opposition parties doing better than 'expected' in 'only' around 40 per cent of *Land* elections from 1949–1990 (and averaging around 98 per cent of their 'expected' vote). This suggests that any 'opposition bonus' was typically less than the penalty effect for national government parties.

Reif and Schmitt suggest one explanation for the difference between governing party loss and opposition party gain: part of the anti-government effect in second order elections may go to smaller and/or new parties as well as the main parties of national opposition. Voters may use the opportunity of second order elections to send messages of protest or dissatisfaction expressed through 'non-establishment' parties. Looking at the data on small parties from 1960–1990,[28] such parties performed better than expected in 55 per cent of our cases. The German data before 1990 therefore provide fairly solid confirmation of the Reif and Schmitt hypothesis that regional elections are a form of 'second order' national election. They are used to 'punish' national government parties for being in office, with the benefits going to a combination of the main federal opposition party and smaller parties which periodically 'flash' into prominence.

In a sense this is what one would expect. Before 1990 Germany was a territorially homogeneous society. With the partial exception of Bavaria, the same political parties stood on much the same political programmes at both national and Land elections. Those parties reflect patterns of social cleavage

[25] For a much fuller analysis both of Dinkel's model and of the German case in general see Jeffery, C. and Hough, D., 'The Electoral Cycle and Multi-Level Voting in Germany', in Padgett, S. and Poguntke, T. (eds) *Continuity and Change in German Politics: Beyond the Politics of Centrality* (London: Frank Cass, 2001), pp. 73–98.

[26] Dinkel, 1977, p.348.

[27] Dinkel, 1977, pp. 351–2 (our translation).

[28] The period 1949–1960 was a period in which a fragmented multi-party system consolidated into a simple three-party system, in part due to adjustments to the electoral system. It is therefore an outlier period which we leave to one side.

which are non-territorial: the Social Democratic Party is historically associated with unionised manual workers; the Christian Democratic Union and its Bavarian sister party the Christian Social Union, with Catholic voters in particular and active Christians more generally, but also farmers; and the Free Democratic Party with the business community. The Greens too are associated with a nation-wide cleavage, albeit of a new kind between 'materialist' and 'post-materialist' value systems. In these circumstances it is unsurprising that voters may have made decisions on Land elections which reflected the terms of an essentially undifferentiated, nation-wide political debate.

Circumstances have changed, though, since unification. The absorption of former communist East Germany into the united German state has introduced a new, territorial, east-west cleavage. This is based in part on differences in material interest that have resulted from the social and economic disruption caused by the unification process. But there are also remnants of the former East German value system. The net outcome is the emergence of eastern Germany as a 'space' for a distinctive territorial politics — more egalitarian, more statist — than in the west.[29] The clearest expression of this is the continued existence of the former communist party of the east, renamed as the Party of Democratic Socialism (PDS), which regularly gains 20 per cent-plus of the vote in eastern Land elections, but which has no significant strength outside the east.

There is some evidence that the wider process and problems of unification have also heightened specifically *territorial* sensitivities, especially on distributional issues, elsewhere in Germany. These have pitched a more affluent southern Germany against a north/east partly dependent on direct and indirect transfers of resources from the south. In this new situation with an east-west and an incipient north-south cleavage, some of the character of Land elections as second-order national elections seems to have been undermined. There has still been a discernible anti-government effect in Land elections since 1990 and there is still plenty of evidence that small parties over-perform (in 56 per cent of Land elections since 1990 they have done *better* than 'expected'). The big difference is that the national opposition party no longer seems to get a bonus. Only in three cases from 1990–1998 did the main opposition party manage to do better than 'expected' in a Land election. The winners in Land elections are the small parties, and these have typically had a limited territorial reach: the PDS in the east; a number of 'flash' parties of anti-system protest in some of the northern Länder; and parties of the far right in both southern Germany and the east.

The growing territorialisation of political debate in Germany and its converse — a weakened capacity of the 'nation-wide' parties to structure

[29] Hough, D., *The Fall and Rise of the PDS in Eastern Germany* (Birmingham: Birmingham University Press, 2002), pp. 106–107.

political debate in the *Länder* in the same way that they do at the national level — arguably brings Germany a little closer to the situation for multi-level electoral competition in Britain. A small number of core parties dominate electoral politics, but are supplemented in some regions by parties with a region-specific identity. In Germany this has meant a partial decoupling of regional elections from the factors that shape national election results. A fuller insight into whether a similar pattern is likely to take shape in the UK can be drawn from Spain.

Spain

Spain is in many respects close to the model of post-devolution UK. It has an asymmetrical regional structure, with fuller devolved powers exercised by regions — 'historic nationalities' — with distinctive territorial identities and histories that set them apart from Spain's Castilian core. In the historic regions there are strong regionalist parties that compete alongside those parties that are active nation-wide. The coexistence of a 'core Spain' and these historic regions adds a quality to multi-level electoral competition that does not occur in Germany.[30] We can show this by looking at regional and national election results from two regions in 'core' Spain — Castilla-La-Mancha and Extremadura — alongside those from two of the historic regions, Catalonia and Galicia.

What we find is that the governing parties at national level manage a little more frequently than in Germany to win more than their 'expected' vote in regional elections (once each in Catalonia, Galicia and Extremadura, and twice in Castilla-La-Mancha over the period since the first regional elections in 1979). The major difference between the German and Spanish cases is, however, to be found in the performances of the opposition parties at the national level and of regionalist parties. The main national opposition party barely out-performs the national governing parties in regional elections (winning on average 91 per cent of their 'expected vote' against the governing parties average of 87 per cent). The explanation for the poor performance of the main national parties — the Socialists and the centre-right Popular Party — appears to lie principally in the strong performances of regionalist parties. These consistently perform better in elections to the regional assemblies than they do in national polls — indeed, in no regional election has a regional party in one of our selected autonomous communities polled less than their 'expected' share of the vote.

In Catalonia, a historic region with an especially sharp sense of identity, regionalist parties (principally the CiU — Convergence and Union) do

---

[30] For further discussion of the German case, see Hough, D. and Jeffery, C. 'Regionalwahlen in Mehr-Ebenen-Systemen', in Conzelmann, T. and Knodt, M. (eds) *Regionales Europa, europäisierte Regionen: Mannheimer Jahrbuch für Europäische Sozialforschung* (Frankfurt am Main: Campus Verlag, Volume 6, 2002), pp. 213–237; See also Jeffery and Hough, 2001, pp. 73–98.

considerably better in regional elections. In the 1987 regional election, for example, the various Catalan regional parties together won 49.9 per cent of the vote, while in the two national elections around it (1986 and 1989) they polled just 34.4 per cent and 35.2 per cent respectively. The same phenomenon is evident in Galicia, where regional parties have until recently managed to register over 200 per cent of their 'expected' vote in regional elections, winning 23 per cent in the regional poll in 1987, and 11.7 per cent and 10.8 per cent in the national contests before and after. This trend is now evident in more or less every autonomous community, excepting Castilla-La-Mancha, Madrid, Murcia and Castilla-Leon, where no electorally significant regionalist parties exist.[31] Citizens of regions such as these do not posses the strong historical identities (and the differing languages that frequently accompany these identifications) that remain very much in evidence in regions such as Catalonia, the Basque Country and Galicia. Voting behaviour in regions such as Castilla-La-Mancha correspondingly fits much better, if still not perfectly, with the second order model of electoral behaviour. The governing party (traditionally the Socialists but in recent times the Popular Party) registered 98.1 per cent and the opposition parties 108.6 per cent of their expected vote in regional elections. While these figures are only based on five series of elections and should therefore be viewed with a degree of caution, the government does appear to perform under par, whereas the main opposition party performs above expectations — much in line with the first/second order model that Reif and Schmitt introduced.

In other words, voters do appear in the historic regions much more than in core Spain to make different decisions about different levels of government. The nation-wide parties which dominate the national parliament and shape national political debate all do less well in regional elections, where voters do seem as it were to want 'Catalan answers to Catalan questions' and to vote according to different, region-specific criteria. Regional elections in the historic nationalities at least are clearly not 'second order' elections, but rather operate according to a distinctive region-specific dynamic.

Canada

To take the point about regional differentiation further, brief consideration of Canada is useful. In Canada there is a very marked incongruence in the relationship between national and provincial party systems. In fact, in Canada it is difficult to speak of a national party system operating across different levels of government. Rather there are ten (often quite distinctive) regional party systems in the ten provinces as well as an over-arching national party system that contests national polls. The national system is comprised of

---

[31] Pallares, F. and Keating, M., 'Multi-level electoral competition: regional elections and party systems in Spain', in Hough, D., Jeffery, C., and Keating, M., 'Territorial Party Systems', Special Issue of *European Urban and Regional Studies*, Summer 2003, forthcoming.

parties that have only quite tenuous links with the parties that are active in the provinces — even if some of them carry the same labels.[32] Parties do not, therefore, say and do the same things at different levels, and voters seem to view the national and provincial levels as unconnected when making their judgments at the ballot box. The most pronounced example of this was in British Columbia in the 1980s, where the Conservative Party polled a derisory 1 per cent of votes in both the 1983 and 1986 provincial elections, but in the intervening 1984 general election scored an impressive 47 per cent. British Columbia is not an exceptional case and a cursory glance at Canadian electoral politics illustrates that the relationship between party systems and voting behaviour across tiers is very strongly uncoupled.[33] Only the Liberals can now claim to be a genuinely national party registering meaningful levels of support in every election at every level.

The three examples above present a 'spectrum' of results in relation to the idea of first and second order elections. In pre-unification Germany, regional elections could be seen as second order elections whose results were shaped by national factors. The subordinate relationship of regional to national elections seems, though, to have begun to break down since German unification. In Spain, there is evidence, especially in the historic regions, that regional elections are uncoupled from the national electoral process and that they should not be considered second order, but as elections with their own, autonomous logic. In some of the less distinctive regions, though, a pattern closer to the first/second order relationship can be seen. In some parts of Spain but not all, national and regional election processes are uncoupled. And in Canada, national and regional elections processes are uncoupled everywhere.

The explanatory variable that would seem to account for these differences clearly has to do with the level of territorial heterogeneity in the states concerned and the consequent impact of territorial cleavage in structuring political debate. In states without significant territorial cleavages, like pre-unity Germany, regional election processes see discussion of much the same political issues by the same set of political parties as in national elections. The stronger the territorial differentiation of society — and the stronger the articulation of territorial difference by distinctive political parties — the more fully is the regional electoral process likely to be uncoupled from the national electoral process. Our three cases show three different levels of territorial differentiation: the increased territorialisation of German politics since unification; the strong territorial distinctiveness of the historic regions in Spain; and the wholesale territorial differentiation of a geographically vast

[32] Robin, M. (ed) *Canadian Provincial Politics* (London: Prentice Hall, 1978). See also Erikson, R. S. and Filipov, M. G., 'Electoral balancing in federal and sub-national elections: the case of Canada', *Constitutional Political Economy*, 12 (4), December 2001, pp. 313–332.

[33] Hough and Jeffery, 2002, pp. 229-30.

and linguistically divided society in Canada. Our assumption would be that the British situation should closely approximate to that in Spain. Scotland and Wales are 'historic nationalities' distinctive from the 'core' British territory of England. In Scotland and Wales party competition pits Britain-wide parties against territory specific nationalist parties. We would expect regional election results here to diverge from the pattern for UK election results. In the next section we present a technique for capturing more precisely the relative level of territorial differentiation of regional elections from the national norm and, we hope, for offering some clearer markers for the future dynamics of multi-level electoral competition in Britain.

THE TERRITORIAL DIMENSION

Research into issues of territorial politics has taken on a new dynamism in the last 30 years and regional institutions and regional parties have become important components of most west European political systems. Yet there has — again — been a conspicuous absence of analysis in European political science into the effect that the territorial dimension may have on electoral behaviour at the regional level as compared to the national level. However, there has been considerable work on the territorial dimension in Canada, where indices of 'dissimilarity' have been devised to capture how far regional election results differ from those at national level.[34] An index of dissimilarity compares the results of a national election in a particular region with the results of the regional election closest to it in time, and expresses the percentage of the regional electorate who would have to change their vote in order to transform the regional result into the national one. Dissimilarity indices provide a benchmark for capturing how far voting behaviour in a particular region is uncoupled from that at national level.

In Figure 10.2, we set out dissimilarity indices for a selection of regions from Germany, Spain and Canada, basing data on all national elections since the Second World War (since 1979 for Spain, since 1990 in east German Brandenburg). The range of dissimilarities is wide. At the top end of the scale, there is a very marked dissimilarity of election results at the national and regional levels in Canada. In British Columbia it would regularly require changes to the votes of over 50 per cent of the regional electorate to replicate a national election result out of the temporally closest regional election result. In 1974 and 1979 the index dissimilarity peaked at over 60 per cent. The average for British Columbia over the post-war period is 39 per cent. In Alberta too there is a record of stark dissimilarity between regional and

[34] Johnston, R., 'Federal and Provincial Voting: Contemporary Patterns and Historical Evolution', in Elkins, D.J. and Simeon, R. (eds), *Small Worlds: Provinces and Parties in Canadian Political Life* (Agincourt: Methuen, 1980), pp. 106–30: Abedi, A. and Siaroff, A., 'The Mirror has Broken: Increasing Divergence between National and Land Elections in Austria', *German Politics*, 8 (1), 1999: 207–28.

Figure 10.2: The index of dissimilarity in selected regions

	Germany				Spain				Canada			
	Bavaria	North Rhine-Westphalia	Baden-Württemb.	Brandenb'g	Catalonia	Galicia	Extremad.	Castilla-La-Mancha	British Columbia	Ontario	Manitoba	Alberta
1949		4.4							7.3	16.5	6.2	33.4
1953	9.9	7.7	16.5						17.3	16.8	13.7	25.3
1957	11.6	6.6	10.2						29.8	6.3	14.6	17.3
1958									46.6	10.4	16	36.1
1961	10.3	6.2	6.6									
1962									27.7	7.3	9.1	30.3
1963									28.7	13.5	5.9	35
1965	9.8	6.9	4.3						31.6	12.7	2.3	32
1968									48.7	16	18.7	51.3
1969	3.6	2.8	14									
1972	8.5	6.6	3.1						33.6	11.1	17.1	36.9
1974									64.3	10.7	20.1	20.9
1976	3.6	2.9	4.6									
1979					19	22.8			62	6.5	12	25
1980	4.3	5.9	8.5						59	8.5	21	24.5
1982					25.6	22.1	8.8	8.13				
1983	4	9.7	2.5									
1984									58.5	11.5	15	18.5
1986					19.4	9.6	9	2.74				
1987	4.5	9	8.2									
1988									41.5	14.5	4	23.5
1989					13.8	10.1	4.1	5.65				
1990	4.8	9.6	13.4	8.21								
1993					18.9	18.3	6.6	8.41	29	42	47	51.5
1994	4.1	5.5	7.9	11								
1996					19	16.7	4.9	3.36				
1997									38.5	28.5	45	52
1998	9.7	6	10.5	8.81								
2000					14.9	6.6	7	12.7				
Average	6.8	6.4	8.5	9.3	18.7	15.2	6.8	6.8	39	14.6	16.7	32.1

national results, producing an average of 32.1 per cent. Even in regions like Ontario and Manitoba there are still averages of around fifteen per cent and, periodically, radical shifts of opinion in elections to the two levels of government, most notably in the 1990s.[35] These high levels of dissimilarity reflect the extent to which the regional and national electoral processes in Canada are uncoupled from one another.

In western Europe levels of dissimilarity are typically much lower than in Canada. In Germany, as would be expected from a territorially more homogeneous society and a party system largely undifferentiated by territory, the dissimilarity index has rarely exceeded ten per cent, and then most of all in the formative years of the West German state when the party system had not yet stabilised. In quite a number of elections, dissimilarities are extremely low at less than five in every one hundred voters. Even in Bavaria, a region where citizens have a well-developed regional identity, voters do not treat regional and national elections that differently. The average scores — with Bavaria, Baden-Württemberg, North Rhine Westphalia and the eastern German Land of Brandenburg each at less than ten per cent — testify to the relative homogeneity of German society and the nation-wide and nation-integrating party system that society has supported (though, as suggested above, the situation may be changing as politics becomes more territorialised since unification; there is as yet no clear evidence for this in the short run of post-unity data on dissimilarity).

The Spanish case is perhaps the most interesting. In regions such as Extremadura and Castilla-la-Mancha the levels of dissimilarity are at or lower than those for Germany. These are regions in 'core' Spain, which lack strong territorial distinctiveness. Regional election results remain on the whole very close to the pattern of national election results. The dissimilarity indices for the two historic regions by contrast approach Canadian levels. The average level of dissimilarity in Catalonia, for example, is 18.7 per cent while for Galicia it is 15.2 per cent. In Extremadura only every sixteenth voter would have to cast their vote differently if the national result were to be replicated, while in Catalonia and Galicia it would be every fifth or sixth voter. And the big difference is accounted for by the regionalist parties in Catalonia and Galicia, which score significantly better (and nation-wide parties rather worse) at the regional level than at the national level.

SCOTLAND AND WALES: LESSONS FROM ABROAD

So what does all this imply for devolved elections in Scotland and Wales? Will these function as second order elections shaped by UK political debates focused on Westminster? If so, we might expect the governing party in

---

[35] See Hough and Jeffery, 2002: pp. 229–30 for further discussion of this data.

Westminster (currently Labour) to lose out in Scottish and Welsh elections, and both the main opposition party (currently the Conservatives) and other smaller parties — including the Scottish and Welsh nationalists — to do better than the results they recorded for Westminster. Broadly though, the dissimilarity between devolved and Westminster results would be modest, with the same parties shaping much the same kind of political debate at both levels of government. The template here would be Germany prior to unification.

Or will the territorial distinctiveness of Scotland and Wales from 'core' Britain (and the territory-specific political parties that exist there) help to 'insulate' and uncouple devolved elections from wider British electoral dynamics? If so we might expect devolved elections to 'penalise' both the government and the opposition party at national level, that nationalist parties will do much better in devolved elections than for Westminster, and that levels of dissimilarity between devolved and UK elections would be rather higher. The template here would be Spain.

Naturally the evidence we have so far to match up against these propositions is thin. The first devolved elections took place in 1999. Since then there has been one Westminster election in 2001 (though the 1997 election could be said to belong to the devolution era not least because of the centrality of devolution in the victorious Labour Party's manifesto and its emergence as one of the prominent themes of the election campaign). At the start of this chapter we set out in Figure 10.1 the results in Scotland and Wales of these elections plus the 1997 Westminster election. We now take a closer look at those results against the background of our data from Germany, Spain and Canada.

Perhaps the most striking feature of Figure 10.1 is the consistency of the Westminster results in 1997 and 2001. This is historically unusual and probably reflects more than anything else the weak performance of the Conservatives as the official opposition at UK level. Nonetheless this stability provides a useful, stable benchmark for identifying territorial variation. And the devolved elections in 1999 do reveal significant territorial variation. Labour clearly under-performed, scoring 75 per cent of its 'expected' vote in Scotland in 1999 and just 68 per cent in Wales. These are, comparatively speaking, very heavy incumbency penalties which outstrip all but four results recorded in Land elections in Germany over the post-war period. Significantly, the Conservatives also did less well than they might have expected on the basis of even a poor Westminster record in Scotland and Wales in recent years, winning 93 per cent of their expected vote in Scotland in 1999 and just 81 per cent in Wales. These are results closer to the Spanish experience (or that of post-unification Germany) and do not match those that the notion of second order elections would predict.

Likewise, the 1999 results of the Scottish and Welsh nationalist parties, the Scottish National Party and Plaid Cymru in Wales, match up better with those in the historic regions in Spain, or even some of the Canadian provinces. The SNP scored 129 per cent of its 'expected' vote and PC a truly exceptional 251 per cent in 1999. SNP and PC results at Westminster in 1997 and 2001 were, though, clearly of a different order. There would seem to be a region-specific dynamic at play here which works to different rules in devolved and Westminster elections, most strikingly in the Welsh case. These regional specifics appear to be confirmed by indices of dissimilarity relating the 1999 devolved election results to those of 1997 at Westminster. In Scotland, 12.5 per cent of the electorate would have to have voted differently to recreate the Westminster result. This is a figure clearly within the range of results from Spain in Figure 10.2. In Wales the index was 21.8 per cent, which is significantly more than the average for Catalonia since 1979, and puts it in the middle of the range of Canadian results in Figure 10.2. Both Wales and Scotland would appear to have electoral processes that are uncoupled from Westminster. Wales in particular does not look like a second order electoral arena.

Figure 10.3: Voting intentions in Scotland: Labour and Conservative

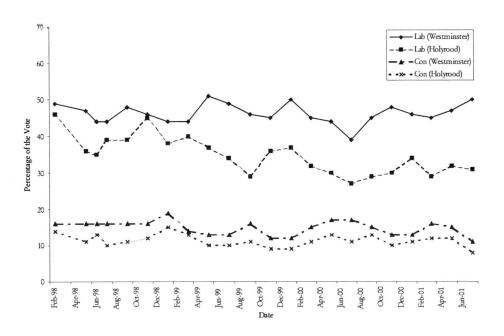

Figure 10.4: Voting Intentions in Wales: Labour and Conservative

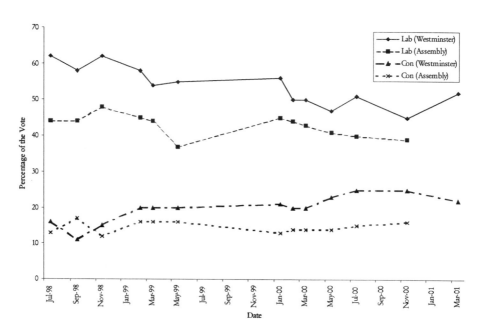

Figure 10.5: Voting Intentions in Scotland: SNP and Liberal Democrats

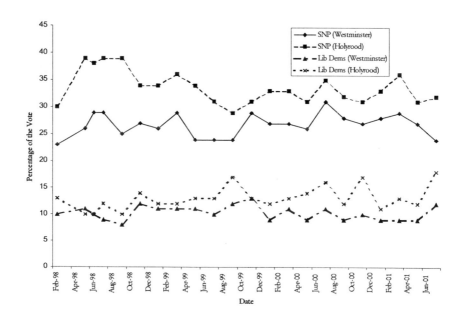

Figure 10.6: Voting Intentions in Wales:
Plaid Cymru and Liberal Democrats

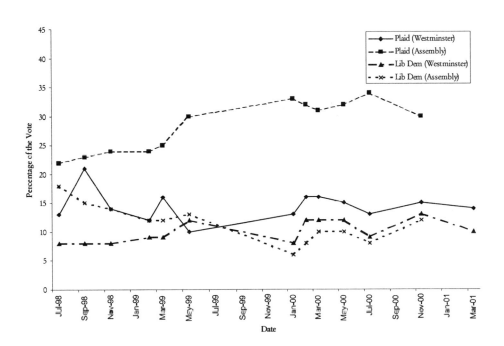

Appearances can of course be deceptive when the dataset is as thin as that so far in post-devolution UK. The 1999 results could prove to be outliers; future results may settle down into something more closely resembling the second order pattern. However, there is some supplementary data available which does seem to point to considerable consistency in the minds of Scottish and Welsh voters in thinking about devolved elections in a different way than they do for Westminster elections. Firstly, commercial opinion polls have pointed to a number of clear patterns in Scotland and Wales by asking simultaneous questions about voting intentions for Westminster and devolved elections. Figures 10.3 to 10.6 reveal the following:

- Labour is significantly more popular in Scotland and Wales in Westminster terms than in terms of voting intentions for Holyrood/Cardiff Bay.
- The Conservatives, the main opposition party at UK-level also has a less pronounced, yet very consistent Westminster 'bonus' (or: devolved 'penalty') in Scotland and Wales.

- The SNP has a steady Holyrood bonus of 5–10 per cent over its support for Westminster.
- PC has a steady Cardiff Bay bonus of 15–20 per cent over its support for Westminster.
- The Liberal Democrats have a slender 0–5 per cent bonus in voting intentions for devolved elections.

It is the steady pattern of these opinion poll findings that is remarkable. There appears to be a systematic distinction in voters' minds about devolved and Westminster elections. Both the main UK parties, Labour and Conservative, are penalised in devolved voting intention, and both nationalist parties have a marked devolution bonus. This pattern is confirmed by specialist opinion research conducted on the two devolved elections in 1999.[36] The Scottish Parliamentary Electoral Survey in 1999 asked voters a) how they had voted for Holyrood and b) how they would vote for Westminster. The results are printed in Figure 10.7 and confirm the pattern of Labour-SNP trade-off. These distinctions were made simultaneously in the course of completing a single survey questionnaire. This reaffirms the point that voting behaviour for Scottish elections is not a snapshot of voters' views about the parties in a 'superior' first order arena. Figure 10.8 sets out equivalent data on Westminster voting intention generated as part of the 1999 Welsh Assembly Election Study and ranged against the actual 1999 results in Wales. Figure 10.9 does so from the 'reverse' perspective of a study of the 2001 general election in Wales, which asked a) how voters had voted for Westminster and b) how they would have voted had there been a Welsh Assembly election. Here the devolved election penalty for Labour is less clear, but the devolution bonus for Plaid Cymru marked. Overall, what is striking is again the systematic distinction voters seem to be making between the devolved and the national arenas.

Figure 10.7: Differential voting intentions in Scotland, 1999[37]

Party	Recalled Vote for Scottish Parliament	Westminster Voting Intention
Conservative	16	16
Labour	39	48
Liberal Democrat	15	14
SNP	28	21

[36] The UK Economic and Social Research Council funded Scottish and Welsh election studies in 1999. Some of their findings are reported in Paterson, 2001, pp. 27–45, and Wyn Jones and Scully, 2002.

[37] Source: Paterson, L. et al, *New Scotland, New Politics* (Edinburgh: Polygon, 2001), p. 32.

Figure 10.8: Differential voting intentions in Wales, 1999[38]

Party	Actual Vote for Welsh Assembly	Westminster Voting Intention
Conservative	16.5	18
Labour	35.5	53
Liberal Democrat	12.5	12
Plaid Cymru	30.6	15

Figure 10.9: Differential voting intentions in Wales, 2001[39]

Party	Actual Vote for Westminster	Recalled Vote for Welsh Assembly
Conservative	17	11
Labour	52	49
Liberal Democrat	16	12
Plaid Cymru	14	26

Both the 1999 election studies offer an explanation for this systematic pattern by honing in on those voters who transfer from Labour to the nationalists in the devolved context. These are not voters especially dissatisfied with Labour at Westminster and indeed see themselves as likely to return to Labour in the Westminster context. At the same time they are not motivated to vote differently by parties' positions on the policy issues that lie in the remit of the Scottish Parliament or Welsh Assembly. Their concern seems to be rather to vote for the party they see as best able to use the institutional platform offered by devolution to pursue Scottish and Welsh interests in a more general sense. As John Curtice has put it: 'Labour's underperformance in the first Scottish election was that it was thought not sufficiently capable of standing up for Scotland's interests within the Union'.[40]

[38] Source: Wyn Jones, R. and Scully, R.: 'Devolution Five Years On: the Case of Wales', paper presented to the 2002 Annual Conference of the Elections, Public Opinion and Parties Specialist Group of the Political Studies Association of the UK, 13–15 September, p. 23.

[39] Source: Wyn Jones, R. and Scully, R.: 'Devolution Five Years On: the Case of Wales', paper presented to the 2002 Annual Conference of the Elections, Public Opinion and Parties Specialist Group of the Political Studies Association of the UK, 13–15 September, p. 24.

[40] Paterson et al., 2001, p. 41.

The SNP in other words takes support from Labour in the devolved context because it is seen as better able to 'stand up for Scotland'. Similarly, 'those switching [in 1999 from Labour] to Plaid tended to place particular importance on Welsh issues' in a wider sense than the particular policy levers available to the National Assembly for Wales.

CONCLUSIONS

This is a pattern familiar to observers of Spanish politics. Strong support for regionalist parties in regional elections in Catalonia and the Basque Country in particular is about building 'clout' for the region in Spain. The early evidence suggests that Scotland and — in particular — Wales are moving in the same direction. The institutional expression through devolution of territorial distinctiveness has created electoral arenas through which voters can make a concern for territorial 'clout' manifest. This new territorialism is stronger than in Germany, where territorial sensitivities have become politically significant only since unification. It is weaker than in Canada, where territorial politics has had such a centrifugal effect that political parties barely act any longer as forces for national integration. In Wales and Scotland the UK parties are still strong, and the Labour Party still the *strongest* party even in the devolved context. Territory-specific and UK-wide dynamics interact to create new questions of relationship of territory and union. Those questions of relationship favour the nationalist parties in the devolved arena and Labour in the UK arena, as they do in Spain. Devolved elections are certainly not second order elections.

Whether the political parties concerned have realised all of this is a different matter. As we suggested at the outset they still tend to view all election results through a Westminster lens. Comparing the devolved elections in 1999 with the Westminster election in 1997 and seeing an electoral 'earthquake' and then seeing the 2001 Westminster election as a resumption of 'normal service' is misconceived. If party strategists are still thinking that way they are in for a surprise come devolved elections in May 2003. The 2001 Westminster results should be compared with the 1997 results for Westminster, not the 1999 results for the National Assembly. And if they are, then the swings from one party to another were fairly unremarkable. And, of course, the 1999 results will need to be compared with the 2003 results in both Wales and Scotland. The trends revealed in 1999 are likely to be repeated. Labour will not do as well as it did in Scotland and Wales for Westminster in 2001, and the SNP and PC will do better in Scotland and Wales than for Westminster. And how far-reaching the trade-off is will depend on how far voters see the parties as capable of 'standing up for Scotland'. Meeting that challenge of 'standing up for Scotland' is inherently more difficult for parties active across Britain and probably most difficult of all for the party in power at Westminster. Labour needs to brace itself again to perform under its Westminster expectations. It perhaps also needs to think more carefully about how a unified, Britain-wide party organisation can develop different messages for different electoral audiences.

BIBLIOGRAPHY

Abedi, A. and Siaroff, A.: 'The Mirror has Broken: Increasing Divergence between National and Land Elections in Austria', *German Politics*, 8 (1) (1999).

Dinkel, R., 'Der Zusammenhang zwischen Bundes- und Landtagswahlergebnissen', *Politische Vierteljahresschrift*, 18 (1977).

Erikson, R. 'The Puzzle of Mid-Term Loss', *Journal of Politics*, 50 (4) (1988).

Erikson, R. S. and Filipov, M. G.: 'Electoral balancing in federal and sub-national elections: the case of Canada', *Constitutional Political Economy*, 12 (4) (2001).

Goodhart, C. and Bhansali, R.: 'Political Economy' in *Political Studies*, 18 (1970).

Heath, A., McLean, I., Taylor, B. and Curtice, J., 'Between First and Second Order: A Comparison of Voting Behaviour in European and Local Elections in Britain', *European Journal of Political Research*, 35 (3) (1999).

Hough, D. and Jeffery, C.: 'Regionalwahlen in Mehr-Ebenen-Systemen', in T. Conzelmann und M. Knodt (eds.): *Regionales Europa, europäisierte Regionen. Mannheimer Jahrbuch für Europäische Sozialforschung* (Frankfurt am Main: Campus Verlag, 2002), pp. 213–237.

Hough, D., *The Fall and Rise of the PDS in Eastern Germany* (Birmingham: Birmingham University Press, 2002).

Jeffery, C. and Hough, D., 'The Electoral Cycle and Multi-Level Voting in Germany', in S. Padgett and T. Poguntke (eds), *Continuity and Change in German Politics: Beyond the Politics of Centrality* (London: Frank Cass, 2001).

Johnston, R., 'Federal and Provincial Voting: Contemporary Patterns and Historical Evolution', in D. J. Elkins and R. Simeon (eds) *Small Worlds: Provinces and Parties in Canadian Political Life* (Agincourt: Methuen, 1980), pp. 106–30

McLean, I., Heath A. and Taylor, B., 'Were the 1994 Euro- and Local Elections in Britain Really Second-Order? Evidence from the British Election Panel Study', in D. M. Farrell, D. Broughton, D. Denver, and J. Fisher (eds) *British Elections and Parties Yearbook 1996* (London: Frank Cass, 1996).

Miller, W. and Mackie, M., 'The Electoral Cycle and the Asymmetry of Government and Opposition Popularity: An Alternative Model of the Relationship Between Economic Conditions and Political Popularity', in *Political Studies*, 21 (1973).

Osmond, J. (ed), *The National Assembly Agenda* (Cardiff: Institute of Welsh Affairs, 1998).

Pallares, F. and Keating, M., 'Multi-level electoral competition: regional elections and party systems in Spain', in Hough, D., Jeffery, C., and Keating, M. 'Territorial Party Systems', Special Issue of *European Urban and Regional Studies*, 10 (2003).

Paterson, L. et al, *New Scotland, New Politics?* (Edinburgh: Polygon, 2001).

Reif, K. and Schmitt, H., 'Nine Second-Order National Elections: A Conceptual Framework for the Analysis of European Election Results', *European Journal of Political Research*, 8 (1) (1980).

Reif, K., 'Ten Second-Order Elections' in K. Reif (ed) *Ten Second-Order Elections* (Aldershot: Gower, 1985).

Robin, M. (ed) *Canadian Provincial Politics* (London: Prentice Hall, 1978).

Soldatos, G., 'The electoral cycle: a brief survey of literature', in *Revue d'économie Politique*, 104 (4) (1994).

Stimson, J., 'Public Support for American Presidents: A Cyclical Model', in *Public Opinion Quarterly*, 40 (1976).

Trench, A., *Devolution and the 2001 General Election. Devolution Commitments of the Major Parties* (London: Constitution Unit, 2001).

Tristan, D. and Wyn Jones, R., 'A Quiet Electoral Earthquake', *Agenda. Journal of the Institute of Welsh Affairs*, Summer (1999).

Tufte, E., 'Determinants of the Outcomes of Midterm Congressional Elections', *American Political Science Review*, 69 (3) (1975).

Wyn Jones, R. and Scully, R., 'Devolution Five Years On: the Case of Wales', paper presented to the 2002 Annual Conference of the Elections, Public Opinion and Parties Specialist Group of the Political Studies Association of the UK, 13–15 September (2002).

11

Devolution Meets the Voters
The Prospects for 2003

John Curtice

INTRODUCTION

There are three obvious questions that we might ask of any election. Who will vote, who will voters support, and who will win power as a result? These questions are particularly worth asking of the second devolved elections that will be held in Scotland and Wales in 2003. For there are doubts about how many people will vote, questions about how well nationalist parties that would prefer more powerful institutions in Edinburgh and Cardiff might do, and a possibility that the electoral system will play a decisive role in determining who has power. The answers to these questions will prove to be important in any evaluation of the success of the devolution project.

A look at the outcome of the last two UK general elections in Scotland and Wales together with that of the first devolved election held in 1999 indicates why our questions are worth asking (see Figure 11.1). In both countries, the turnout in 1999 was disappointingly low. In Scotland it was 13 points lower than the already relatively low figure that was recorded in the 1997 general election, while in Wales it was no less than 27 points lower, with less than half of the principality's registered electorate participating in its first devolved elections. True, the turnout in the subsequent 2001 general election indicated that Westminster too was now having difficulty persuading voters to go to the polls. Indeed in Scotland turnout was no higher than it had been in 1999. But this perhaps simply underlined the doubts, raised by the 1999 result, about whether devolution would prove an effective means of helping to reconnect voters with the political system.

Nationalist parties did far better in both countries in 1999 than might have been expected, given their past performance in previous UK general elections. Plaid Cymru caused an 'electoral earthquake' by moving from being the fourth party in Wales to the principal opposition to Labour. In winning well over a quarter of the vote it far outstripped its previous best Westminster result of 11.4 per cent recorded in 1970. And while the SNP's progress was more modest, registering a 5-6 per cent increase in its vote on 1997, its share of the vote was still higher than it had secured at any previous Westminster election apart from October 1974.

Figure 11.1: Recent election results in Scotland and Wales[1]

Scotland							
	1997		1999			2001	
	Votes	Seats	1st vote	2nd vote	Seats	Votes	Seats
	%	%	%	%	%	%	%
Conservative	17.5	0.0	15.6	15.4	14.0	15.6	1.4
Labour	45.6	77.8	38.8	33.6	43.4	44.0	77.8
Lib Dem	13.0	13.9	14.2	12.4	13.2	16.3	13.9
SNP	22.1	8.3	28.7	27.3	27.1	20.1	6.9
Others	1.9	0.0	2.7	11.3	2.3	4.0	0.0
Turnout	71.3		58.2			58.1	
Wales							
	1997		1999			2001	
	Votes	Seats	1st vote	2nd vote	Seats	Votes	Seats
	%	%	%	%	%	%	%
Conservative	19.6	0.0	15.9	16.5	15.0	21.0	0.0
Labour	54.7	85.0	37.6	35.4	46.7	48.6	85.0
Lib Dem	12.4	5.0	13.5	12.5	10.0	13.8	5.0
Plaid Cymru	9.9	10.0	28.7	27.3	28.3	14.3	10.0
Others	3.4	0.0	4.7	5.1	0.0	2.3	0.0
Turnout	73.4		46.4			61.4	

Yet, in contrast to the low turnout, this feature of the 1999 elections was not repeated in the 2001 UK general election. Although still higher than at any previous Westminster election, Plaid Cymru's share of the vote was only half of what it had been in 1999. Meanwhile the SNP fared worse than at any

[1] Note: In Scotland, votes cast for the Speaker in Glasgow Springburn in 2001 are counted as Labour.

time since 1987. Perhaps then the nationalist surge in 1999 was a one-off event that has died now that voters have come to appreciate the benefits of devolution within the Union. But equally it could be the case that devolution has provided those parties that would ultimately wish to see the dissolution of the Union with an electoral arena in which they can prosper more easily. Far from helping to strengthen the Union, it may have provided a lifeline to the Union's principal political opponents.

The nationalists gained votes in the 1999 devolved elections, and in so doing appear to have harmed Labour in particular, but they did not win power. True, in stark contrast to its near monopoly of Scottish and Welsh representation at Westminster, Labour failed to win a majority of the seats in either the Scottish Parliament or the Welsh Assembly. To that extent the additional member electoral system that was used in the devolved elections, instead of the traditional single member plurality system, supplied a more proportionate outcome. But at the same time Labour still won a significantly higher share of seats than it did of votes. In Wales it secured 47 per cent of the seats on just 35 per cent of the decisive second or party list vote, while in Scotland it won 43 per cent of the seats with no more than 34 per cent of the party list vote. These bonuses helped ensure that in both countries the party could form a majority coalition government with the Liberal Democrats, even though in both countries the two parties together won less than half the vote. It seems then that despite the use of a different, supposedly more proportional, electoral system, Labour may still have what some might consider an unfair advantage when it comes to winning seats and thus power.

So it appears that devolution has won the indifference of voters and provided succour to nationalists, but also that it is saddled with an electoral system that is biased towards Labour. Such an outcome would seem to disappoint hopes that devolution would help reconnect people in Scotland and Wales with both politics in general and the Union in particular. In this chapter we attempt to account for the trends revealed in Figure 11.1 in order to establish how far this characterisation is correct, and if so what this might mean for the outcome of the second devolved elections in 2003. In so doing, we will make particular use of surveys of public opinion undertaken immediately after the 1999 devolved elections and again after the 2001 general election. Between them these surveys enable us to chart how public opinion in Scotland and Wales may have changed since the first devolved elections and to compare how people voted in the 1999 devolved elections with how they voted in 2001. Further details about these surveys are given in the appendix at the end of this chapter.

TURNOUT

Voters are unlikely to feel that it is worth voting in an election if they do not think that the outcome matters. Thus we can anticipate that fewer people will vote in an election for an institution that is thought to have little power than will do where the institution is thought capable of making a difference. And indeed, elections to institutions that are deemed to be 'second order', such as the European Parliament, regularly secure lower levels of voter participation than do elections to those thought to be 'first order', such as national parliaments.[2]

Where do the Scottish Parliament and the Welsh Assembly lie on this spectrum? Are they thought to be institutions that matter? And perhaps most importantly, how important do voters think they are now that they have some experience of seeing them in action? Has the reality persuaded voters that the devolved institutions do matter? Or has the opposite happened?

Figure 11.2: Perceptions of power

1999: Which do you think will have influence over the way Scotland/Wales is run?
2000, 2001: Which do you think has most influence over the way Scotland/Wales is run?

Scotland	1999 (%)	2000 (%)	2001 (%)
Scottish Parliament	41	13	15
UK government	39	66	66
Local Councils	8	10	9
European Union	4	4	7

Wales	1999 (%)	2000 (%)	2001 (%)
Welsh Assembly	30	na	16
UK government	44	na	61
Local Councils	12	na	15
European Union	7	na	3

na: not available

[2] Reif, K. and Schmitt, H. 'Nine Second Order Elections', in K. Reif (ed) *The European Elections: Campaign and Results of the 1979/81 First Direct Elections to the European Parliament*, (Aldershot: Gower, 1980), pp. 3-44; see also Chapter 10 in this volume.

Further evidence that voters in Scotland and Wales do not consider their new devolved institutions to be as influential as Westminster can be seen in Figure 11.3. It shows the answers that respondents gave when in 2001 they were asked whether they thought that changes since 1997 in the standard of the NHS, in the quality of education, and in living standards in Scotland/Wales were mainly the result of the UK government's policies at Westminster or mainly the result of the policies of the Scottish Executive/National Assembly. Even though health and education at least are areas where significant power and responsibility has been given to the devolved institutions, in each case far more felt that credit and blame for recent trends lay with Westminster than with their devolved institution. There was some apparent recognition in Scotland that decisions about that country's distinctive educational system are made in Edinburgh, but even on this itcm a little under one in five felt that principal responsibility for recent trends lay with the Scottish Executive, while as many as two in five felt that the UK government was responsible. On all of the other instances in Figure 11.3, over a half said that responsibility lay mainly with the UK government.

Figure 11.3: Perceived responsibility for outcomes since 1997[3]

	Scotland		Wales	
	UK Govt.	Scottish Executive	UK Govt.	National Assembly
	%	%	%	%
Standard of the NHS	53	11	58	10
Quality of Education	40	19	52	8
Standard of living	53	12	58	8

Still, we should perhaps not exaggerate the importance of what we have found so far. After all, to say that the UK government is more influential than the devolved institutions is not necessarily to say that the latter are unimportant. Certainly, in the 1999 elections, perceptions of which body would be the more important had only a marginal impact on whether people voted or not. Thus in Scotland the reported level of participation amongst those who said that they thought the Scottish Parliament would have most influence over the way Scotland was run was only seven points higher than it was amongst those who expected the UK government to have most influence. In Wales the equivalent figure was only three points. So perhaps many of those who

---

[3] Note: Those answering ' both' or 'some other reason' not shown.

thought in 1999 that the UK government would still have most influence believed at the same time that the devolved institutions would matter as well. And perhaps many of those who now think that the UK government is most influential still believe the devolved institutions matter as well. Even so, the decline in the perceived importance of the devolved institutions as compared with Westminster seems unlikely to do anything to enhance the turnout in 2003.

In any event, there is evidence that there has not just been a decline in the perceived relative importance of the devolved institutions but in their absolute importance too. One such piece of evidence is that perceptions of the achievements of the devolved institutions to date do not match the expectations that people had of them in 1999. In both Scotland and Wales fewer people now think that devolution has given their country a stronger voice in the UK, given ordinary people more say in how they are governed or increased the standard of education in their country, than expected in 1999 would be the case. Unrealistically high as they may have been, having positive expectations of the devolved institutions does seem to have helped persuade people to go to the polls in 1999, especially in Wales.[4] That expectations have since declined can only make it harder to persuade people that it will be worth turning out in 2003.

---

[4] For example, turnout amongst those who thought that having a National Assembly would give ordinary people more say in how they are governed was thirteen points higher than it was amongst those who did not. The equivalent figure for Scotland is ten points. The equivalent differences for having a stronger voice are ten points (Wales) and six (Scotland) and for increasing the standard of education, sixteen and three.

Figure 11.4: Expectations and reality

1997, 1999: Will a Scottish Parliament/National Assembly give ... ?

2000: Is having a Scottish Parliament going to give ... ?

2001: Do you think having a Scottish Parliament/National Assembly is giving ... ?

Scotland

	1999	2000	2001
	%	%	%
... Scotland a stronger voice in the UK	70	52	52
... ordinary people more say in how Scotland is governed	64	44	38
... improvements in the standard of education	56	43	27

Wales

	1999	2000	2001
	%	%	%
... Wales a stronger voice in the UK	62	na	49
... ordinary people more say in how Wales is governed	56	na	34
... improvements in the standard of education	42	na	22

na = not available

A second and perhaps more important piece of evidence that suggests there has been a decline in the perceived importance of the devolved institutions (or at least in the elections to those bodies) comes from the answers that people give when they are asked how much of a difference they think it makes who wins an election. As Figure 11.5 shows, fewer people now think that it matters who wins a Scottish or a Welsh election than was the case in 1999. In 1999 56 per cent of people thought that it mattered a 'great deal' or 'quite a lot' who won elections to the Scottish Parliament, but that figure had fallen to 43 per cent in 2001. In Wales the equivalent figure fell from 46 per cent to just 35 per cent.

Figure 11.5: Does it matter who wins?

	Scotland			
	Scottish Parliament Elections		House of Commons Elections	
	1999	2001	1999	2001
	%	%	%	%
Great deal	28	15	27	16
Quite a lot	28	28	28	29
Some	19	22	18	19
Not very much	18	25	22	25
None at all	5	8	4	8
	Wales			
	National Assembly Elections		House of Commons Elections	
	1999	2001	1999	2001
	%	%	%	%
Great deal	24	13	29	20
Quite a lot	22	22	28	27
Some	19	20	16	17
Not very much	22	30	20	26
None at all	9	11	7	8

Moreover, as Figure 11.6 reveals, feeling that the outcome of an election is thought to matter makes a substantial difference to the probability that someone votes. In 1999 no less than 86 per cent of those who felt that it mattered a great deal who won the Scottish election turned out to vote compared with just 43 per cent of those who said it did not matter at all. Equally, the equivalent figures for Wales are 75 per cent and 35 per cent respectively. So, other things being equal, any decline in the proportion who think that the outcome of devolved elections matters points towards a decline in the level of turnout in such elections.

**Figure 11.6: Perceived importance of who wins and turnout,
1999 and 2001**

How much it matters who wins elections	% voting in			
	Scotland		Wales	
	1999	2001	1999	2001
	%	%	%	%
Great deal	86	84	75	85
Quite a lot	78	75	70	77
Some	64	69	50	75
Not very much	61	60	40	59
Not at all	43	38	35	36
1999 = Scottish/Welsh election; 2001 = UK election				

Not that the decline in the perceived importance of devolved elections is necessarily simply the result of a decline in the perceived importance of the institutions themselves. Whether it makes a difference who wins an election depends not simply on whether the institution being elected is thought to have significant powers but also on whether there are thought to be important differences between the principal protagonists in the way that they would use those powers in office. Indeed, not only do the devolved institutions seem to have declined in importance in the public mind, but so also have the perceived differences between the principal protagonists. Thus, whereas 41 per cent thought that there was a great deal of difference between Labour and the SNP in 1999, only 33 per cent did so in 2001. Further evidence that the decline in the perceived importance of the outcome of devolved elections is not simply a product of perceptions of the institutions themselves can also be gleaned from Figure 11.5, which shows that the perceived importance of Westminster elections has also declined since 1999. In short, devolved elections are then probably subject to the same currents that produced the low turnout in the 2001 UK general election.[5] But while this might help absolve

---

[5] On what those currents might be see Bromley, C. and Curtice, J., 'Where have all the voters gone?', in A. Park, J. Curtice, K. Thomson, L. Jarvis and C. Bromley (eds) *British Social Attitudes: the 19th report* (London: Sage, 2002); Bromley, C. and Curtice, J., 'The Lost Voters of Scotland: Devolution Disillusioned or Westminster Weary?', *British Elections and Parties Review* (forthcoming).

the devolved institutions from some of the blame for any decline in turnout in 2003, at the same time it indicates that those institutions are not sufficiently attractive or important in the public mind to rekindle their interest in the electoral process.

It appears then that turnout could well be lower in 2003 than it was in 1999. True, none of the individual pieces of evidence that we have been able to cite points to a large drop in turnout. The decline in the perceived importance of the outcome of devolved elections would on its own for example point to just a two point fall. Equally, not all of the individual pieces of evidence are unproblematic. But cumulatively they all point in the same direction. It appears that, unless the political climate changes significantly in the final months of the devolved administrations, the electorate is likely to be harder to motivate in 2003 than it was four years previously — and that perhaps even in Scotland less than half the voters might go to the polls this time around.

PARTY CHOICE

What will those voters who do go to the polls do with their votes? Will the 2003 election demonstrate that the nationalist upsurge of 1999 is a busted flush? Or will it provide evidence that in establishing devolved elections the UK government has unwittingly provided succour to Scottish and Welsh nationalism, with the likely consequence that devolution will fail to end the debate about the constitutional status of Scotland and Wales?

Figure 11.7 provides strong evidence that the latter conclusion is closer to the truth. The table shows the difference between how those who voted in the 1999 and 2001 elections cast their ballot and how they said they would have voted if a different kind of election had been taking place. Thus in 1999 as well as being asked how they voted in the devolved election, voters were also asked how they would have voted if it had been a UK general election that had been held that year. The table indicates for each party the difference between the proportion saying they had actually voted for that party on the first vote of the devolved contest and the proportion saying they would have done so if they had been voting in a House of Commons election.[6] Meanwhile, in 2001, as well as being asked how they voted in the UK general election, voters were asked how they would have voted if it had been a Scottish Parliament or National Assembly election that had been held that year. Similarly, the table shows for each party the difference between the proportion

---

[6] Note that those who said they would not have voted in a UK general election or did not know how they would have voted have been excluded from the denominator used in calculating the share for each party in a Westminster election. The differences reported in Figure 11.7 in part reflect the potential impact of differential abstention in a Westminster abstention amongst those who voted in the Scottish Parliament election.

saying they would have voted for that party on the first vote of a devolved election and the proportion saying they had actually voted for that party in the UK general election.[7] In each case a plus sign indicates that more people are inclined to vote for that party in a devolved election, while a negative sign indicates that fewer are minded to do so.

Figure 11.7: Voting differences

Difference between Devolution and Westminster vote				
	Scotland		Wales	
	1999	2001	1999	2001
	%	%	%	%
Conservative	-2	-1	-4	-6
Labour	-6	-4	-11	-3
Lib Dem	0	-2	+1	-2
Nationalist	+6	+7	+13	+11

The plus signs appear in the nationalist columns. More people said they voted nationalist in 1999 than said they would have done in a UK general election that year. Equally, more people said that they would have voted nationalist if a devolved election had been held in 2001 than said they actually did so in that year's Westminster election. Meanwhile, Labour in particular appears to find it more difficult to win votes in a devolved election than in a Westminster one, though in Wales at least that mantle may be passing to the Conservatives. In any event, the lower level of support registered for the nationalist parties in the 2001 UK general election does not mean that the nationalist upsurge of 1999 will not reappear in 2003. Rather, devolved elections appear to provide a new arena in which political nationalism can prosper in a manner that it has never done before.

Indeed not only does it appear that the SNP and Plaid Cymru can win at devolved elections the support of those who vote for a different party at Westminster elections, they also appear to be relatively more successful than their opponents at persuading their supporters to go to the polls in a devolved election. Figure 11.8 indicates that in Scotland the proportion of those who say they are SNP supporters who went to the polls was higher in 1999 than in 2001. In contrast supporters of other parties were no more likely to vote in 1999 than they were in 2001. Meanwhile in Wales turnout amongst Plaid Cymru supporters was more or less the same in 1999 and in 2001, while other

---

[7] The comment in footnote 6 applies here also, mutatis mutandi.

parties' supporters were much more likely to go to the polls on the latter occasion. In short, nationalist supporters are more likely to vote in a devolved election, thereby contributing further to their ability to win a higher share of the vote in such elections.

Figure 11.8: Turnout by party identification

% voting				
	Scotland		Wales	
Party Identification	1999	2001	1999	2001
Conservative	76	75	59	73
Labour	71	75	53	73
Lib Dem	81	83	72	82
Nationalist	79	70	77	79

These results are not the isolated findings of the surveys being analysed in this chapter. In Scotland they are regularly replicated by the regular monthly polls undertaken by NFO System Three for *The Herald* newspaper. Over the six months to the end of August 2002, the proportion saying they would vote for the SNP on the first vote of a Scottish Parliament election was on average seven points higher than the proportion saying they would do so in a House of Commons election.[8] There seems then every reason to anticipate that the SNP will represent a more serious challenge to Labour's position as the most popular party in Scotland in the 2003 election than the party was able to offer in the 2001 general election.

Why do the nationalist parties find it easier to win votes in a devolved election? Figure 11.9 provides one possible clue. By their own report, voters had rather different considerations in mind when deciding how to vote in 1999 than they did in 2001. In 1999 more said that they voted mostly on the basis of what was happening in their part of the UK than said they were doing so according to what was happening in Britain as a whole. In 2001, in contrast, the very opposite was the case. This difference between the two elections was particularly marked in Wales, where the proportion who in 2001 said that they voted mostly on the basis of what was going on in the principality was half what it was in 1999.

---

[8] In the same polls, Labour's share of Scottish parliament voting intentions on the first vote was eight points lower than its share of Westminster intentions, the Conservatives' share three points lower, while the Liberal Democrats were two points higher.

Figure 11.9: Deciding how to vote

	Scotland		Wales	
% who decided to vote mostly according to	1999	2001	1999	2001
what was going on in Scotland/Wales	53	34	41	22
what was going on in Britain as a whole	31	44	31	62

So it seems that voters may be voting differently in devolved elections because they have different motivations. Certainly, as Figure 11.10 shows, if voters are principally focused on what is happening in their particular part of the UK, they are more likely to vote for a nationalist party. Thus, for example, in the 1999 election in Scotland, nearly two in five of those who said that they decided how to vote according to what was happening in Scotland backed the SNP, compared with little more than one in seven of those who said they were voting according to what was happening in Britain as a whole. Indeed, as revealed by the figures for 2001, if voters are thinking primarily about what is happening in Britain as a whole and are voting in a Britain wide contest then they are very unlikely indeed to vote nationalist. In devolved elections, however, the opposite is true.

Figure 11.10: Deciding how to vote and nationalist support

	Scotland		Wales	
% voting nationalist if mostly deciding on what is happening in:	1999	2001	1999	2001
Scotland/Wales	39	33	48	38
Britain as a whole	15	5	12	4

Even so, this analysis still rather begs the question as to why voters who are focusing on what is happening in their part of the UK should be more inclined to support a nationalist party. One possibility presumably is that the nationalist parties appear more significant and credible political actors if voters' attention is concentrated on what is happening in Scotland or Wales rather than across Britain as a whole, and particularly so in a devolved election when all that is at stake is the future of Scotland and Wales. But perhaps also the nationalist parties are thought to pay greater attention to the interests of their part of the UK and to be more likely to stand up for Scottish or Welsh interests than are parties that also have to appeal to electorates elsewhere in the UK.[9] If voters are most concerned about what is happening in their part of the UK, rather than Britain as a whole, then perhaps they feel they have more reason to vote for a party that will promote the interests of their part of the UK, and especially so in a devolved election.

Figure 11.11: Who looks after Scotland and Wales?

Scotland					
% who believe party looks after interests of Scottish people in general					
	New Labour at Westminster		Labour Party in Scotland		SNP
	1999	2001	1999	2001	1999	2001
Very closely	3	3	7	8	22	21
Fairly closely	37	36	53	58	45	49
Not very closely	43	51	27	28	21	22
Not at all closely	12	8	6	3	7	6
Wales					
% who believe party looks after interests of Welsh people in general					
	New Labour at Westminster		Labour Party in Wales		Plaid Cymru
	1999	2001	1999	2001	1999	2001
Very closely	6	3	13	7	45	22
Fairly closely	37	37	51	53	36	45
Not very closely	38	43	20	27	5	21
Not at all closely	11	12	5	6	2	7

Figure 11.11 indicates that the first part of this argument at least is correct. Both the SNP and Plaid Cymru are more likely to be thought to look after the interests of their part of the UK closely than not only 'New Labour' at Westminster, but also the Labour Party in Scotland or Wales. Thus, for example,

---

[9] For further elaboration of this argument and further evidence in its support see Paterson, L., Brown, A., Curtice, J., Hinds, K., McCrone, D., Park, A., Sproston, K., and Surridge, P., *New Scotland, New Politics?* (Edinburgh: Polygon, 2001) and Curtice, J., 'Is Devolution Succouring Nationalism?' *Contemporary Wales*, 14, 2001, pp. 80-103.

in 1999 over one in five people in Scotland thought that the SNP looked 'very closely' after the interests of Scottish people in general, compared with only around one in fifteen who thought the same of the Labour Party in Scotland and just one in thirty who thought the same of New Labour at Westminster. Moreover, this picture has changed little since. Meanwhile, Plaid Cymru appears to have been particularly successful at promoting itself as a party that looks after the interests of people in Wales in general, despite traditionally being particularly associated with the Welsh speaking population in the country, though there are some signs that the party's advantage on this count may have declined since 1999.

**Figure 11.12: Reasons for voting, who looks after
Scotland and Nationalist support**

% voted SNP				
Decided vote on basis of what is happening in:	Who is thought to look after Scottish people's interests more closely			
	New Labour	No difference	SNP a little	SNP a lot
1999				
Scotland	10	21	40	71
Britain	4	9	26	24
2001				
Scotland	5	17	40	58
Britain	0	1	8	19

Meanwhile, Figure 11.12 illustrates how this perception of the parties makes a difference to the way that people vote if what they primarily have in mind is what is happening in their part of the UK rather than Britain as a whole. The table shows the proportion voting SNP in 1999 and in 2001, broken down according to both what they most had in mind when they decided how to vote and whether they thought New Labour or the SNP were the more likely to look closely after the interests of Scottish people in general. Thus, for example, someone who says that New Labour looks after the interests of Scottish people 'fairly closely' but the SNP 'not very closely' is classified as believing that New Labour looks after the interests of Scottish people more closely. Those who give the same answer for both parties (irrespective of what that answer is) are counted as seeing 'no difference' between the parties. So far as those who think the SNP look more closely after the interests of Scottish people are concerned, these are divided into those who only see 'a little' difference between the parties and those who see 'a lot'. The former comprise those who simply put the SNP one rung higher on our scale than New Labour (such as saying that the SNP look after the interests of Scottish people 'very closely' and New Labour 'fairly closely') while the latter are those who put the two parties two or three rungs apart.

The SNP is evidently most successful at winning votes amongst those who are both focusing on what is happening in Scotland and believe that the party looks after the interests of Scottish people more closely than Labour. Taken on their own, these two factors — voting on the basis of what is happening in Scotland or believing that the SNP looks more closely after the interests of Scottish people — have at most only a modest impact on someone's chances of voting SNP. It is the presence of the two in combination that matters. And while people might always be inclined to think that the SNP are more likely to look after the interests of Scottish people, it is only in devolved elections that most Scots are focused as well on what might be best for their part of the UK in particular.

Similar results to those shown in Figure 11.12 can also be found in Wales. Thus for example in 1999 no less than two-thirds of those voters who felt that Plaid Cymru looked after the interests of Welsh people in general 'a lot' more closely than New Labour, and who said they were voting on the basis of what was happening in Wales, backed the nationalists. In contrast, amongst those who thought Plaid Cymru looked a lot more closely after the interests of Welsh people, but who also said they were voting on the basis of British issues, only 22 per cent supported the nationalists. Even if a voter said they were voting according to what was happening in Wales but they also saw no difference between the parties in how closely they looked after the interests of Welsh people, only 15 per cent backed Plaid Cymru. Also, as we might expect, we find analogous results if we look at how people rated the nationalists and the Labour Party in Scotland/Wales rather than the nationalists and New Labour at Westminster.

It seems then that in all likelihood the nationalist parties will again find the devolved elections fertile ground in 2003. Holding an election for specifically Scottish or Welsh institutions perhaps almost inevitably invites voters to put first in their minds what they think are the interests of their particular part of the UK, and in this 2003 is likely to resemble 1999. True, the nationalists' opponents might try and enhance the degree to which they are thought by voters to have the interests of their part of the UK in particular in mind, but despite the presence of Labour-led administrations in both

Scotland and Wales, there is no sign as yet that this has significantly increased the degree to which the Labour Party is associated with the interests of those living in Scotland or Wales. And without such a development, the devolved elections look as though they will give succour to the nationalists once more.

THE ELECTORAL SYSTEM

As we remarked at the beginning of this chapter, while Labour might find it relatively difficult to win votes in devolved elections, it still seems to have an advantage over its opponents when it comes to winning seats. Why does this happen? And what are the implications both for the prospects for 2003 and for any evaluation of the fairness of the additional member electoral system?

The principle behind the additional member electoral system (AMS) is simple. Each of Scotland's and Wales' parliamentary constituencies elects someone to represent it in the Scottish Parliament and the National Assembly, using the same single member plurality electoral system that is used to elect MPs to the House of Commons.[10] But at the same time, additional members — 56 in Scotland and 20 in Wales — are elected from party lists, such that the total number of constituency and additional seats won by each party is as proportional as possible to its share of the party list vote. It would seem then rather surprising that a party should win a far higher share of seats than of votes as Labour did in both Scotland and Wales in 1999.

There are, however, two significant constraints on the proportionality of the AMS system used in Scottish and Welsh elections. The first arises from the fact that rather than being distributed on the basis of votes cast across the country as a whole, the additional seats are allocated in separate regional constituencies, of which there are eight in Scotland and four in Wales. One consequence is that the share of the vote that a party has to win to secure an additional member seat is raised. In Scotland, where the average region contains 16 constituency and additional seats, a party has in practice to win a little over 5 per cent of the vote to win an additional seat, while in Wales, where there are typically only 12 seats in a region, the de facto threshold ranged in 1999 between 7.7 and 11.1 per cent.[11] Little wonder then that despite winning 11 per cent of the party list vote between them in 1999, only two representatives were elected in Scotland from party lists nominated by other than the four largest parties.

The second significant constraint on the proportionality of AMS is that if a party does particularly well in the constituency contests there may well be too few additional seats available to ensure that the overall outcome is

[10] Except that the Orkney and Shetland Islands each elect their own MSP whereas they are represented by one MP at Westminster.

[11] Curtice, J. and Steed, M., 'And now for the Commons? Lessons from Britain's First Experience with Proportional Representation', *British Elections and Parties Review*, 10, 2001, pp. 192-215.

proportional. This happened frequently in 1999, and nearly always to Labour's advantage. The party won no less than seven more seats across four regions of Scotland than it should have done, had the outcome been proportional, and four extra seats across three regions in Wales. In the absence of these 'misallocations' Labour would have had just 38 per cent of the seats in Scotland and 40 per cent in Wales, much closer to the 34 and 35 per cent respectively of its share of the party list vote.

There is little reason to believe that Labour will not continue to have a more effectively distributed vote in Scotland and Wales in 2003 and thus will once again win more seats than a strict application of the D'Hondt rule that is used to allocate additional seats would imply. Indeed, the distribution of Labour's vote that pertained in 2001 left it somewhat less vulnerable to a nationalist challenge than was the case in 1999. As a result even if there were to be an even bigger nationalist challenge than happened in 1999, the party looks likely to be able if it so wishes to put together once again a majority coalition with the Liberal Democrats in both countries. This is illustrated in Figure 11.13, which shows how many seats would be won by each party if Labour and the nationalists won equal shares of both the first and second votes in both countries and that this happened as a result of a uniform movement of votes in each constituency and region compared with 1999. Thus, for example, in Wales we assume that Labour's share of the vote falls by 4.6 points in every constituency compared with 1999, while support for Plaid Cymru increases by the same amount, a switch that would be enough to put both parties on 33 per cent of the vote. At the same time we assume a similar movement of 2.5 per cent on the party list vote, putting the two parties on 33 per cent apiece here too. In Scotland the equivalent movements are 5.0 and 3.2 per cent respectively. We assume that in all other respects — including votes cast for all the other parties, the electorate and the turnout — the outcome is exactly the same as it was in 1999.

Figure 11.13: Hypothetical seat outcomes if Labour and nationalists tie

	Seats	
	Scotland	Wales
Conservative	18	9
Labour	48	24
Liberal Democrat	18	7
Nationalist	42	20
Others	3	0

Despite the fact that under these assumptions Labour would not win a single vote more than their nationalist opponents, they would emerge at a significant advantage in the battle for power. Labour would have six more seats than the SNP in Scotland and four more than Plaid Cymru in Wales. These additional seats would be crucial. It would mean that in both countries Labour and the Liberal Democrats together would be able to put together a majority coalition whereas the Nationalists and the Liberal Democrats (or indeed the Nationalists and the Conservatives) would not.

The additional member system that has been introduced into devolved elections cannot be relied upon to treat Labour and the nationalists equally. While it provides Labour with far less of an advantage than would the single member plurality system alone, it does not necessarily eliminate all of the bias in Labour's favour that single member plurality creates, and in some circumstances at least this bias could have a decisive impact on the race for power.

CONCLUSIONS

It appears that the devolution settlement may well be found guilty at the 2003 election on each of the charges that we have laid against. The 2003 election threatens to stir up apathy and to record a nationalist 'success', and yet still see Labour along with their Liberal Democrat allies safely restored to power. Of course events may yet intervene to alter this picture. But if our predictions are proved correct, the hopes of devolution's advocates, that the new political settlement would strengthen rather than weaken the Union, will look fragile indeed.

APPENDIX

The analysis in this chapter is based on the results of the following surveys:

1999 Scottish Parliamentary Election Study/Scottish Social Attitudes Survey

A random sample of 1,482 adults aged 18 plus and resident in Scotland was interviewed in the weeks immediately after the 1999 Scottish election. Interviews were conducted face to face using a computer assisted questionnaire, while respondents also completed a supplementary self-completion booklet. Conducted by the National Centre for Social Research Scotland, the directors of the survey were John Curtice, David McCrone, Alison Park, Paula Surridge and Lindsay Paterson. Funding was supplied by the Economic and Social Research Council.

1999 Welsh Assembly Election Study

A random sample of 1,256 adults aged 18 plus and resident in Wales was interviewed in the weeks immediately after the 1999 Welsh elections. Interviews were partly conducted face to face and partly by telephone. Conducted by the National Centre for Social Research, the directors of the survey were Anthony Heath, Katarina Thomson and Richard Wyn Jones. Funding was supplied by the Economic and Social Research Council.

2001 Scottish Social Attitudes Survey

A random sample of 1,605 adults aged 18 plus and resident in Scotland was interviewed by the National Centre for Social Research Scotland in the summer and early autumn of 2001. Interviews were conducted face to face using a computer assisted questionnaire, while respondents also completed a supplementary self-completion booklet. Most of the questions here were financed by a grant from the Economic and Social Research Council to John Curtice, David McCrone, Alison Park and Lindsay Paterson under its Devolution and Constitutional Change Research programme.

2001 Welsh Life and Times Survey

A random sample of 1,085 adults aged 18 plus and resident in Wales was interviewed in the summer of 2001. Interviews were conducted face to face using a computer assisted questionnaire, while respondents also completed a supplementary self-completion booklet. Conducted by the National Centre for Social Research, the directors of the survey were Anthony Heath, Katarina Thomson and Richard Wyn Jones. Funding was supplied by the Economic and Social Research Council under its Devolution and Constitutional Change programme.

Figures 11.2 and 11.4 also quote results from the *2000 Scottish Social Attitudes Survey*. This interviewed a random sample of 1,663 adults resident in Scotland in the summer and early autumn of 2000. Funding was provided by the Economic and Social Research Council supplemented by funding from the Leverhulme Trust under its Nations and Regions programme.

The author would like to acknowledge his debt to the directors of these surveys and to the funding bodies involved.

BIBLIOGRAPHY

Bromley, C. and Curtice, J.,'The Lost Voters of Scotland: Devolution Disillusioned or Westminster Weary?', *British Elections and Parties Review* (forthcoming).

Bromley, C. and Curtice, J., 'Where have all the voters gone?', in A. Park, J. Curtice, K. Thomson, L. Jarvis, and C. Bromley (eds) *British Social Attitudes: the 19th report* (London: Sage, 2002).

Curtice, J., 'Is Devolution Succouring Nationalism?', *Contemporary Wales*, 14, 2001, pp. 80-103.

Curtice, J. and Steed, M., 'And now for the Commons? Lessons from Britain's First Experience with Proportional Representation', *British Elections and Parties Review*, 10, 2000, pp. 192-215.

Paterson, L., Brown, A., Curtice, J., Hinds, K., McCrone, D., Park, A., Sproston, K. and Surridge, P., *New Scotland, New Politics?* (Edinburgh: Polygon, 2001).

Reif, K., and Schmitt, H., 'Nine Second Order Elections', in K. Reif (ed) *The European Elections: Campaign and Results of the 1979/81 First Direct Elections to the European Parliament* (Aldershot: Gower, 1980), pp. 3-44.

12

Conclusion

The Devolution Scorecard as the
Devolved Assemblies Head for the Polls

Robert Hazell

This final chapter draws up a report card on devolution's first term. What are devolution's main achievements so far? What successes will the devolved governments want to highlight as they head for the polls in May 2003? What have been the difficulties, and the failures of devolution? And what will be the main challenges facing the devolved administrations in their second term?

DEVOLUTION'S MAIN ACHIEVEMENTS

Devolution has made a difference, in broadly the ways it was intended to. It has brought government closer to the people of Scotland, Wales and North-ern Ireland; it has enabled the devolved governments to introduce policies more closely tailored to the needs of the local people; and it has introduced a new kind of politics to the United Kingdom. But before discussing what form the new politics takes, it is worth recording the main achievement of devolution, which is how quickly it has taken root.

Devolution is Here to Stay
Devolution is here to stay. The passionate opposition of the Conservatives, expressed so forcefully by John Major in the 1992 and 1997 elections, already seems light years away. It has not led to the break up of Britain which he and Tam Dalyell forecast. If anything the loosening of the internal ties has led to a strengthening of the Union: opinion polls in Scotland and Wales show there is now less support for independence than there was in the days before devolution.

The other great achievement is its smooth introduction. Although the devolved governments have faced internal difficulties, with several changes of First Minister, externally their relations with the UK government have been extraordinarily smooth. There have been no major rows, no bitter constitutional or financial disputes, no public posturing of the kind that char-acterises federal state relations in many more mature systems. It is of course early days, but in these early days devolution has had an easy ride. This has been thanks to two unusually benign sets of circumstances: the coincidence of Labour-led administrations in London, Edinburgh and Cardiff; and successive comprehensive spending reviews which have seen quite unprecedented increases in public expenditure, shared in by the devolved governments.

Devolution has Introduced a More Responsive Kind of Politics

The 'new politics' takes different forms in different parts of the country. The common characteristic of all three devolved assemblies is that, thanks to being elected by proportional representation, no single party had an overall majority in their first term. This creates a very different atmosphere from the domination of single party government at Westminster, whether it is the triumphalism of Mrs Thatcher in the 1980s or the easy supremacy of New Labour now. In all three devolved assemblies a coalition government was formed in the first term. Coalition governments have to accommodate the views of the coalition partners and have to listen more carefully to other strands of opinion within the assembly.

But it goes further than that. The 'new politics' has also pioneered new forms of civic engagement: it has attempted to build elements of participatory democracy into the work of the devolved assemblies, alongside the traditional forms of representative government. The advocates of devolution promised that it would usher in a new kind of politics: more consensual, more participatory, more inclusive than the adversarial party politics and political games played at Westminster. So great were the hopes of some of the founding fathers in the Scottish Constitutional Convention that there was a sense of disillusionment when post-devolution the 'new politics' was found to contain a lot of the old political knockabout. But those who decry the new politics as an empty shell are missing something important. There is still conflict, there are still sharp clashes of interest and of ideology; but the way the new assemblies go about their business is very different from Westminster. They are significantly more open and accessible to outside organisations and individual citizens, and seek to be a lot more participatory in the way they operate.

Openness and Accessibility in the Scottish Parliament

This is most clearly evident in the Scottish Parliament, which from the start was determined to be different from Westminster. The Scottish Constitutional Convention in 1995 and the Consultative Steering Group which advised on the Standing Orders in 1998 both stressed the need for defining principles of openness, responsiveness, accessibility and accountability.

Figure 12.1:Participation in the Scottish Parliament

The new, participatory politics is most evident in the way the Scottish Parliament scrutinises legislation, in the work of its committees, and in its handling of public petitions. At Westminster the public have no opportunity to make any direct input into the legislative process, except on the small minority of bills which are published in draft and then subject to pre-legislative scrutiny. In the Scottish Parliament extensive efforts are made to ensure the public are engaged. As part of the Stage 1 procedure on a bill the lead committee enquires into the adequacy of the consultations so far, and will often invite further representations from interested parties. The purpose was simply stated by the Consultative Steering Group: 'By making the system more participative, it is intended that better legislation should result'.

Similarly the committees of the Scottish Parliament are more active in stimulating and facilitating public involvement in their work than their counterparts at Westminster. This can be seen in their websites and use of on-line consultation; in their use of reporters, members of the committee who are expressly charged with seeking out views, especially from sections of the public who would not normally submit evidence to a parliamentary inquiry; and in their willingness to travel outside Edinburgh. In the first year of the Scottish Parliament its committees held eight meetings outside Edinburgh, and made 40 visits to other parts of Scotland.[1]

The Scottish Parliament's strong desire to engage with the public is exemplified in its innovative system for handling public petitions. This could not be more different from Westminster, where the procedure for petitions has atrophied to an empty formality. In Scotland, by contrast, there is a Public Petitions Committee which provides a gateway for all petitions, and which ensures they are taken seriously by the relevant committee or public authority. In the words of its Convener,

> [The] committee exists to ensure that people have the right to directly petition the parliament and its committees, and, more importantly, to ensure that when they do so their petitions are treated respectfully and seriously . . . [It] has no agenda of its own other than to assure access to the parliament for petitioners and action by the parliament in response to those petitions.[2]

Partnership Councils in Wales

In Wales the emphasis is as much on engaging with stakeholders as with the wider public. The National Assembly is under a statutory duty to consult with key partners in local government, the voluntary sector and the business community. It has done so through establishing partnership councils with each of these sectors. To boost their input, the Assembly has also helped to

---

[1] Winetrobe, B., *Realising the Vision: A Parliament with a Purpose* (London: Constitution Unit October 2001), p. 65

[2] McAllion, J., 'Public Petitions Committee', *SCOLAG Journal*, September 2000, p5.

create and to fund dedicated support centres for the voluntary sector and business organisations.[3]

2002 saw the publication of a study into the relationship of the National Assembly with local government commissioned by the Joseph Rowntree Foundation, alongside a parallel study of the relationship between the Scottish Parliament and local authorities in Scotland.[4]

These two studies both suggest that devolution has produced political institutions which are a lot more accessible than the closed worlds of Whitehall and Westminster. The Scottish study found the great majority in local government were supportive of the Parliament and devolution: 'local government reported that, post devolution, government was more open and inclusive, and ministers and civil servants had become more accessible.' And in Wales the researchers found that 'Collectively, local government, primarily through the WLGA [the Welsh Local Government Association], has been able to influence the Assembly on significant issues.' In both cases two common factors were in play: the geographic closeness of the devolved institutions, and the small number of local authorities involved. As the Welsh report added, 'The contrast with local–central relations in England is striking. Central government there is much more remote from the more numerous local authorities. Labour ministers do not see local government . . . as an especially important constituency.'

Stakeholder Participation in Regional Chambers in England

England is unaware of these developments, as it is unaware of the constitutional innovation taking place in its own regions, where the new Regional Chambers provide our last example of the 'new politics'. Two thirds of the members of these assemblies are local authority leaders from the region, while one third are drawn from the 'social and economic partners': business, the voluntary sector and environmental organisations. What is innovative about the Regional Chambers is the inclusion of the social and economic partners as full members of the assembly. In Scotland, in Northern Ireland and in the Greater London Authority the attempt has been made to convene the partners in a separate Civic Forum; but so far these Forums have found themselves marginalised and still searching for a role.

By contrast the stakeholder members of the 'partnership assemblies' (as they themselves describe the Regional Chambers in England) are developing a role, providing chairs or vice chairs of committees and proving their worth and their expertise in the work of the new scrutiny commissions. They are

---

[3] Shaw, K., *et al*, *The Engagement of Economic and Social Partners in a Directly Elected Regional Assembly for the North East* (Newcastle: CURDS, June 2002), ch. 4.

[4] Laffin, M., *et al*, *A new Partnership? The National Assembly for Wales and Local Government*; Bennett, M. *et al*, *Devolution in Scotland: the Impact on Local Government*. Both reports published by Joseph Rowntree Foundation, 2002.

also effective conduits, cascading information down to their respective communities of interest and feeding their views back in; and using groups outside the plenary chamber and committees to enhance their 'inclusiveness'.[5] Few have noticed, but this is the only example outside the House of Lords of appointed stakeholders being engaged directly in the democratic process. Increasingly they see themselves as taking part in a political process, as full members and equal partners with the local government leaders. It is an interesting model, which so far seems to offer more promise for the partners than a stand-alone Civic Forum. But it is early days, and the model will not properly be tested until Regional Chambers have significant power. That may never happen in those regions which opt for a directly elected Regional Assembly, because the government does not believe that appointed stakeholders should be full members of directly elected assemblies.[6]

Impact of the 'New Politics'

Have people noticed any difference in the 'new politics' offered by devolution? The early signs are not encouraging. In Scotland in summer 2000 only one third of Scots believed that the creation of the Scottish Parliament had improved the way that Britain is governed, with over four in ten (44 per cent) believing that the parliament had made no difference.[7] And expectations of what the Scottish Parliament and Welsh Assembly are likely to deliver have fallen sharply compared with back in 1997. After two years of devolution, only 38 per cent of Scots and 34 per cent of Welsh people believed that the parliament/assembly were giving ordinary people more say in how Scotland/Wales was governed.[8]

But it is very early to be coming to judgement on such new institutions. These polls were conducted just one and two years into devolution's first term. To assess whether devolution is delivering a new kind of politics, we may need to wait a lot longer for the institutions to impinge on people's lives. We may also need to ask a battery of questions directed at the issue of participation and citizen engagement, and to ask for direct comparisons between Westminster and the devolved institutions, to see if people notice a difference, and in what respects. And we may need to ask those same questions of interest groups and organisations which have direct dealings with the Westminster Parliament and with the devolved assemblies, because they are in the

[5] Sandford, M., *Inclusiveness of Regional Chambers* (London: The Constitution Unit, October 2002).

[6] White Paper, *Your Region, Your Choice*, May 2002, para 7.11.

[7] Bromley C., Curtice J. and Seyd B., *Has Constitutional Reform 'Reconnected' Voters with their Government?* (London: The Constitution Unit, February 2002).

[8] Curtice J., 'Devolution, The Union and Public Opinion', report submitted to House of Lords Constitution Committee, 2002. See also Surridge P., 'Society and Democracy: The New Scotland' in J. Curtice et al, *New Scotland, New Society? Are Social and Political Ties Fragmenting?* (Edinburgh: Polygon Press, 2001).

best position to make direct comparisons. Elite groups may notice differences where the general public do not.

Devolution has Produced Different Public Policies

Even if from the outside the political process looks much the same, the public should start to notice a difference in terms of policy outputs. As the politicians head for the polls, they will be trumpeting their first term achievements, and promising more to come. The Scots will be reminded of their government's different policies on tuition fees in higher education (following the Cubie report); their more generous policy on free nursing care for the elderly (see Chapter 9), following the recommendations of the Sutherland Royal Commission on Long Term Care; and their long term settlement of teachers' pay. For budgetary reasons none of these policies has been introduced in England.

Figure 12.2: Different public policies in Scotland 1999–2003

- Free long term personal care for the elderly
- Abolition of tuition fees for students in higher education
- Three year settlement for teachers pay & conditions ('McCrone' settlement)
- Less restrictive freedom of information Act
- Abolition of fox hunting, by the Protection of Wild Mammals (Scotland) Act 2002
- 'One stop shop' for Public Sector Ombudsman (2002)
- Reforming law to protect property and welfare of adults with mental incapacity
- Abolishing feudal system of land tenure
- Abolition of the ban on 'promoting homosexuality' in schools by repeal of Section 2A of the Local Government Act (known as 's28' in England)

Wales has fewer such big policy items. In part this reflects the Assembly's lack of legislative power, in part its smaller per capita budget, which allows less room for manoeuvre, and in part the lesser policy making capacity in Wales. In the first year under Alun Michael's leadership there was little attempt to be different. The only thing to show in terms of distinctive policy was the Children's Commissioner for Wales. But when Rhodri Morgan became First Minister and then entered the partnership agreement with the Liberal Democrats in October 2000 some distinctive policies began to emerge, and the list in Figure 12.3 is quite long. The partnership agreement has delivered free school milk for all children under seven, a freezing of prescription charges, and free bus travel for pensioners from 2002. In April 2001 it delivered free opening of the national museums and galleries of

Wales, and free prescriptions for those under 25 and over 60. In the health service the National Health Plan for Wales is to replace the existing five health authorities with 22 local health boards, to take effect by April 2003. This last may result in maximum disruption just in the run up to the elections, with any electoral payoff much further down the track. With the new health boards sharing the same boundaries as Wales' 22 local authorities, they should be better placed to tackle the wider determinants of public health; but that is not a strategy which will have much appeal for the public, who will see only another round of health service reorganisation.

Figure 12.3: Different public policies in Wales in the Assembly's first term

- UK's first Children's Commissioner
- Creation of 22 local health boards, to work alongside Wales' 22 local authorities
- Education and Learning Wales (ELWa), new body to oversee post 16 education and training; and Careers Wales, to provide careers advice and guidance to all ages
- Homelessness commission, and extending support for the homeless
- Abolition of school league tables
- Free medical prescriptions for those under 25 and over 60
- Freezing all other prescription charges
- Free bus travel for pensioners
- Free school milk for children under seven
- Means tested learning grants for people in higher and further education
- Six weeks free home care for the elderly after discharge from hospital
- Finance Wales established as a 'user-friendly bank' for small business
- Piloting a new Welsh Baccalaureate in 19 schools and colleges

And even in Northern Ireland, despite all its difficulties, the Executive and Assembly can claim credit for the following.

Figure 12.4: Public policy changes in Northern Ireland

- Abolition of school league tables
- Free fares for the elderly
- Establishment of single economic development agency
- Introduction of more egalitarian student-finance package
- Direction that 11+ examination be abolished
- Planned establishment of Children's Commissioner
- Executive Programme Funds to promote joined-up government

Finally, devolution should be understood as providing a policy laboratory. It enables policy experiments in different parts of the UK, which if successful can be adopted in other parts. Examples of policy transfer can be seen in the lists above: different packages to help with student tuition fees, free bus travel for the elderly, abolition of school league tables, and the spread of the Children's Commissioner. Before devolution there were policy differences, but they were far fewer, they were less visible, and there was no formal machinery to facilitate policy transfer. Post devolution the differences are much more visible: it is in the interest of the devolved governments to high-light the differences, to show how much difference they have made. This leads them to be given more prominence in the media (always eager to denounce 'anomalies'), and amongst the professional networks who can be important vectors of policy change.

Post devolution there is also formal machinery, in the Joint Ministerial Committee, in which policy differences can be discussed between the UK government and the devolved administrations. The sharing of ideas and policy transfer has not been its primary purpose (which was dispute resolution); but as chapter 6 describes, UK ministers are still experimenting with the JMC in different formats. The JMC (Health) has been convened several times to share experience and discuss solutions to issues like bed-blocking, winter pressures, and performance measures. On occasion the devolved administrations have been invited to lead the discussion with an example of innovative practice, and the JMCs on Health briefly developed into a forum for the exchange of information and best practice. For the ministers attending from Scotland, Wales and Northern Ireland the JMC could provide opportunities to present and share innovation and research in a way that did not exist pre-devolution. It remains to be seen whether the revived JMC on Poverty (see chapter 6) similarly develops into a forum for information exchange and policy transfer, or whether it is more bluntly used by Gordon Brown to drive forward his own social policy agenda, as he is used to doing with his UK ministerial colleagues.

DEVOLUTION'S DIFFICULTIES AND FAILURES

In previous volumes we have written about the instability of the devolution settlement. By this I do not mean that the whole devolution project is at risk of collapsing; but simply that devolution is a dynamic process, that the initial settlement cannot endure for ever, but will continue to evolve. We have already seen signs of stresses and strains, of the growth pains of devolution, emerging during devolution's first term. In Wales the limitations of 'executive devolution' have become increasingly evident, and in 2002 a review was established into the adequacy of the Assembly's powers. In Scotland there is an issue of downsizing of the Scottish Parliament, and there too a review has been established. In Northern Ireland devolution has teetered from crisis to crisis, and in autumn 2002 the devolved institutions were suspended for the fourth time. Meanwhile in England the devolution dynamic is slowly working its way through: six regions have now established constitutional conventions, and in summer 2002 the Government published a White Paper setting out its plans for how they might move forward to establish elected Regional Assemblies.

Wales Contemplates the Need for Stronger Legislative Powers
There is a common myth about the settlement in Wales, that the National Assembly was granted very limited powers because the people of Wales were not ready for more, and that was underlined in the narrow referendum result in 1997. In truth the half way house of executive devolution was a compromise solution to try to bridge the unbridgeable gulf between the pro and anti devolution factions inside the Wales Labour Party. Labour in Wales had long been deeply divided over devolution, going back to the 1970s, and a small Assembly with limited powers was the most that Ron Davies could get past his anti-devolution colleagues. So it was that the Assembly was created as a body corporate to take over the executive functions of the Secretary of State. These extend to powers of subordinate legislation, but do not include any primary legislative powers.

It soon became apparent that the body corporate model wasn't working. John Osmond has described how the first year of devolution saw the Assembly gradually turn itself into a constitutional convention. In the second and third years the convention got down to work. Rhodri Morgan as the new First Minister announced two reviews: an internal review of the Assembly's procedures; and an external review of the Assembly's powers. The first, the Assembly Review of Procedure, reported in February 2002. The review set the seal on a series of developments in 2000 and 2001 which had gradually introduced a separation of powers within what is still technically a body corporate. On the executive side, the Cabinet is now called the Welsh Assembly Government, with ministers and deputy ministers to whom the bulk of civil servants report. On the legislative/scrutiny side, the Assembly is governed by a Presiding Office with its own separate budget and small staff.

The external review of the Assembly's powers is potentially a more important development. The independent commission, chaired by Lord (Ivor) Richard, cannot duck the central question in its terms of reference, which is whether the Assembly needs primary legislative powers. In its report, due by the end of 2003, it will also have to consider the size of the Assembly and its electoral arrangements: there is a presumption that an Assembly with legislative powers would need more than the existing 60 members, who are already pretty stretched.

The commission started work in autumn 2002, and is beginning to get to grips with the complexity and obscurity of the present arrangements, in which few people in Wales or in Whitehall have a proper understanding of the scope of the Assembly's powers. The internal review of procedure had emphasised how dependent the Assembly is on primary legislation made at Westminster, and had recommended the adoption of a set of principles to try to ensure greater consistency and parity of treatment for Wales in Westminster legislation.[9] The commission will need to come to a view about the workability of these arrangements, as well as the willingness of Whitehall or Westminster to adopt a new set of drafting rules for Wales.

Northern Ireland Collapses for the Fourth Time

The repeated breakdown of devolution in Northern Ireland has been because of failures in the peace process rather than failures of the devolution settlement itself. As chapter 4 describes, the unionists' confidence in the Belfast agreement was fragile from the start, and it has taken repeated knocks because of the IRA's reluctance to put their arms beyond use, and because of Sinn Féin's apparent reluctance to give up some of its old habits. Each suspension of the devolved institutions resulted from the IRA's failure seriously to engage with the decommissioning process, which in turn put severe pressure on the unionist leadership from their own supporters; but each suspension eroded confidence in devolution's capacity to deliver peace through working together and trying to break down the huge barriers of mistrust which separate the two communities.

The latest suspension in autumn 2002 seems likely to be longer lasting. The British government clearly thinks so, as shown by its appointment of two new junior ministers to help bear the load on the Northern Ireland Office engaging once more in direct rule. Paul Murphy is not the heavyweight John Reid was as Secretary of State, and Blair is going to have less time for Northern Ireland as he has to devote more time to international affairs and the war against terrorism. So although it will be led by NIO and the British government, any review of the peace process and any attempt to re-start devolution will depend primarily on the political players in Northern Ireland, and whether the unionists can re-enter a power sharing executive with Sinn Féin when the IRA have still not laid down their arms.

It seems unlikely that any review will include a review of the machinery created by the Belfast agreement. But if it does, there are three features which might be worth re-examining. The first is the power-sharing executive itself, and the requirement that the coalition is compulsory rather than voluntary. Second is the requirement that Assembly members designate themselves as 'nationalist', 'unionist' or 'other', which may have served to reinforce the ethno-religious divide. Third is the electoral system: STV contains no

---

[9] *Assembly Review of Procedure*, Final Report, Feb 2002 ch. 4 and Annex 5.

incentives towards political accommodation, and there is a real fear that fresh elections may see a further erosion of the political centre. The nightmare scenario if elections are held in May 2003 is that in place of the moderate UUP and SDLP, the two largest parties may turn out to be the DUP and Sinn Féin.

The English Regions Move Slowly Forward

England continues to be the gaping hole in the devolution settlement, and the English Question is the biggest piece of unfinished business. It is unfinished business going back to 1997, when Labour's manifesto promised to 'introduce legislation to allow the people, region by region, to decide in a referendum whether they want directly elected regional government'. Blair's first government introduced Regional Development Agencies, and voluntary, non-statutory Regional Chambers with a purely consultative role; but John Prescott received no support from his Cabinet colleagues to move towards elected regional assemblies, and no further progress was made on this in Labour's first term.

The 1997 commitment appeared in much the same form in the 2001 manifesto, and John Prescott's long awaited White Paper on regional government finally appeared in May 2002. It proposes slimline, strategic regional assemblies with relatively small budgets and few executive powers. In the Whitehall battles which had preceded the White Paper Prescott had persuaded few of his colleagues to give up any substantial powers or functions, and most of the powers on offer to regional assemblies come from Prescott's own department. This raises a big question mark over whether, come the referendum, voters will be willing to support the creation of assemblies with such slender powers; but (as with the GLA and the London Mayor) they may not realise how ineffective these bodies are destined to be until they are brought into existence.

The other respect in which regional assemblies may be stifled at birth is in the requirement that they should be accompanied by unitary local government. Here government policy has hardened. It used to be for 'predominantly' unitary local government, with the suggestion that local government restructuring might come after the introduction of regional government.[10] That left some room for manoeuvre. Now that the government has insisted on local government reorganisation as a precondition of regional government, they risk a re-run of the bloodbath which accompanied the Banham reviews of local government 10 years ago. The Conservative Party will raise the standard to save the counties, and regional referendums will be much harder to win.

---

[10] See eg the statement of Beverley Hughes MP, Parliamentary Under-Secretary at DETR, Westminster Hall, 16 January 2001.

Whitehall Muddles Through

It has been a continuing difficulty of devolution that there is no coherent approach at the centre, with no one who thinks about devolution in the round, and no one to give strategic vision. In the best traditions of Whitehall pragmatism ministers and civil servants deal with the day-to-day problems, in a piecemeal and incremental way, and tomorrow is left to look after itself. With three separate territorial Secretaries of State, plus the Office of the Deputy Prime Minister (ODPM), Whitehall has not one but four 'centres' to handle policy on devolution: one dealing with Scotland, one with Wales, one with Northern Ireland, and one with the English regions. There used to be a small devolution team in the Cabinet Office, but since the creation of ODPM they have joined its Nations and Regions division, and find themselves in a line department whose main focus is the English regions. John Prescott chairs the Cabinet Committee on Nations and Regions, but his own interest in and knowledge of devolution is pretty small, and his political energy is focused on regional government in England.

Does this matter, other than symbolically? It matters because there is no capacity to think about devolution in the round, to understand the dynamics of devolution, to think about how devolution links up with other constitutional change. The machine is good at managing the detail, but weak on the broader strategy. Two examples will suffice to make the point: Lords reform, and the bigger devolution issues mentioned in this chapter. If (as the government proposes) elected members in a reformed second chamber are to represent the nations and regions, that needs to connect with the policy on devolution and regional government. But it became clear after publication of the White Paper on Lords Reform in November 2001 that the government had held no discussions with the devolved governments or assemblies, and had made no connection with devolution policy. Other current devolution issues — reviewing the legislative framework for Wales, reducing the size of the Scottish Parliament, the funding formula for devolution and regional government — all have wider implications, and call for a more joined up approach, but ministers at the centre have neither the will nor the capacity to join them up.

The Lords Ride to the Rescue

At Westminster the structures of the House of Commons are just as fragmented as those in Whitehall. Reflecting the three territorial departments, the Commons still have three separate Select Committees for Scottish Affairs, Welsh Affairs and Northern Ireland respectively, and a fourth (the Standing Committee on Regional Affairs) for the English regions. Chapter 7 describes how these continue to operate in separate compartments; and more generally, how little impact devolution has had on the business of the House of Commons. Robin Cook, the new Leader of the House since 2001, has been keen to modernise the legislative process, the scrutiny work and the sitting hours of the House of Commons, but the dense framework of territorial committees (which all date from pre-devolution days) is something which he has been content to leave alone.

It has been left to the Lords to take a more synoptic view. As described in chapters 6 and 7, the new Constitution Committee in the Lords has chosen as the subject for it's first major inquiry inter-institutional relations in the devolved UK. They have taken evidence from the chairmen of the territorial Committees in the Commons, from John Prescott and the territorial Secretaries of State, and from the First Ministers and their colleagues in the devolved administrations, and the Presiding Officers in the devolved assemblies. Their first volume of evidence is a rich compendium of information about the working out of devolution in its first three years.[11] Parliamentary comity prevents them passing judgement on the fragmented committee structure in the Commons, but they are more likely to say something about the fragmented structures in Whitehall, and the weakness of the machinery at the centre if devolution enters choppier waters.

CHALLENGES AHEAD IN THE SECOND TERM OF DEVOLUTION

What will the Manifestos Say? Challenges Facing the Parties in 2003

In Scotland and in Wales the main challenge to the incumbent Labour/Liberal Democrat coalition governments comes from the nationalist parties. Figure 10.1 in chapter 10 shows how in 1999 Labour lost out dramatically, by comparison with its performance in general elections, while the SNP and Plaid Cymru made dramatic gains. Despite the lacklustre opposition performance of the SNP and Plaid under their new leaders, both parties are likely to benefit from the devolution 'bonus' which appears to accrue to them at devolved-level elections. As chapter 10 explains, Labour voters seem willing to switch to the nationalist parties in the devolved assembly elections because of a perception that they are more likely to 'stand up for Scotland' and to put Wales first. Labour is particularly disadvantaged as the party in power nationally, and Scottish Labour and Welsh Labour will have to strive doubly hard to distance themselves from the party in London. In the past the Labour party headquarters in London took a close and sometimes a guiding interest in the conduct of campaigns in Scotland and Wales. It will be interesting to see how many of Labour's national figures from Scotland (Gordon Brown, Robin Cook, Alistair Darling) are deployed in the 2003 elections, or whether they are advised to stay away.

The Labour 2003 manifestos will emphasise their Scottish, and Welsh, credentials on every page. They will make the most of their distinctive

[11] House of Lords Constitution Select Committee on the Constitution Session 2001–02 *Devolution: Inter-institutional relations in the United Kingdom* Evidence complete to 10 July 2002 HL Paper 147.

policies on tuition fees, long term care, free bus passes etc; and will promise more for the second term. The one to watch is the Labour manifesto in Wales, for what it says — or fails to say — on the powers of the National Assembly. Rhodri Morgan has long been in favour of the Assembly having powers of primary legislation, but many in his party still have doubts. Labour has avoided giving evidence to the Richard Commission on the Powers of the National Assembly until after the elections, and their manifesto may duck the issue, take credit for setting up the commission, but say the matter now rests with Lord Richard and his colleagues. This is the kind of issue which Plaid Cymru and the Liberal Democrats could exploit in arguing that Labour is not standing up sufficiently for Wales.

The other manifesto to watch is that of the SNP in Scotland, and how much prominence it gives to Scottish independence. The SNP are divided between a fundamentalist wing, for whom independence is all, and realists who want to win Scottish elections and form a government in Scotland, even if it is still under the umbrella of Westminster. Chapter 10 shows that Plaid Cymru's devolution 'bonus' in Wales is twice that of the SNP in Scotland, but does not explore the reasons why. Could one reason be that Plaid eschews the word 'independence' and espouses a softer form of nationalism? The SNP might feel it has little to learn from Plaid. But if it could emulate their much bigger devolution bonus it would be the largest party in Scotland, and able to form a government: much like the nationalist parties which have successfully governed in Catalonia and the Basque country for most of the last 20 years. What can the SNP learn from their success, and are they willing to make any electoral compromises to get there?

Wales Needs a New Settlement
The Richard commission on the powers of the National Assembly is due to report by the end of 2003, six months after the Assembly elections in May. On the central issue it is hard to see how it can avoid recommending primary legislative powers. The evidence from Welsh ministers may suggest that they can carry on muddling through, and that so far they have not felt unduly circumscribed; but Lord Richard is wise enough to see the difficulties in Wales being so reliant on Whitehall and Westminster for all its primary legislation. The settlement is precarious, because it is completely dependent on the goodwill of the British government to find legislative time (always in short supply) and their willingness to accommodate Welsh concerns. Sooner or later the fountain of goodwill will dry up, and the National Assembly will find itself stymied.

The Commission will search for a compromise, but on the central issue there is no satisfactory half way house. Nor is there a quick legislative fix to confer primary legislative powers: it cannot be done through tinkering with the Government of Wales Act, but requires fresh legislation on the lines of the Scotland Act. Before being so bold the Commission will want to test the water with the new government which assumes power in Wales after the elections. If Rhodri Morgan continues to be First Minister, he will get the answer he wants in a report which recommends primary legislative powers; and he will use the Commission's report to win over his more cautious Labour colleagues.

Whether Rhodri Morgan can use the report to win over the British government is another matter. Tony Blair has never shown much interest in devolution, and will not welcome a request to tear up the Welsh settlement and start all over again. Morgan may need to keep up his sleeve the weapon of a referendum on the commission's proposals. The Commission has been asking whether a new settlement would require a new referendum. There is no principle or precedent which says that it must. But if the British government proves reluctant, it could be a useful device for the Welsh Assembly to deploy in reserve, to demonstrate the wishes of the people of Wales.[12]

English Regions Must Make up their Minds

England stands at a crossroads. The government is pressing ahead with legislation to enable regional referendums to be held. The English regions will then be presented with a choice to vote in a referendum for a directly elected regional assembly, or to stick with the existing structures which include an indirectly elected Regional Chamber. The timing of the referendums will be left to the government to decide, after consultation with the Regional Chamber. But first the Boundary Committee of the Electoral Commission must draw up a plan for local government restructuring in the region. That is likely to take at least a year. If the legislation authorising referendums is passed in 2002–03, and if the Boundary Committee can complete its task in 2003–04, then the first regional referendums could be held in autumn 2004. But the government will want to see how opinion shapes up before firing the starting gun; and in 2004 the government will be in pre-election mode, and may not want to risk any electoral upsets in the run-up to the next general election.

The government will also want to consult the Regional Chambers, not all of whom will be in favour of the move to Regional Assemblies. The likelihood is that most will not, because an elected Assembly would take over their prime function of scrutinising the Regional Development Agency, and in time could take over their other functions. Regional Chambers, which are still developing their own role, may become more assertive in the debate on regional government and make the case for strengthening their own role as a forum for regional stakeholders. The Regional Development Agencies,

---

[12] But the referendum question would need to be very carefully worded to come within the Assembly's powers. S 36 of the Government of Wales Act empowers the Assembly to hold a poll of the electorate in Wales about any of the Assembly's existing functions; but it excludes matters coming within s 33, which is the general provision enabling the Assembly to 'consider, and make appropriate representations about, any matter affecting Wales'.

which are mainly business-led, are likely to come out against elected Regional Assemblies, following the lead already set by the CBI. Local government leaders, who comprise 70 per cent of the membership of Regional Chambers, could also come out against elected Regional Assemblies when the implications of local government restructuring are brought home to them.

This is why it is too early to judge the outcome of any regional referendum, even in a vanguard region like the North East. The coalition of forces who are likely to be opposed is potentially formidable. Even among the regional elites who have been making the case for regional government, some may prefer at least initially to work at strengthening the Regional Chamber as a proto-Assembly, rather than take a risk at this stage on an elected assembly from which the economic and social partners will be excluded.

CAN THE SYSTEM TAKE THE STRAIN?

We noted at the beginning that devolution has enjoyed an extraordinarily smooth introduction. With the exception of the on-off nature of devolution in Northern Ireland, there have been no disasters, no major rows between governments, no public stand-offs of the kind which many had feared. There have of course been disagreements, but these have mostly been dealt with behind the scenes. The formal machinery for resolving disputes has yet to be tested: the Joint Ministerial Committee has not been convened in dispute resolution mode, and the Judicial Committee of the Privy Council has yet to hear a devolution case on division of powers. The UK government continues to dominate intergovernmental relations, and the mood in Whitehall is one of quiet satisfaction at a job well done.

How long can it last? Three things have contributed to devolution's extended honeymoon period. First, the coincidence of Labour being in power in London and heading the coalition governments in Edinburgh and Cardiff. Second, the extraordinary electoral success of New Labour and the continuing popularity of Blair as Prime Minister. Third, the unprecedented increases in public expenditure which have resulted in substantial additional funding being passed on to the devolved governments every year since they came into office.

The conventional wisdom notes only the first of these circumstances, and remarks that devolution will not be properly tested until there are governments headed by different political parties in London and Edinburgh or Cardiff. That may well be right; but it is worth asking what would happen in the absence of the other two. If Blair's luck runs out, and New Labour becomes an electoral liability; or if Brown's luck runs out, and the devolved governments begin to feel the financial squeeze . . . What will then happen to the cosy and harmonious system of intergovernmental relations? Labour in Scotland and Wales would certainly need to put some distance between themselves and New Labour in London. And the devolved governments might demand a review of the funding system which keeps them so closely tied to the Treasury's purse strings once those purse strings start to tighten.

There may not be a single defining moment when the honeymoon period comes to an end. But one defining moment will be the 2003 elections, and the subsequent behaviour of devolved governments who have sought election on a mandate to make a difference. Other defining moments will be when they feel confident enough to call themselves governments;[13] and when they first come together and support each other in a combined challenge to the British government. These things may happen in their second term, even if we still have Labour administrations ruling in all three capitals. And when these things happen, and when the devolved governments become more self-confident and more self-conscious of their own powers, then we can say that the devolved governments will have come of age.

BIBLIOGRAPHY

Official Documents
National Assembly Review of Procedure, Final Report, Feb 2002 ch. 4 and Annex 5.
House of Lords Constitution Select Committee on the Constitution Session 2001–02 *Devolution: Inter-institutional relations in the United Kingdom* Evidence complete to 10 July 2002 HL Paper 147.
White Paper, *Your Region, Your Choice*, May 2002, para. 7.11.

Secondary Sources
Bennett, M., *et al*, *Devolution in Scotland: the Impact on Local Government* (Yorkshire: The Joseph Rowntree Foundation, 2002).
Bromley, C., Curtice, J. and Seyd, B., *Has Constitutional Reform 'Reconnected' Voters with their Government?* (London: The Constitution Unit, February 2002).
Curtice J., 'Devolution, The Union and Public Opinion', report submitted to House of Lords Constitution Committee, 2002.
Laffin M., *et al*, *A new Partnership? The National Assembly for Wales and Local Government* (Yorkshire: Joseph Rowntree Foundation, 2002).
McAllion, J., 'Public Petitions Committee', *SCOLAG Journal*, September 2000.
Sandford, M., *Inclusiveness of Regional Chambers* (London: The Constitution Unit, October 2002).

---

[13] Instead of the timidity and confusion of the 'Scottish Executive' and the 'Welsh Assembly Government'. Jack McConnell tried to introduce the term 'Scottish government' but was warned off by the British government. Strangely, there was no such objection when Rhodri Morgan re-christened the Welsh executive, even though its new name has no statutory foundation.

Shaw K. *et al, The Engagement of Economic and Social Partners in a Directly Elected Regional Assembly for the North East* (Newcastle: CURDS, June 2002), ch. 4.

Surridge P., 'Society and Democracy: The New Scotland' in J. Curtice et al, *New Scotland, New Society? Are Social and Political Ties Fragmenting?* (Edinburgh: Polygon Press, 2001).

Winetrobe, B., *Realising the Vision: A Parliament with a Purpose* (London: Constitution Unit October 2001).

Index

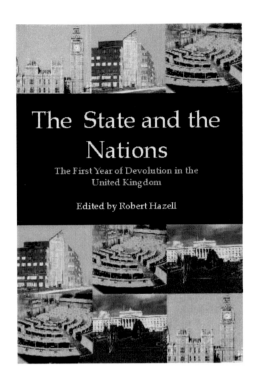

The State and the Nations

The First Year of Devolution in the United Kingdom

Edited by Robert Hazell

Director of the Constitution Unit,
Professor of Government
and the Constitution
University College London

ISBN 0907845 800   304 pages
now half price (£7.50/$12.50)

TABLE OF CONTENTS

> 'An invaluable volume of record for all serious students of the changing United Kingdom'
> **Vernon Bogdanor**

www.imprint-academic.com/state

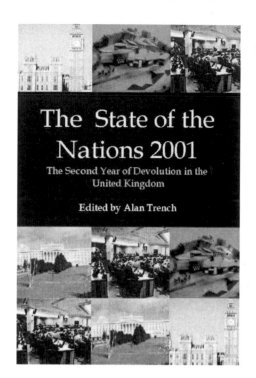

The State of the Nations 2001

The Second Year of Devolution in the UK

Edited by Alan Trench

Senior Research Fellow,
The Constitution Unit
University College London

ISBN 0907845 193   304 pages
£14.95/$24.95